America Alone

The Neo-Conservatives and the Global Order

This book explores how George W. Bush's election and the fear and confusion of September 11, 2001, combined to allow a small group of radical intellectuals to seize the reins of U.S. national security policy. It shows how, at this "inflection point" in U.S. history, an inexperienced president was persuaded to abandon his campaign pledges and the successful consensus-driven, bipartisan diplomacy that managed the lethal Soviet threat over the past half-century and adopt a neo-conservative foreign policy emphasizing military confrontation and "nation building." To date, the costs – in blood, money, and credibility – have been great and the benefits few. Traditional conservatives deplore this approach. This book outlines the costs in terms of economic damage, distortion of priorities, rising anti-Americanism, encroachment on civil liberties, domestic political polarization, and reduced security. Then it sets out an alternative approach emphasizing the traditional conservative principles of containing risk, consensus diplomacy, and balance of power.

Stefan Halper is a Fellow of Magdalene College, University of Cambridge, and a Senior Fellow of the Centre of International Studies, where he directs the Donner Atlantic Studies Programme. He holds a B.A. from Stanford University and doctorates from both Oxford and Cambridge Universities. He was a White House and State Department official during the Nixon, Ford, and Reagan administrations. For twelve years he was executive editor and host of the weekly radio program *This Week from Washington* and then was executive editor and host of *WorldWise*, a weekly TV program on foreign affairs. He has made contributions to numerous print media, including the *American Spectator*, *Chicago Tribune*, *Christian Science Monitor*, *Dallas Morning News*, *International Wall Street Journal*, *Los Angeles Times*, *National Interest*, *National Review*, *Wall Street Journal*, *Washington Post*, *Washington Times*, and *Weekly Standard*. Dr. Halper is senior editor at the *Cambridge Review of International Affairs* and a contributing editor at the *American Spectator*. He is the co-editor of *Latin America: The Dynamics of Social Change*.

Jonathan Clarke is a Foreign Affairs Scholar at the CATO Institute in Washington, D.C. He received a B.A. and an M.A. from Oxford University and has also been a Counselor, British Diplomatic Service, with assignments in Germany, Zimbabwe, and the United States. He is the coauthor of *After the Crusade: American Foreign Policy for the Post-Superpower Age* and has made numerous contributions to various forms of print media, including *Foreign Affairs*, *Foreign Policy*, the *Los Angeles Times*, *National Interest*, *Orbis*, and the *Washington Post*.

Stefan Halper
dedicates this book to his parents
and to the late William D. Roosevelt,
patriot, philanthropist, and friend

and

Jonathan Clarke
dedicates this book to
his parents, Richard and Nora,
in this year of their 60th wedding anniversary

America Alone

The Neo-Conservatives and the Global Order

STEFAN HALPER
University of Cambridge

JONATHAN CLARKE
CATO *Institute*

CAMBRIDGE
UNIVERSITY PRESS

CAMBRIDGE UNIVERSITY PRESS
Cambridge, New York, Melbourne, Madrid, Cape Town, Singapore, São Paulo

Cambridge University Press
40 West 20th Street, New York, NY 10011-4211, USA

www.cambridge.org
Information on this title: www.cambridge.org/9780521838344

First published 2004
First paperback edition 2005

Printed in the United States of America

A catalog record for this publication is available from the British Library.

Library of Congress Cataloging in Publication Data

Halper, Stefan A.
America alone : the neo-conservatives and the global order / Stefan Halper, Jonathan Clarke.
    p.   cm.
Includes bibliographical references and index.
ISBN 0-521-83834-7
1. Conservatism – United States.   2. United States – Foreign relations – 2001–3.
United States – Politics and government – 2001–   I. Clarke, Jonathan, 1947–   II. Title.

JC573.2.U6H34   2004
320.52'0973 – dc22   2004040795

ISBN-13   978-0-521-83834-4 hardback
ISBN-10   0-521-83834-7 hardback

ISBN-13   978-0-521-67460-7 paperback
ISBN-10   0-521-67460-3 paperback

Contents

Preface		*page* vii
Acknowledgments		xi
List of Abbreviations		xiii
	Introduction	1
1	The Neo-Conservatives: A New Political Interest Group	9
2	Origins and Early Development	40
3	The Nineties: From Near Death to Resurrection	74
4	The Neo-Conservative Ascension	112
5	The False History	157
6	Outreach to the Media and Evangelicals	182
7	Iraq: The False Pretenses	201
8	America: Perception and Counterperception	232
9	The Neo-Conservative "World War IV" and Its Impact on American Society	273
10	The Balance Sheet and Looking Ahead	296
Bibliography		341
Index		351

Preface to Paperback Edition

In the conclusion to *America Alone* written in early 2004, we described the forces of neo-conservatism as having reached a high water mark. We anticipated that the foreign policy pendulum would start to swing back to more established norms. Under these the United States would, in a prudent calculation of national interest, re-emphasize the value of working with the grain of international opinion, would give a less prominent place to unilateral action, and would treat military intervention more cautiously.

In its first steps, the second Bush administration has indeed started to act on these lines – with obvious benefits. Relations with Europe have improved; a more constructive exchange has opened on Middle East questions, and China's responsibilities as a global citizen have been given added focus. Whether our book had any influence on these positive developments is not for us to calculate. The trend, however, is a welcome one. Furthermore, a more practical tone has seen the administration soften its strident "March of Democracy" rhetoric, thus allowing democratic aspirants in various parts of the world to have the confidence to pursue the path of democracy without portraying themselves as acting on instructions from Washington. All this suggests that the trauma of 9/11 has begun to abate and that a nuanced period in which real interests are balanced with idealized aspirations may lie ahead.

Does this mean neo-conservatism is finished, destined to join other failed "isms" like Marxism as just another momentary entry in the historical archives? As some of the movement's leaders transition from the Pentagon and State Department to less formative roles in the policy process, this may seem to be the case. Can, therefore, Americans and their well-wishers around the world heave a sigh of relief, happy that the outcome of the neo-conservative experiment in Iraq could have been worse and that the excesses of neo-conservative ambition in Syria, Iran, North Korea and elsewhere seem unlikely to eventuate? Clearly not.

To do so would represent the height of complacency. At the end of the Cold War, the neo-conservatives were thought to be headed for oblivion – a round trip from Trotskyism to anachronism, as one commentator put it. Instead, they regrouped. During the 1990s they operated through a carefully constructed network of think-tanks, media outlets and academic outposts, re-inventing themselves as tenacious advocates of US military power in the service of neo-Wilsonian interventionism. When 9/11 struck, they were the ones with a strategic response.

Today, they are hardly vacating the field. Institutionally, they have re-created the Committee on the Present Danger and leading neo-conservatives proponents speak of the need for the US to commit itself to World War IV. Iran remains in their sights; they are ready with new "regime change" plans if diplomatic efforts falter. Moreover, they continue to drag the center of US foreign policy into a single region of the world. Thus, the tenets of neo-conservatism and the dangers represented by its unbalanced instrumentality live on. So we must remain familiar with them.

This is particularly important in an age when a dramatic revolution in American military technology has taken place. America's power-projection preeminence is now the nation's main comparative advantage, much increasing the temptation to utilize military force as an early policy option. Neo-conservatives are not the only advocates of this militarized culture, but they have deep intellectual roots in a predisposition to see military force as the decisive – even the desirable – element in international relations. And they have drawn few if any cautionary lessons from the Iraq experience.

This means that the administration's current approach may not survive new tensions, let alone another major terrorist attack. New conflicts may lie before us. In turn this means that we need to remind ourselves of how the 2003 Iraq War was presented to the public. Here the idealistic objective of removing Saddam and injecting a democratic government in the center of the Arab world seemed saleable if only the American people believed US national security interests required it. Thus a "conditional reality" in which Saddam "might" have weapons of mass destruction; "might" have links to al-Qaeda; and "might" have been complicit in 9/11 was advanced by the Administration and, eventually, believed by a majority of Americans. This was a process in which the government created a false reality and then mobilized the nation to war against that background.

This book details that process – and does so on the basis of the record. In the sense that to misunderstand or be ignorant of one's history is to risk repeating it, this is a cautionary tale about the excesses of zealotry and, in this case, the damage done to national interests both foreign and domestic. It is all the more important, in the light of the fragile outcome in Iraq, as neo-conservative elites have started to rewrite the record. Though not the only decision-makers behind the first Bush administration's Iraq policy, the neo-conservatives were the most committed, the most tenacious and the most willing to use subterfuge to gain their ends. Their accountability cannot be air-brushed out of history.

Finally, the preoccupation of the neo-conservative policy elite with one region of the world has effectively diverted the nation's attention from a challenge soon upon us that will alter the quality of life in America if not properly addressed. China's dramatic growth, its economy expanding at 9% per year for over a decade, its exhaustive need for commodities, its massive hard currency reserves, its vast holdings of US Treasury bonds, its growing high tech prowess, and newly modernized military represents more than an afterthought for Americans. China represents the central challenge to the American way of life in the 21st Century. As such, we need to give pride of place in allocating the nation's research and analytic resources to understanding China in all its facets. Other regional issues, however central to neo-conservative hearts, cannot be allowed to assume a disproportionate importance.

As we preface this paperback edition of *America Alone: The Neo-Conservatives and the Global Order*, we invite readers to enter a conversation; an examination of the interests that have played upon the policy process, the dynamic relationship between the White House the media and opinion, and the choices going forward. Amidst an intense foreign policy debate obscured at times by partisan interest, our hope is to demystify and clarify. For the lessons drawn here and the policy that results will have much to do with the quality of life, values and freedoms surrounding our children and their children.

Acknowledgments

The ambiguities of the concept commonly called "intellectual property" strike home as we consider how properly to thank those who have assisted us in this book's creation. The names of those who have rendered direct help are well known to us. But what of those who, over the years, with a word of advice, a friendly gesture, an unusual perspective, or a touch on the shoulder have shaped our ideas in decisive but less tangible ways? Let us simply say to them that we are grateful – wherever they may be.

To our friends and colleagues who have assisted us so generously with their time, encouragement, and advice, we are deeply grateful. These include a particularly brilliant group of postgraduate students at the Centre for International Studies at Cambridge University: Joel Rogers, Lezlee Brown Halper, Michael Gottesman, Ben Reiter, Annaliza Tsakona, and Christopher Waddington.

Dr. Tarak Barkawi, Fellow of the Centre of International Studies, reviewed the manuscript in its entirety, providing an indispensable blend of criticism, focus, and encouragement without which the book would not exist in its present form. Professor Jonathan Haslam, Fellow of Corpus Christi College, Cambridge, helped to conceptualize the book's thesis at the time of its genesis. Dr. Barbara Bodenhorn, Fellow of Pembroke College, helped greatly with the discussion of anti-Americanism, carefully reviewing the anthropological implications of the arguments presented.

Professor James B. L. Mayall, Director of the Centre of International Studies at Cambridge, Dr. Philip Towle, Senior Fellow, Centre of International Studies, and Dr. Charles Jones, Fellow of the Centre of International Studies, each offered a distinct perspective on the issues at hand and helpful comments on the manuscript, bringing greater clarity to the argument. The authors thank Dr. John Dumbrell, University of Keele, and Dr. Richard

Crockatt, University of East Anglia, for their guidance and perspective. In addition, thanks are due to Mr. Uwe Bott and Dr. Joe DiVanna, who advised us on economic issues, and to Mr. John Forsyth, a Fellow of the Centre of International Studies, who debated the complex economic matters associated with the book's argument and provided a critical final review of these issues.

The authors thank Mrs. Anne Lonsdale, President of New Hall and Pro-Vice Chancellor of Cambridge University, Professor Eamon Duffy, President of Magdalene College, Cambridge, and Mr. Dennis Murphy, a Fellow and former Bursar at the college, for their insight and encouragement, making the task that much easier.

In Washington, D.C., Dr. Ted Galen Carpenter, Mr. James Fallows, Mr. Alfred Regnery, Mr. Ben Tyree, Mr. Max Boot, Rear-Admiral Ronald Christiansen (U.S. Navy, ret.), Dr. Armeane Choksi, Mr. James Clad, Dr. Charles Horner, Mr. Barry Jacobs, Captain Robert Mercker (101st Airborne, ret.), Ms. Hella Dale, and Mr. John O'Sullivan offered their encouragement or special perspectives, as did Mr. Curtin Winsor III. Ms. Michelle Hunsicker-Blair, librarian at the Metropolitan Club, searched out and provided many a journal. Our editor at Cambridge University Press, Lewis Bateman, patiently endured our outbursts. Vanessa Clarke, sister of Jonathan, provided advice at a vital time.

The book's central thesis was ours, but the contributions of these others were indispensable in allowing such merits as it has to shine through. We are deeply grateful to them.

To our families, we also say a heart-felt thank you. Stefan would like to thank his wife, Lezlee, for her early inspiration, for coordinating the research effort in the United Kingdom, for her sage advice, and for her patience through the long Cambridge winters. He also thanks his children, Elizabeth and Marin, to whose collective hand the torch will soon pass. Jonathan expresses deep appreciation to his wife, Suzanne, and children, Crispin, Tiffany, and Robin, who, in travels around the world with him in bonds of love and fun, have taught him that their vision of global peace is a goal profoundly worth striving for.

List of Abbreviations

ABM	anti-ballistic missile
AEI	American Enterprise Institute
BSA	Bosnian Serb Army
CAPPS II	Computer Assisted Passenger Pre-screening II
CDM	Coalition for a Democratic Majority
CIA	Central Intelligence Agency
CSP	Center for Security Policy
DARPA	Defense Advanced Research Projects Agency
DIS	Defense Intelligence Staff
DPG	*Defense Planning Guidance*
E.U.	European Union
FCC	Federal Communications Commission
FDOD	Foundation for the Defense of Democracy
FISA	Foreign Intelligence Surveillance Act
HBC	Hispanic Broadcasting Network
HSARPA	Homeland Security Advanced Research Projects Agency
IAEA	International Atomic Energy Agency
ICC	International Criminal Court
IFCJ	International Fellowship of Christians and Jews
IFOR	Implementation Force
IMF	International Monetary Fund
INC	Iraqi National Congress
INF	Intermediate-Range Nuclear Forces
JINSA	Jewish Institute for National Security Affairs
MEF	Middle East Forum
MEMRI	Middle East Media Research Institute
NATO	North Atlantic Treaty Organization

NESA	Near East and South Asia
NMD	National Missile Defense
NSC	National Security Council
NSS	*National Security Strategy*
OSP	Office of Special Plans
Patriot II	Domestic Security Enhancement Act
PNAC	Project for the New American Century
SDI	Strategic Defense Initiative
TIA	Terrorist/Total Information Awareness
UNOSOM II	U.N. Operation in Somalia
UNPROFOR	U.N. Protection Force
WINEP	Washington Institute for Near East Policy
WMD	weapons of mass destruction
WTO	World Trade Organization

Introduction

Any veteran of the Cold War trenches will tell you that the reason the war was worth fighting over so many years and in so many obscure venues around the world was that it was an existential struggle. Not only was it a struggle for the usual things that have throughout history compelled men to fight – family, territory, resources, and so on – but, more important, it set our values of human decency against forces whose first instinct was to imprison the human spirit and toss away the key. Such was the titanic scale of the struggle that defeat would be total. When nations were absorbed by communism there was, until 1989, no second chance. For those who ventured into these dark places, morality provided the guiding light.

Turning to the practical instruments that made victory possible, these veterans will tell you that the indispensable ingredients were the availability of U.S. power and the superior performance of the U.S. free market economic model. But the key lesson is that America's most effective weapon was its moral authority. Specifically, this was the sense that America was a force for good in the world – and the other side implicitly acknowledged the truth of this reality. Thus, while military and economic power were indispensable, for victory to be durable, there was no substitute for moral authority.

The results speak for themselves. The Soviet Gulag is no more, the communist deceits that enslaved minds and bodies for the best part of a century are over, and regime change – though this is not our term – took place in Moscow and in more than a dozen capitals under its suzerainty. All without a single hostile sortie from NATO.

That is, in essence, why we feel this book is worth writing. America's military might, dominant for nearly a century, has attained new, unchallengeable heights; its economic mass remains preeminent. While this is a laudable state of affairs, however, its moral authority is at risk. That is because the policies adopted in response to the catastrophic horror of September 11, 2001, have rested on a series of critically flawed premises, namely that the challenges we face are essentially military in character and that military power alone can deliver victory. And while that may be true when barbarian fights barbarian for strips of territory, it is a profound mistake when civilization hopes to emerge triumphant.

This book therefore is about America and about the changes that have come over the country in the past three years. These changes have been incremental, so the drama of the totality may have eluded those of us who live here. But overseas visitors, who love America and Americans, tell us that they barely recognize the country they thought they knew so well. Our context is America's relations with the outside world. This is the arena where we spent our professional careers at the heart of Cold War governments. But our theme is America in the round: What do the ways in which we conduct ourselves with others and the state of our foreign relationships say about who we are as a nation and about the direction in which we are traveling? The book asks Americans to stand back from the emotions generated by that terrible day and to hold up a mirror to themselves, their surroundings, and their relations both within their neighborhoods and with their more distant friends overseas. It invites them to reflect on the changes that have taken place and to question whether these are the qualities and the future they wish America to pursue.

For, consciously or otherwise, in this relatively brief time since 9/11 we have changed as a people and as a society. Sights on our streets include troops in combat fatigues patrolling public places, their weapons at the ready; concrete barriers around government buildings and synagogues; the drastic changes to air travel; flashing highway signs urging drivers to report suspicious behavior; vanity license plates proclaiming "fight terrorism"; and daily reminders on our TV screens of a seemingly permanent color-coded Terrorist Threat Level, subject to inexplicable change as unnamed experts sense movement in the pattern of potential terrorist "chatter."

In America's relations with the wider world, much also has changed. The spontaneous and unrestrained wave of post-9/11 sympathy has transformed itself into anti-Americanism, with its more sinister cousin, counter-Americanism, being made ready in the wings; alliances painstakingly built up over half a century have been deconstructed, and multilateral institutions, most brought into life by American inspiration, have been diminished; our foreign embassies are less and less able to function as accessible havens of American culture but hide behind redoubts and tank-proof chicanes. Americans themselves are hesitant to travel abroad, not surprisingly in the light of the many official warnings against overseas travel. When they do, they are often taken aback at the professional or personal hostility they encounter.

Economically, the price on our society has been high. The federal budget is buffeted by ballooning deficits and state governments are reeling from un-bridgeable gaps between revenue and spending, a substantial part of these caused by unfunded federal security-related demands; progress toward freer movement of goods, services, and foreign human capital is stalled as a result of onerous visa procedures and tighter administrative processing at ports of entry; in places American products are resisted simply because they are American; and trade agreements with foreign partners are increasingly de-pendent on non-trade-related issues, including the degree to which they sup-port Washington's foreign policy.

It is on the political front, however, that change has been most subtle and remarkable. A decade ago, it was a proud Washington boast that well-fashioned American policy toward Latin America had moderated that re-gion's love affair with its generals and returned the military to its barracks. Today, the trend in America is in the opposite direction. Few political rallies or speeches are complete without a military accent. The only extraordinary aspect of this is how ordinary it now seems to us, persuaded as we have been to forget that one of the unifying threads of our political culture, ex-emplified by Washington's resignation of his commission in 1783, has been an avoidance of military intrusion into politics. But now times have changed so that we observe passively when, in defiance of the underlying grain of the American political ethos, movement is in the direction of tighter central control. New bureaucratic structures include a Department of Homeland Security, whose broad remit has stimulated an intense effort by both liberals and conservatives to limit its powers lest it approach those once dreaded security ministries in Eastern Europe that so many Americans worked to eliminate. The Department of Justice sits astride new powers of intrusiveness and surveillance unprecedented in peacetime. Little-known offices within the Pentagon have devised catchall technology for mining electronic information about Americans' daily lives. All this has proceeded in the name of the "war on terrorism."

This of course is the rub. The greatest change is psychological. Today we have convinced ourselves (with a massive assist from cable news and talk radio) that, as Americans, our natural state is war – war that has no dimensions, with elusive enemies who may be equally residents of Damascus or Detroit and with no definition of what constitutes victory and thus with no end in sight. Having absorbed a siege mentality, we live our lives in crisis mode. "It's the terror, stupid," is the defining political slogan. Yet we are left with a stark paradox. Despite the massive application of American firepower overseas and an equally massive diversion of resources toward homeland security, Americans feel not a whit more secure – quite the opposite. Poll after poll shows Americans feeling more personally threatened than at any time in their history.

Our contention is that this state of siege reflects a range of developments – of which 9/11 is only one. To be sure, the events of September 11 demand a decisive and sustained response. This is common ground. But this is only half of the explanation. The full truth is very different. The situation of unending war in which we find ourselves results in large part from the fact that the policies adopted after 9/11, the initial strike against the Taliban aside, were hardly specific to that event. Unlike the policy of containment that evolved in direct response to Soviet moves in Central and Eastern Europe and involved radical new thinking on the part of those involved, the post-9/11 policy was in fact grounded in an ideology that existed well before the terror attacks and that in a stroke of opportunistic daring by its progenitors, has emerged as the new orthodoxy. The paper trail is unambiguous. Minds were already made up. A preexisting ideological agenda was taken off the shelf, dusted off, and relabeled as *the* response to terror. The reality is that it has little or nothing to do with combating terror and in fact may make the terror threat all the worse. An ideology that highlights conventional state-against-state conflict as its one-size-fits-all policy option has been adapted for an era when threats are unconventional, transnational, and non-state-specific. Little wonder that no one feels safer.

This ideology – usually described as neo-conservative, though its adherents who are aware of the negative flavoring of this word prefer the term "American internationalist" or "democratic globalist" – purposefully places the United States on a war footing. Viewing diplomacy as a tiresome constraint on American "unipolarity," it embraces a risky and adventurous policy that utilizes military power as the instrument of first resort for a wide range of policy challenges. Neo-conservatives (if we may use this term) and their hangers-on lose no sleep that this places the United States in a state of constant tension with the outside world and inclines to a climate of intolerance and conformity at home. Indeed, neo-conservative advocates speak of World War IV, enthusiastically embrace the notion of "neo-war," and question the patriotism of those who dare to raise questions. Although premised on a formidable internal logic, the neo-conservatives and their cheerleaders in the media are not above reinterpreting or downright falsifying history (they accuse Richard Nixon of being soft on communism) and jumping on passing bandwagons to accomplish their purposes. So long as a state of war or a state of crisis endures or can be argued to endure, debate (let alone dissent) is chilled; the alternatives go unexamined.

Our professional careers gave us a privileged position at the heart of the U.S. and U.K. governments' fight against communism. Our philosophic anchoring is a conservative one. We have lived and worked in the same culture from which many of the neo-conservatives have emerged. As often as not we have been colleagues. We have fought many of the same battles that they have fought. We too have locked horns with shadowy emanations of the Soviet Union and seen the inside of the beast; we have been on the ground in North Korea and Cuba, stood in the same trenches taking the incoming fire from European protests over Pershing missiles; we too know our way around the wars and revolutions of Central America; we too know how to defend ambitious aims against the counsels of timidity and defeatism.

But we did so first and foremost in defense of the values exemplified by America's open society. We recognized that cooperation with our allies overseas was the essence of America's strength, not an optional extra or a bothersome constraint. When we rallied to Ronald Reagan's clarion cry of the "Evil Empire," we did not imagine that a generation later we would see the nation embark on a perilous course of power projection and intimidation, treating friends and allies much as though they were Soviet-style satellites. We never supposed that, when we thrilled to Reagan's demand to Mikhail Gorbachev to "tear down this wall," we would see a day when new walls would be built in our own society. As we gave the lie to the communist *nomenklatura*, we did not do so in the name of widening differences in our own country. A decade and a half later we never thought to see a small group of neo-conservative policy makers appropriate Reagan's multilayered legacy as though it were their exclusive property and, careless of history, boil it down to a few simplistic slogans. We never anticipated the day when Americans, as a result of their interventions around the world, would be held in lower esteem than if they had simply stayed at home.

This is not our memory of how we conducted business in that period nor, as we show below, is it the historical record. Whatever the merits of their service under Presidents Gerald Ford, Reagan, and George H. W. Bush, this group has today, in a different time and under a different president, substituted "ideology" for "interests" in a way that has left the nation isolated outside and polarized within.

This is a second reason the book is worth writing. We are at an unusual juncture in American history. The character of our society is in play. The combination of unprecedented technological capability in the U.S. military and a formidable set of highly dynamic, carefully articulated ideas advocated by the neo-conservatives has created a treacherous situation. Given their access to military power and the instruments of domestic authority, this relatively small group has the ability to put its ideas of a force-based, war-oriented America into practical effect.

It might be thought that this is a foreign policy issue, that this is a debate on the outermost fringes of the American political universe. That would be a mistake. America's overseas posture has changed the domestic context. Authoritarianism overseas generates authoritarianism at home. By capturing the nation with their vision of permanent external war, the neo-conservatives and their ideological bedfellows on the home front have cast a shadow over our entire domestic polity. As advocates of limited government conservatism, we are dismayed at the flow of power toward the center. In this way, the neo-conservative ideology has outgrown its roots in the foreign policy community. All Americans and their overseas allies and friends are now involved.

Though founded as a reaction to empire – a notion rejected a century ago – Washington's undisciplined rhetoric and awkward diplomacy has left much of the world with the impression that it nurses global ambitions of dominance and seeks to impose a "made in America" version of democratic governance, often overlooking history and local cultural and political preferences. The empires of history vary in reputation, with a bevy of new historians painting them in ever more positive ways, but they share one characteristic: They are, in the words of the poet laureate of imperialism, "one with Tyre and Nineveh." Literally, they are history. Yet America's founding premise was that it truly was a different political organism capable of resisting the path trod by the imperial powers of yesteryear.

The casualty in all of this, of course, is America's moral authority. As noted earlier, those who negotiated the Cold War in Washington, London, and across Asia and Africa understand the broad support commanded by the American "brand." In conversation with the Soviets, East Germans, Chinese, Cubans, and the like, there was little doubt about who held the high ground. They simply could not defend the mass murder that had taken place in defense of their ideology. This is why we are dismayed that the neo-conservatives place so little value on this priceless asset and instead treat power – raw, military power – as the alpha and omega of America's interaction with the world. This reminds us of Stalin's cynical question about how many divisions the Pope can field. We doubt that this is the company our nation wishes to keep.

The dramatic American military successes recorded by the world's media – though condemned by many – may lend some specious confirmation to this force-centric thesis. But it ushers in the complex nation-building problems we have sought to avoid in Somalia, Haiti, Kosovo, East Timor, and Afghanistan, and this against a background significantly eroded by the collapse of moral authority. Far from being seen as liberators, U.S. forces have encountered hostility and danger on raising the Stars and Stripes.

By any objective measure, recent experience demonstrates that Washington neither understands the technology of nation building nor has demonstrated the will to finance sustained and costly administrative and reconstructive efforts in the places where it has intervened over the past decade. And thus either there must be a compelling rationale for this administration's policy – or that of any administration – that links means to ends identifying realizable objectives or today's neo-conservative policies must be subjected to radical surgery and replaced with new productive and achievable objectives.

Inevitably, this will happen. For this is the other side of our story. We speak of the neo-conservative "moment." That is, we are talking about something that, so long as the normal checks and balances of the American political genius hold sway, is transient. For the fatal error of neo-conservatism is its lack of a coherent and accurate history. Although presented with biblical authority, the neo-conservative ideology is little more than an aberration. It runs counter to the political society crafted over half a century by Republican and Democratic administrations alike. But like all special interests and temporary infatuations over the course of American history – we are thinking of the "yellow press" that marked America's last flirtation with empire or Clinton's fitful flirtations with "assertive multilateralism" – they run their course. The pendulum swings back.

This book is written in the expectation of that swing of the pendulum. This is the area in which we acknowledge a personal ambition: to help American conservatism swing back to its moderate roots after the detour on which the neo-conservatives have led it. Far too often, contemporary political debate pigeonholes proponents and opponents such that the resulting argument is a simple and unproductive clash of rigid, ideological stovepiped positions. We urge our readers to look beyond these stereotypes at the ideas themselves, but, to the extent that our political orientation is relevant, let us put on record that we approach these issues not from the left, as many have. Our critique arises from the "center-right" and asserts the virtues of the interest-driven, consensus-seeking, risk-conscious policies adopted by American administrations with great success since World War II. They are policies in which alliances and the international process are vital assets permitting the United States additional platforms and contexts to advance its interests.

We do not write merely to pick logical holes or to tease out minor inconsistencies in the neo-conservative ideology. We do not question the good faith of its acolytes and devotees. We know them well. As hosts and guests, we have joined them on radio and TV programs and shared platforms with them in the conservative think-tanks.

This is neither a work of academic theorizing nor is it inside-Washington payback. There is a need for something much broader. We need to change the questions that Americans are asking themselves. These questions go beyond the events of the moment, however dramatic they may seem at the time – Saddam's capture and the bombing of the U.N. headquarters in Baghdad come to mind. Such events impelled many to ask whether they signify that the administration's policies are either succeeding or failing. Would that it were that simple.

Rather, we as Americans confront complex questions with a trajectory longer than that of a TV image. Many are found in America's current debate over the nature of its global responsibilities, its objectives in the Middle East, the circumstances and modalities attendant to the use of force abroad, the rise of China and India, the integrity of global markets, the tenuous nature of today's foreign policy consensus, relations with multilateral institutions such as NATO and the U.N. that we helped to create, and the vital challenge of how to preserve U.S. credibility in a world increasingly mistrustful of American initiatives.

We believe that the neo-conservatives propose an untenable model for our nation's future. Their recent writings indicate that, as Tallyrand observed about the Bourbons, they remember everything but have learned nothing from the nation's experiences in 2003 in Afghanistan and Iraq. We embrace an alternative based on the interest-focused centrist policies that have guided both Republican and Democratic administrations from 1945 to 2000. At stake is the continuing capacity of the United States to advance democratic ideals and the principles of liberal government on which the United States was founded without unleashing a backlash that will render any short-term gains null and void. This is an ambitious agenda, a worthy fit with America's noblest aspirations. We write in hopes of helping Americans to understand the changes around them, to assess the new structures being put in place, and to stimulate them to action before the ugly hallmarks of our new society become part of our permanent condition, well after the neo-conservatives themselves have left the scene.

I

The Neo-Conservatives

A New Political Interest Group

The neo-conservatives have become a *cause célèbre* in both American and international politics. Conspiracy theories about their influence abound, but well-grounded accounts remain few and far between. In the coming chapters we set out to demystify the neo-conservatives. We ask how and when they came by that name. We examine their beliefs and objectives and how they reached their positions of influence. We look at their history, ponder their strengths and weaknesses, and assess their impact on policy, on our lives at home, and on our national security.

The neo-conservative story to date spans a period of over thirty years. It is complex and diverse, comprising as it does a fascinating intellectual migration from the left to the right and from domestic to foreign policy. Occasionally, it includes wild-eyed obsessives: Dr. Strangeloves propelling the nation into uncharted waters. But more often we encounter mild-mannered East Coast academics of formidable ability serving conservative administrations in senior positions. The story's climax comes after the moment of national crisis on September 11, 2001, when many of the same people found themselves, half by design and half by accident, in positions of high influence and moved to take charge of America's war machine. We chart their actions from that time forward in some detail.

The conclusion to which the facts of our story unmistakably point is that the neo-conservatives have taken American international relations on an unfortunate detour, veering away from the balanced, consensus-building, and resource-husbanding approach that has characterized traditional Republican internationalism – exemplified today by Secretary of State Colin Powell – and acted more as a special interest focused on its particular agenda. We reach this conclusion reluctantly inasmuch as it implies that the American global role, to which we attach great value as a force for good, has not been as effective as it should have been – even when due credit is given for heart-warming successes, such as the capture of Saddam Hussein and progress in Libya. This is a sad event for all Americans and especially distressing for people such as ourselves who have felt comfortable under past Republican administrations and who had been expecting something better. Rather than constituting an enduring trend, however, the facts also suggest that the neo-conservative influence should be momentary and containable. Indeed, one neo-conservative writer has already concluded that the end result of the unipolar policies advocated by the neo-conservatives since the mid-1990s is that "America, for the first time since World War II, is suffering a crisis of international legitimacy."[1] Providing that the normal democratic checks and balances remain effective and providing that the American people in general and mainstream conservatives in particular see neo-conservatives for the aberration they are and demand a restoration of balance to the nation's affairs, the neo-conservative influence will gradually dwindle.

Let us now proceed to meet the neo-conservatives. Their movement is not a card-carrying organization. They do not hold meetings or conventions. There is no absolute dividing line between who is and who is not a neo-conservative. Indeed, the word "movement" may exaggerate the degree of intellectual cohesion. Irving Kristol, who accepts the title of neo-conservatism's "godfather," prefers to describe neo-conservatism as a "persuasion."[2] Whether movement or persuasion, it certainly does not apply an ideological straightjacket on its members or an admittance test. There is no Cardinal Joseph Ratzinger or Marshal Mikhail Suslov figure presiding sternly over doctrinal rectitude. No Curia, no Politburo. The neo-conservatives are prolific writers, but acknowledged canonical texts are in short supply. No Bible, Koran, or Torah. Furthermore, corporate media ownership (Fox News, the *Weekly Standard*, and the *London Times* are under the same ownership) has led to some homogenization of views on the right.[3] But to get the reader started, even at the risk of some initial simplification, the following are three sets of headlines that express the common denominators of modern neo-conservatism.

[1] Robert Kagan, "A Tougher War for the U.S. Is One of Legitimacy," *New York Times*, January 24, 2004, p. A17.

[2] Irving Kristol, "The Neo-Conservative Persuasion," *Weekly Standard*, August 25, 2003, pp. 23–25.

[3] James Fallows, "The Age of Murdoch," *Atlantic Monthly*, September 2003, p. 90.

Today's neo-conservatives unite around three common themes:

1. A belief deriving from religious conviction that the human condition is defined as a choice between good and evil and that the true measure of political character is to be found in the willingness by the former (themselves) to confront the latter.
2. An assertion that the fundamental determinant of the relationship between states rests on military power and the willingness to use it.
3. A primary focus on the Middle East and global Islam as the principal theater for American overseas interests.

In putting these themes into practice, neo-conservatives:

1. Analyze international issues in black-and-white, absolute moral categories. They are fortified by a conviction that they alone hold the moral high ground and argue that disagreement is tantamount to defeatism.[4]
2. Focus on the "unipolar" power of the United States, seeing the use of military force as the first, not the last option of foreign policy.[5] They repudiate the "lessons of Vietnam," which they interpret as undermining American will toward the use of force, and embrace the "lessons of Munich," interpreted as establishing the virtues of preemptive military action.[6]
3. Disdain conventional diplomatic agencies such as the State Department and conventional country-specific, realist, and pragmatic analysis. They are hostile toward nonmilitary multilateral institutions and instinctively antagonistic toward international treaties and agreements. "Global unilateralism" is their watchword.[7] They are fortified by international criticism, believing that it confirms American virtue.[8]
4. Look to the Reagan administration as the exemplar of all these virtues and seek to establish their version of Reagan's legacy as the Republican and national orthodoxy.

---

[4] William Bennett, *Why We Fight: Moral Clarity and the War on Terrorism* (Washington, D.C.: Regnery, 2003), p. 56.

[5] Robert Kagan, *Of Paradise and Power: America and Europe in the New World Order* (New York: Knopf, 2003), p. 3.

[6] Lawrence F. Kaplan and William Kristol, *The War over Iraq* (San Francisco: Encounter, 2003), p. 118.

[7] Irving Kristol quoted in Eric A. Nordlinger, *Isolationism Reconfigured* (Princeton, N.J.: Princeton University Press, 1995), p. 18.

[8] Richard Perle, public speech in New York City, February 13, 2003; William Safire, "Nixon on Bush," *New York Times*, July 7, 2003, p. A17.

Based on these beliefs and approaches, neo-conservatives tend to find themselves in confrontational postures:

- with the Muslim world now, but who knows with whom in the future,
- with America's allies and friends, with the need for cooperation in the United Nations and elsewhere to reach U.S. objectives,
- with deficit hawks who urge restraint on discretionary spending, and
- with those fellow Americans who disagree with them and their objectives.[9]

Underlying these themes and these policy approaches, we detect a deep pessimism among neo-conservatives about human nature and human society – and one that is much darker than the skepticism about human perfectibility common in much conservative thinking. This is in complete contrast to their patron saint, Ronald Reagan, and to the general cast of the American temperament as embodied in the Declaration of Independence.[10] Though they say that their message of "freedom, democracy and human rights" is an optimistic one, this is largely rhetorical.[11] The here-and-now world in which neo-conservatives see themselves is a world of Hobbesian state-of-nature primitivism and conspiracy where perpetual militarized competition for ascendancy is the norm, and moderation (even of the sort envisioned by Hobbes) by the community of nations is impossible, where the search for a social contract à la Locke or Rousseau is illusory, where trust (even Reagan's "trust but verify") among human beings is elusive, and where adversaries (defined as anyone who does not share the neo-conservative worldview) must be preemptively crushed lest they crush you.[12] "We should not try to convince people that things are getting better," comments Kenneth Adelman.[13] Domestically, they see America on a path to perdition, with education, sexual mores, morality, and the judiciary all in grip of an alien modernist and secular culture.[14] In many important respects, they still inhabit the gunpowder-impregnated sixteenth-century world of one of their love-hate heroes, Machiavelli, escape from which formed so much of America's early founding philosophy that looked optimistically to the future and understood

[9] Robert H. Bork, "Civil Liberties after 9/11," *Commentary*, July–August 2003, pp. 29–35.
[10] Gary Wills, *Inventing America: Jefferson's Declaration of Independence* (New York: Doubleday 1978).
[11] Ibid., p. 23.
[12] Joshua Muravchik, "The UN on the Loose," *Commentary*, July–August 2002, p. 29.
[13] Dana Milbank and Mike Allen, "Security May Not Be Safe Issue for Bush in '04," *Washington Post*, August 22, 2003, p. A1.
[14] Robert H. Bork, *Slouching toward Gomorrah: Modern Liberalism and American Decline* (New York: Regan Books, 1996).

that progress lies in bringing out the best in people, not forever expecting the worst.

Neo-conservatives, furthermore, are very clear about the tenets of international affairs with which they do not agree. As the Bush administration was still savoring its first days in office, a group of neo-conservatives sent the new president a letter advising him to pay little attention to notions such as "stability" and "normalcy."[15] "Good relations" is a term of suspicion. "Deterrence," "containment," "realism," "collective security," "confidence building," "dialogue," and "consensus" are thought largely unworkable in today's world.[16] The word "humble" used by then candidate George Bush is regarded as little more than campaign rhetoric. The Middle East "peace process," always mentioned in obligatory quotation marks, is regarded as a suspect notion pursued by reflexive "peacemongers."[17] They see treaties and conventions as seeking to "constrain and control American power" rather than as underpinning world order.[18] They pay little heed to the role of non-military factors such as economic incentives, poverty alleviation, soft power, environmental loss, or international commerce.[19] They show little or no interest in the economic implications of their policies. Iraq's oil resources, for example, were only a minor factor in their thinking about that country. Further, they do not simply agree to disagree with Americans who value these aspects; they stigmatize them as "gloomsayers," "saboteurs," or defeatists. They question their patriotism and, in the case of the BBC, suggest that it is in league with Saddam Hussein.[20]

A common charge laid at the neo-conservative door is that they are an exclusive "in group" or "cabal." They are sufficiently sensitive to this description to react with vigorous defense against it.[21] They argue that, based on their writings, speeches, voluminous public pronouncements, and generous media accessibility both domestically and internationally, they cannot be accused of acting as a Soviet-era conspiracy or cabal. This is fine as far

---

[15] Steven Mufson, "Bush Urged to Champion Human Rights: Conservatives Call on President to Promote Democracy, Freedom in Foreign Policy," *Washington Post*, January 26, 2001, p. A 5.

[16] Robert J. Lieber, "The Folly of Containment," *Commentary*, April 2003, pp. 15–21.

[17] Norman Podhoretz, "Oslo: The Peacemongers Return," *Commentary*, October 2001, pp. 21–33.

[18] Jeane J. Kirkpatrick, "American Power – For What?" *Commentary*, January 2000, p. 34.

[19] Donald Kagan and Frederick W. Kagan, "Peace for Our Time," *Commentary*, September 2000, pp. 42–46.

[20] Martin Peretz, "The Passive Saboteurs," *Wall Street Journal*, September 8, 2003, p. A18; Josh Chafetz, "The Disgrace of the BBC," *Weekly Standard*, August 25, 2003, pp. 18–22.

[21] Joshua Muravchik, "The Neo-Conservative Cabal," *Commentary*, September 2003, pp. 26–33.

as it goes. It is certainly true that they do not shrink from the limelight. But we argue that this media blitz conceals – deliberately or otherwise – a less spoken-about agenda. This reticence about their true objectives introduces an important criticism of the neo-conservatives, namely that they have not come clean and are not coming clean with the country.

The positive side of their public availability is that they and their views are easy to identify. They include individuals who hold or held positions in government: Chief of Staff to the Vice-President, I. Lewis Libby; Special Advisor to the President, Elliott Abrams; Deputy Secretary of Defense, Paul D. Wolfowitz; State Department officials John R. Bolton and David Wurmser. On governmental advisory bodies one finds Richard Perle and Eliott A. Cohen on the Defense Policy Board; in the academy Yale professor Donald Kagan, Princeton professors Bernard Lewis and Aaron Friedberg, Pepperdine professor James Q. Wilson and others; in the media *Weekly Standard* editor William Kristol, *Washington Post* columnist Charles Krauthammer, and most foreign policy editorialists on the *Wall Street Journal* editorial pages and the Fox News Channel; in business former CIA Director James Woolsey, among others; and in research institutions Max Boot at the Council on Foreign Relations, Norman Podhoretz and Meyrav Wurmser at the Hudson Institute, any member of the Project for the New American Century, and most foreign or defense studies scholars at the American Enterprise Institute. The latter, incidentally, has moved a great distance away from the principles of transatlantic cooperation symbolized by the mural outside the conference room depicting a gathering of President Ford, British Prime Minister Callaghan, German Chancellor Schmidt, and French President Giscard d'Estaing.

Vice-President Dick Cheney and Defense Secretary Donald Rumsfeld, who would be better described as American nationalists than as neo-conservatives, have found that many of their deeply held beliefs about American exceptionalism and unilateralism parallel neo-conservative thought and have been decisive in their support for the underlying neo-conservative ideological thrust. Both their signatures can be found on a key neo-conservative document, the 1997 Statement of Principles by the Project for the New American Century. Rumsfeld signed the Project's January 1998 letter to President Bill Clinton calling for the removal of Saddam Hussein. Cheney shares the neo-conservative absolutist antipathy to international organizations as sources of encroachment on U.S. sovereignty. Without their support, the neo-conservative agenda could never have been implemented.[22]

---

[22] David Halberstam, *War in a Time of Peace: Bush, Clinton and the Generals* (New York: Touchstone, 2002), pp. 86–94; James Mann, *The Rise of the Vulcans: The History of the Bush War Cabinet* (New York: Viking, 2004), pp. 138–45.

A notable omission from these names is significant representation in the Senate or House of Representatives. When the neo-conservative movement was first forming, Representative Jack Kemp (later Robert Dole's running mate) interested himself in their ideas, especially on economic issues, and Senator Daniel Patrick Moynihan played an important part. Representative Tom Foley, later Speaker of the House, was associated with the Committee for a Democratic Majority. Today, however, with the possible exception of former Speaker Newt Gingrich in his postcongressional manifestation, or Senator Joseph Lieberman in his robust support for American military action in the Middle East, the creative dynamic is not located on Capitol Hill. Neo-conservatism is primarily an East Coast intellectual phenomenon (with modest outposts within the Hoover Institution at Stanford and at the University of Chicago). The modern neo-conservative status as an intellectual movement carries a minor historical irony given that one of its founding fathers, Irving Kristol (who, unlike the present neo-conservative generation, had himself served in the military) railed against the influence of intellectuals on foreign policy, describing this as "not a healthy situation."[23] From modest beginnings when neo-conservatism was seen as something of a view from the fringe, it has now achieved, as we show below, significant political traction through its affiliation with the national security views of the late Senator Henry M. "Scoop" Jackson and its association with social conservatives and evangelical Protestants in the heartland.[24]

AREAS OF AGREEMENT WITH THE NEO-CONSERVATIVES

As we open our debate with the neo-conservatives, we do not intend to pull any punches. But our discussion will not resemble the no-holds-barred tracts that tear at an opponent's throat and that have become such an ugly scar on the American political landscape. We have no intention of further disfiguring discourse. But as the neo-conservatives have shifted from philosophy to polemics, they have lost interest in the middle ground. Their often-repeated credo is you are either "with us or against us." Central to our concern is that the neo-conservatives have betrayed long-established Republican foreign policy principles in which pragmatism and balance play key roles and that, in doing so, they have poorly served the nation and the world beyond.

Having said this, there are broad areas of policy where we agree. While neo-conservatives were not the first to note the fallibility of the communist

---

[23] Irving Kristol, *Neoconservatism: The Autobiography of an Idea* (New York: Free Press, 1995), pp. 75–91.
[24] Walter Russell Mead, *Special Providence: American Foreign Policy and How It Changed the World* (New York: Knopf, 2001), pp. 218–63.

system – in 1947 George Kennan had already pointed out that the communist system bore within the "seeds of its own decay"[25] – John Foster Dulles in 1952 and the Dwight Eisenhower in 1956, to name just two others, were also there before them – they were among the first to grasp the importance of underscoring Moscow's moral bankruptcy. They understood that Khrushchev's admissions of Stalin's purges made communism virtually impossible to defend, even by the most committed. In the 1970s, for example, Daniel Patrick Moynihan identified the Soviet Union's moral fallibility and set the stage for Reagan's dramatic and crucial Evil Empire speech. Jeane Kirkpatrick's useful distinction between authoritarian and totalitarian states powerfully operationalized the Soviet Union's human rights Achilles heel in a way that President Jimmy Carter's eloquent (for example, his May 1977 Notre Dame speech) but empty rhetoric on the same subject never could. Elliott Abrams's sustained efforts to bring freedom to Central America in the early 1980s were ill and unjustly rewarded as he fell personal victim to political revenge seeking.

With regard to the present group, we draw a distinction between the sophisticated strategic analysis found in the thinking of "practitioner" neo-conservatives such as Paul Wolfowitz, Lewis Libby, and John Bolton and their "pamphleteer" colleagues in the academy manqué and the various talk-show hosts whose simple-minded catering to America's baser instincts devalues the neo-conservative coin – and, which pains us more, the Republican coin. We rarely walk the full distance with Wolfowitz, Libby, or Bolton, but it is rare when we do not travel some of the way with them. We acknowledge the logic, the moral purpose, and dynamism of their arguments. For example, the logic of Bolton's arguments on the International Criminal Court is impeccable (so impeccable indeed that the French have quietly secured for themselves an American-style opt-out), but we doubt the practicality of his vendetta against the court.[26] His stewardship of the Proliferation Security Initiative shows that he can operate effectively in multilateral groupings. Strategically, we like the neo-conservative conjunction of values with power. Finally, while we dislike the bombastic, self-congratulatory tone of some of their pronouncements and hope that they will tone down their *ad hominem* attacks on fellow Americans, we do not question their patriotism or that they are working for what they see as America's best interests.

[25] George Kennan, "Sources of Soviet Conduct," *Foreign Affairs*, July 1947, pp. 572–82.
[26] John R. Bolton, "Courting Danger: What's Wrong with the International Criminal Court," in R. James Woolsey, ed., *The National Interest on International Law and Order* (New Brunswick, N.J.: Transaction, 2003), pp. 93–108.

OUR DIFFERENCES WITH THE NEO-CONSERVATIVES

To turn now to our differences with the neo-conservatives: Much of what they say amounts to reiterations of certain timeless principles that have been the staple of American foreign policy since at least the McKinley administration. Few will disagree with the propositions that the United States should remain militarily strong, should reserve the right to self-defense (in common with all other countries in accordance with Article 51 of the U.N. Charter), and should pursue policies based on American moral values (has any President or aspiring presidential candidate failed to say that these were his guiding light?).[27]

The boilerplate bromides are, however, simply the entry point into the neo-conservative matrix. As the authors learned when appearing with John Bolton on America's Voice's weekly *WorldWise* foreign affairs debate, the seemingly uncontroversial premises have a purpose. They draw in the unwary and, before he or she knows it, far more ambitious ideas are in the mix: unipolarity, preemptive militarism, imperialism, rollback, unilateralism, expeditionary-ism. America has flirted with many of these ideas before and, mainly under the influence moderates within the Republican mainstream, has kept them in a proper equilibrium with other concepts that adhere more closely to the principles on which America was founded and stands for today. It is well to repeat this process now by identifying neo-conservative directions precisely and providing enough information and perspective about them for people to decide whether they wish to proceed along this path. Subsequent sections set out the detail of the argument.

THE UNSPOKEN STRATEGY

Neo-conservatism is not a modest ideology. In their writings and speeches, neo-conservatives offer a blueprint for a comprehensive revamping of American foreign policy around their objectives. In their book *Present Dangers: Crisis and Opportunities in American Foreign and Defense Policy* (which, in the light of the range of neo-conservative contributors, provides something close to the contemporary neo-conservatism canon), Robert Kagan and Bill Kristol speak of establishing the "standard of a global superpower that intends to shape the international environment to its own advantage." They decry a narrow definition of America's "vital interests" and argue that America's moral purposes and national interests are identical. They pour cold water on efforts

---

[27] Walter A. McDougall, *Promised Land, Crusader State: The American Encounter with the World since 1776* (New York: Houghton Mifflin, 1997), pp. 172–98.

to define American priorities for intervention by what Henry Kissinger calls "criteria for selectivity" involving, for example, distinctions between vital interests and those judged less important.[28] In operational terms, Kagan and Kristol assert this "will require an American foreign and defense policy that is unapologetic, idealistic, assertive and funded well beyond existing appropriations. America must not only be the world's policeman or its sheriff, it must be its beacon and guide."[29] In their book *An End to Evil*, which appeared in late 2003 after the Afghan and Iraq Wars, David Frum and Richard Perle reiterate these themes as the neo-conservative matrix for future foreign policy.[30]

This may strike many in the Republican mainstream who did not arrive at their views from way-stations on the left as dangerously close to what has been called the utopian "social work" of the Clinton administration[31] or the "bear any burden, pay any price" euphoria of the Kennedy administration. There is no hint of the conservative virtues of either balance and caution nor of the academic work highlighting the difficulties inherent in transplanting democracy.[32] Indeed, there is a case to be made that, far from being conservative, modern neo-conservatism is better understood as a phenomenon of the "humanitarian liberal, Wilsonian" left.[33] Certainly, the movement's liberal beginnings suggest that there is substance in this interpretation, as do Kagan and Kristol's self-declared affinities with Wilsonian impulses.[34] Some neo-conservatives describe themselves as "hard Wilsonians," that is, advocates of American power to enforce American liberalism.[35] "Liberal imperialists" might be a better term.

Interestingly, as neo-conservatism's first generation completed its rightward migration, it ended in a position highly critical of a foreign policy based on "human rights," regarding this as a manifestation of a leftist "hidden agenda."[36] Today's neo-conservatives such as Wolfowitz revert

---

[28] Robert Kagan and William Kristol, eds., *Present Dangers: Crisis and Opportunity in American Foreign and Defense Policy* (San Francisco: Encounter, 2000), pp. 13–23.

[29] Kaplan and Kristol, *War over Iraq*, p. 121.

[30] David Frum and Richard Perle, *An End to Evil: How to Win the War on Terror* (New York: Random House, 2003).

[31] Michael Mandlebaum, "Foreign Policy as Social Work," *Foreign Affairs*, January–February 1996, pp. 16–32.

[32] Amy Chua, *World on Fire: How Exporting Free Market Democracy Breeds Ethnic Hatred and Global Instability* (New York: Doubleday, 2002), pp. 259–88.

[33] Norman Podhoretz, "Strange Bedfellows: A Guide to the New Foreign Policy Debates," *Commentary*, December 1999, pp. 19–31.

[34] Robert Kagan and William Kristol, "American Power – For What?" *Commentary*, January 2000, pp. 30–32 and 35–36.

[35] Max Boot, "Neocons," *Foreign Policy*, January/February 2004, p. 20.

[36] Irving Kristol, "Human Rights: The Hidden Agenda," *National Interest*, winter 1986/87.

to the movement's roots in the left by elevating human rights to center stage, for example, on U.S. China policy, precisely the approach followed by the Carter and Clinton administrations without great success.[37] What happened was that, following the 1972 McGovern debacle, one faction of the left regrouped around moderate progressivism (exemplified, perhaps, in the Carnegie Endowment for International Peace where Robert Kagan has a perch), while the other faction, calling themselves neo-conservatives, migrated to the Republican Party where they now reside. Once ensconced there, they adopted conservative jargon but retained their original leftist instincts. There is nothing to divide them from Madeleine Albright's thinking over Kosovo nor from her moralistic self-congratulation at having "done the right thing."[38]

The reality, however, is that while the neo-conservatives' globalist and idealist trappings provide a discourse that mobilizes political sentiment and patriotic emotion, they are little more than window dressing. In actual practice their focus is narrow, in fact distilled: the Middle East and military power, most of all the use of military power in the Middle East. They represent a new phenomenon in American foreign policy analysis, something that might be called "agenda-ism." Search *Present Dangers* and there is no mention of Latin America, Mexico, or Africa. Japan and Southeast Asia attract peripheral comment. India and Pakistan are viewed as "nonproliferation" problems. The European Union surfaces only inasmuch as it conflicts with NATO. When regional issues such as those clustered around North Korea's nuclear program are considered, the problem of proliferation is employed largely to underscore the neo-conservative willingness to act unilaterally, using preemptive force if necessary. In fact, Richard Perle suggests that he favors a unilateral attack on North Korea even at the cost of sacrificing the ten million plus inhabitants of Seoul.[39]

The economic dimension is almost entirely absent. Fully 80 percent of the book deals with the Middle East or the need for a strong military. The same pattern is repeated elsewhere. *An End to Evil* treats Islamic-inspired terrorism as the sole foreign policy challenge to the United States. Scholars at the Project for the New American Century pour most of their energies into the Middle East. Members of Americans for Victory over Terrorism do so exclusively. When attention turns elsewhere, for example, to a possible military deployment to Liberia, the neo-conservatives' unanimity

---

[37] Paul D. Wolfowitz, "Statesmanship in the New Century," in Kagan and Kristol, *Present Dangers*, pp. 318–20.

[38] Madeleine Albright, *Madam Secretary: A Memoir* (New York: Miramax, 2003), pp. 393–407.

[39] Frum and Perle, *An End to Evil*, pp. 99–100.

dissolves.[40] Suddenly, the longtime U.S. historical connections and the possibility that military activism might contain a human catastrophe and moderate regional destabilization from Nigeria to Sierra Leone, as detailed by Robert Kaplan, are of little importance.[41] As Owen Harries, the former editor of the *National Interest*, observed about Irving Kristol, "Australia along with a great deal of the rest of the world's surface, including all of Asia, Latin America, Africa and Canada does not draw his serious attention which is reserved for what goes on in the United States, Europe and Israel."[42]

Within the Middle East, neo-conservatives hold highly specific views clustering around open hostility to the peace process and Islam. Amid the various encomia they have penned in favor of the 2002 "Bush doctrine," the only criticisms emerge with regard to his Middle East policy, which is described as the "low point" and "unrealistic."[43] Several prominent neo-conservatives, including Richard Perle and Douglas Feith, took part in a 1996 study prepared for the Israeli Prime Minister Binyamin Netanyahu recommending a turn away from the Oslo peace process.[44] In 2001, Feith wrote a chapter titled "Land for No Peace" in *The Mideast Peace Process: An Autopsy*.[45] In his then capacity as Chairman of the Defense Policy Board, Perle sponsored in July 2002 an anti-Saudi briefing from Rand Corporation analyst Laurent Murawiec.[46] The eminent historian Bernard Lewis, although primarily a historian of the Ottoman period, has lent his considerable authority to the broad-front neo-conservative assault on Islam, his position as Princeton professor emeritus obscuring the fact that he is an influential, tactical, and partisan player in the contemporary policy debate.[47] And as signs emerged of real American engagement on the Israeli-Palestinian roadmap, they were there to limit administration action.[48] Perle has detailed ideas for the application of American power in every corner of the world, but when it comes to finding

[40] Charles Krauthammer, "Liberal Democrats' Perverse Foreign Policy," *Washington Policy*, July 11, 2003, p. A21.
[41] Robert Kaplan, *The Coming Anarchy: Shattering the Dreams of the Post–Cold War World* (New York: Vintage, 2001), pp. 7–15.
[42] Owen Harries, "The Australian Connection," in Christopher DeMuth and William Kristol, eds., *The Neo-Conservative Imagination* (Washington, D.C.: AEI Press, 1995), p. 35.
[43] Norman Podhoretz, "In Praise of the Bush Doctrine," *Commentary*, September 2002, pp. 19–28.
[44] "A Clean Break: A New Strategy for Securing the Realm," Strategic Research Publications, Institute for Advanced Strategic and Political Studies, June 1996.
[45] Neal Kozodoy, ed., *The Mideast Peace Process: An Autopsy* (New York: Encounter, 2001).
[46] Thomas E. Ricks, "Briefing Depicted Saudis as Enemies: Ultimatum Urged to Pentagon Board," *Washington Post*, August 6, 2002, p. A1.
[47] Peter Waldman, "A Historian's Take on Islam Steers U.S. in Terrorism Fight," *Wall Street Journal*, February 3, 2004, p. 1.
[48] Daniel Pipes, "Does Israel Need a Plan?" *Commentary*, February 2003, p. 19.

peace between Arabs and Israelis, he says that the United States is confined "at best . . . to use its influence to help broker the creation of a neutralized, disarmed Palestinian ministate."[49]

As an example of where these thoughts can sometimes lead in superheated moments, and to reflect views sometimes arising from the midlevels, it is instructive to consider extracts from a document entitled "Should Islam Be the Religion of the New Iraqi State?" circulating among the staff of the civilian administration in Baghdad in May 2003. Having stated that "our liberation of Iraq gives us the opportunity to revolutionize Muslim thinking on the role of Islam in the state," the document sets out two options: either "agree that Islam be declared the state religion" or "ensure that Islam is not declared the state religion." In other words, active consideration was given not simply to removing Saddam Hussein or eliminating the threat from weapons of mass destruction but additionally to revising the religious basis on which the Iraqi state was constituted.

The document looks at the first option's advantages in terms of "denying the Wahhabis, Iranian Mullahs and other fundamentalists the opportunity of claiming the US is trying to make Muslims into non-believers." However, the document perceives difficulties with this option arising from the "question of whether the state should support . . . what type of Islam (i.e. Shiite or Sunni), and permanent enshrinement based on today's percentages of Shiites and Sunnis which will likely change in the future, due to the seemingly higher birthrate among the Shiites, especially in the South." It comes to the firm conclusion that "only as a last resort should we agree that Islam should be the religion of the state."

The document was sent to Paul Wolfowitz, Richard Perle, Elliott Abrams, Bernard Lewis, Abe Shulsky, Douglas Feith, Paul Bremer (not then the U.S. Administrator in Baghdad), and others and was reflected in Iraq's draft constitution.[50]

This document sets some remarkably ambitious goals for an American-prescribed transformation of an ancient culture. It does not establish any modalities of how they are to be achieved; there is no mention of the region's history in which in the period 1952–79 five pro-Western kings or emperors were overthrown; and there is no discussion of whether there might be any negative consequences. The document contains ideas going far beyond the proclaimed goal of eliminating Iraq's weapons of mass destruction. We treat it therefore as emblematic of the fatal neo-conservative flaw: conceptual overreach and the absence of pragmatism.

---

[49] Frum and Perle, *An End to Evil*, p. 182.
[50] The document is in the authors' possession.

The document also reveals the neo-conservative unspoken agenda. If we may interpret what may lie behind the document:

The Middle East is a region of great strategic interest to the U.S. The security of Israel is a core commitment of the U.S. and access to Middle East energy resources is a vital strategic interest. Yet the region is highly unstable and successive attempts at intervention by past American administrations have come to nothing. Our friends in Israel tell us that the Palestinian *intifada* is exacting an insupportable economic and human burden. Our friends in Saudi Arabia tell us that they are sitting on a fundamentalist powder keg. The status quo is not an option. Imaginative new approaches are needed. The unelected governments comprising the Arab League must be persuaded to reform, to embrace democratic pluralism. Change is essential – by persuasion if possible, by force if necessary. The second step will be a reinvigoration of the peace process.

In an interview with the *Jerusalem Post*, Wolfowitz presented this general line of argument.[51] And, in his sympathetic account of neo-conservative views within the Bush administration, William Shawcross summarizes their Middle East view in broadly these terms.[52] Yet, even if it makes some strategic sense, we doubt that it is practicable. Regardless, if this does correspond to neo-conservative strategy, then it should be clearly articulated to the American people before the event and others throughout the world impacted by American policy. The endless parade of dissembling, misleading, or manufactured facts and policy pretense we have seen so far is unproductive and has injected the question of credibility into the political calculus. This is what is meant by saying that for all their claimed transparency, the neo-conservatives have an unspoken agenda that should be seen in the light of day where it can be properly scrutinized and debated. The foreign policy of a great country cannot be based on the sort of prevarication that has recently corrupted American decision making. That direction, as the neo-conservatives will themselves acknowledge, leads to perdition.

MORAL ARROGANCE

Neo-conservatives make much of their claim to have invented "moral clarity" for the purposes of foreign policy – or at least to have revitalized it following a period of dormancy after the Reagan administration. The reality is that, as Henry Kissinger (someone of intense suspicion to

---

[51] Janine Zakariah, "Interview with Paul Wolfowitz: Building a Free and Democratic Iraq Is Going to Be a Huge Victory in the War on Terrorism," *Jerusalem Post*, September 29, 2003.

[52] William Shawcross, *Allies: The U.S., Britain, Europe and the War in Iraq* (New York: Public Affairs, 2004), p. 56.

neo-conservatives) writes: "Moral purpose was a key element of motivation behind every American policy and every war in the twentieth century."[53] The neo-conservative claim of having uniquely placed the ambitions of nations around the world into categories of good and evil is, thus, without foundation. In his first inaugural address President Dwight Eisenhower stated that "the forces of good and evil are massed and armed and opposed as rarely before in history."[54] Go back further than that. The sense of American exceptionalism, the sense that America is seeking to be a society as none other in history, has existed since the earliest days and has been embraced and espoused by Abraham Lincoln, Teddy Roosevelt, and Woodrow Wilson, among many others. It is hardly unique to the neo-conservative elite. We will not treat an illegitimate claim on a patent they do not own as a hanging offense. But we would ask them to agree that others, including ourselves, have found their own, unaided way to a conviction of America's special place in the world. One of us has grown up with it implanted in his genes; the other has moved himself and his family here to breathe that air.

Indeed, by making special claims about their own moral virtue, the neo-conservatives tread on dangerous ground. The issue of "moral clarity" – who has it, who claims it – has haunted the presidency since its inception. It is, without question, a tricky political commodity – easily claimed as the neo-conservatives have, but seldom sustained. Every president has maintained that he has adhered to the nation's moral ideals more firmly than his predecessor – but have they? Bill Clinton campaigned on the theme that, unlike President George H. W. Bush, he would not buckle to the "butchers of Beijing." The result was that the Chinese gained Permanent Normal Trade Relations status under his administration.[55] Decrying this, George W. Bush said that he would treat China as a "competitor, not a strategic partner."[56] Three months into his administration he dealt very pragmatically with China over the EP-3 spy-plane incident, and relations have grown increasingly pragmatic as the Bush administration has realized that it needs Chinese cooperation to contain North Korea's nuclear ambitions. In a gesture toward China, the United States worked with the Chinese to designate the East Turkestan Islamic Movement as a terrorist movement. In a speech

---

[53] Henry Kissinger, *Does America Need a Foreign Policy?* (New York: Simon and Schuster, 2001), p. 272.

[54] Stephen E. Ambrose, *Eisenhower: Soldier and President* (New York: Simon and Schuster, 1990), p. 297.

[55] James Mann, *About Face: A History of America's Curious Relationship with China. From Nixon to Clinton* (New York: Knopf, 1999), pp. 292–314.

[56] Governor George W. Bush, "A Distinctly American Internationalism," speech at Ronald Reagan Library, Simi Valley, Calif., November 19, 1999.

at Qinghua University in February 2002 President Bush stated: "China is on a rising path, and America welcomes the emergence of a strong and peaceful and prosperous China." In December 2003, he came closer to endorsing China's position on Taiwan than any of his immediate predecessors. Moreover, emblematic of the above, President Bush has made himself available to the Chinese, meeting with them more often than President Clinton did.[57]

The point here is that in foreign policy the moral straight and narrow is difficult to maintain. All too quickly, events overwhelm ideologically driven intentions. Hypocrisy and double standards lurk at every corner and decision makers who are forced to make trade-offs are not thus, necessarily, morally bankrupt. Some minor spluttering aside, the neo-conservatives, for example, have been remarkably silent about the evaporation of President George W. Bush's high moral tone regarding the authoritarian regime in China despite in a collection of essays published in early 2000 having unambiguously identified China as a political, military, and moral adversary.[58] They have not hesitated, however, to criticize others who do not accept the neo-conservative agenda in the war on terrorism, including Republicans in good standing, as somehow lacking a proper moral dimension in their policy prescriptions. This is certainly the case when considering the Middle East where ideological prescriptions are inextricably bound with morality in advancing a policy that combines America's moral obligations to Israel with the objective of imposing market democracy on the entire region. They beg the question of whether such a policy is realistic, whether it is achievable given the resource constraints facing the United States and the enormous task of recasting the vast and alien political culture that permeates the region. They brush off the concern that invasive policies of this kind may in fact fan the flames of Islamic fundamentalism. The political debate cries out for a distinction between the desirability of pursuing an ideologically driven policy and which approach might best constitute a realistic one. Overextension is a very real danger and one that has made more than one appearance in the history of nations with global aspirations. And this leads to the question of the conditions under which this debate has proceeded in the United States, particularly the implication that those who disagree with the neo-conservative view harbor ill will toward Israel's effort to maintain a democratic, market-oriented state.

Those who do not accept the neo-conservative agenda but rather propose a return to the realism that has guided Republican foreign policy for half a

57 David M. Lampton, "The Stealth Normalization of U.S.-China Relations," *National Interest*, fall 2003, pp. 37–48.
58 Elliott Abrams et al., "American Power – For What?" *Commentary*, January 2000, pp. 21–47.

century do not, by definition, lack a moral compass nor are they defeatist. Both the authors criss-crossed Eastern Europe during the Cold War. When we transited the Friederickstrasse underground crossing between West and East Berlin, we had no illusions. We knew we were crossing from a society in which humanity was valued to a society where it was held in contempt. We also knew that we were not alone in thinking this. In the United States, the Cold War, informed by idealism but grounded in realism, reflected a balanced policy that was sustained on a bipartisan basis. The same was true in Britain where both Conservative and Labour Prime Ministers were equally committed to the struggle. In continental Europe it was two Socialist leaders, François Mitterrand of France and Helmut Schmidt of West Germany, who were the most active proponents of intermediate-range nuclear forces. And of those on the left or the right, who did not agree? They forced delays and brought political tension, but they were a strength to us, because they showed the Soviets that, unlike them, we could cope with dissent without the Gulag. We certainly agree that Ronald Reagan turned up the heat on the Soviets and, in crucial ways, was the author of its demise, but we also agree with Margaret Thatcher, a woman not known to be a shrinking violet on the issue of communism, that "the communist system contained within it the sources of its own destruction – its denial of human rights, its crushing of innovative thought, its suppression of nationalities."[59] What must be considered is that the Arab tyrannies dominating the region also contain the seeds of their demise and that our posture should be one of managing the transition or, at a minimum, influencing it, rather than imposing it.

Moral purpose has illuminated American foreign policy throughout the nation's history. For all their concerns about American moralizing, double standards, and hypocrisy, foreigners acknowledge that, at times of crisis, it is American values that saved the day. But for moral purpose to work best, it needs to be inclusive. We do not begrudge the neo-conservatives their values, although we would invite them to reflect that their principles may be less authoritative and somewhat more personal than they acknowledge. William J. Bennett, for example, is sometimes called by his admirers "America's Morality Czar." He belongs to a doctrinally hierarchical church that grounds its authority on its apostolic descent from the Jesus Christ of the New Testament. But when his personal preferences in favor of violence diverge from his church's interpretations of Christ's teachings, he does not hesitate to tease out legalistic interpretations that support his own views.[60]

---

[59] Caspar Weinberger and Peter Schweiz, *The Next War* (Washington, D.C.: Regnery, 1996), p. ix.
[60] Bennett, *Why We Fight*, pp. 33–36.

Neo-conservatives are passionate attackers of what they call "moral relativism," but the disjunction in the principles underlying policy prescriptions
for the Middle East, when compared with those informing policy in other regions, evidence just that. As we discuss in our chapters of anti-Americanism
and the impact on the homeland, morality should be a rallying point, not a
weapon, as the neo-conservatives have used it, to divide America from the
rest of the world and Americans from other Americans.

SHRINKING THE FOREIGN POLICY INSTRUMENTALITY

The emphasis on unilateral military force ("preemptive and unilateral war")
as the first and often the only option is the "joker" in the neo-conservative
deck.[61] From its early beginnings, a proclivity toward the use of force has
been an identifying badge of the neo-conservative ideology, with the early
neo-conservatives bolting the Democratic Party in the 1970s primarily because of what they described as its "culture of appeasement." This represented a much needed corrective to the prevailing liberal culture, made all the
more persuasive by the then neo-conservative recognition that "power begets
responsibility – above all, the responsibility to use this power responsibly."[62]

Today's neo-conservatives present a less subtle version of the ideology than
their intellectual progenitors. They reject what they regard as the Democratic
Party's "reflexive opposition to the use of force" and today instinctively embrace force, almost as an end in itself and, seemingly, regardless of its consequences.[63] (Afghanistan and Iraq are cases in point.) Due to the unparalleled
dominance of American military technology, their ideas are now enforceable
with, at least in the belligerent phase, unprecedented ease. Wars, such as in
Afghanistan and Iraq, can be fought with remarkable speed, fewer casualties
(including on the enemy side), and the utter certainty of victory.

This state of affairs shows all the signs of having gone to the collective
neo-conservative head. Max Boot writes that the Iraq campaign has made
"fabled generals such as Erwin Rommel and Heinz Guderian seem positively
incompetent by comparison." He looks forward to a new era when America,
like the British Empire, will always be fighting some war, somewhere,
against someone.[64] The neo-conservative fascination with war would make

---

[61] William Kristol, "Taking the War beyond Terrorism," *Washington Post*, January 30, 2002,
p. A25.
[62] Irving Kristol, *Neoconservatism*, p. 91.
[63] Lawrence F. Kaplan, "The Neo-McGovernites," *Wall Street Journal*, July 8, 2003, p. A16.
[64] Max Boot, *The Savage Wars of Peace: Small Wars and the Rise of American Power* (New York:
Basic Books, 2002), pp. 348–52.

an interesting psychological study, for, as a group, they exhibit few warrior norms. But add up their collective recommendations and the result would be a five-front war, including with China.[65]

In questioning this approach, Americans must be clear that the level of pre-Iraq defense spending, for example, is not at issue in this debate. As the world's leading nation, the United States will inevitably face crises that it alone must resolve. For any conservative and for most Republicans, the prerequisite is a strong, adequately funded military. Neo-conservatives have made much of the reductions in military spending during the Clinton administration (which the 1993 Regional Defense Strategy shows were actually initiated by then Defense Secretary Dick Cheney – "we are reducing our forces significantly") and have achieved a substantial increase in the defense budget – albeit one that keeps defense spending at about 3.5 percent of GDP and that is being implemented with broad bipartisan support.[66] And while it remains unclear at this writing whether additional troops may be required in Afghanistan and Iraq, the U.S. military is not in critical disrepair – at least according to the White House. Even at a somewhat lower proportion of GDP, 3.2 percent, Bruce Berkowitz from the Hoover Institution concludes that "we are keeping our edge without even breathing hard."[67] The questions revolve far more around how this awesome force is to be used.

The practical question is how effectively force settles the challenges facing the United States. World War II provides an unambiguous answer that wars are sometimes necessary and effective. But subsequent experience is less clear-cut. The Korean War may best be described as a standoff, and Vietnam is obviously the paradigm warning against a rush to war. The lessons of post-9/11 wars have yet to play out other than to make clear that America's fighting prowess has made the belligerent period the easy part. Neo-conservatives write glowingly about the rapid twenty-six-day victory in Iraq. Without question the military performance was remarkable, even unprecedented. To use the Pentagon's jargon, America's fighting forces have no "peer competitor." However, the follow-up – even when punctuated by heart-warming successes such as the capture of Saddam Hussein – is much more problematic, with long-term, truly grounded success proving elusive.[68]

---

[65] Kagan and Kristol, *Present Dangers*, pp. 3–24.

[66] Project for the New American Century, *Rebuilding America's Defenses: Strategy, Forces and Resources for a New Century* (Washington, D.C.: PNAC, 2000), p. 75.

[67] Bruce Berkowitz, *The New Face of War: How War Will Be Fought in the 21st Century* (New York: Free Press 2003), p. 5.

[68] Max Boot, "The New American Way of War," *Foreign Affairs*, July–August 2003, p. 44.

Afghanistan illustrates this point well. After the successful ejection of the Soviet army in 1991, one of the authors took part in British efforts to persuade the United States to stay engaged. At first our representations were heard respectfully as we warned about the dangers of a fundamentalist recrudescence in the wake of the corruption, incompetence, rapacious warlords, and underfunding of the Afghan government. But gradually we were received lower and lower down the bureaucratic hierarchy. Other than recovering unspent Stinger missiles, it was clear that no one was interested. As a senior CIA officer put it to one of the authors, "we don't do doors and windows," that is, the unglamorous follow-up was not part of CIA's job description. It was not that this neglect led directly to the Taliban and their harboring of Osama bin Laden, but it certainly helped.

The clear lesson here is that force, even when it can be deployed with such devastating and clinical effect, does not produce the clear-cut results that its advocates advertise. War, as an instrument of change, cannot address enduring political and cultural problems – the resolution of which is a precondition to market democracy – efficiently or effectively. If the nation-destroying aspect of war is to work, it can do so only in conjunction with the nation-building aspects of after-war. This is a reason to beware the flood of books describing the campaign aspects of the Iraq war in vivid Technicolor but which descend into grayer tones when dealing with politics.[69] The corollary is that if neo-conservatives believe that war is the preferred option to resolve conflict, then they must also believe in sustaining the peace through nation building – but that is a technology that neither they nor anyone else understands.

This means, of course, that the cost of war is not simply that of the belligerent phase; it extends into what, as we have seen, will be an extended and very costly period of postwar administration. Between them, Afghanistan (which is being done on the cheap) and Iraq are costing the American taxpayer sums of money, the orders of magnitude of which are being felt across the entire American macro-economy. These aspects of the neo-conservative policy are rarely mentioned in their writings. It is for this reason that we ask whether it is sensible to neglect, as the neo-conservatives would have us do, the other instruments of foreign policy that are available to the American government. Diplomatic, economic, allied cooperation, commercial, cultural: These are all levers of immense power. We look at this question in a chapter dedicated to the Iraq war. This was a popular war, but its instigation is found very

---

[69] Williamson Murray and Robert H. Scales, *The Iraq War: A Military History* (Cambridge, Mass.: Harvard University Press, 2003), pp. 251–56.

close to the neo-conservative heart. Preemptive military action in this case preempted the national policy process.

The second set of questions that need to be asked about the neo-conservative predilection for force is whether this distorts their analysis of international problems. If the dominant policy instrument is military, then the policy mindset is to look for enemies. China, in all its complexity and ambiguity, is caricatured as an adversary against which the only option is to "counter, confront and challenge."[70] The ongoing struggle between hardliners and reformists in Iran is ignored, rather than subtly analyzed for where this might be pushed in America's direction. Instead of this, Michael Ledeen of the American Enterprise Institute puts forward the flamboyant military option suggesting that "far more than the overthrow of Saddam Hussein, the defeat of the mullahcracy and the triumph of freedom in Tehran would be a truly historic event."[71] John Bolton brushes aside possible openings in the North Korean position as not worth knowing and indulges in personal recrimination against those with whom he is meant to be negotiating (while the authors share his views on Kim Jong-Il, they would have preferred a different venue to present them). In each case there is sound argument that the neo-conservative emphasis on force lacks credibility, principally because of the likely devastation that an attack would unleash. Is it likely, for example, that the United States would risk the annihilation of Seoul (against which some 11,000 North Korean artillery pieces are arrayed along the demilitarized zone thirty-three miles to the north) by an attack on North Korea? This is highly improbable. But by talking of military options that do not in fact exist, the neo-conservatives undo American credibility, making the search for solutions that much more difficult to obtain.

The last set of questions concerns the impact of neo-conservative views on the applicability of force on American global relations and on American society. Two neo-conservatives, Professor Eliot Cohen of the Defense Policy Board and former CIA Director James Woolsey (like Gingrich, more an ideological fellow-traveler than a founding member), have suggested that the United States is now "on the march" in "World War IV."[72] Clearly, this grabs headlines and, in its evocation of the Trotskyite notion of permanent revolution, keeps us alert. But is this, in fact, the most useful way of looking at the global problems facing the United States? As ordinary

---

[70] Ross H. Munro, "China: The Challenge of a Rising Power," in Kagan and Kristol, *Present Dangers*, pp. 68–69.

[71] Michael Ledeen, "Back the Freedom Fighters," *Washington Post*, June 23, 2003, p. A21.

[72] James Woolsey, speech at seminar at UCLA organized by Americans for Victory over Terrorism, April 2, 2003.

Americans ponder the ways in which they can promote American interests and values – whether in business, offering technologically advanced goods; in the arts, offering recording artists attracting crowds of young people; as hosts welcoming foreign students to witness the best of America; or in a thousand other capacities – we wonder, as discussed in our chapter on contemporary anti-Americanism, whether the best image the world can have of America is engagement in warfare twenty-four hours a day, seven days a week, 365 days a year.

When war is more than a slogan, one must ask, What are the implications? Domestically, many stand mute as the Justice Department proceeds to implement far-reaching limitations on Fourth Amendment rights of privacy and due notification of search and seizure, all in the name of a combined "war on terror" and the war in Iraq. Just as this state of constant warfare has the effect of transferring power to the center,[73] the very constraints on federal power that lay at the heart of America's founding philosophy are being eroded in the name of an alleged defense of our freedoms. Is this a trend we wish to embrace? Are these sacrifices that Americans are ready to make? Throughout this book we raise these and other questions about the implications of neo-conservative policy. Most involve matters of judgment rather than fact. Of course, this suggests part of the answer. Anyone who says that he or she has easy answers to these questions is not providing the full facts.

By embracing force and military methods generally, one of the main neo-conservative goals is to banish the "Vietnam syndrome" once and for all. Neo-conservatives do not accept President George H. W. Bush's assertion that Desert Storm moved the United States beyond Vietnam. To the contrary, writes Eliot Cohen, "the Gulf War did not end the Vietnam syndrome, but, if anything, strengthened it."[74] By which he means that, while Desert Storm showed that the United States could fight a post-Vietnam war that was forced upon it by external causality, it did not yet show that the United States could fight a discretionary war such as that in Kosovo or Iraq. They have little interest in any so-called lessons of Vietnam that inhibited such undertakings. One of their objectives is to repudiate these lessons.

As we move forward to our next section where we look at the applicability of force as the default weapon against terrorism, it may be worth reminding ourselves of three lessons drawn by the chief architect of the Vietnam

---

[73] Charles Tilly, "Reflections on the History of European State-Making," in Charles Tilly, ed., *The Formation of Nation States* (Princeton, N.J.: Princeton University Press, 1975), p. 42.

[74] Eliot A. Cohen, *Supreme Command: Soldiers, Statesmen and Leadership in Wartime* (New York: Free Press, 2002), p. 199.

policy, Robert McNamara, who occupied the office now held by Donald Rumsfeld:

We failed then – as we have since – to recognize the limitations of modern, high-technology military equipment, forces and doctrine in confronting unconventional highly motivated people's movements.

We did not hold to the principle that U.S. military action – other than in response to direct threats to our own security – should be carried out only in conjunction with multinational forces supported fully (and not merely cosmetically) by the international community.

Underlying many of these errors lay our failure to organize the top echelons of the executive branch to deal effectively with the extraordinarily complex range of political and military issues . . . associated with the application of military force under substantial constraints over a long period of time.[75]

In our view, these are key points on which neo-conservatives need to be questioned. Force has its place in the foreign policy of any country, but for fifty years it has been a goal of American foreign policy to minimize the incidence of international violence. If, in the world according to neo-conservatism, this is no longer to be the default goal of American foreign policy, this represents a significant change. Neo-conservatives happily say, "[N]ow that the U.S. is powerful, it behaves as powerful nations do."[76] Perhaps. There is a certain obvious inevitability about this. But we think it is worth asking whether this is the future Americans would choose. Or might it be something different? Was America always destined merely to follow down the same paths followed by those once great, now no more powers? As we see it, this is a betrayal of both Republican and conservative principles, producing outcomes that resemble the restless, half-committed half-apologetic, no follow-up interventionism practiced by the Clinton administration – and roundly and rightly criticized by the neo-conservatives. In the following chapters we invite our readers to see the impact of these prescriptions on national policy.

THE RESPONSE TO SEPTEMBER 11

Immediately following the shock of September 11, an extremely important development took place. In his address that night to the nation, President Bush said: "The search is under way for those who are behind these evil acts. I've directed the full resources of our intelligence and law enforcement communities to find those responsible and to bring them to justice. *We will*

---

[75] Robert McNamara, *In Retrospect: The Tragedy and Lessons of Vietnam* (New York: Times Books, 1995), pp. 322–23.
[76] Kagan, *Of Paradise and Power*, pp. 20–21.

make no distinction between the terrorists who committed these acts and those who harbor them" (emphasis added). By the time of Bush's address to the nation on October 7, 2001, as the Afghan war opened, this thought was solidified. "Today we focus on Afghanistan, but the battle is broader. *Every nation has a choice to make. In this conflict, there is no neutral ground. If any government sponsors the outlaws and killers of innocents, they have become outlaws and murderers, themselves.* And they will take that lonely path at their own peril" (emphasis added).

There is, however, some evidence that, at least momentarily, thought was given to framing the U.S. response to 9/11 as a challenge posed fundamentally by nonstate actors. After meeting with his national security team on September 12, Bush said, "The American people need to know that we're facing a different enemy than we have ever faced. This enemy hides in shadows." In his address to a joint session of Congress on September 20 he stated: "Americans are asking: How will we fight and win this war? . . . *This war will not be like the war against Iraq a decade ago, with a decisive liberation of territory and a swift conclusion. It will not look like the air war above Kosovo two years ago*" (emphasis added).

How U.S. policy transitioned from a position in which the focus should have been on a messy, long-term engagement against the perpetrators of terrorism – which parallels the policies of many of the closest allies of the United States who have faced and still face acute and chronic terrorist challenges (Britain with the IRA, France with the OAS, Germany with the Red Brigade, Spain with ETA) – into its final position of concentrating on the claimed state sponsors of terrorism, in which conventional state-on-state war became the norm and the war on Iraq inevitable, remains to be explained by future historians. They will also be better able to assess whether the adopted approach proved effective or whether it deepened the terrorist threat to the United States and to individual Americans. What is already known, however, is that the transition closely reflected the established neo-conservative position and neo-conservative interventions in the policy process. As we show below in our analysis of the rise of the neo-conservatives under George W. Bush and in the case-study on Iraq, Deputy Secretary of Defense Paul Wolfowitz advocated an attack on Iraq on September 15, just four days after September 11 and before any sure lines of responsibility were established. On September 11 itself presidential speechwriter David Frum spent an hour on the telephone with Richard Perle, whose first response to the events was to counsel that the United States go after "not just terrorists, but whoever harbors those terrorists."[77] Perle was among the first to draw public attention to the significance

---

[77] Sam Tanenhaus, "Bush's Brain Trust," *Vanity Fair*, July 2003, p. 117.

of the administration's decision to go after states.[78] We also show how the language used by the top policy makers made the eventual policy outcome inevitable.

As Donald Rumsfeld stated in congressional testimony on July 9, 2003, "the coalition did not act in Iraq because we had discovered dramatic new evidence of Iraq's pursuit of weapons of mass murder. We acted because we saw the existing evidence in a new light, through the prism of our experience on September 11th." Whether or not this is true, the fact remains that the neo-conservatives succeeded in focusing attention on those *states*, such as Iraq, Iran, and Syria, that had been in the neo-conservative sights for at least a decade rather than on the *causes* of 9/11 about which no one knew very much – and indeed about which there is still some uncertainty today. By directing attention to what they called the "terror masters," the neo-conservatives were able to influence the decision-making process toward their long-held positions involving attacking Iraq.[79] These positions go back to at least the 1992 draft Defense Planning Guidance paper (which after a troubled gestation eventually was published as the Regional Defense Strategy of 1993), when the neo-conservatives, with the support of then Defense Secretary Dick Cheney, already had the possibility of a "rejuvenated Iraq" in their sights.[80] Wolfowitz acknowledges that he personally started worrying about Iraq in 1979, even though he "knew the country only from books."[81] In a letter to President Clinton of July 26, 1996, masterminded by the Project for the New American Century and signed by several prominent neo-conservatives, but with the addition of such names as Donald Rumsfeld and Richard Armitage, this thinking was significantly developed. It said: "The only acceptable strategy is one that eliminates the possibility that Iraq will be able to use or threaten to use weapons of mass destruction. In the near term, this means a willingness to undertake military action as diplomacy is clearly failing." In the following years the neo-conservatives cultivated close relations with the Iraqi National Congress, a longtime advocate of the overthrow of Saddam Hussein.

September 11, therefore, found the neo-conservatives well prepared. Far better than anyone else, they had their response in place and targets fixed. In a very real sense, Saddam's coordinates were already entered into the computer. The result therefore was that the United States found itself fighting not a new or different kind of war but a straight-up reprise of Desert Storm, the only

[78] Richard Perle, "The US Must Strike at Iraq," *New York Times*, December 28, 2001, p. A19.
[79] Michael Ledeen, *The War against the Terror Masters* (New York: St. Martin's Griffin, 2003), pp. 269–88.
[80] Dick Cheney, "Defense Strategy for the 1990s: The Regional Defense Strategy," p. 21.
[81] Jim Hoagland, "Getting to Know the Iraqis," *Washington Post*, July 20, 2003, p. B7.

difference being that on this occasion military technology delivered an even swifter kill. We have already dealt with the fact that, in many respects, this represented an implementation of the preexisting neo-conservative agenda rather than a de novo response to an unfolding emergency, as was the case with Pearl Harbor and the post–World War II containment policy. But the open question is what this has to do with fighting and defeating terrorism, the goal that unites all of us.

Terrorism experts, both perpetrators and preventers, come in all shapes and sizes, but if there is a point of commonality, it is that, in the age of the Internet, cellular communications technology, miniaturization technology, mass airline transportation, and global financial transfer networks, modern terrorism has been "democratized" in the sense that attacks can be mounted through virtual networks without the need for state resources or centralized leadership structures. Whereas Abu Nidhal needed the support of the various Libyan People's Bureaus to communicate securely and to make financial transactions, this support is no longer needed. The first director of British Intelligence's Counter Terrorism Center told us that he now believes that "state sponsorship" is an obsolescent idea.[82] Modern terrorism can achieve devastating effects with micro inputs. The devastation of 9/11 was brought by nineteen terrorists at a cost that some estimate as low as $500,000. The 1993 attack on the World Trade Center is thought to have cost as little as $20,000.[83] The idea current in neo-conservative circles that terrorism needs to be a multibillion-dollar business is highly suspect.[84] British antiterrorism experts estimate that, even at the height of its terrorism, the IRA had less than 100 hard-core members. Israel has killed or imprisoned hundreds of "senior Hezbollah leaders," yet the suicide bombers keep coming. The Russian military has conducted sweep after sweep through the streets of the Chechen capital of Grozny, but the explosions in Moscow continue. Once terrorism has become a mass-based phenomenon, "leadership is superfluous."[85] We show below how these realities have, among our allies, elicited very different policy responses.

President Bush was right when he said that this enemy hides in the shadows. Leaders are barely necessary when, with a single key stroke, a million

---

[82] Jessica Stern, "The Protean Enemy," *Foreign Affairs*, July–August 2003, pp. 27–40.

[83] "Terrorist Financing: Foxes Run to Ground," *Journal of Money Laundering Control*, winter 2003 (London: Howard Stuart Publication), p. 275.

[84] Rachel Ehrenfeld, *Funding Evil: How Terror Is Financed and How to Stop It* (Chicago: Bonus Books, 2003).

[85] Roger D. Petersen, *Understanding Ethnic Violence: Fear, Hatred, and Resentment in Twentieth-Century Europe* (Cambridge: Cambridge University Press, 2002).

e-mail instructions can be sent out to "kill an American." There are multiple Web sites that provide the motivation for terrorists. This is why the neo-conservative ideology is so inappropriate for this challenge. It is retrogressive. Not only have neo-conservative policies stimulated anti-American sentiment worldwide, imposing strain on our commercial relations and diplomatic efforts, it harks back to an earlier age when military competition between nation-states was the main component of international relations. Rather than putting its faith in the classic antiterrorism tools of police and intelligence work fortified by political engagement with the causes of terrorism, the neo-conservative model is taken from the classic wars of nineteenth- and twentieth-century Europe.

THE FALSE HISTORY

Though passionately interested in ideas, neo-conservatives tend to be "more concerned with influencing public debate and elite policy making than with producing knowledge for other intellectuals."[86] This approach shows clearly in the strenuous efforts made by neo-conservatives to adorn their ideology with the legitimacy of American history. Theodore Roosevelt, Harry Truman, and certainly Ronald Reagan are their heroes. This is not true history, however, but a pastiche of selective citations or cherry-picked highlights designed to prove a point. On Roosevelt we hear much of his "big stick" but little of his cautionary words about the use of force in his second inaugural address. We hear absolutely nothing about Roosevelt's intense personal diplomacy in the Russo-Japanese War, for which he was awarded the Nobel Peace Prize.[87] Regarding Truman, they applaud his tough stance against the Soviets but tell us nothing about his means, namely his intimate connection with the creation of the United Nations.[88] As for Reagan, here the neo-conservative have boiled down his presidency to a few simplistic slogans and have airbrushed out their own keen misgivings about him. As Reagan's administration was drawing to a close, for example, Norman Podhoretz was proclaiming that "the communists were winning."[89] It is little more than a historical mugging that we discuss further in a subsequent chapter. Certainly, Reagan prized

---

[86] Sara Diamond, *Roads to Dominion: Right Wing Movements and Political Power in the US* (New York: Guilford, 1995), p. 179.

[87] Edmund Morris, *Theodore Rex* (New York: Random House, 2001), pp. 386–428.

[88] Stephen C. Schlesinger, *Act of Creation: The Founding of the United Nations* (Boulder, Colo.: Westview, 2003), pp. 5–16.

[89] Amy E. Ansell, *Unraveling the Right: The New Conservatism in American Thought and Politics* (Boulder, Colo.: Westview, 1998), p. 63.

military strength highly, but, as his Secretary of State George P. Shultz, himself a patron of at least two of today's neo-conservative leaders, summed up Reagan's foreign policy, Reagan "believed in being strong enough to defend one's interests, but he viewed that strength as a means, not an end in itself. He was ready to negotiate with his adversaries."[90] In other words, the support they seek from Presidents Roosevelt, Truman, and Reagan for their ideology that military force should be the primary option simply is not there.

Ironically, one of the neo-conservative group, Donald Kagan, is a serious historian. In his splendid book *The Peloponnesian War*,[91] he sets out a good case that the real lesson for empires at the top of their game is to be wary of overconfidence, and specifically overreliance on their military dominance. The land battle of Delium in 424 B.C., he argues, hastened Athens's decline as a military power. When the neo-conservatives recycle their endless mantra of "Munich," Delium might be a novel way to inject new life into a rather tired conversation. Kagan himself might assist this progress by repudiating his contribution to *Present Dangers* where, in order to accord with neo-conservative ideology, he presented what he must know is a sadly bowdlerized version of the events leading up to Munich.

THE NEO-CONSERVATIVES AS A SPECIAL INTEREST?

Against this background, we suggest that the most appropriate way to view neo-conservatism is as that staple of American political life: a special interest. What do we mean by this?

When George Washington was preparing to leave office for the final time in September 1796 he awarded himself the luxury of a Farewell Address in which to communicate some cautionary remarks to his fellow countrymen. Among them was a strong warning about the undemocratic tendencies of "factions" or, as we would call them today, "special interests":

All combinations and associations, under whatever plausible character, with the real design to direct, control, counteract, or awe the regular deliberation and action of the constituted authorities are destructive of this fundamental principle and of fatal tendency. They serve to organize faction, to give it an artificial and extraordinary force – to put in the place of the delegated will of the nation, the will of a party; often a small but artful and enterprising minority of the community; and, according to the alternate triumphs of different parties, to make the public administration the mirror of the ill concerted and incongruous projects of faction, rather than the organ

[90] George P. Shultz, *Turmoil and Triumph* (New York: Scribners, 1993), p. 1136.
[91] Donald Kagan, *The Peloponnesian War* (New York: Viking, 2003), pp. 167–70.

of consistent and wholesome plans digested by common councils and modified by mutual interests. However combinations or associations of the above description may now and then answer popular ends, they are likely, in the course of time and things, to become potent engines, by which cunning, ambitious and unprincipled men will be enabled to subvert the power of the people, and to usurp for themselves the reins of government."[92]

Americans, be they Supreme Court justices, talk-show hosts, or book authors, tend to react selectively to the pronouncements of the Founding Fathers. They quote those they like as examples of eternal verities to be ignored at their peril by succeeding generations. Where they are less enthusiastic, they quietly say that times have changed. Michael Hirsh, not a neo-conservative but a sympathizer, writes: "A great deal of what Thomas Jefferson and George Washington once thought is not terribly relevant today, at least as concerns foreign policy. Nor is what happened in the Philippines in 1899 or to Rome and Byzantium."[93]

We believe that historical amnesia is a major gap in American foreign policy conceptualization. But we know what Hirsh means. We do not wish to become slaves to history. So, in this case, perhaps we can have it both ways. Of course, Washington was talking about a country very different from that which we know today. He remarks, for example, that his readers (the address was never given orally) had the "same religion, manners, habits, and political principles," a state of affairs that obviously no longer prevails today. But the prescient genius of his insight was to anticipate what has turned out to be a continuing feature of American politics, namely the striving by associations representing the interests of their members to secure for themselves a privileged seat at the national decision-making table. Today we call these associations "special interests" to distinguish them from political parties that are accountable to the people and are part of the open democratic process. In general, Americans whether of the left or the right react badly to any mention of the influence of special interests, and legislative efforts to check their activities are constantly in motion. Antitrust legislation, introduced at the end of the nineteenth century and still powerfully active today, is the classic example of legislation introduced to check the influence of an overmighty agglomeration of power.

What constitutes a special interest? Political science offers varying definitions, but MIT professor Gene Grossman offers a usefully flexible

---

[92] John C. Fitzpatrick, *The Writings of George Washington* (Washington, D.C.: US Government Printing Office, 1934–40), vol. 35: pp. 214–38.

[93] Michael Hirsh, *At War with Ourselves: Why America Is Squandering Its Chance to Build a Better World* (New York: Oxford University Press), p. 13.

interpretation as "any minority group of voters that shares identifiable characteristics and similar concerns."[94] The neo-conservatives fit this definition:

- They covet similar policy outcomes;
- They advocate unchanging ideological solutions to multiple problems whatever the changing circumstances;
- Although holistic in presentation, their policy recommendations are highly focused on certain regions and certain policy instruments;
- They seek to exclude alternative options.

It is a sad fact of modern American politics that special interests tend to produce a zero sum game. I cannot win unless you lose. If steel producers gain a tariff that raises import prices, they win but consumers of imported steel – car and refrigerator buyers, for example, or anyone who drives over a bridge built with steel girders – lose, to say nothing of frayed tempers inside the World Trade Organization. In the battle between special interests, the complexity and interdependence of problems becomes lost. The only required value is clarity, however ersatz in quality. As people who have been frequently interviewed on the telephone for appearance on a cable news show, we know that the line goes very quiet if we make the mistake of remarking that an issue might have more than two sides. For cable news hosts interested solely in playing to their demography, black or white are the preferred, indeed, the only choices. Anything else risks losing viewers or listeners. So special interests all too often dominate the public discourse. In his book *The Dust of Empire*, Karl Meyer relates the tale of a Central Asian peasant who, on fortuitously freeing a genie from a beautiful jar while tilling his field, is granted a wish – on condition that he agrees that his neighbor will be awarded twice anything he receives. The peasant reflects carefully and finally asks, "Genie, take my right eye."[95] This story is usually cited to illustrate the hopelessly noncooperative basis of life on the steppes. But it can equally be applied to the scorched-earth outcomes that emerge from the relentless competition among rival special interests in American politics.

Our argument is that America today faces this dangerous special interest phenomenon in the field of foreign affairs where adherents of neo-conservatism have established a remarkable ascendancy over the decision-making process. In doing so, they have succeeded in imposing an artificial

94 Gene M. Grossman and Elhanan Helpman, *Special Political Interests* (Cambridge: MIT Press, 2001), p. 75.
95 Karl E. Meyer, *The Dust of Empire: The Race for Mastery in the Asian Heartland* (New York: Public Affairs, 2003), p. 201.

clarity of their own invention on the highly complex network of interactions that constitute America's relations with the rest of the world.

Some may interject that special interests are well known in American foreign policy. President Eisenhower famously warned of the influence of the "military-industrial complex." An obvious contemporary example is the Cuban-American community has established a forty-year stranglehold over U.S. policy toward Cuba. The electoral arithmetic is so finely balanced in South Florida that no administration, even the Bush administration, which is being pushed for change by its natural allies in the business community, can hint that it might be ready to discontinue its ritual round of "Cuba libre" toasts with the exile community on May 20 each year.[96] During the Clinton administration, national security strategy resembled a grab bag of every liberal constituency on earth, from the environment, family planning, biological diversity, collapsing states, and AIDS.[97]

Furthermore, with foreign policy an elite endeavor (the requirements of national security and diplomatic confidentiality, not to mention language skills, necessarily limit the numbers of those fully in the know), it is clear that foreign policy will always be a minority undertaking. At several points in American history, crucial "transformatory" moments, for example, America's emergence on the world stage through the 1898 Spanish-American War or the evolution of the containment policy after World War II, have been directed by a relatively small number of individuals, often from privileged backgrounds. It is hardly unusual for such people to absorb a sense of mission. But what is dangerous is when the debate becomes constricted and exclusionary. When this happens, the danger we face is that we do not recreate the Truman and Reagan administrations but, instead, risk resuscitating the "best and brightest" generation that brought us the prolonged engagements in Southeast Asia.

---

[96] Ann Louise Bardach, *Cuba Confidential: Love and Vengeance in Miami and Havana* (New York: Random House, 2002), pp. 101–25.

[97] William J. Clinton, *National Security Strategy of Engagement and Enlargement* (Washington, D.C.: U.S. Government Printing Office, 1996).

2

Origins and Early Development

The terrorist attacks of September 2001 brought neo-conservatism and neo-conservatives in from the cold. In the wake of that national trauma, they and the belligerent mindset associated with them gained a prominence and influence that they had been striving for, mostly with only moderate success, for over thirty years. From being an intellectually dynamic but little known movement struggling to be heard above and differentiated from Goldwater conservatism, neo-conservatives suddenly found themselves with increasing access to real power. Celebrity beckoned. Well-composed photographs of the main neo-conservative figures appeared in glossy magazines normally dedicated to teen models and the goings-on of the rich and glamorous.[1] The words "neo-conservative agenda" became a fashionable media sound bite. Diplomats in many an anxious Washington chancery analyzed neo-conservatives' views with the attention they once gave to the Kremlin. The European Union Delegation even composed a dossier of some of the more provocative neo-conservative *bons mots*.[2] But below the hype, the neo-conservative creed remains a much-misunderstood phenomenon. To their friends, neo-conservatives are "super hawks"; those less well disposed call them "warmongers." In short, neo-conservatism has become the stuff of cable news label mongering, a form of journalistic shorthand for policies favoring war fighting and regime change mainly but not exclusively in the Middle East.[3]

---

[1] Sam Tanenhaus, "Bush's Brain Trust," *Vanity Fair*, July 2003, pp. 114–69.
[2] Fraser Cameron, *US Foreign Policy after the Cold War* (New York: Routledge, 2002).
[3] Jonah Goldberg, "State of Confusion: Brouhahas – Intellectual and Otherwise," *National Review*, May 16, 2003.

How neo-conservatives reached their current positions of influence and how their beliefs have evolved over the years provides the material for this chapter. We set out to explain who they are and what they believe in. Some of the names may be unfamiliar, and, inversely to their influence, the numbers are relatively few. Neo-conservatism is not a mass movement.

Neo-conservatives have traveled along a circuitous path, as befitting the elusive character of their philosophy. As the neo-conservatives were starting out in the 1960s, scholars struggled to define the newly emerging term. One noted that neo-conservatism had "no common manifesto, credo, religion, flag, anthem or secret handshake."[4] Another was more blunt, asserting that neo-conservatism simply could not be coherently defined.[5] Yet another commented that they "can speak bitterly about each other's work and opinions."[6] Nonetheless, neo-conservatives were making an impact; they were seen as the "men who are changing America's politics."[7] And the description was not unmerited. As we show below, first-generation neo-conservatism was a philosophical movement of political significance to American society at large. America's neo-conservative founders – Irving Kristol, Norman Podhoretz, Daniel Bell, Daniel Patrick Moynihan, Midge Decter, Michael Novak, Gertrude Himmelfarb, Peter Berger, et al. – addressed the many challenging questions facing American society. In international affairs, two of their defining concepts were staunch defense of Israel and a depiction of détente as a failure of nerve and a spineless reluctance to stand up to the evils of communism.

Within the discourse of these prolific intellectuals were debates over whether man now suffered from spiritual chaos rather than an amalgam of institutional failures; whether one could understand the social conditions of the modern West while ignoring the central place that religion held in past societies; and how to achieve a successful balance between social control and individual freedom.[8] They dissected the contradictions raised by the tenets of their own thinking: Can one support free market capitalism and accept a welfare state? Do we still advocate democratic freedom if we

---

[4] Quoted in Jonah Goldberg, "The Neoconservative Invention: No New Kid on the Block," *National Review*, May 20, 2003.

[5] Seymour Martin Lipset, "Neoconservatism: Myth and Reality," *Society* (July–August 1988), p. 28.

[6] Irving Howe quoted in Joseph Dorman, *Arguing the World: The New York Intellectuals in Their Own Words* (New York: Free Press, 2000), p. 1.

[7] From the title of Peter Steinfels, *The Neo-Conservatives: The Men Who Are Changing America's Politics* (New York: Simon and Schuster, 1979).

[8] Cited in ibid., p. 107.

criminalize the institutional outlets used by the nation's most dangerous enemies? Can society truly support free speech if it censors pornography?[9] In refreshing contrast to today's more constricted debate topics, their interests extended beyond the use of force or a modern interpretation of Machiavelli's *Prince*. They asked as many questions as they offered answers. Not all parts of neo-conservatism have worn equally well – there are early passages of such stridency opposing multiculturalism that they come close to racism – but there is no doubt that in the 1970s neo-conservatism represented one of the most extensive and sophisticated bodies of American political discourse.

These intellectuals stood out from other stands of contemporary right-wing thought, for arguing with more reason than sensation and slogan. They looked at a world defined not only by its malcontents in the Middle East or North Asia, but also by the complexity of human behavior and the substance of human systems.[10] In his autobiographical collection of selected essays and publications from almost half a century of writing, Irving Kristol discusses interrelated and separate questions of welfare, race, sex, socialism, nihilism, social reform, corporate capitalism in America, the definitions of social justice, Adam Smith, the moral sources of capitalism, urban civilization plus its discontents, Christianity, Judaism, and the role of religious orthodoxy within society.[11] Kristol gave early space in the *Public Interest* to the young advocates of a then obscure theory of economic growth called "supply side economics," which jumped to prominence under Ronald Reagan and which continues to be influential today.[12] Whereas the critic Lionel Trilling once described American conservative thought as "irritable mental gestures which seek to resemble ideas," there is no doubt that the early neo-conservatives helped to establish a genuinely American brand of conservatism that broke free of European roots.[13]

In an ironic development, the advent of today's neo-conservatives in positions of influence has coincided with a marked diminishment in their

---

[9] Mark Gerson, *The Neo-Conservative Vision: From the Cold War to Culture Wars* (London: Madison, 1996), p. 11.

[10] Ibid., pp. 16–23.

[11] Irving Kristol, *Neoconservatism: The Autobiography of an Idea* (New York: Free Press, 1995), see preface and contents.

[12] Jude Wanniski, "The Mundell-Laffer Hypothesis: A New View of the World Economy," *Public Interest*, spring 1975, pp. 31–52.

[13] Gary Dorrien, "Inventing an American Conservatism: The Neo-Conservative Episode," in Amy E. Ansell, *Unraveling the Right: The New Conservatism in American Thought and Politics* (Boulder, Colo: Westview, 1998), p. 56.

intellectual range. America's current expression of neo-conservatism is intellectually dwarfed by the shadow of its progenitor. It is assertively binary in formulation: us versus them, good versus evil, Mars versus Venus, Hobbes versus Kant, right versus left, and so on. Contrary to the expectations of the early neo-conservatives who at the end of the Cold War saw the international agenda as "mission accomplished" but wrote that "in the realm of domestic policy only a beginning has been made on the work of the conservative revolution,"[14] today's neo-conservatives focus heavily on foreign affairs. They continue to pursue interests in other spheres, such as human genetics, welfare, and crime, but somehow these seem like sideshows largely unintegrated with their main pursuits.

Even on foreign policy, modern neo-conservatism focuses narrowly. It pays scant attention to the world beyond defense budgets and select areas of the world where its ideology is applicable. Today's children of the early neo-conservatives (in many instances this is literally the case) demonstrate little desire for the sort of interpretive framework that their intellectual forefathers sought in order to explain the world around them. Indeed, for the sake of advancing their foreign policy beliefs, they have entered marriages of convenience with populist conservative elements far removed from the intellectual rigor espoused by the neo-conservative founding generation and with whom they had bitter disputes on social issues throughout the Reagan administration.

One reason for this is that today's generation has a narrower range of intellectual experimentation than their predecessors. Irving Kristol records that on his graduation in 1940, the "honor I most prized was the fact that I was a member in good standing of the Young People's Socialist League (Fourth International)." At the same time he was also reading the King James Bible and was coming under the influence of the Catholic theologian Reinhold Niebuhr.[15] The modern neo-conservatives, however, give the appearance of having been born intellectually middle-aged. Not for them the frivolity of Woodstock or the iconic music of the time. Today, at the risk of a slight caricature, a neo-conservative is a contributor to the *Weekly Standard* who takes his intellectual cue from the American Enterprise Institute and agrees that the French are a "strategic enemy."[16]

---

[14] Norman Podhoretz, "Neo-Conservatism: A Eulogy," *Commentary*, March 1996, p. 26.
[15] Kristol, *Neoconservatism*, pp. 5 and 470.
[16] Michael Ledeen, quoted in "The War Party," BBC *Panorama* transcript, May 18, 2003.

ALCOVE I: THE EARLY BEGINNINGS

The term "neo-conservative" originally was a biographical as much as an ideological description. It entered the Modern American lexicon in the 1970s to define a new breed of political animal who had turned toward the right as a former liberal disenchanted with the left's reluctance to stand up to the Soviets and the anti-American radicals.[17] Although he did not invent the term, the sticker "neo-conservative" was first used by Michael Harrington and the editors of *Dissent* as a derogatory term for former comrades.[18] Norman Podhoretz asserts that the name was intended as "pejorative,"[19] and even today modern neo-conservatives such as Elliott Abrams accept the designation more as an act of daring than as a badge of honor.[20] The term did not instantly define the genus. Moynihan complained that while his friends on the left, such as Harrington, called him a neo-conservative, his friends on the right, such as the conservative thinker William F. Buckley, Jr., called him a "left-liberal" – after all, as a senior White House adviser he pushed Nixon toward income support programs for the poor.[21] Buckley, however, in a characteristic gesture of support for early neo-conservatives, defended Moynihan and his co-author Norman Glazer against charges of racism that were raised after publication of their book *Beyond the Melting Pot*.[22] Interestingly, Irving Kristol thought that Buckley, though a conservative icon, was in fact a closet liberal.[23]

But to take the biographical analogy one step further, the biography of a neo-conservative is also a biography of American twentieth-century history. One political observer remarked that the vital statistics of a "neo-con" comprise a college education in Marxism, a fervent sense of anticommunism, support for civil rights, and an experimentation with radicalism followed by a total repudiation of it.[24] This gives a clue to neo-conservative psychology, both at its founding and in its contemporary version. It inhabits a Manichean world where there is no place for half-measures and no holds are barred, even against their fellow conservatives. Michael Ledeen writes that he was "sickened by the grotesque spectacle" of the G. H. W. Bush administration after

---

[17] David Frum, *Dead Right* (Toronto: HarperCollins, 1994), p. 127.
[18] Goldberg, "The Neoconservative Invention."
[19] Podhoretz, "Neo-Conservatism: A Eulogy."
[20] Elliott Abrams, "American Power – For What?" *Commentary*, January 2000, p. 21.
[21] Daniel Patrick Moynihan, *A Dangerous Place* (New York: Secker and Warburg, 1975), p. 49.
[22] John B. Judis, *William F. Buckley Jr.: Patron Saint of the Conservatives* (New York: Simon and Schuster, 1988), pp. 326–27.
[23] Ibid., p. 169.
[24] Gerson, *Neo-Conservative Vision*, p. 192.

the end of the Cold War.[25] Moynihan describes Oliver North, anonymously but unmistakably, as a "mindless apparatchik."[26]

The founders of neo-conservatism had briefly associated with the Trotskyist left in the 1930s. Some of the original neo-conservative thinkers first became an identifiable group during this decade while gathering in a small section of the City College of New York cafeteria called Alcove 1. This was where the noncommunist socialists gathered to debate the nature of their anti-Stalinism, while the Communists exercised their suzerainty over Alcove 2. It was here that America's future neo-conservative intellectuals such as Daniel Bell, Nathan Glazer, Irving Kristol, Melvin Lasky, Seymour Martin Lipset, Seymour Melman, Daniel Patrick Moynihan, and Philip Selznick received enduring parts of their education.[27]

But one must dispel the popular misconception that Trotsky became in any way a guiding intellectual influence on neo-conservatives. He was never quoted in subsequent neo-conservative articles or essays and never featured in the philosophical ideas that they brought to bear on American society.[28] It was more that this experience helped to shape these students' intellectual style as aggressive debaters in a highly politicized environment where sympathy for communism and even Stalin himself was common.[29] It was from discussing the finer points of Marxism in the 1930s among formidable intellectual colleagues that they learned to use the sophisticated application of theory as a form of political combat and the conception of politics as something that should be instructed by theory.[30] Ideas were the stock in trade. As Irving Kristol put it, "what rules the world is ideas, because ideas define the way reality is perceived."[31] As we show below, this interpretation assumed critical importance in the way that the neo-conservatives constructed the political discourse to represent their version of reality in the public debate before the Iraq war.

Two essential ways to identify the early neo-conservatives are what they wrote and where they wrote it. A look at where the neo-conservatives wrote

[25] Michael Ledeen, "American Power – For What?" *Commentary*, January 2000, p. 37.
[26] Daniel Patrick Moynihan, *Pandaemonium: Ethnicity in International Politics* (New York: Oxford University Press, 1993), p. 46.
[27] Gary Dorrien, *The Neoconservative Mind: Politics, Culture and the War of Ideology* (Philadelphia: Temple University Press, 1993), p. 69.
[28] Goldberg, "The Neoconservative Invention."
[29] Quoted in Dorrien, *Neoconservative Mind*, p. 70. See also Gillian Peele, *Revival and Reaction: The Right in Contemporary America* (Oxford: Clarendon, 1984), pp. 24–25.
[30] John B. Judis, "Trotskyism to Anachronism: The Neoconservative Revolution," *Foreign Affairs*, July–August 1995, p. 126.
[31] Kristol, *Neoconservatism*, p. 233.

delineates a journey from intellectual circles in New York in the 1930s to Washington's corridors of power in the 1970s. As Steinfels wrote in one of the first comprehensive studies on the phenomenon of neo-conservatism, the geography of the intellectuals' world is the geography of journals. For the neo-conservatives, this space expanded gradually but considerably from the 1950s until it occupied a prodigious place in American political discourse by the time Ronald Reagan took office. When Podhoretz was named editor in chief of *Commentary* in 1959, it had a profound effect on the journal's intellectual direction. Published by the American Jewish Committee (although with its own editorial board and separately financed), it henceforth became one of a cluster of leading intellectual fora for neo-conservatives. By the late '60s, *Commentary* was launching regular assaults on the New Left and the emerging counterculture. Six years after Podhoretz arrived at *Commentary*, Kristol and Bell founded the *Public Interest,* designed to be a "nonideological" approach to issues of the social and political sciences and aimed at providing information necessary for public policy decisions. Although not every writer in these journals could be considered neo-conservative, a comparison between the first issue of the *Public Interest* and the bicentennial issue ten years later gives a sense of the tightly knit intellectual clique that evolved among the contributing academics. While the first issue featured articles by Kristol, Glazer, Bell, Moynihan, Robert Nisbet, Martin Diamond, and Robert Solow, the issue ten years later featured articles by Moynihan, Glazer, Diamond, Bell, and Nisbet. Thus, *Commentary* and the *Public Interest* shared many of the same writers from the 1960s onward and helped to create an intellectual infrastructure of neo-conservative writers that included other leading academics, such as Midge Decter, Diana Trilling, Edward Shils, Novak, Milton Himmelfarb, and Lipset.

A 1979 study on the seventy most prestigious contemporary American intellectuals suggested that about one in every four of the intellectual elite was a neo-conservative.[32] This comment reflected just how far the intellectual reach of neo-conservatism had grown. When Nixon took office, he recommended that his cabinet read an article by Peter Drucker that had recently been published in the *Public Interest*. When Reagan took office, he appointed Jeane Kirkpatrick to the position of U.S. ambassador to the U.N. largely on the basis of an article that she had published in *Commentary*. It was not simply that these presidents came across these articles as they perused the morning papers; in Kirkpatrick's case, National Security Adviser Richard V. Allen drew Reagan's attention to the article. These journals, and

[32] Steinfels, *Neo-Conservatives*, p. 4; Gerson, *Neo-Conservative Vision*, pp. 94–95.

the intellectuals who wrote for them, occupied an essential space in America political discourse that reached the highest levels of government.[33] In just over a decade *Commentary* had turned from a provincial New York intellectual periodical into a journal read and discussed by presidents and their immediate advisers.[34] Alongside *Commentary* and the *Public Interest*, neo-conservative thinkers and writers established ties with *Encounter*, the *New Leader*, *American Scholar*, and *Foreign Policy*. By the end of the 1970s, neo-conservative articles were appearing in *TV Guide*, *Reader's Digest*, *Fortune*, *Business Week*, and *U.S. News & World Report*.

ENTER THE THINK TANKS

Arm in arm with the extending influence of neo-conservative thought across American literature in the 1970s was the increasingly visible presence of the think tank. Only a few think tanks had operated in Washington up to the beginning of the 1970s. The subsequent ascendance of the policy think tank to a higher position in America's political order was representative of the socio-political changes of the time. These institutions expanded and multiplied as ideological conservatives and like-minded thinkers began to conduct nationwide campaigns against policies and ways of life that they felt threatened America. For example, the American Enterprise Institute (AEI) had been founded in 1943 but remained at a modest level of activity until 1971, when then Secretary of Defense Melvin Laird began an intense fund-raising campaign. AEI's budget subsequently increased from $1 million in 1970 to $10.4 million in 1980.[35]

The campaign continued when Jimmy Carter defeated Gerald Ford, and, in a foreshadowing of its uncompromising opposition to Bill Clinton, AEI assumed a markedly oppositional role toward government. Ford subsequently became a fellow at AEI where he joined a number of leading intellectuals, including Irving Kristol, Novak, Kirkpatrick, and Herbert Stein. Just as neo-conservative ideas were gaining greater purchase on the political debate in Washington, so they were becoming ingrained in an emerging think-tank culture. Large and steady business contributions were becoming more forthcoming from corporations such as those now represented in the Business

---

[33] Paul Gottfried, *The Conservative Movement* (New York: Twayne, 1993), pp. 83–84; Steinfels, *Neo-Conservatives*, pp. 5–10; and David M. Ricci, *The Transformation of American Politics: The New Washington and the Rise of the Think Tanks* (New Haven: Yale University Press, 1993), pp. 160–64.

[34] Gottfried, *Conservative Movement*, p. 85, and Steinfels, *Neo-Conservatives*, p. 83.

[35] Ricci, *Transformation*, p. 169.

Roundtable. With more money and larger staff by the latter 1970s, AEI published several periodicals, such as *Foreign Policy and Defense Review* and *Public Opinion*.[36] But although AEI offered a range of conservative opinions including those of increasingly prominent neo-conservatives, it was still funded largely by older corporations and foundations that adhered to moderate Republican sentiments.

In response, a group led by Paul Weyrich, which claimed to represent the real sentiments of conservatism, established the Heritage Foundation in 1973. Heritage immediately specialized in the advocacy industry producing well-referenced bulletins and essays on current issues that made detailed research accessible in short memoranda to busy government officials, journalists, and academics.[37] As think tanks progressively found their new niche in the political life of Washington, so did many neo-conservatives find themselves ensconced within the growing network. Leading neo-conservatives developed strong links with AEI, Heritage, the Georgetown Center for Strategic Studies, the Aspen Institute, the Hudson Institute, and Freedom House. With a spreading influence across Washington's body politic, these prominent academics were not simply intellectuals who wrote articles and books. They had the ear of officeholders and political candidates. They contributed to speeches, recommended programs, helped to draft legislation, and served on special commissions.

THE PHILOSOPHICAL UNDERPINNINGS

In looking at what the early neo-conservatives wrote, a general discussion of ideas is problematical since these intellectuals were by definition highly independent thinkers and drew from an "admixture of themes from liberal, conservative and socialist traditions."[38] Neo-conservatives have often grumbled at attempts to place them into an ideological pigeonhole. As Irving Kristol said in 1979, "when two neo-conservatives meet they are more likely to argue with one another than to confer or conspire."[39] Well-identified neo-conservatives at times joke – in tones reminiscent of testimony before the House Un-American Affairs Committee – "I was not and never have been a neo-conservative."[40]

---

[36] Ibid.
[37] Ibid., pp. 161–62.
[38] Steinfels, *Neo-Conservatives*, p. 3.
[39] Quoted in Goldberg, "The Neoconservative Invention."
[40] Daniel Bell, "Neoconservatives: Then and Now," *New York Times*, October 19, 2003, sec. 4, p. 10.

This tradition certainly continues today with neo-conservatives disagreeing among themselves about whether or not to call themselves Wilsonians. Some, such as Robert Kagan and William Kristol, seek to have it both ways, sometimes identifying with the Wilsonian tradition and sometimes distancing themselves from it.[41] There is, therefore, always something slightly arbitrary about summarizing neo-conservative thought. However, it is possible to group the tenets of neo-conservative thought around the five fundamental categories: protection of democratic capitalism, the purpose of government, desegregation and ethnicity, moral values and religion, and America's role in the world.[42]

In response to this confused analytic situation, Irving Kristol published an essay titled "Confessions of a True, Self-Confessed Neo-Conservative."[43] As a leading figure in neo-conservatism, he went further than many in establishing a definitive classification of it. In an attempt to define what he saw as the rudiments of neo-conservative thinking, Kristol described a "vague consensus" of five principles that had helped to transform a number of liberals into certified neo-conservatives. First, he emphasized that neo-conservatism was "not at all hostile to the idea of a welfare state." As he asserted: "[I]n general, it approves of those social reforms that, while providing needed security and comfort to the individual in our dynamic, urbanized society, do so with a minimum of bureaucratic intrusion in the individual's affairs." Second, Kristol underlined the neo-conservative belief that the market is an essential instrument for spreading resources while protecting individual liberty. The third tenet was an emphasis on being "respectful of traditional values and institutions: religion, the family," and so on. According to Kristol, avoiding undermining the moral value system was "one thing that neo-conservatives are unanimous about." Fourth, his definition rejected the insistence that everyone must have "equal shares of everything." The last element of consensus was foreign policy, where neo-conservatism believed that "American democracy is not likely to survive long in a world that is overwhelmingly hostile to American values."[44]

Although these are general statements, they provide a framework for understanding both the body of issues that occupied the early neo-conservative thinkers and the social and political circumstances that induced

---

[41] William Kristol and Robert Kagan, "Reject the Global Buddy System," *Washington Post,* October 25, 1999, and "American Power – For What?" *Commentary,* January 2000, pp. 30–33 and 35–36.

[42] Peele, *Revival and Reaction,* pp. 32–33.

[43] Quoted in Goldberg, "The Neoconservative Invention."

[44] Steinfels, *Neo-Conservatives,* pp. 51–53.

the conversion from liberal to neo-conservative. The last element also gives a clue to an abiding aspect of neo-conservatism. It is born out of a deep Spenglerian pessimism that far transcends the mild pessimism that may be found in many conservative circles. In February 1975, Moynihan, following his tempestuous tenure as U.S. Ambassador to India, said on New Delhi's airport ramp, "I am delighted to be departing a country whose principle export is communicable disease." *Commentary* published Moynihan's article titled "The United States in Opposition," in which he described his experience as an American diplomat confronting opposition at every turn. Echoing this gloomy assessment, Podhoretz commented that the United States was "hated because of who and what we are."[45]

This sense that the United States was losing the war of values not just with the Soviet Union but also against the ravages of extreme liberalism in the United States and Western Europe deeply permeates neo-conservative thinking. Leo Strauss, whose ethereal but pervasive influence is outlined below, went so far as to worry that the entire construct of post-Enlightenment liberal civilization – which he called the "Modern Project" – was faltering under the onslaught of communism. In a foreshadowing of modern neo-conservative obsession with military strength, Strauss counseled, "The only restraint in which the West can put some confidence is the tyrant's fear of the West's immense military power."[46] This pessimism about the sustainability of Western ideas unsupported by the bayonet conditioned the early neo-conservative migration from left to right, and remains crucially influential today. In this way, neo-conservatism differs radically from the essential optimism of their chosen role models, such as Ronald Reagan. In parallel with his defense buildup Reagan was, like Theodore Roosevelt, Franklin Roosevelt, and Jack Kennedy, incurably optimistic about the eventual triumph of American values – and not simply because they had more firepower behind them. He liked to quote Lord Acton in saying that history is the march of liberty. They have little in common with the neo-conservative fretfulness that all too often resembles that of the inhabitants of a gated community.

In response to what they saw as an undermining of America's moral values and the increasing appeal of reactionary ideologies in American society, the first-generation neo-conservatives wrote prolifically on the question of capitalism in modern society. Kristol published *Two Cheers for Capitalism* in 1978, which suggested that capitalism may not be perfect but was better

45 Norman Podhoretz quoted in Ian Buruma, "How to Talk about Israel," *New York Times Magazine*, August 21, 2003, p. 32.
46 Moynihan, *Pandaemonium*, p. 237.

than any alternative for the provision of both material wealth and personal liberty. Daniel Bell's "Unstable America" questioned why governing institutions were progressively losing their legitimacy in the eyes of various sections of society. George Gilder published an explanation of why capitalism did not corrode society but, through its spreading wealth, tended to improve the lot of everyone. Published in 1981, Gilder's *Wealth and Poverty* argued that successful economy depends on the proliferation of the rich and that entrepreneurs were the heroes of economic life. In 1982, Michael Novak's *The Spirit of Democratic Capitalism* defined the capitalist model as something beyond materialism and utilitarian efficiency. It was a system with spiritual and moral foundations, which bound together the market economy, the democratic polity, and society's ethical values.[47]

The tumultuous course of events in American society through the 1960s defies any identification of a single incident or collection of events as the stimulus for the neo-conservative conversion. The enormous buildup of American forces in Vietnam, a new era of political activity across schools and universities, the civil rights movement leading to civil unrest and the articulation of discontent among African Americans, the perceived infiltration of radical left-wing ideas from student movements into middle-aged intellectuals, massive protest marches, occupied campuses, and barbed wire and tanks on the streets of Chicago all seemed to herald the arrival of an adversarial and dangerous culture for a number of elite intellectuals.[48] They believed that liberals were failing to defend liberalism from the assault of the New Left. Neo-conservatives were rapidly becoming critics of modern American liberalism in their efforts to defend what they saw as liberalism under siege, and by the end of the 1960s, the intellectual discourse between right and left was more like intellectual war.[49] By the turn of the decade, liberal politics seemed to be moving progressively in two directions: the radical liberals were demanding that American society push beyond the boundaries of contemporary liberalism in order to attain its potential; and those such as Irving Kristol and the intellectual coterie associated with him had become increasingly vocal in their assertion that America must act in response to the ever more

---

[47] Peele, *Revival and Reaction*, pp. 33–35; Steinfels, *Neo-Conservatives*, p. 53; and George Nash, "Twenty Years of Great Conservative Thought," *Policy Review*, the Heritage Foundation, December, 12, 2002.

[48] Jerome Himmelstein, *To the Right: The Transformation of American Conservatism* (Berkeley: University of California Press, 1990), p. 70; Mary C. Brennan, *Turning Right in the Sixties: The Conservative Capture of the GOP* (Chapel Hill: University of North Carolina Press, 1995), p. 131; Steinfels, *Neo-Conservatives*, pp. 44–45; and Gerson, *Neo-Conservative Vision*, p. 115.

[49] Will Hutton, *The World We're In* (London: Little, Brown, 2002), p. 93; Steinfels, *Neo-Conservatives*, p. 4; and Gerson, *Neo-Conservative Vision*, p. 128.

visible adversarial culture in order to preserve liberalism's heritage.[50] By the early 1970s, Irving Kristol and Gertrude Himmelfarb had endorsed Richard Nixon for president. Although the majority of like-minded intellectuals did not follow them in this move, the gesture confirmed a conceptual evolution among a number of Democrats and liberals.[51]

THE MOVE FROM LEFT TO RIGHT

Of course, what animated the ideas and impulses of these intellectuals were their opinions on America's role in the world. By the end of the '60s, this issue was occupying ever more space on the neo-conservative agenda. In reaction to the groundswell of left-wing and liberal protest against American involvement in Vietnam, numerous neo-conservatives began in the 1970s to voice the opinion that defeat in Vietnam was a failure of circumstance, not motive or morality. Although some had previously revealed dovish positions on American entanglement in Southeast Asia, prominent intellectuals such as Podhoretz now reacted against the movement of liberals and radicals who described America's role in the war as an example of evil: "That there were many things wrong with the country I had been saying for a long time now. But evil?"

Moynihan complained that advances by the Vietcong were being "welcomed in the *Harvard Crimson*."[52] Podhoretz announced a turning point in 1970, when he refashioned *Commentary* to reflect his response to reactions from the left. Liberals and social democrats that had contributed to the journal for over a decade suddenly ceased to appear in it.[53] Podhoretz and others reacted against what they saw as the incorrect interpretation of failure in Vietnam as delegitimizing American military commitment abroad in general. For many neo-conservative thinkers, the debate over Vietnam was a mechanism to identify people who were anti-American, not only within the United States, but also abroad.[54] Today, the Vietnam War remains a hot button for neo-conservatives, with persistent emphasis laid on the falsity of drawing lessons from that experience.

Although the Vietnam question reflected in some measure where an individual stood in the spectrum of debate across America between radical

---

[50] Fred Halliday, *The Making of the Second Cold War* (London: Verso, 1983), p. 113, and Steinfels, *Neo-Conservatives*, p. 4.

[51] Halliday, *Making*, p. 113, and Gerson, *Neo-Conservative Vision*, p. 135.

[52] Moynihan, *Pandaemonium*, p. 59.

[53] Dorrien, *Neoconservative Mind*, p. 164.

[54] Peele, *Revival and Reaction*, pp. 46–47.

left and neo-conservative right, there were those such as Irving Kristol who did not see the conflict as a root cause for the emergence of an adversarial culture. He considered the counterculture not to have originated in response to any sense of crisis in economics, politics, or even America's serious involvement in Vietnam, "since the emergence of a counterculture antedated it by several years." Instead, he believed that it came from elements belonging to the very fabric of society. As Kristol suggested, "the counterculture was not caused, it was born."[55] This idea emphasized the intense desire among early neo-conservatives to understand and explain where the inherent failures and fault lines of society lay. Frequently discussed across the pages of the *Public Interest* and *Commentary* were the issues of desegregation and ethnicity. As one of Kristol's co-editors at the *Public Interest* and professor at the department of education at Harvard, Glazer wrote various works concerning the debate on ethnicity in American culture, including his 1982 publication *Ethical Dilemmas*.[56] Both he and Moynihan also produced *Beyond the Melting Pot*, in which they asserted that race and ethnicity were among the essential mechanisms with which people group themselves and would always constitute an immovable obstacle to the liberal conception of integration.[57] Moynihan induced controversy in 1965 when he wrote a report on the challenges faced by African Americans in the United States. In it he argued that discrimination against African Americans could not be eliminated simply through legislation, owing to the very nature of their position within American society. Both Glazer and Moynihan agreed that the social life of the American polity was largely designated by ethnicity, which therefore made antidiscrimination laws difficult.[58] Glazer was at pains to stress the limitations of social policy.[59]

Other neo-conservative thinkers such as Bell examined the relationship between what they saw to be a shrinking emphasis on class and the strengthening of "national, cultural, linguistic, religious, communal, tribal or primordial attachments."[60] The politics of targeting racial discrimination with legislation troubled many neo-conservatives because they believed that the prospect of integration relied on a misconception of society that ignored natural ethnic and religious allegiances. Many of them viewed the concept of positive discrimination and affirmative action in universities and workplaces

[55] Kristol, *Neoconservatism*, p. 136.
[56] Peele, *Revival and Reaction*, p. 38.
[57] Gerson, *Neo-Conservative Vision*, p. 86.
[58] Ibid.
[59] Nathan Glazer, "The Limits of Social Policy," *Commentary*, September 1971, pp. 51–58.
[60] Daniel Bell, *Sociological Journeys: Essays 1960–1980* (London, 1980), p. ix.

as a threat to the concept of opportunity. They regarded the emerging notion of multiculturalism as abhorrent. Neo-conservatives such as Moynihan and Glazer emphasized the need to protect the opportunities for mobility within American society from false liberal assumptions about progress that might ensue from forced integration.[61]

In their efforts to understand the constructs of society and the challenges that modern America was facing, a number of neo-conservatives also debated what the government's position within the political system should be. In 1973, Kristol wrote, "I am thinking of such questions as: How do we know whether or not a social reform has worked? What are the general characteristics of successful reforms? Are there any general principles of reform that can guide us towards success and steer us away from failure? After our experience of the past decade, such questions are certainly in order."[62] This is not to say that all neo-conservatives believed in the unchecked power of the free market across all social spheres. It is more that Irving Kristol and others were concerned with the degree of governmental intervention in welfare.[63] They believed that it needed to be set within constraints and doubted its capacity to combat an existing culture of poverty. One particular neo-conservative idea suggested that society contained within it an unemployable subsection that was impervious to the alteration of its status. This implied a world-view among some of those living in the worst conditions that determined their status regardless of any chances to escape it. Neo-conservatives questioned whether there might even be some inherited factors that predisposed society's underclass to welfare.[64]

The neo-conservative discourse often considered discussion of the social and political conditions of modern society to be connected in some way to the question of religion. The original neo-conservatives had an intense interest in religion and the debates surrounding its position within society. The manner in which those such as Bell, Glazer, and Podhoretz tackled the questions of religion in America differed significantly from the approaches of the New Right and religious right.[65] The latter two strands focused on particular social and political issues and actively sought to secure the election of conservative candidates; the neo-conservatives, meanwhile, adopted

---

[61] Nathan Glazer and Daniel Patrick Moynihan, *Beyond the Melting Pot: The Negroes, Puerto Ricans, Jews and Irish in New York* (Cambridge: MIT Press, 1963), pp. 290–93.

[62] Kristol, *Neoconservatism*, p. 200.

[63] Peele, *Revival and Reaction*, pp. 36–37.

[64] Kristol, *Neoconservatism*, pp. 42–46, and Steinfels, *Neo-Conservatives*, p. 61.

[65] Jonathan Schoenwald, *A Time for Choosing: The Rise of Modern American Conservatism* (Oxford: Oxford University Press, 2001), p. 256.

a more intellectual approach, explaining the general contribution that religious values make to the health of society and the human character. Whereas the New Right was an exclusively Republican organization and sought to bend the Republican Party to their views, neo-conservatives as true intellectuals divided their party political loyalties. As late as 1992 several neo-conservatives endorsed Bill Clinton over George Bush.[66] Increasingly from the 1970s, neo-conservative writing articulated a dislike for right-wing religious fundamentalism in American society. Irving Kristol, Richard John Neuhaus, and Norman Podhoretz examined what they saw as the social value of religion and its function as a basis for virtue, self-responsibility, and morality in society.[67] Many neo-conservatives also expressed great concern over what they viewed as the undermining of this basis. Irving Kristol considered there to be a surrendering of religion to the spirit of modernity "at the very minute when modernity itself is undergoing a kind of spiritual collapse."[68]

ANTICOMMUNISM AND FOREIGN POLICY

Thus, from the social function of religion to the culture of poverty, from the mechanisms of integration to the limitations of welfare systems, neo-conservatism's first generation showed a capability for enormous scope within its "vague consensus." However, for the last of Irving Kristol's five principles – America's role in the world – the 1972 elections were a turning point. George McGovern seemed to illustrate everything that was wrong with American liberalism. Intellectuals such as Podhoretz and Jeane Kirkpatrick considered McGovern's slogan of "Come home, America" as defeatist and isolationist.[69] A handful of Democrats, such as Hubert Humphrey, Senator Henry Jackson, Max Kampelman, Penn Kemble, Evron Kirkpatrick, Jeane Kirkpatrick, Moynihan, Podhoretz, and Ben Wattenberg, formed the Coalition for a Democratic Majority (CDM) as a way to pull the Democratic Party away from the younger generation of McGovern supporters. Although some of these individuals shared views only in the most general of terms, they had begun the movement against what they regarded as spineless foreign policy that would eventually define neo-conservatism. Here the influence of Reinhold Niebuhr's work, *The Children of Light and the Children of Darkness*,

---

[66] Peele, *Revival and Reaction*, p. 44.
[67] Gerson, *Neo-Conservative Vision*, p. 284.
[68] Kristol, *Neo-Conservatism*, p. 440.
[69] Dorrien, *Neoconservative Mind*, p. 166.

with its emphasis on the human capacity for evil, played a key role in providing a Cold War theology[70] for the early neo-conservatives. The CDM in turn spawned offshoots such as the Institute on Religion and Democracy, founded by Penn Kemble, Richard Neuhaus, and Michael Novak.

Richard Nixon's emerging policies of reconciliation and peaceful coexistence with the Soviet Union were subsequently described in the pages of *Commentary* as almost exactly that. Podhoretz went on to assert that Nixon "would no doubt much rather be presiding over the growth of an empire, but who finds no realistic alternative to the withdrawal of the United States from the role it has played since the end of World War II in checking the expansion of Communist power."[71] By the middle of the 1970s, a recognized political grouping of Jackson, Kirkpatrick, Moynihan, and Podhoretz had emerged as fiercely aggressive toward the Soviet Union and profoundly critical of détente.[72] In 1975, Podhoretz published "Making the World Safe for Communism." This was a caustic condemnation of the American failure in the conflict with communism. The Soviet enemy was apparently winning without a fight. An inherent neo-conservative pessimism-based distrust in the intrinsic power of American ideas was beginning to show through. Podhoretz and others argued that a crippling hesitancy was affecting American foreign policy and that "the Vietnam syndrome was eating away at the American sense of self."[73] Many neo-conservatives supported Senator Henry M. (Scoop) Jackson, a Democrat from the state of Washington, in the 1976 primary campaign, and subsequently found that the Democrat who won the nomination greatly exacerbated the malfunctions in American foreign policy making.[74] Jimmy Carter became as much a focus for neo-conservative accusations of failing nerve as Nixon. Podhoretz published "The Culture of Appeasement" in the first years of Carter's presidency, in which he portrayed the apparent weakness that derived from the residual influence of Vietnam on policy making in Washington.[75] He reflected the attitudes of many neo-conservatives in asserting that a rising tide of pacifist sentiment had permeated not only American critical consciousness at the generalized level, but also the upper echelons of the Carter administration. He contended that in order to counter this phenomenon and encourage a more

---

[70] Michael Novak "Needing Niebuhr Again," *Commentary*, September 1972.
[71] Quoted in Dorrien, *Neoconservative Mind*, p. 169. See also Gerson, *Neo-Conservative Vision*, p. 178.
[72] Halliday, *Making*, p. 117.
[73] Gerson, *Neo-Conservative Vision*, p. 180.
[74] Dorrien, *Neoconservative Mind*, p. 167.
[75] Gerson, *Neo-Conservative Vision*, p. 182, and Dorrien, *Neoconservative Mind*, p. 170.

activist foreign policy, which the threat of communism around the globe demanded, Americans needed a more visibly patriotic culture.[76] A meeting between a group of leading neo-conservatives and Carter in January 1980 that was designed to heal the rift between them and the Democratic Party ended disastrously and, in a sense, legitimized the migration to the Republicans. It was at this stage that a further rift opened between those who were leaving the Democrats and those who were remaining, notably Moynihan.[77]

In November 1979, *Commentary* published Kirkpatrick's "Dictatorships and Double Standards." This article (which built on ideas outlined a year earlier by Ernest Lefever in his article "The Trivialization of Human Rights") described what she saw as a basic paradox in Carter's policy of punishing countries such as El Salvador, Nicaragua, and Iran for human rights abuses while also trading and negotiating with the Soviet Union and various other communist governments. She argued that it was pointless to refuse engagement with dictators and apply moralistic standards if the only consequence was the replacement of that regime with a communist-oriented, totalitarian state. The article strongly suggested that American national interests should not be undermined by support for movements in other countries likely to produce regimes hostile to the United States. Kirkpatrick maintained that Carter's human rights policies and Nixon's détente amounted to a sense of naïveté in American foreign policy. During Reagan's preparation for the presidential debates with Carter, Kirkpatrick had played Carter's role in discussing foreign policy, but it was largely on the basis of this *Commentary* article that Reagan appointed Kirkpatrick as ambassador to the U.N. when he assumed office.[78] This was a highly innovative and operationally dynamic contribution to U.S. diplomatic practice. With the transition of countries such as the Philippines (where Paul Wolfowitz in his State Department capacity played a key role), South Korea, Argentina, and Brazil from authoritarian rule to a more liberal civil society, it is a theory that remains relevant – even if its hard edge has been blunted somewhat by the emergence of democracies from the former Soviet empire.

The question of U.S. relations with the U.N., however, had already witnessed the hard edge of neo-conservative realism in foreign policy before Kirkpatrick's appointment. The 1970s had seen a groundswell of neo-conservative criticism against the U.N. as an effective governing body. For

---

[76] Ibid.

[77] Robert G. Kaufman, *Henry M. Jackson* (Seattle: University of Washington Press, 2000), pp. 397–98 and 444.

[78] Gerson, *Neo-Conservative Vision*, p. 177; Peele, *Revival and Reaction*, p. 48; and Nash, "Twenty Years."

a number of years, Kirkpatrick, Podhoretz, and Moynihan had been particularly skeptical toward the U.N., and demanded a realistic reassessment of America's relations with the world body.[79] They believed that the Soviet Union had no intention of respecting the U.N. as a conflict-resolution mechanism or system of checks and balances and that America was therefore persisting in an erroneous belief in the U.N. charter as a useful instrument for the conduct of American foreign policy.

ISRAEL, ANTI-SEMITISM AND THE U.N.

Although the role of the U.N. in world affairs constituted a neo-conservative preoccupation in itself, the issue was closely related to another key focus of their intellectual attention: a keen interest in the affairs of Israel. Intellectuals such as Podhoretz argued that the American commitment to Israel derived from Israel's democratic rather than religious nature. He emphasized that the profound neo-conservative commitment to Israel's security transcended individual religious status.[80] This is not to say that neo-conservatism at any point in its history was or is a purely or even predominately Jewish phenomenon. To depict it as such is a sloppy and false characterization – one that has been abused by tabloid polemicists of both left and right to distract attention from the substance of neo-conservative ideas. Neo-conservatism attracts adherents from a wide variety of religious backgrounds, and commitment to Israel's security has been a core principle of all American administrations ever since Harry Truman's recognition of Israel in 1949. Some neo-conservatives allege that the hostility to them is a disguise for hostility toward Israel.[81] It is not. It is possible to be a neo-conservative or to support neo-conservative views without being Jewish or a Zionist, just as it is possible to be critical of neo-conservatives without being anti-Semitic or hostile to Israel.

In relation to Israel, the 1970s also witnessed an increase in the number of neo-conservative publications that focused on defense of American policies concerning the Israel. Following the 1973 Yom Kippur War, the Jewish Institute for National Security Affairs was established, partially at the prompting of the Pentagon for a counterbalance to liberal sniping at defense spending. Podhoretz, for one, played an active role in providing a visibly pro-Israeli voice in what many neo-conservatives of the time considered to

---

[79] Peele, *Revival and Reaction*, p. 47.
[80] Ibid., p. 187.
[81] David Frum and Richard Perle, *An End to Evil* (New York: Random House, 2003), p. 120.

be an intellectual community lacking in support for Israel as the only genuine democracy in the Middle East.[82] Intellectuals such as Peter Berger, Murray Friedman, and Irving Kristol had been suggesting for a number of years that American society was witnessing a rise in the negative stereotyping of Jewish people across various segments of society. In the 1970s, Podhoretz published numerous articles in *Commentary* that discussed the manner in which Israel's victory in the Six Days' War had engendered both a great sense of unity within the American Jewish community and a wave of anti-Zionism throughout the intellectual communities of the world, including in the United States. Podhoretz was also certain that anti-Zionism was simply a thin veil to cover expressions of anti-Semitism and that it was often a sentiment found among those who were generally anti-American in their radical orientation.[83] Thus, commitment to Israel's security and right to exist and a patriotic support of American values were inextricably linked in the eyes of many neo-conservatives.

By 1975, Moynihan, Podhoretz, and others were convinced that the same phenomenon afflicted the U.N. They considered that the anti-Israel bias visible within America's own intellectual community was reflected in the attitudes of Third World nations at the U.N. General Assembly, who accordingly regarded the U.N. as a forum to be used against the United States and Israel. Indeed, the 1974 U.N. resolution "Zionism Is a Form of Racism and Racial Discrimination" heralded intimidating verbal attacks on Israel from other U.N. members. The Ugandan leader, Idi Amin, who had led the passage of the resolution, announced to the General Assembly: "I call for the expulsion of Israel from the United Nations and the extinction of Israel as a State, so that the territorial integrity of Palestine may be ensured and upheld."[84] Podhoretz subsequently contributed to the drafting of Moynihan's speech as U.S. ambassador to the U.N. in 1975, in which Moynihan severely berated the U.N. and described it as "a place where lies are told."[85] (His later position on the U.N. was somewhat more mellow.)[86]

The issues surrounding Israel's position in the Middle East functioned as a catalyst for other neo-conservative foreign policy impulses. The oil crisis of 1973 and the increasing awareness of Europe's dependence on the region for energy encouraged the long-standing tilt among European governments

---

[82] Halliday, *Making*, p. 117, and Gerson, *Neo-Conservative Vision*, p. 162.
[83] Dorrien, *Neoconservative Mind*, pp. 270–71, 190.
[84] Quoted in Gerson, *Neo-Conservative Vision*, p. 170.
[85] Ibid.
[86] Moynihan, *Pandaemonium*, pp. 143–74.

toward more pro-Arab policies. The perception that Europe was reassessing its own commitment to Israeli security helped to nurture the seeds of anti-European sentiment among certain neo-conservative intellectuals, which already existed based on what they saw as the European embrace of socialist economic models. They questioned why America should remain so supportive of Europe when Europe was reluctant to support Israel. Intellectuals such as Midge Decter, Moynihan, and Podhoretz wrote various articles arguing that the U.N., Communism, and much of the Third World was anti-Semitic, as were large swathes of America's intellectual community.[87] For neo-conservatives, America and Israel therefore shared a common ideological struggle against common enemies. The 1970s saw the vague consensus of neo-conservatism described by Irving Kristol wrap itself tightly around the belief that America must have a self-assured and robust elite, which must be willing to employ U.S. power promptly and resolutely, if need be, and prepared to stand up to the USSR along with its anti-American and anti-Semitic allies at the U.N. and beyond.[88]

THE NEXT GENERATION

Opposition to the Nixon-Kissinger strategy of peaceful coexistence with the Soviet Union had marked a significant period in the development of both neo-conservatism as an entity and as an important element in American foreign policy.[89] Jackson's Coalition for a Democratic Majority became the basis for other groups of the same ilk, such as the Committee on the Present Danger and the Committee for the Free World. These bodies constituted a kind of Who's Who for right-leaning Democrats and neo-conservative intellectuals and some Republicans, who all advocated a much stronger policy toward the USSR.

In 1973, Jackson and a number of like-minded senators and neo-conservatives became concerned over the issue of Jewish emigration and the plight of Soviet Jewry. Jewish emigration had increased from 1971 to 1973 largely on account of the improved relations between East and West that had surrounded the period of détente. In August 1972, however, the Soviet government instituted a new diploma tax for emigrants by claiming excessive education reimbursement fees on its citizens wishing to emigrate,

---

[87] Steinfels, *Neo-Conservatives*, p. 278; Gerson, *Neo-Conservative Vision*, p. 192; and Dorrien, *Neoconservative Mind*, pp. 190–92.

[88] Gottfried, *Conservative Movement*, p. 69.

[89] Judis, "Trotskyism," p. 126.

which primarily targeted the Soviet Union's Jewish population. In a campaign to pressure the Soviet Union to end the diploma tax and eliminate barriers to free emigration by linking trade concessions to the Soviet Union with explicit Soviet concessions on Jewish emigration, Jackson worked with Democratic Representative Charles Vanik, along with a coalition of major Jewish organizations and various neo-conservative allies, to pass the Jackson Vanik Act, later known as the Normal Trade Relations Act.[90] In the group working with Jackson was a young political aide, Richard Perle. It was throughout the 1970s that a number of neo-conservative offspring began to make their political names in Washington. Joshua Muravchik became Executive Director of the Coalition for a Democratic Majority in 1977 and served there until 1979. Housed in this organization's offices during that period was also Team B. Authorized in 1976 by Gerald Ford and organized by then CIA Chief George Bush, this group had the purpose of developing an independent judgment of Soviet capabilities and intentions. Team B was headed by Richard Pipes but also included, among others, the young Paul D. Wolfowitz of the Arms Control and Disarmament Agency. The embryos of the next generation of neo-conservatives were in utero.

Perle and Wolfowitz shared important elements of their curricula vitae. They had both been disciples of Albert Wohlstetter, a professor of political science at the University of Chicago. Wohlstetter was a conservative nuclear strategist who had worked for RAND and believed that nuclear deterrence was not sufficient. As a consultant to the Pentagon for many years during the Cold War, Wohlstetter believed that America must plan to fight a nuclear war in order to deter it, and he strongly advocated the view that the military power of the USSR was underrated. Wolfowitz became the protégé of Wohlstetter as a doctoral student at the University of Chicago in the late 1960s, although Perle had encountered Wohlstetter earlier when he met the professor's daughter as a high school student in Los Angeles. When Perle was subsequently a graduate student at Princeton, Wohlstetter invited him to Washington to work with Wolfowitz on a paper about the proposed Anti-Ballistic Missile Treaty, which Wohlstetter vehemently opposed. The professor later helped to position Perle in Washington's political circles by introducing him to Senator Jackson.[91] Perle dedicated his book, *An End to Evil*, to Wohlstetter.

[90] Jacob Heilbrunn, "Eclipse of a Statesman: Why Dr. K's Star Has Fallen," *Washington Monthly*, May 1999.
[91] Elizabeth Drew, "The Neocons in Power," *New York Review of Books*, June 12, 2003.

The maturation of neo-conservatism's next generation began in this period. But it was as the various advocates of neo-conservative philosophy subsequently climbed Washington's political ladders that the movement began to depart from its roots. The shared background of Wolfowitz and Perle is only partially representative of the extensive network of intellectual and professional connections that developed in the 1970s among those who would eventually carry the baton of neo-conservatism. Along with Wohlstetter, another University of Chicago academic named Allan Bloom also tutored Wolfowitz. The link between these two scholars has subsequently been described as the most important root that supports the modern neo-conservative tree. Both Wohlstetter and Bloom were protégés of the influential German-born academic Leo Strauss. By the 1970s, as Wolfowitz rose through the ranks of the arms control bureaucracy, so did other Straussians and Wohlstetter protégés across various Senate committee staffs. As Perle went to work at Jackson's office, Steven Bryen joined Republican Clifford Case, and Elliott Abrams served on Moynihan's staff.[92] Strauss's students and their students went on to occupy various positions in the administrations of Reagan and George H. W. Bush, such as Caspar Weinberger's former speechwriter, Seth Cropsey, National Endowment for the Humanities Deputy Chairman John T. Agresto, National Security Council adviser Carnes Lord, Assistant Secretary of State for International Organization Affairs Alan Keyes, legal scholar and judge Robert Bork; Justice Clarence Thomas of the Supreme Court, and former Secretary of Education William Bennett.[93] Also among those who studied with Strauss at the Chicago school was Harry Jaffa, who introduced fellow intellectual Harvey Mansfield to Straussian ideas. Mansfield subsequently went on to Harvard and educated the high-profile neo-conservatives William Kristol and Andrew Sullivan, who became a senior editor at the *New Republic*.

WOHLSTETTER AND STRAUSS

Wohlstetter is a man to whom some of today's neo-conservatives attribute a great deal of significance in terms of both their own intellectual maturation and their concepts of moral strategy. Although Wohlstetter was, for public purposes, a comparatively little-known figure in the Cold War, those on the inside described him as a "brilliant analyst" who overturned

---

92 Jeffrey Steinberg, "The Ignoble Liars," *Executive Intelligence Review*, January 18, 2003.
93 Shadia B. Drury, *Leo Strauss and the American Right* (New York: Palgrave Macmillan, 1997), p. 3.

conventional thinking on the Soviet military.[94] In a *New York Times* obituary after his death in 1997, he was credited with helping to lure the Soviets into Afghanistan, presiding over Reagan's defense buildup with his protégés, Perle and Wolfowitz, and playing a decisive role in the many and various circumstances that led the Berlin Wall to fall and the Soviet Empire to implode.[95] For some of the prominent neo-conservatives, Wohlstetter's intellect and his insight had a recognizable influence. Wolfowitz and Perle saw in their mentor two modes of thought that would become inherent characteristics in the modern expression of neo-conservatism after the end of the Cold War. Wohlstetter represented to these young intellectuals a blend of pragmatism and moralism that made an attractive strategy for approaching international affairs. As Wolfowitz remarked on his evolving impressions of Wohlstetter, "I thought, well, maybe he was also associated with these sort of cold-blooded systems analysts who kind of seemed to leave the moral piece of politics and strategy as though it wasn't part of the equation. It was terrifically gratifying to me as I got to know him better, to realize that there were intensely moral considerations in the way he approached these issues."[96]

Wohlstetter also had tremendous significance for neo-conservatives because of his strategic approach and personal contribution to the development of America's ability to wage high-technology wars. The imaginative employment of military technology subsequently became a central plank in neo-conservative thinking on how increased capabilities in precision targeting expanded the scope for American military intervention around the world. Neo-conservatives would later view the two Gulf Wars, the campaign in Afghanistan, and the limited air campaigns against the Bosnian Serb Army as expressions of this theory. Wolfowitz described Wohlstetter as being one of the first people to understand what a dramatic difference it would make to have accurate weapons. Wohlstetter advocated two ideas: to adapt the delivery systems – for example, cruise missiles, originally designed for nuclear weapons so that they could deliver conventional payloads – and to have technology that minimized collateral damage while maximizing strike capability, the sort of which became manifest in the U.S. interventions of the 1990s.

Two decades earlier, Wohlstetter had set up a group called the New Alternatives Workshop in order to examine the implications of new technology.

---

[94] Henry A. Kissinger, *The White House Years* (Boston: Little, Brown, 1979), p. 197.
[95] Cited in Jude Wanniski, "Albert Wohlstetter, RIP," *Polyconomics*, January 16, 1997.
[96] Paul Wolfowitz, interview with *Vanity Fair*, May 15, 2003.

Neo-conservatives subsequently saw the manner in which the first Gulf War was fought as an expression of this forward thinking. As Wolfowitz contended, "it was a considerable matter of personal satisfaction to watch those missiles turn right-angles in the Gulf War in '91, doing what Albert envisioned 15 years before."[97] Wolfowitz explained that without Wohlstetter, the Tomahawk cruise missile would have been traded away in the SALT II talks in 1976. Moscow had suggested that it would make an agreement only if Washington banned all cruise missiles at ranges greater that 600 kilometers, thereby including the Tomahawk. The Navy was happy to give it up as a largely unnecessary nuclear delivery system carried by submarines with limited torpedo space. The neo-conservatives credit Wohlstetter with preventing this decision and having the creative foresight to recognize that an accurate delivery system using conventional weapons could help to transform the way America fought its wars.[98]

There has been endless debate on the nature and extent of Strauss's influence on neo-conservatism. While some political analysts depict him as the intellectual godfather of second-generation neo-conservatism, others claim that his influence is overstated, that his books are obscure, and that there is no direct link between the professor and those with offices on Washington's corridors of power.[99] Certainly, today's neo-conservatives show no signs in their policy advocacy of adhering to Strauss's caution that "the philosopher ceases to be a philosopher when certainty of a solution becomes stronger than his awareness of the problematic character of that solution."[100] Moynihan and Irving Kristol both acknowledge their debt to him. Today's neo-conservatives generally write affectionately about him as a philosopher but become intensely defensive when it is suggested that modern neo-conservatism owes any debt to Strauss.[101] Some modern neo-conservatives have told us that "they do not know who Strauss is." They see the suggestions of Straussian influence, alongside similar claims of Trotskyite influence, as part of a dastardly campaign by their adversaries to blacken their reputations.[102]

---

97 Quoted in Tanenhaus, "Bush's Brain Trust," p. 141.

98 Wolfowitz, interview, *Vanity Fair*.

99 Ivo H. Daalder and James M. Lindsay, *America Unbound: The Bush Revolution in Foreign Policy* (Washington, D.C.: Brookings Institution, 2003), pp. 46–47.

100 Leo Strauss, *What Is Politics and Philosophy?* (New York: Glencoe, 1959), pp. 115–16.

101 Steven Lenzner and William Kristol, "What Was Leo Strauss Up To?" *Public Interest*, fall 2003, pp. 19–28.

102 Joshua Muravchik, "The Neo-conservative Cabal," *Commentary*, September 2003, p. 28.

Strauss's political ideas may, indeed, be elusive; understanding him has been described as a "task of overwhelming complexity."[103] One admirer talks of Strauss's "initial obscurity and rather alien character."[104] His influence was derived principally from the personal effects of his teaching at the University of Chicago. A classical scholar, with a reflexive disdain for the "horrors of mass culture,"[105] he used his studies of the classical texts to reflect on the nature of twentieth-century tyrannies. For Strauss, these were the product of modernity's rejection of the essential values of classical society; instead, he advocated a social system hierarchically ordered and steeped in religiosity.[106] Strauss seldom turned his attention directly toward current politics. He mostly focused on Christian, Jewish, and Muslim sacred writings and Greek classical texts. The arguments for a correlation between his writing and the tenets of neo-conservative thought center on two aspects of his philosophy, both inherently and deeply pessimistic. First, he had experienced the dissolution of the Weimar Republic as a young man and had drawn the conclusion that democracy was without the requisite capacity to enforce its own paradigm if it could not directly confront tyranny. To this assertion he added the belief that tyranny was inherently expansionist by nature. Second, he coupled the fact that the twentieth century had produced two totalitarian regimes with his belief that modernity had induced a denunciation of moral values. He argued that virtue was the basis for democracy and that the European emphasis on human reason deriving from the Enlightenment represented a decline in religion-based values, not an advance. He deplored a secular political order as a "movement away from the recognition of a superhuman authority – whether of revelation based on Divine will or a natural order – to a recognition of the exclusively human based authority of the State."[107] In this sense, he shared his emphasis on the utility of religion in society with those such as Irving Kristol, who acknowledged the profound influence of Strauss on his thought.[108]

---

[103] Eugene F. Miller, "Leo Strauss: The Recovery of Political Philosophy," in Anthony de Crespigny and Kenneth Minogue, eds., *Contemporary Political Philosophy* (New York: Dodd Mead, 1975), p. 69.

[104] Thomas L. Pangle, *The Rebirth of Classical Political Rationalism* (Chicago: University of Chicago Press, 1989), p. vii.

[105] Leo Strauss, *Liberalism Ancient and Modern* (New York: Basic Books, 1968), p. 4.

[106] Drury, *Leo Strauss*, p. 11.

[107] Leo Strauss, *The Political Philosophy of Hobbes: Its Basis and Genesis* (Chicago: University of Chicago Press, 1952), p. 17.

[108] Kristol, *Neoconservatism*, pp. 6–7.

Strauss's many works include three well-known texts: *Natural Right and History*, *The City and Man*, and *Thoughts on Machiavelli*. In the first, Strauss discusses what he calls the issue of natural right and contends that reality largely derives from a distinction between right and wrong in ethics and politics. *The City and Man* comprises a collection of provocative essays on Thucydides' *Peloponnesian Wars*, Plato's *Republic*, and Aristotle's *Politics*, in which Strauss compares a historian, a philosopher, and a political scientist. Scholars contend that Strauss essentially argued for a renewal of ancient political philosophy. In the introduction to *The City and Man*, Strauss suggested that we are forced to turn "toward the political thought of classical antiquity" because of the "crisis of our time, the crisis of the West."[109] Published in 1958, Strauss's *Thoughts on Machiavelli* discussed, among other things, how Machiavelli's writings were not just a significant turning point in modern political philosophy, but that his texts were defined by hidden writing. Strauss suggested that Machiavelli was essentially a teacher of evil by linking the outset of modernity and the manner in which modern forms of thinking undermine civilization.[110] Many of Strauss's ideas were popularized by his student, Allan Bloom, in his book *The Closing of the American Mind*, and influenced both Wolfowitz and Francis Fukuyama. Wolfowitz subsequently became the inspiration for a minor character in *Ravelstein*, a novel based on Bloom by fellow Chicago academic Saul Bellow.

It is possible to see the manner in which Strauss's ideas might relate both to the moral battle between American democracy and Soviet communism during the Cold War and to the "civilizational" battle now under way against terrorism and tyranny. But one can only speculate on the extent to which Straussian philosophies have really affected the minds of policy makers over the years. It would also be far-fetched to suggest that all students of Strauss are neo-conservative or vice versa. Wolfowitz has stated implicitly that the suggestion of a Straussian link to the essential tenets of modern neo-conservative foreign policy is "a product of fevered minds who seem incapable of understanding that September 11 changed a lot of things and changed the way we need to approach the world." He argues that the approach to foreign affairs shared between himself and his colleagues derives "not from reading Plato" nor "from any ideological prejudices whatsoever." Wolfowitz defined his own approach as being "the difference between ideological thinking and

---

[109] Neil Robertson, "Leo Strauss's Platonism," *Animus*, February 17, 2000.
[110] Steven Lenzner, "Leo Strauss and the Conservatives," *Policy Review: Hoover Institution*, April 2003.

pragmatic thinking."[111] Nevertheless, by affiliation or derivation, Strauss's ideas occupied a space in the education of many students and intellectuals who subsequently progressed to the highest levels of Washington's political elite.

Furthermore, the networks of political associations that emanate from the University of Chicago during the 1970s present a framework of interrelated biographies for many of those considered to be among the rank and file of today's neo-conservatives. Disciples of Strauss who have become associated with the more recent neo-conservative ascendancy are Lewis Libby, chief of staff and chief national security adviser to Vice President Cheney (who was introduced to the world of Strauss by his own Yale University professor and mentor, Wolfowitz); John Podhoretz, editorial page editor of the *New York Post*, former editor of the *Weekly Standard*, and son of first-generation neo-conservatives Norman Podhoretz and Midge Decter; Pentagon intelligence officer Abram Shulsky; Gary Schmitt, executive director of William Kristol's Project for the New American Century (PNAC); David Brooks, formerly of the *Weekly Standard* and now a columnist for the *New York Times*; Werner Dannhauser, a protégé of Strauss who left academia to take on editorship of *Commentary* after the retirement of Podhoretz; and Robert Kagan, also of the *Weekly Standard* and the son of leading Yale University Straussian Donald Kagan.[112]

For a number of reasons, this new generation of neo-conservatives reflected a break from the cultural milieu that started in Alcove 1. Generally speaking, the older neo-conservatives were not a force in the Republican Party. Although Irving Kristol and Gertrude Himmelfarb gave their backing to Nixon in 1972, many other neo-conservatives did not. It was a different story twenty years later, however, with William Kristol's assertion on behalf of most neo-conservatives that "any neo-con who drifts back to the Democratic Party is a pseudo-neo-con."[113] Even though the majority of older neo-conservatives twice voted for Reagan and a number worked for him, most had avoided becoming Republicans.[114] Furthermore, although the first generation neo-conservatives belonged to a highly influential academic elite, they remained in the academy all the same. Apart from one or two notable exceptions such as Wolfowitz, the next generation of neo-conservatives avoided academia and sought to hold positions in Republican administrations. As Irving Kristol observed in 1995, Strauss's original students had

[111] Wolfowitz interview, *Vanity Fair*.
[112] Steinberg, "Ignoble Liars."
[113] Quoted in Dorrien, *Neoconservative Mind*, p. 390.
[114] Gerson, *Neo-Conservative Vision*, pp. 135 and 249.

produced another generation of political theorists who chose to relocate in Washington.[115] Thus, the children of the original neo-conservatives left the academy in favor of politics.

Dozens of those who followed or were influenced by Strauss in the 1960s and 1970s joined the federal government to initiate a new conservative political outlook.[116] William Kristol clearly stated that he was unable to think of himself as being a scholar for the rest of his life.[117] He left Harvard following his doctorate to join William Bennett's staff at the Department of Education, later to become the chief policy adviser of Vice President Quayle. There is also a long list of other neo-conservatives who transferred from faculty to government office and brought Strauss's influence with them. Carnes Lord left the University of Virginia to serve on the National Security Council in the first Reagan administration. He also became chief foreign policy adviser of Vice President Quayle in the administration of George H. W. Bush. Nathan Tarcov left the University of Chicago to join the State Department Policy Planning Staff. David Epstein left Chicago's New School for Social Research and became an analyst in the Pentagon's Office of Net Assessment. Gary Schmitt left the University of Dallas to be part of Reagan's National Advisory Board for Foreign Intelligence. Abram Shulsky left Chicago to become director of Strategic Arms Control Policy at the Department of Defense. Michael Malbin left the University of Maryland to become the Associate Director of the House Republican Conference.[118]

NEO-CONSERVATIVES UNDER REAGAN

Looking at the biographies of many neo-conservatives, one could be forgiven for believing that the Reagan era was the time when neo-conservative ideas moved to the forefront of policy making. As Podhoretz himself remarked, by giving important positions to neo-conservatives such as Kirkpatrick, Eugene V. Rostow, Perle, and Abrams, Reagan seemed "to be forging a living link between the Democratic mainstream and his own administration."[119] Neo-conservatives also entertained high hopes for the youthful Director of the

---

[115] Kristol, *Neoconservatism*, p. 7.
[116] John Ehrman, *The Rise of Neoconservatism: Intellectuals and Foreign Affairs 1945–94* (New Haven: Yale University Press, 1995), p. 174, Robert Devigne, *Oakeshott, Strauss and the Response to Postmodernism* (New Haven: Yale University Press, 1994), pp. 58–59.
[117] Drury, p. 180, note 4.
[118] Devigne, *Oakeshott*, p. 221, n.76.
[119] Norman Podhoretz, "The Reagan Road to Détente," *Foreign Affairs*, America and the World, 1984, p. 449.

Office and Management and Budget David Stockman, who had studied at the Harvard Divinity School, where he was thought to have absorbed some neo-conservative thought, evidenced by his writings on welfare policy in the *Public Interest*. It is certainly true that Reagan's election as president in November 1980 looked like a major victory for American conservatism across the spectrum of policy issues. His resolve to diminish the extent of government intrusion into people's lives, cut taxes, reduce the regulation of savings and loans, lower the budgets for federal social programs, and remove the bureaucratic red tape of an overly centralized system of government convinced the true-blue guardians of conservatism that they finally had a man in the White House who shared their views. Podhoretz praised Reagan as a "political figure offering himself as the legitimate heir to Richard Nixon's usurped throne."[120] Reagan also looked like a victory for neo-conservative foreign policy. In contrast to the three presidents who had gone before him, Reagan seemed to share neo-conservative perceptions of the present danger and how to confront it.[121] The central tenet in his foreign policy was anti-Sovietism and the imperative of standing up to the Soviet threat in every part of the world. Podhoretz and others saw in Reagan "the hope that the Republican Party would now assume the responsibility for containing Soviet expansionism that had originally been shouldered by the United States under Democratic leadership but that the Democrats since Vietnam had been increasingly eager to evade."[122]

Because today's neo-conservatives believe the tenets advanced by Reagan's foreign policy validate their emphasis on preemptive war fighting, we discuss this claim (which we reject) in full detail in a later chapter. But in the 1980s foreign policy was not – yet – the neo-conservatives' exclusive realm. It makes sense therefore to look at how the neo-conservatives fared under the first Republican president with whom the neo-conservatives felt properly in tune. We look in particular at some of the tensions that arose with other elements of the conservative movement who also thought their time had come.

For an administration in which the neo-conservatives invested such high hopes and on which they now look back with awe, the Reagan period saw only moderate advances. True, they saw neo-conservatives such as

---

[120] Podhoretz, "The New American Majority," *Commentary*, January 1981, pp. 19–28.
[121] Norman Podhoretz, "The First Term: The Reagan Road to Détente," *Foreign Affairs*, America and the World, 1984, p. 451; Ehrman, *Rise of Neoconservatism*, pp. 137–38; Peele, *Revival and Reaction*, p. 2; and Robert Dallek, *Ronald Reagan: The Politics of Symbolism* (Cambridge, Mass.: Harvard University Press, 1999), pp. xv–xvi.
[122] Podhoretz, "The Reagan Road," p. 449.

Kirkpatrick and William Bennett appointed to high positions, but they never joined the inner sanctum. In both 1981 and again in 1983 when, as Reagan records, there were "conservative pressures to give the National Security Council job to Kirkpatrick," he resisted, as there was "bad chemistry between her and George Shultz."[123] Bennett became Secretary of Education only after it was clear that Reagan had abandoned his pledge to abolish the Department of Education. But the neo-conservatives made one crucial advance that endures to this day and that in part explains their position of influence. In the course of the Reagan administration, the conservative camp around Pat Buchanan with its roots in nativism and isolationism began to dig itself into a hole from which it was never to extricate itself. At the end of the first Bush administration it was in its death throes, not yet so lifeless that it could not poison Bush's reelection bid but reduced to an angry chorus on the sidelines. This opened the way to an alliance – one is tempted to call it a marriage of convenience – between the neo-conservatives and Christian evangelicals who, drawing on their missionary roots, including Christian proselytization in the Muslim world, shared their ideas of forceful external interventionism. They joined forces in pushing the Clinton administration into the Balkans. Notwithstanding the number of eschatological incompatibilities to be swallowed on both sides, this alliance proved politically potent. With the isolationist wing in disarray, the neo-conservatives were able to nibble away at the Republican realist school to the extent that, in the wake of September 11, they found themselves in the ascendant.

In 1980, however, all this lay ahead. At that point the neo-conservatives were anticipating early gratification. The impediments, including groups such as the American Conservative Union, the New Congress Foundation, and the National Taxpayers Limitation Committee, however, were many. The New Right deeply believed that they, rather than those whom they regarded as Democratic interlopers, were the real architects of the Reagan victory. Moreover, many who were members of Barry Goldwater's campaign staff and had joined Reagan, in addition to Goldwater himself, could justifiably claim to have created much of the new energy on the conservative side. This was generously acknowledged by Reagan, who had chaired Goldwater's California campaign in 1976.[124] There were, thus, serious differences between the New Right and the neo-conservatives. The former believed passionately in goals such as school prayer and the right to life and looked

---

[123] Ronald Reagan, *An American Life* (New York: Simon and Schuster, 1999), p. 448.

[124] Frances Fitzgerald, "The Triumphs of the New Right," *New York Review of Books*, November 19, 1981.

to Reagan to push these. Irving Kristol, by contrast, breezily concluded that "most parents do not really care whether their children pray in school."[125] Moreover, anti-abortion crusading, especially attempts to criminalize the procedure, was not central to most neo-conservatives.

Also expecting to benefit by Reagan's victory in advance of the neo-conservatives were large numbers of professional Republican campaign consultants such as Richard Viguerie, who proclaimed that "the simple truth is that there is a new majority in America – and it is being led by the New Right,"[126] together with those who were longtime friends of Ronald Reagan, such as Phyllis Schlafly. The New Right directed some choice insults at the neo-conservatives: "[I]t is splendid when the town whore gets religion and joins the church. Now and then she makes a good choir director, but when she begins to tell the minister what he ought to say in his Sunday sermons, matters have been carried too far."[127]

A more formidable obstacle to both the neo-conservatives and the New Right lay in the team immediately around Reagan. Men such as Richard Allen, Marty Anderson, Michael K. Deaver, Paul Laxalt, Edwin Meese, Lyn Nofziger, and William French Smith simply did not share the analysis that Reagan's victory owed much to anyone other than the candidate himself. They dismissed the pretensions of the New Right "successfully . . . creating the widespread impression that they were the basic components of Reagan's support."[128] Citing the advice in *The Godfather* to "hold your friends close, hold your enemies closer," a White House aide commented, "we want to keep the Moral Majority types so close to us that they can't move their arms."[129]

It was hardly surprising therefore that both the New Right and the neo-conservatives were soon voicing reservations about Reagan. Barely one year into the administration, Viguerie noted, "I am disappointed that the majority of policy-making positions in the Reagan administration have gone to moderates and liberals."[130] Kristol commented of Reagan that "every now and then he shows a flash of the Ronald Reagan that might have been but these intermittent flashes are quickly dimmed." He asked the question, "was the critical election of 1980 merely a mirage?"[131] The climactic event came in

[125] Kristol, *Neoconservatism*, p. 362.
[126] Richard A. Viguerie, *The New Right* (Falls Church, Va.: Viguerie, 1981), p. 7.
[127] Gerson, *Neo-Conservative Vision*, p. 314.
[128] Lou Cannon, *Ronald Reagan: The Role of a Lifetime* (New York: Putnam, 1982), p. 315.
[129] Ibid., p. 316.
[130] Viguerie, *New Right*, p. 174.
[131] Kristol, *Neoconservatism*, p. 357.

1981 with the appointment to the Supreme Court of Sandra Day O'Connor, whose views, in the opinion of the Moral Majority, were insufficiently hard-line on abortion. But they were quickly slapped down. In response to the complaints of Moral Majority leader Jerry Falwell, Goldwater commented that "every good Christian ought to kick Falwell in the ass."[132]

Of the two groups, the neo-conservatives handled their disappointment better. While they did not hold back their criticism (which, as shown else-where, was especially vociferous on foreign policy and which undermines their invocation of the Reagan legacy as their model), they foresaw what Kristol later described as the "coming conservative century."[133] They bided their time and did not overreach. This was quite unlike the Buchananite wing, which seething under its grievances during the Reagan administration and growing ever more frustrated under the G. H. W. Bush administration, moved to the attack, citing the neo-conservatives for dual loyalty ("mistak-ing Tel Aviv for the capital of the United States") and for being fixated on Israel.[134] Other than among the bigoted, this attack went nowhere. While it has always been the case that the neo-conservative movement has attracted and continues to attract a number of Jewish adherents (although, accord-ing to opinion surveys provided by the American Jewish Committee, the vast majority of Jewish Americans do not share neo-conservative views), the movement itself is manifestly open to all comers and has been from its in-ception. Further, the notion spread by the Buchananites that commitment to the well-being of Israel is an exclusively Jewish or neo-conservative phe-nomenon flies in the face of half a century's solid, bipartisan support for Israel. Not surprisingly, these attacks provoked a strong reaction not just among neo-conservatives but from the William F. Buckley, Jr., wing of the conservative movement, which had consistently sought to distance itself from the anti-Semitism of the old right.[135]

With the great military success of the Gulf War, the Buchananite accu-sations took on an alarmist arm and have faded from view. Which gives rise to the corollary of Buchanan's argument. Today, it should not be con-sidered legitimate to imply that any criticism of neo-conservatism is nec-essarily tainted by anti-Semitism.[136] Neo-conservatism (and the question-ing of it) stands on its own feet. However, the failure to carry the war to

---

[132] Cannon, *Reagan*, p. 315.

[133] Kristol, *Neoconservatism*, p. 364–68.

[134] Judis, *William F. Buckley Jr.*, p. 263.

[135] William F. Buckley, Jr., "In Search of Anti-Semitism," *National Review*, December 31, 1991.

[136] Lawrence Kaplan, "Toxic Talk on War," *Washington Post*, February 18, 2003, p. A25.

Baghdad gave fresh energy to the neo-conservative agenda for the rest of the Bush administration and throughout the Clinton administration. As we will show in the next chapter, the neo-conservatives used these years well. By the end of the Clinton administration the neo-conservatives had successfully re-grouped, primed with a far-reaching agenda to be put into action at the first opportunity.

3

The Nineties: From Near Death to Resurrection

As the Cold War wound down in the 1980s and in the early 1990s, those who had defined the neo-conservative movement moved on to a variety of new interests, acknowledging that the defining themes and directions had faded. Jay Winik wrote in 1989 that "with the warming of U.S.-Soviet relations and the ratification of the treaty on Intermediate-Range Nuclear Forces (INF), America is witnessing the end not just of the Reagan era, but perhaps of the neo-conservatives as well."[1] Five years later, John Judis argued in *Foreign Affairs* that the neo-conservative journey from Alcove 1 to Soviet collapse was a transition "from Trotskyism to anachronism."[2] Even Norman Podhoretz pronounced that neo-conservatism "no longer exists as a distinctive phenomenon."[3]

These predictions turned out to be premature. Quite unexpectedly, the neo-conservatives used the last decade of the twentieth century to reinvent and redefine themselves as force-based "hard" Wilsonians focused on foreign policy – two attributes that would have surprised neo-conservatism's founding fathers. Their analysis of the events of the time, notably the wars in Somalia and Yugoslavia, led them to a policy palette based on three interconnecting elements: force as the preferred policy option, black-and-white moralism as the preferred form of analysis, and unilateralism as the preferred mode of execution. The process by which they came to these conclusions is the subject of this chapter.

---

[1] Jay Winik, "The Neoconservative Construction," *Foreign Policy*, Winter 1988/89, p. 135.

[2] John Judis, "From Trotskyism to Anachronism," *Foreign Affairs*, July–August 1995, pp. 123–29.

[3] Norman Podhoretz, "Neo-Conservatism: A Eulogy," *Commentary*, March 1996, pp. 19–27.

Neo-conservatives had made valuable contributions to fighting the Cold War during the Reagan years. As Assistant Secretary of Defense for international security policy, Richard Perle helped to shape arms control agreements for over six years, while playing a central role in stemming the flow of sensitive technology to the Eastern Bloc. George Shultz, Reagan's Secretary of State, records that, after some early tensions with him were resolved, he found Perle to be "one of the most helpful members" of the team.[4] As successive heads of the Arms Control and Disarmament Agency, Eugene Rostow and Kenneth Adelman were both key advocates of a military buildup as the prerequisite for successful arms reductions and stable U.S.-Soviet relations. Max Kampelman became head of the U.S. delegation to the negotiations on nuclear and space arms with the Soviet Union. Abrams was instrumental in securing aid for the Contras in their war against the Sandinista regime in Nicaragua, and Kirkpatrick used her position at the U.N. to its full capacity in convincing the other member states that they were fully accountable for their behavior toward America.[5]

However, as John Ehrman noted in his book *The Rise of Neoconservatism*, the movement entered a state of confusion in the second half of the 1980s. Mikhail Gorbachev became leader of the Soviet Union in March 1985 and began to implement a series of domestic reforms and a more conciliatory approach toward the West. Conservatives with impeccable anticommunist credentials, such as Margaret Thatcher, proclaimed that Gorbachev was "a man with whom we can do business." Partially under her influence, Reagan started to move beyond his early Evil Empire rhetoric to a process of sustained diplomacy between the two superpowers. This directly blunted the credibility of the neo-conservative opposition to the concept of arms control agreements between Washington and Moscow. Kirkpatrick's departure from the U.N. in 1985 deprived the neo-conservatives of their highest-level celebrity. Growing congressional opposition to the administration's hard line in Central America and an absence of public support undermined neo-conservative hopes for a sustained campaign of backing the Nicaraguan Contras. The Iran-Contra scandal in 1986 subsequently assured this. As the Soviet bloc crumbled, so did Podhoretz's authority as a foreign policy commentator. The severity of his and of other commentators' line in *Commentary* on the Soviet Union started to look like inflexibility in the face of changed

---

[4] George Shultz, *Turmoil and Triumph: My Years as Secretary of State* (New York: Charles Scribner, 1993), pp. 512–13.
[5] Winik, "Neoconservative Construction," p. 135.

international events. In the later 1980s the journal rapidly lost both credibility and contributors. At decade's end, the era in which an article in *Commentary* might establish the basis for a policy initiative or lead to an appointment in government was over.[6]

In 1986, it had been easy for Peter Berger to articulate the thrust of neo-conservative thinking on foreign affairs: "We believe that the most important political and moral challenge of our time is the struggle for the survival of freedom. In the international context this struggle has its focus in the resistance to the spread of Soviet-style totalitarianism."[7] But with the Soviet empire in collapse by the end of the decade, neo-conservatism had lost its compass. The movement now confronted a question it had not faced for half a century: What should the basis of American foreign policy be? The neo-conservative Cold War consensus subsequently collapsed into disagreement. The debate fell between those who advocated the narrower definition of national self-interest and those who believed that America's role in the post-Soviet world should be a democratic crusade. Long-established neo-conservative voices of some twenty years, such as those of Glazer, Kirkpatrick, and Irving Kristol and of academicians with close neo-conservative associations, such as Robert W. Tucker, now argued for a reduced role for American foreign policy. Meanwhile, younger intellectuals such as Joshua Muravchik, Ben Wattenberg, Charles Krauthammer, and Carl Gershman believed that the advancement of democracy should be "the touchstone of a new ideological American foreign policy." In phraseology that set the tone for today's neo-conservative attitudes, Krauthammer described America's foreign policy as one of "universal dominion" in a "unipolar" world.[8]

THE DEBATE: MISSION ACCOMPLISHED OR PERPETUAL STRUGGLE?

Irving Kristol contended that this emphasis on enhancing democracy was a "chastened and revised version of liberal internationalism." As he suggested, it had appeal "not only to liberals but to many conservatives who are ideologically adrift in the post–Cold War era." Kristol cautioned that

---

[6] John Ehrman, *The Rise of Neoconservatism: Intellectuals and Foreign Policy 1945–94* (New Haven: Yale University Press, 1995), pp. 170–74.

[7] Brigitte Berger and Peter Berger, "Our Conservatism and Theirs," *Commentary*, October 1986, p. 66.

[8] Charles Krauthammer, "Universal Dominion: Toward a Unipolar World," *National Interest*, winter 1989/90, p. 47, and Ehrman, *Rise of Neoconservatism*, pp. 173–78.

while prodemocratic capitalism was "a tempting move for those who wish to remain engaged in world politics," it was also a dangerous manifestation of Wilsonianism.[9] Intellectuals such as Krauthammer and Muravchik also opposed the Wilsonian concept of using multilateral bodies such as the U.N., which Muravchik later described as "almost wholly feckless," as the basis for regulating international relations.[10] Kristol continued, arguing that the "inspirational rhetoric in which this foreign policy is clothed . . . is Wilsonian enough to run into all the older Wilsonian dilemmas – dilemmas resulting from the disjunction between the ideal and reality, general principles and particular issues." Instead, he recommended the notion of an American "national interest." He argued that "there is no balance of power for us to worry about" and that "monitoring and maintaining a balance of power among other nations, large and small, in Europe, the Middle East, Asia, and elsewhere . . . would make the United States the world's policeman." He concluded, "We are simply not going to be that kind of imperial power."[11] Similarly, Tucker believed that an imperial temptation had arisen in Washington. He believed that because of the concern over "the fate of free institutions and the conditions of world order," military power had "assumed a role that is excessive in the light of the traditional conceptions of the national purpose." Echoing the sort of realism encouraged by Irving Kristol, Tucker asserted, "The principle aim of American security policy today ought to be a devolution of substantial responsibilities to alliance partners, together with the retention of existing security commitments."[12] Norman Podhoretz

---

[9] This term originated from the fourteen-point war aims enunciated before Congress by President Woodrow Wilson in January 1918. Wilson advocated a number of principles as the basis for a new world order. While eight points related to the geographical and political specifics of the peace settlement of the First World War, six points also formed the tenets of Wilsonianism. These were self-determination of colonial populations, a standing concert of nations to provide collective security, open covenants of peace, freedom of navigation upon the seas, removal of economic barriers to trade, and massive reduction in armament levels. Although many of Wilson's objectives were subsequently compromised in negotiation, the fourteenth point regarding a prospective assembly of nations for the purpose of collective security became the basis for the Covenant of the League of Nations, inaugurated at the Treaty of Versailles in Paris on June 28, 1919, by the leaders of Great Britain, Italy, France, and the United States of America. Wilson's vision of a postwar international order has become known as the "Wilsonian triad," encompassing the three basic principles of peace, democracy, and free trade.

[10] Joshua Muravchik, "The Bush Mandate," *Commentary*, December 2002, p. 28.

[11] Irving Kristol, "Defining Our National Interest," in Owen Harries, ed., *America's Purpose: New Visions of US Foreign Policy* (San Francisco: Institute of Contemporary Studies, 1991), pp. 53–69.

[12] Robert W. Tucker and David C. Hendrickson, *The Imperial Temptation: The New World Order and America's Purpose* (New York: New York University Press, 1992), pp. 6–17, 198–211.

wrote that there are "only a tiny handful who still advocate the expansive Wilsonian interventionism."[13]

Another advocate for this brand of neo-conservative realism was Kirkpatrick. In an article titled "A Normal Country in a Normal Time," she suggested, "It is not within the United States' power to democratize the world." She said, "the time when Americans should bear unusual burdens is past. With a return to 'normal' times, we can again become a normal nation.... Most of the international obligations that we assumed were once important are now outdated." Kirkpatrick said that it is "enormously desirable for the U.S. and others to encourage democratic institutions wherever possible." But in direct response to the alternative genesis of neo-conservative thinking that was growing out of Soviet collapse, Kirkpatrick asserted that "it is not the American purpose to establish 'universal dominance' in the provocative formulation of Charles Krauthammer – not even the universal dominance of democracy."[14]

Also among the established neo-conservatives who argued against continued American activism abroad or a democratic crusade was Glazer. As he suggested, "Whatever our commitment to governments of freedom and democracy, it would never have justified the enormous expansion of American military power were it not for the threat of communism." While saying, "We should maintain our democracy and our commitment to free government," Glazer also asserted, "In promoting and recommending those universal principles to which we are attached, it is now time to withdraw to something closer to the modest role that the Founding Fathers intended." Glazer believed that America was "not to be the policeman of the world." In his view, "it is not to become enmeshed in permanent alliances, whether based on the balance of power, some presumed geopolitical conflict, or an assumption of permanent or unchangeable ideological division."[15]

However, on the other side of the fence from the new realism among older neo-conservatives, an entirely different view of America and the world was emerging from the neo-conservative "Young Turk" faction. Krauthammer believed that "communism may be dead, but the work of democracy is never done." As he put it, "With the decline of communism, the advancement of democracy should become the touchstone of a new ideological American foreign policy."[16] In laying out the basis for a more activist American role,

[13] Podhoretz, "Neo-Conservatism: A Eulogy," p. 26.
[14] Jeane Kirkpatrick, "A Normal Country in a Normal Time," *National Interest*, fall 1990, pp. 40–43.
[15] Nathan Glazer, "A Time for Modesty," in Harries, ed., *America's Purpose*, pp. 133–41.
[16] Krauthammer, "Universal Dominion," p. 47.

he contended, "Foreign entanglements are indeed a burden. But they are also a necessity." Krauthammer was instrumental in focusing the debate on "the proliferation of weapons of mass destruction and their means of delivery." He argued that this "will constitute the greatest single threat to world security for the rest of our lives." In terminology that now is familiar to all, he asserted in early 1991, "Iraq, which (unless disarmed by Desert Storm) will likely be in possession of intercontinental missiles within the decade, is the prototype of this new strategic threat, what might be called the Weapon State." He suggested, "With the rise of the Weapon State, there is no alternative to confronting, deterring and, if necessary, disarming states that brandish and use weapons of mass destruction." In opposition to the narrower views of older neo-conservatives, Krauthammer declared, "If America wants stability, it will have to create it" because "the alternative to such a robust and difficult interventionism . . . is chaos."[17]

The neo-conservative movement had fractured. As we have remarked earlier, it is an open question whether this new brand was a phenomenon of the left or the right. Today it attracts liberal adherents such as Michael Ignatieff, who, remarkably, goes as far as to excuse any untruths that the administration may have been told to bolster its case for war against Iraq.[18] At the time, Norman Podhoretz, worried that neo-conservative names were appearing on Balkan-related appeals in the company of the likes of *New York Times* columnist Anthony Lewis, whom he regarded as belonging to the unreconstructed left, tried to explain that what distinguished neo-conservative interventionism from humanitarian liberal interventionism was the former's "emphasis on interests as well as values."[19]

But there was something half-hearted in this assertion as the new generation, led by scholars such as Muravchik, proposed a conceptual alternative to the views of older neo-conservatives that went significantly beyond traditional interests-based analysis. In stark contrast to Tucker's *Imperial Temptation*, Muravchik contended, "If, conversely, communism soon completes its demise, U.S. foreign policy still should make the promotion of democracy its main objective." As he explained, "we should concentrate on continuing to spread democracy in a post-Communist world for three good reasons. . . . The first is empathy with our fellow humans. . . . Second, the more democratic the world, the friendlier America's environment will

---

[17] Charles Krauthammer, "The Unipolar Moment," *Foreign Affairs*, America and the World, winter 1990/91, pp. 23–33.
[18] John Lloyd, "Between Iraq and a Hard Place," *Financial Times*, August 30–31, 2003, p. W5.
[19] Norman Podhoretz, "Strange Bedfellows: A Guide to the New Foreign Policy Debates," *Commentary*, December 1999, pp. 19–31.

be. . . . Third, the more democratic the world, the more peaceful it is likely to be." Muravchik described Irving Kristol and Tucker as conservative neo-realists who were more like "right isolationists" and rhetorically declared, "Can America export democracy? It can." His thesis was that democracy "is created; it does not just arise." As he argued, it comes "as a result of political, cultural, or intellectual structures," and these processes "are manifestly subject to influence." While Muravchik made the point that "no one advocates that the United States take it upon itself to subdue other countries solely to democratize them," he added, "This is not to say that we should accept a blanket prohibition against military interventions to change the internal order in another state. It would have been a blessing if outside powers had overthrown Hitler and Pol Pot and Lenin before they had done their worst." With the views of Krauthammer and Muravchik, therefore, the younger neo-conservative movement established the two ideas that would eventually constitute a basis for the second and final war against Saddam Hussein twelve years later: U.S. interventionism against the weapon state and the export of democracy as a central purpose of American foreign policy.

Other intellectuals were to join neo-conservatism's camp of Young Turks. Carl Gershman asked, "Is the objective of supporting democracy sufficient to serve as a 'central purpose' for the United States in its relations with the world? The question should answer itself, for this already *is* our central purpose."[20] Meanwhile, Ben Wattenberg posed the question, "Doesn't the spread of democracy enhance our national interest?" He promptly added: "As the last superpower, we should try to shape evolution. . . . We ought not be passive players." As Wattenberg saw it, "in the future, the Number One country will be the one that is most successful in shaping the global democratic culture."[21]

It was because of this narrowing preference for the activist projection of American power among the younger neo-conservatives that they turned against George H. W. Bush and toward his presidential challenger in 1992. Muravchik wrote in November 1992, "Much to my surprise, I'm supporting Bill Clinton for president." He outlined his disappointment about the weakness and incompetence of Bush Senior in handling America's role in the post–Cold War era. As he remarked, "When Chinese students demonstrated for democracy in 1989, Bush was inert." He declared, "When Communist regimes fell, Bush did not rush to shore up new democracies."

[20] Carl Gershman, "Freedom Remains the Touchstone," in Harries, ed., *America's Purpose*, p. 42.
[21] Ben J. Wattenberg, "Neo-Manifest Destinarianism," in ibid., pp. 107–13.

Muravchik also highlighted what became the deepest neo-conservative grievance against the first Bush administration: "Bush kept democracy off Desert Storm's agenda."[22] The president's failure to end the Gulf War in Baghdad with the removal of Saddam Hussein became a regular gripe in the pages of neo-conservative publications such as *Commentary*. As Arthur Laffer wrote in an article supporting candidate Clinton, "Saddam Hussein today thrives as Iraq's leader. And it was Bush's decision not to press the military campaign in order to depose Saddam."[23] Meanwhile, Muravchik was also disgusted with Bush's approach to the Middle East: "Bush's courtship of Iraq was justified in part by the need to counterbalance Iran; but we have learned that we also courted Iran.... Bush calls this foreign policy realism. But since both of these regimes remain bloodily repressive, internationally mischievous, and implacably hostile to America, just what is realistic about it?"[24]

THE BALKANS: TEST BED FOR THE NEW DOCTRINE

Thus, one gets an insight into an evolving neo-conservative proscription for the Middle East that predates George W. Bush's war on terror by over a decade. Although today's president may not himself have been fully mindful of these debates at the start of the 1990s, the intellectuals who would eventually dominate his discourse on the humanitarian pursuit of democracy in hot and dangerous places were already cultivating the doctrine-to-be in the wake of Soviet collapse. To understand their policies of today, it is essential to see how they formed in the years after 1990.

Besides the failure to remove Iraq's dictator during the Gulf conflict, the new thrust of neo-conservative debate also focused on Washington's inactivity over the Yugoslav wars of succession. Fragmentation of the bipolar order had quickly ushered in a new era of regional conflict around the globe as governments lost their superpower benefactors and peoples demanded their rights to self-determination. With the disappearance of superpower tension, the Bush administration was intent that the United States remain a great power but avoid the strain of such a broad security umbrella. Absent the fear of Russian intervention or the expansion of Soviet influence, policy makers in Washington now felt able to leave much of the responsibility for maintaining regional stability to multilateral institutions that had previously enjoyed no

---

[22] Joshua Muravchik, "Conservatives for Clinton," *New Republic*, November 1992, p. 22.
[23] Arthur B. Laffer, "Conservatives for Clinton," *New Republic*, November 1992, p. 23.
[24] Muravchik, "Conservatives for Clinton."

such role, namely the European Union (E.U.) in the Balkans, or to the U.N., the track record of which was not unblemished.[25] Furthermore, for senior members of the Bush administration, such as President Bush himself, Secretary of State James Baker, and National Security Advisor Brent Scowcroft, the prospect of fragmentation in the former parts of greater Russia was more important than Yugoslavia.[26] As the Bush administration saw it, American recognition of Croatia and Slovenia might set a precedent for potential breakaway provinces still within Moscow's sovereign orbit, which would severely compound Gorbachev's political problems in handling the breakup of the Soviet empire.[27] So the Bush administration steered clear of Bosnia.

Many neo-conservatives were quick to condemn this as an ideological anathema. Muravchik described the Bush administration's advocacy of Yugoslav unity as "encouraging Serbia's bloody aggressions."[28] Frank Gaffney wrote, "Western inaction in the face of extreme atrocities and human rights abuses ... has already communicated an unmistakable green light to would-be aggressors elsewhere." Daniel Pipes argued that "our stake is moral, not practical. It is no less real for being abstract. Accordingly, we should get involved." Similarly, Richard Pipes wrote, "The United States should quickly assert its role as guarantor of peace." Dov Zakheim suggested, "For 45 years, the United States had demonstrated ... that stability and freedom in Europe remain vital American interests. These interests are no less vital today after Communism's fall than they were during the Cold War."[29] Later, some European politicians, for example, David Owen, who co-chaired the International Conference on Former Yugoslavia, credited neo-conservatives such as Krauthammer for bringing a moral clarity to the table that others did not.[30]

Another cause of neo-conservative discontent with the Bush administration was its policies toward Israel. In early 1992, the Bush administration demanded from Tel Aviv that the $10 billion in U.S. loan guarantees to Israel

---

[25] For in-depth analysis of the Bush administration's foreign policy in the wake of Soviet collapse, see David Halberstam, *War in a Time of Peace: Bush, Clinton and the Generals* (London: Bloomsbury, 2001), and Wayne Bert, *The Reluctant Superpower* (New York: Macmillan, 1997).

[26] George Bush and Brent Scowcroft, *A World Transformed* (New York: Knopf, 1998), p. 541.

[27] Halberstam, *War*, p. 33; William Durch, "Faultlines: UN Operations in the Former Yugoslavia," in *UN Peacekeeping, American Politics and the Uncivil Wars of the 1990s* (Basingstoke: Macmillan, 1997), p. 2.

[28] Muravchik, "Conservatives for Clinton," p. 22.

[29] "To Die in Sarajevo: US Interests in Yugoslavia: A Symposium," *Foreign Policy*, fall 1992, pp. 37–40.

[30] David Owen, *Balkan Odyssey* (New York: Harcourt Brace Jovanovich, 1995), p. 329.

not be used in the building of Israeli settlements in the occupied territories. Kirkpatrick consequently suggested that this marked a point of departure from traditional American support for Israel: "[I]t's flipped. George Bush is putting the pressure on Israel now."[31]

If Bush Senior alienated neo-conservatives with his foreign policy, his domestic policies were also a disappointment for mainstream conservatives. In 1988, he had campaigned with the slogan "Read my lips. No new taxes." Then in 1990, he had been responsible for exactly that, which created a sense of betrayal among core Republican voters. As some antitax, anti-big government conservatives subsequently ended up voting for the insurgent campaign of Ross Perot, many neo-conservatives became willing to vote for Clinton to save America's role abroad. As Muravchik declared, "on foreign policy, Clinton's stands are preferable to Bush's. On what I care about – human rights and promoting democracy, keeping some sense of ideals in our foreign policy – Clinton is more amenable than Bush."[32] In his campaign speeches, Clinton was highly critical of Bush's failure to stand up for human rights in the Balkans, China, Haiti, and parts of Africa.[33] The increasing scale of the war in Yugoslavia amid growing evidence of atrocities against civilians and the parallel emergence of a humanitarian crisis in Somalia caused by civil war were key points of focus for Clinton's moral attack on the Bush administration.[34] There was also word among neo-conservatives such as Richard Schifter that Clinton discreetly advocated military action against Saddam Hussein. The *New Republic* published articles with titles such as "Neocons for Clinton: They're Back!" to suggest that the Reagan Democrats – the name used during the 1980s to describe the neo-conservatives who went to work for the Reagan administration – were returning to the Democratic Party.

In fact, Clinton made a concerted effort to woo the neo-conservatives. Schifter resigned from the Bush administration in April 1992 and immediately became foreign policy adviser to Clinton's campaign. He then undertook the job of recruiting other neo-conservatives, with varied success. David Ifshin and Peter Rosenblatt – both veterans of the Coalition for a Democratic Majority – also joined Clinton. Even though some of the well-established neo-conservatives such as Kirkpatrick, Irving Kristol, Podhoretz, Bennett,

---

[31] Quoted in Fred Barnes, "Neocons for Clinton: They're Back!" *New Republic*, March 7, 1992, p. 12.

[32] Barnes, "Neocons for Clinton," p. 14.

[33] Will Hutton, *The World We're In* (London: Little, Brown, 2002), pp. 110–11; Halberstam, *War*, pp. 13–15, 251–52.

[34] William Durch, "Faultlines: UN Operations in the Former Yugoslavia," and Bert, *Reluctant Superpower*, pp. 164–66.

and Abrams refrained from supporting the Democratic candidate, they accepted that there was potential in Clinton's bold approaches to various issues. Wattenberg asserted, "I'd love to vote for a Democrat.... Clinton's got to show he's not just going to talk the talk, he'll walk the walk." Bennett said of those neo-conservatives joining Clinton's campaign, "They have less reason not to go home to the Democratic Party. It's understandable. Clinton and Gore are hardly subversives."[35] But if Clinton thought that he had found support among the ranks of Washington's neo-conservatives, the moment was brief. By the end of his first year in office, they were all unambiguously against him.

When the first shots of what was to become the Yugoslav war were fired in June 1991, Washington initially welcomed Europe's enthusiasm to take responsibility for its own security. By the autumn of 1991, however, the E.U.'s venture into conflict prevention had fallen apart. A progression of ceasefires navigated by E.U. mediator Lord Carrington between the warring factions in Croatia had broken.[36] Without armed forces, common purpose, and established machinery for concerting foreign policies, the E.U. was exposed as unprepared for the responsibilities it had embraced.[37] When the U.N. subsequently took the major role in handling the crisis, its first measure was an embargo on the delivery of arms to all warring parties, which favored the better-armed Serbs. The U.N. entered Bosnia not to monitor a cease-fire as in Croatia, where it effectively froze the status quo, but to keep the population alive while the war continued and to act as a cosponsor for diplomatic efforts. The new U.N. Protection Force (UNPROFOR) that arrived in October 1992 aimed to protect the aid agencies but to keep out of the fighting.[38] Britain and France were the major troop contributors and determined that the intervening force could not sustain more aggressive rules of engagement because of the troops' physical vulnerability to reprisals.[39]

By the summer of Clinton's first year in office, neither Somalia nor the Balkans looked like successful examples of his bold approach to foreign affairs. In response to the administration's "lift-and-strike" proposal of lifting the arms embargo on Bosnia and undertaking air strikes against the Bosnian Serb Army as an alternative to committing American ground troops, the administration encountered British and French opposition in the belief that

---

35 Quoted in Barnes, "Neocons for Clinton," p. 12.
36 Durch, "Faultlines," pp. 204–5.
37 Peter Calvocoressi, *World Politics: 1945–2000* (London: Longman, 2000), p. 341.
38 Durch, "Faultlines," pp. 223–24.
39 Ivo Daalder, "Fear and Loathing in the Former Yugoslavia," in Michael Brown, ed., *The International Dimensions of Internal Conflict* (Cambridge, Mass.: MIT Press, 1996), p. 461.

they would be ineffective, would endanger troops, and would spread the war to hitherto unaffected areas. Both Britain and France believed that the best way to resolve the conflict was to maintain neutrality and particularly to avoid being perceived as anti-Serb. Sustaining the position of UNPROFOR in Bosnia and continuing with negotiations to end the conflict was viewed in Paris and London as the approach of least risk and smallest cost.[40] Accordingly, early U.S. plans to drop supplies to the ill-equipped Muslim-Croat positions were strongly opposed by Britain.[41] Washington's growing concern ran counter to the basic idea of British policy, which was predicated on Muslim-Croat capitulation in one form or another. Meanwhile, U.S. officials became ever more convinced throughout the conflict that French objections to U.S. proposals reflected a conscious disregard for transatlantic relations and comity in NATO and an ambition to place France at the center of an alternative power structure designed to challenge Washington.[42]

In Somalia, meanwhile, U.S. casualties were mounting in an operation that was supposed to illustrate the administration's new magic bullet for post–Cold War collective security: multilateral peace-keeping. When Siad Barre's unstable regime finally toppled in 1991, the chaos that ensued within a country where no single group had legitimate claim to power manifested itself in media images of mass starvation and struggling international relief efforts. Barre's remnants had fled south with General Mohamed Farah Aideed's forces in pursuit, and as leader of the military wing of the United Somali Congress, Aideed then retuned to fight against the USC's president, Ali Mahdi Mohammed, for control of the country.[43] Provoked by the pressure of TV images and harsh criticism from Democrats over human rights violations around the world, in December 1992 the (lame-duck) Bush administration authorized an armed international expedition of some 35,000 troops to Somalia as the United Task Force to ensure that relief reached its destination. To avoid getting mired in a civil war indefinitely, the Bush administration had pressed in its December planning for rapid transfer of responsibility to the U.N. by the following May. The Bush administration stated clearly that the United States was proposing not to fix what was broken in Somalia, but only to deal with the visible consequences of the breakdown that was stalking

---

[40] Bert, *Reluctant Superpower*, pp. 170, 201.

[41] Brendan Simms, *Unfinest Hour: Britain and the Destruction of Bosnia* (London: Penguin, 2002), pp. 60–61.

[42] Ibid., pp. 65–66, 110.

[43] William Durch, "Introduction to Anarchy: Humanitarian Intervention" and "State-Building in Somalia," in *UN Peacekeeping, American Politics and the Uncivil Wars of the 1990s* (Basingstoke: Macmillan, 1997), pp. 311–15.

Western consciences. Only five months into the new Democratic presidency, the establishment of the U.N. operation in Somalia (UNOSOM II) rapidly came unstuck. It was immediately apparent that creating a secure environment meant doing more than helping the food to reach its distribution centers. Aid became a prime political currency for militias who capitalized on starvation while the U.N. rules of engagement restrained peace-keepers' triggers. Aideed duly increased the level of hostility in conjunction with the departure of most American forces, and the remaining U.S. support force shared in the casualties with other U.N. peace-keeping forces.[44]

DISENCHANTMENT WITH CLINTON

If neo-conservatives favored the unashamed demonstration of American strength in a unipolar world, the Clinton administration was a disappointment. In March 1993, then Ambassador Madeleine Albright spoke at the U.N. about the importance of nation building in Somalia and the need for a new and more democratic model.[45] Later in the month, Clinton told Dan Rather of CBS News in a conversation about Bosnia that he was "convinced that anything we do would have to be done through the United Nations."[46] Secretary of State Warren Christopher announced in April that the administration was placing a "new emphasis on promoting multinational peacekeeping and peacemaking."[47] Clinton asserted at a news conference in May: "We must work together through the United Nations."[48] These adamant expressions of support for multilateralism and U.N. peacekeeping became the basis for the administration's first review of international peace enforcement in Presidential Review Directive-13 (PRD-13), signed in February 1993. While this document was not a policy statement, it considered the commitment of American support to an expanded military role for the U.N. The proposed expansion included the notion of placing American forces under U.N. command, and although U.S. commanders would have the right to decline orders that were considered too dangerous or reckless, they would be unable to disagree with decisions of strategy made by the U.N. Moreover, policy would not be set by Washington concerning its own

44 Durch, "Introduction to Anarchy," p. 321.
45 Cited in Halberstam, *War*, p. 257.
46 *Interview with Dan Rather of CBS News*, Weekly Compilation of Presidential Documents (United States Government Printing Office, vol. 29, no. 12, March 29, 1993), pp. 457–501.
47 Quoted in Daalder, "US Policy," p. 40.
48 *The President's News Conference*, Weekly Compilation of Presidential Documents (United States Government Printing Office, vol. 29, no. 19, May 14, 1993), pp. 856–65.

troops when under U.N. command. PRD-13 was a clear demonstration of the administration's commitment to using military force in concert with other nations rather than unilaterally.[49] When Albright outlined some of the proposed new features in a speech to the Council on Foreign Relations in early June, she declared that "the time has come to commit the political, intellectual and financial capital that U.N. peacekeeping and our security deserve."[50]

PRD-13 was not a popular document in many parts of Washington. Along with a growing bipartisan coalition in Congress, the neo-conservatives' critique of Clinton's approach to world affairs focused on his apparent aquiescence in the paralysis of multilateralism and his reluctance to employ military power. Their criticisms were certainly not unjustified. UNPROFOR and the arms embargo on the former Yugoslavia had become a "fig leaf" for independent British and French foreign policies.[51] Bosnia demonstrated that the ability of the U.N. to operate effectively in the post–Cold War era was still impeded by Great Power rivalries. Countries could hide behind the U.N., neutralize its capability to use force, and subvert its mandates to suit their interests. After National Security Advisor Anthony M. Lake managed to convince European allies on the general idea of NATO air strikes against the Bosnian Serbs in 1994, French, British, and American officials had to negotiate around European objections to full NATO control of operations by establishing a U.N. veto in the decision-making process. The decision to use air power proceeded under a dual arrangement between the U.N. command in the former Yugoslavia and the North Atlantic Council. Before NATO could act, the call for air strikes had to originate with the U.N.[52] But since the U.N. command was dominated by France and Britain as UNPROFOR's largest contributors, they had de facto control over the use of NATO's air power.

The dual key mechanism proved to be an easy way for Paris and London to manipulate NATO's airpower. U.N. commanders on the ground diluted and altered NATO ultimata in accordance with their own views or those of their governments. The ultimatum that followed the mortar attack on the Sarajevo market in February 1994 demanded complete withdrawal by the Bosnian Serb Army (BSA) of heavy weapons from within twenty kilometers of the city. When the ten-day deadline passed without full compliance, U.N. Special

[49] Jeffrey Smith, "United States Plans Wider Role in UN Peacekeeping," *Washington Post*, June 18, 1993.
[50] Quoted in ibid.
[51] Simms, *Unfinest Hour*, p. 86.
[52] Bert, *Reluctant Superpower*, p. 165.

Representative Yasushi Akashi and General Michael Rose decided that the removal of several hundred weapons was sufficient to forgo requests for air strikes. Although BSA shells were killing Sarajevans at an average of six a day, Rose considered that compliance with the spirit of the ultimatum was more important than total and strict compliance. The British and French positions not only frustrated NATO military headquarters, but also encouraged BSA violations of exclusion zones and safe areas with their reluctance to use decisive force. Over thirty cease-fires were broken, NATO's air forces failed to stop 3,000 violations of the no-fly zone, and in parts of Bosnia over 50 percent of the food aid fell into the hands of local factions. The BSA effectively managed to hold NATO air power hostage by threatening U.N. personnel who were limited by their rules of engagement. The manner in which one or the other of the British and French field commanders could veto U.N. field units' calls for air support or NATO staff suggestions for air strikes meant that they were essentially directing the politics of response coming out of Washington by controlling the amount of force used on the ground.[53]

These details were not lost on neo-conservatives, who scrutinized the daily evolution of American power in the post–Cold War era as closely as anyone in the White House. For the editors of the *New Republic*, the follies of Clinton's foreign policy were obvious: "The administration – in practice, if not in theory – has abided by the notion that it has two options in foreign policy: inaction or ambitious multilateralism. It has chosen inaction in Bosnia and overly ambitious multilateralism in Somalia."[54] In another article the editors stated that "the U.N. will not punish aggressors with reasonable consistency so long as unanimity among the Security Council's permanent members is required for action."[55] As Patrick Glynn contended, "Despite heady campaign rhetoric on Bosnia, the Clinton administration has essentially repeated the Bush pattern of inaction and obfuscation – only in a more obvious, embarrassing and potentially destructive fashion."[56] In the *Washington Post*, Kirkpatrick argued, "The reason the Clinton administration's foreign policy seems indecisive is that multilateral decision-making is characteristically complicated and inconclusive. The reason Clinton's policy seems ineffective is that U.N. operations – in Bosnia or Somalia or wherever – are

[53] Ivo Daalder, *Getting to Dayton: The Making of America's Bosnia Policy* (Washington: Brookings Institution Press, 2000), p. 21; Simms, *Unfinest Hour*, p. 116; Daalder, "Fear and Loathing in the Former Yugoslavia," pp. 243, 249; Durch, "Faultlines," p. 245.
[54] "Notebook," *New Republic*, October 25, 1993, p. 8.
[55] "Good Cop, Good Cop," *New Republic*, June 7, 1993, p. 7.
[56] Patrick Glynn, "See No Evil," *New Republic*, October 25, 1993, p. 29.

characteristically ineffective."[57] Edward Luttwak cynically exclaimed, "If the Bosnian Muslims had been bottle-nosed dolphins, would the world have allowed the Croats and the Serbs to slaughter them by the tens of thousands?"[58] Meanwhile, both Muravchik and Glynn accused Clinton of repeating his predecessor's ploy in using Somalia as "a cover for inaction in Bosnia." Muravchik contended that the Clinton administration's embrace of what Albright called "assertive multilateralism" was a "kind of poor man's internationalism." He also believed that it was an "isolationist's internationalism," in that Clinton "welcomed international action but not the exertion of American power."[59] The editors of the *New Republic* were also quick to accuse Clinton of being soft on Saddam Hussein. They criticized the president's "obsession with the U.N. requirements" and his "preferred style of opposing this tyrant" with what they branded "legalism." They maintained that in foreign policy, "legalism is almost always another instance of innocence."[60] As Wolfowitz wrote in *Foreign Affairs*, "A sense of confusion about defining the national interest is the most troubling aspect of Bill Clinton's first year as president." He argued that the Clinton administration had "squandered military prestige on issues of little importance in Somalia and Haiti. In Bosnia, Wolfowitz noted that Clinton had "failed to reconcile American interests with the dangers of military intervention." As a precursor to what he would inject into the post-9/11 discourse on U.S. national security, Wolfowitz also stressed that the real questions facing American foreign policy were not being addressed: "In the future, the real threats to U.S. interests are 'backlash states' like North Korea, Iraq and Iran...."[61]

Thus, the period of détente between neo-conservatism and the Democratic Party was short. Before the end of Clinton's first year in the White House, they solidly opposed him. He had also upset certain neo-conservatives by keeping them out of his administration after seeking their support. In their stead, he chose former members of the Carter administration such as Christopher, Anthony Lake, and Cyrus Vance for the highest positions. Muravchik declared, "With the appointment of Christopher and his team, my fond hopes for a vigorous Clinton foreign policy...were all but out the window." He articulated personal disappointment at the absence of neo-conservatives on the Clinton team: "Having actively supported Clinton, and having written books about human rights and democracy as issues in foreign policy, I felt I

[57] Jeane Kirkpatrick, "Where Is Our Foreign Policy?" *Washington Post*, July 30, 1993.
[58] Edward N. Luttwak, "If the Bosnians Were Dolphins," *Commentary*, October 1993, p. 27.
[59] Joshua Muravchik, "Beyond Self-Defense," *Commentary*, December 1993, p. 21.
[60] "Clinton and Saddam," *New Republic*, February 8, 1993, p. 7.
[61] Paul D. Wolfowitz, "Clinton's First Year," *Foreign Affairs*, January/February 1994, pp. 28–43.

was a plausible candidate for the position of Assistant Secretary of State for Democracy and Human Rights." It was a matter of months after Muravchik had optimistically announced his support for Clinton that he published the article "Lament of a Clinton Supporter." In it, he described Clinton's failure to win European support for military action in Bosnia as "not a setback but rather the opening of a new era of deliberately reduced American leadership."[62]

Muravchik was not alone in his concern. On September 2, 1993, the *Wall Street Journal* published an open letter to Clinton on what America must do in Bosnia, which was signed by over a hundred politicians, diplomats, writers, and scholars. Besides the coterie of neo-conservative names such as Kirkpatrick, Kampelman, Wohlstetter, Bell, Gaffney, Muravchik, Perle, Rostow, and Wolfowitz, the signatories also included such prominent international figures as Margaret Thatcher, George Shultz, and Zbigniew Brzezinski. The letter attacked Clinton's complete failure to act, and derided the efforts of the U.N. to keep the peace. The signatories were adamant that "Western governments should act now substantially to reduce Serbia's immediate and future power of aggression." They concluded, "if the West doesn't use force... 'the message' received will only bring American and Western resolve into contempt."[63] Less than a month after the letter was published, eighteen American soldiers died in a single incident in Somalia. As the world watched, angry Somali mobs dragged the body of an American soldier through the streets of Mogadishu while a bipartisan congressional offensive erupted against the White House from the other end of Pennsylvania Avenue in response to the culminating failures of Somalia and Bosnia. Clinton's bold and multilateralist approach to foreign policy had foundered.

UNILATERALISM: THE NEO-CONSERVATIVE EMBRACE

Just as Clinton underwent his Balkan learning curve in the 1990s, so did the neo-conservatives. While their entry point into the Balkans was moral outrage rather than any detailed familiarity with the issues, the key lesson they derived from this period was that multilateralism was doomed to ineffectiveness. In this way, they distanced themselves from liberals who shared their moral motivations and drew the lesson that giving more teeth to international institutions, such as the International Criminal Court, was

---

[62] Joshua Muravchik, "Lament of a Clinton Supporter," *Commentary*, August 1993, p. 20.
[63] "What the West Must Do in Bosnia," *Wall Street Journal*, September 2, 1993.

the right response.[64] Thus, a basic ideological foundation for the Bush administration's instinctive preference for "with-us-or-against-us, go-it-alone" was laid in the Clinton interventions of the 1990s. The specific nature of Washington's recent military campaigns in Afghanistan and Iraq reflect what the neo-conservatives and others learned while watching Clinton. American reluctance to embrace the painstaking diplomacy needed to win U.N. Security Council approval, the disinclination to allow the U.N. any control over policing a postbellum order, the perceived disjunction between effective action and the requirement for unanimity, lack of faith in European allies, and the preference for taking unilateral action were embedded in the neo-conservative paradigm for world order well before George W. Bush moved into the White House. The one point they kept relatively quiet – perhaps to maintain solidarity with the then Republican orthodoxy – was their at least implicit enthusiasm for nation building.

Wolfowitz, Perle, Muravchik, Krauthammer, Gaffney, and others felt utterly vindicated when the Bosnian war finally ended. They had all been signatories to the open letter published in the *Wall Street Journal* that argued, "Air power directed against the present and future sources of such (Bosnian Serb) attack could be used selectively and discriminately . . . with minimal danger to Serbian civilians or to UNPROFOR." Indeed, they were right. Under the kind of sustained American leadership that stood in contrast to the seemingly headless coagulation of political forces that had previously handled the response to Bosnian Serb aggression, NATO's Operation Deliberate Force lasted for only three weeks in the middle of 1995, before the Serbs agreed to enter into serious negotiations. It also vindicated the neo-conservative argument that American power was indispensable in the crisis and that U.N. primacy was an obstruction. Although NATO and UNPROFOR joined with the Croat-Bosnian army to defeat the Bosnian Serbs, it was the substance of NATO's air campaign driven by Washington that delivered the Bosnian Serbs to the table. The Bosnia-wide cease-fire was brokered by a U.S. negotiating team, the final accords were reached on American soil, and the real extent of the U.N.'s contribution to bringing the war to an end was its blessing for a NATO mandate to enforce the peace agreement.[65]

For many neo-conservatives, however, this success was more than simply moral vindication. They viewed the high-technology, precision-guided form of limited intervention that Washington was able to undertake against the

---

[64] Geoffrey Robertson, *Crimes against Humanity: The Struggle for Global Justice* (New York: New Press, 1999), pp. 324–67.

[65] Almon Leroy Way, "How America Goes to War," *Progressive Conservative*, December 10, 1999.

BSA, which was similar in strategic approach to the high-altitude precision war that America would later wage over Kosovo, as representative of a new military age for the United States. Starting with the first Gulf war, many of the second-generation neo-conservatives considered that the coming of this age owed a great deal to the work of their intellectual forefather, Wohlstetter (as discussed in Chapter 2). As Perle later contended after the second Gulf war, "that it was won so quickly and decisively, with so few casualties and so little damage, was in fact an implementation of his [Wohlstetter's] strategy and vision."[66]

As this chapter argues below, although interventions in both Bosnia and Kosovo were undertaken primarily by NATO, it was American military power and American technology that provided the capability. This military edge stemmed in part from Wohlstetter. Much of his original work had focused on building the most accurate nuclear and conventional weapons possible for Cold War strategic purposes at a time when the dominant thinking had been that increasing weapon accuracy would only make nuclear war more likely. Wohlstetter countered this thinking with the argument that policy makers had to be able to respond to regional conflicts with nonsuicidal options and that it was better to have more accurate technology that targeted Soviet weaponry rather than civilians. In the period of détente, Wohlstetter had greater difficulty in influencing the executive, but his ideas and his vision gained considerable purchase under Reagan, who awarded Wohlstetter the Presidential Medal of Freedom. When the United States consequently graduated from the bipolar era with the highest level of military force, capability, and technology in the world, the neo-conservatives envisaged this emerging expression of precision-targeted and high-technology American power as not merely a strategic reality. It was the basis for a new logic regarding the use of military force in the post–Cold War era. For the younger neo-conservatives, the unipolar landscape after Soviet collapse was to be combined with America's surgical and specialized weapon – capabilities to define a new agenda of the possible for U.S. foreign policy.[67] Missiles could turn corners and gun emplacements could be destroyed while the adjacent houses were left intact. Thus, the opportunities for intervention were increased. These intellectuals viewed the level of technological capability manifest in the first Gulf war and both NATO interventions in the Balkans as representative of what Washington could now achieve at little or even no human cost.[68]

---

[66] Neil Swidey, "The Analyst," *Globe Magazine*, May 18, 2003.

[67] Ibid.

[68] Although the estimates of collateral damage on the ground during the Kosovo War suggest the death of around 500 people, no NATO personnel were lost during the war.

The argument that American capability would make certain wars a "cake-walk" and that intervention could be undertaken at negligible cost to the U.S. forces involved would later become a central plank in the neo-conservative case for a Second Gulf War as sold to Congress and the American public.

A further reality surrounding Bosnia that would later become fundamental for neo-conservatives was that there could not have been greater contrast between the success of NATO's Implementation Force (IFOR) and the failures of UNPROFOR. IFOR contained a clear chain of command operating under a unified structure without any dual-key mechanism. Because it had the ability to respond forcefully and without the political interference of the U.N. Security Council or the national field commander's private orders, it enjoyed early and persistent success in executing its mandate. The central role of the U.N. and its command structure had been the ultimate reason why forceful air strikes had not materialized against the BSA in 1994 and early 1995 and why European obstructionism had been so successful. Of enormous significance for the future of armed intervention in the 1990s and beyond was the new assumption among a majority of American policy makers that prohibiting the U.N. from any decision-making role was essential to the success of military operations. As James O'Brien, Special Presidential Envoy to the Balkans in Clinton's second administration, described it: "The U.N. had become a byword in Washington for neutrality to evil."[69]

For the neo-conservatives, this was all the proof that anyone could ever need to demonstrate why a multilaterally directed security process was not feasible. The primacy of the U.N. Security Council in the post–Cold War order had been undermined by its own performance in Bosnia and Somalia. Krauthammer argued early in Clinton's second term that "the actions of the Democratic administration of the past six years . . . reflect a vision of the world that is at odds with the realities of the international system. . . . It is truly a world imagined."[70] As suggested by a statement of the Washington-based Action Council for Peace in the Balkans in 1995, on whose roster sat prominent neo-conservatives such as Perle, Rostow, Wolfowitz, Wohlstetter, and Kampelman, "the West's refusal to use force has relegated the U.N. to irrelevancy at best and complicity at worst."[71]

---

[69] Interview with James O'Brien, Washington, D.C., April 10, 2003.

[70] Charles Krauthammer, "A World Imagined," *New Republic*, March 15, 1999.

[71] Marshall Harries and Stephen Walker, "Fingers in the Dark: Renewing Ceasefires and UN Mandates," *Bosnia Institute*, April–May 1995. The Action Council for Peace in the Balkans was not by any means a solely neo-conservative group. Its members included a variety of individuals, such as Stephen Morris Abram, Morton Abramowitz, Fouad Ajami, Richard Allen, Daniel Bell, Zbigniew Brzezinski, Richard Burt, Frank Carlucci, Hodding Carter,

ATLANTIC RELATIONS

Of equal significance to the neo-conservative influence on foreign policy after September 11 was how the Balkan wars of the 1990s defined the post–Cold War relationship between Europe and the United States.[72] Until the Iraq war, it ranked among the worst chapters in transatlantic relations ever. In the four years that war raged in Bosnia, the region transitioned from a peripheral concern to the central transatlantic security problem.[73] Violence between the BSA and Bosnian government forces never threatened the core security of any NATO member. But it threatened to demolish the idea of the West. A war that was directed chiefly against civilians seemed to challenge essential values on both sides of the Atlantic, while the disparities in U.S./European policy perspectives provoked an acute crisis in alliance relations. The very credibility of the West seemed in jeopardy as these differences led to paralysis. If the transatlantic alliance could not prevent such violence within Europe, what use was it?[74] For neo-conservative intellectuals such as Kagan, the answer was obvious: "The 1990s witnessed not the rise of a European superpower but the decline of Europe into relative weakness[,] ... military incapacity and political disarray."[75] He noted, "whatever Europe can or cannot offer in terms of moral and political support, it has had little to offer the United States in strategic military power since the end of the Cold War.... Europe could not even act in Bosnia without the United States."[76]

Although NATO went to war as an alliance and won in 1999, Kosovo failed to ameliorate the discord in transatlantic relations that had sharpened over Bosnia. It revealed underlying and systemic weaknesses in the half-century-old alliance, and just as Bosnia had been for many in Washington the first and last test case for U.N.-led multilateralism in the post–Cold War era, so Kosovo became the first and last opportunity for NATO to demonstrate its effectiveness at fighting wars. Even so, nervous European politicians had once again seemed to hinder the employment of decisive military power. Many in

Walter Cronkite, Dennis DeConcini, David Dinkins, Frank Fahrenkopf, Geraldine Ferraro, Henry Louis Gates, Leslie Gelb, Marshall Harris, Bianca Jagger, Barbara Jordan, Patt Kerian, Lane Kirkland, Jeane Kirkpatrick, John Lehman, Ron Lehman, Eugene McCarthy, Frank McCloskey, George McGovern, Edmund Muskie, Paul Nitze, John O'Sullivan, Martin Peretz, Norman Podhoretz, Eugene Rostow, Donald Rumsfeld, Carl Sagan, Albert Shanker, George Shultz, Henry Siegman, John Silber, Helmut Sonnenfeldt, Susan Sontag, William Howard Taft, Paul Volcker, Elie Wiesel, and Elmo Zumwalt.

[72] Richard Holbrooke, *To End a War* (New York: Random House, 1998), pp. 360–61.

[73] Dana H. Allin, *NATO's Balkan Intervention* (Oxford: Oxford University Press, 2003), p. 13.

[74] Ibid., p. 9; Robert Kagan, *Of Paradise and Power: America and Europe in the New World Order* (New York: Knopf, 2004), p. 49.

[75] Robert Kagan, "Power and Weakness," *Policy Review*, June 2002, pp. 3–28.

[76] Kagan, *Of Paradise*, pp. 42, 98.

Washington believed that disagreements among allies over what targets to hit affected the campaign throughout its course and that the inherent political constraints of the nineteen-member alliance revealed the follies of waging war under transatlantic consensus.[77] There was also great concern over the acute imbalance in military capacity that the war had made so apparent. Operation Allied Force was run and largely conducted by Americans. U.S. aircraft flew two-thirds of the strike missions. Almost all of the targets were identified using U.S. intelligence assets and virtually every precision-guided weapon was launched from an American platform.[78] The campaign greatly weakened European credibility, reflecting its political inadequacy, material inferiority, and dependence on America's military capacity. This made political interference from European capitals during the campaign even harder to swallow in Washington.

Simply put, based on the Kosovo experience, the neo-conservatives concluded that the Atlantic alliance was more a hindrance than a help. As Kagan wrote, "the Kosovo war showed how difficult it was going to be for the United States and its European allies to fight any war together." He suggested that Kosovo posed a number of questions that were answered after September 11: "What if Americans believed their vital interests were directly threatened? What if Americans suffered horrendous attacks on their own territory and feared more attacks were coming? Would Americans in such circumstances have the same tolerance for the clumsy and constrained NATO decision-making and war-fighting process? Would they want to compromise again with the European approach to warfare, or would they prefer to 'go it alone'?"[79] The answer for Kagan was obvious: "With almost three thousand dead in New York City, and Osama bin Laden on the loose in Afghanistan, the U.S. military and the Bush administration had little interest in working through NATO. This may have been unfortunate from the perspective of transatlantic relations but it was hardly surprising." As Perle said of the Europeans after September 11, "we no longer need them in the way that we once did. They are no longer vital to the defense of our interests in the world."[80]

---

[77] Halberstam, *War*, pp. 444–45, and Ivo Daalder, *Getting to Dayton: The Making of America's Bosnia Policy* (Washington, D.C.: Brookings Institution Press, 2000), p. 123.

[78] Ivo Daalder, "Unlearning the Lesson of Kosovo," in *American Foreign Policy Journal* (New York: McGraw-Hill, 2000), p. 60.

[79] Kagan, *Of Paradise*, p. 51.

[80] Quoted in Ted Galen Carpenter, "The European Policy of the Bush Administration: A Superpower Doesn't Do Windows," in Julian Lindley-French, ed., *Transatlantic Relations and the Bush Administration* (Paris: Institute for Security Studies of the Western European Union, 2001), p. 13.

William Kristol correctly linked the matter of disparity in U.S./European capability with the other fault line in transatlantic relations that became a chasm in the 1990s: divergent policies toward rogue states and crisis zones. As Kristol commented about European allies, "they spend on social programs and allow the United States to guarantee their security, and then condemn their American cousin for being too aggressive."[81] This issue of America's being "too aggressive" became a running sore in the 1990s.[82] Where the Europeans argued that dialogue and trade constituted better tools of leverage to deal with undesirable regimes, Washington contended that this provided resources to them and sent a dangerous message to the world's other malcontents. While the United States has not traded with Cuba for the best part of forty years, the E.U. was the source of more than half of Cuban annual imports during the 1990s. The E.U. alone was doing more than a combined total of $20 billion in annual trade with Iran and Libya, accounting for over 20 percent of E.U. oil imports. Large French and Italian companies, such as Total, Elf, and Agip, have investments of hundreds of millions of dollars in both countries, while Iran has debts with Germany of $8.6 billion. As Britain gave full support to U.S. preparations in 1998 to respond militarily after Saddam Hussein expelled U.N. weapons inspectors, Italian and French construction and oil companies were making visits there to position themselves for contracts following the lifting of sanctions. Support for the United States toward Iraq in early 1998 isolated Blair's government from France and other European allies.[83] London was criticized by continental allies for being the sole supporter of U.S. policy in the region. Kristol's diagnosis of this was simple: "Absent the United States, who else could uphold decency in the world? Europe? . . . Having proclaimed in the 1990s the 'hour of Europe,' its leaders spent the decade failing to deal with ethnic cleansing on their own continent, while cutting lucrative trade deals with a gallery of rogue states and refusing to boost their defense budgets or take the other necessary steps to establish an independent foreign policy."[84]

However, such views in Washington, as reflected in Kagan's argument that "Europe lacked the wherewithal to introduce and sustain a fighting

[81] Lawrence F. Kaplan and William Kristol, *The War over Iraq: Saddam's Tyranny and America's Mission* (San Francisco: Encounter, 2003), p. 92.

[82] Philip Gordon, "Rogue States and Transatlantic Relations," in Frances Burwell and Ivo Daalder, eds., *The United States and Europe in the Global Arena* (London: Macmillan, 1999), p. 109.

[83] John Dumbrell, *A Special Relationship: The Anglo-American Relations in the Cold War and After* (Basingstoke: Macmillan, 2001), p. 121.

[84] Kaplan and Kristol, *War over Iraq*, p. 120.

force in potentially hostile territory," that "the European role was limited to filling out peacekeeping forces after the United States had, largely on its own, carried out the decisive phases of a military mission," and that organizations such as the U.N. and NATO "constrained" American capability, were not confined to neo-conservatives.[85] From the early stages of Clinton's first term, Congress had been instrumental in setting the terms of debate on American unilateralism. Republican Senators Robert Dole, Mitch McConnell, John McCain, John Warner, Alfonse D'Amato, and others had worked with Democratic Senators such as John Kerry, Joseph Lieberman, and Robert Byrd in campaigning for a greater unilateralism abroad. They saw American support for the embargo on all arms to the former Yugoslavia as utterly immoral because it deprived Bosnia of the ability to defend itself. Although the eighteen U.S. soldiers in Somalia had been lost on an operation under U.S. control, the rapid reaction force sent out to rescue them was under U.N. command, and its tardy appearance sealed the Rangers' fate. The Mogadishu debacle helped to fuel a groundswell of opposition in Congress to the viability of multilateralism and, more generally, the U.N. as a global conflict resolution system. As Clinton tried to ignore them, their voices grew, until the White House had to pay attention to the veto-proof congressional bill of June 1995 in favor of unilaterally lifting the embargo. With burned fingers over Somalia and Bosnia, the Clinton administration subsequently made every effort to take the heat out of the potential congressional uproar. The absence of a ground force and a campaign fought at 15,000 feet over Kosovo was the end result.

Unilateral tendencies became woven into the fabric of American foreign policy after Soviet collapse because of circumstance rather than doctrine. As presidential candidate in 1992, Clinton had declared: "the cynical calculus of pure power politics is ill-suited to a new era." Seven years later, the war in Kosovo demonstrated the administration's migration from idealism to Realpolitik.[86] NATO launched Operation Allied Force in spite of Belgrade's recognized sovereignty over Kosovo, against the wishes of powerful nations such as Russia, China, and India, and without authorization from the U.N.[87] As Lake admitted after leaving office, "There was in Bosnia, and there was in Kosovo and there has been now in Iraq a constantly recurring tension between the desire of the United States to get things done for

---

[85] Kagan, "Power and Weakness."

[86] Stephen M. Walt, "Two Cheers for Clinton's Foreign Policy," *Foreign Affairs*, March–April 2000, p. 78.

[87] Dana H. Allin, *Nato's Balkan Interventions* (Oxford: Oxford University Press, 2003), p. 48.

humanitarian or other purposes and a dedication to the U.N. as an important instrument."[88]

Nor was the idea that NATO fought wars badly purely a neo-conservative conception. Much of Washington's political elite agreed with Kagan's interpretation. In a hearing before the Senate Committee on Foreign Relations shortly after the war, Eliot Cohen said, "We are not going to march into the future thinking that NATO is now the cohesive military instrument which we can bring to solve all kinds of military issues." William Taft told the same committee, "NATO is not a thing for everywhere. It is not for the Middle East. It is not for Africa, but to keep the peace in Europe and keep stability." Similarly, Brzezinski asserted that NATO's primary role should now be in enlarging "the zone of stability and peace and security in Europe." As he saw it, "I do not believe that in the longer run it is in their [Europe's] interest and in our interest that NATO be truly a joint-American-European partnership and an alliance that binds the U.S. in a reciprocal relationship with 18 other states with an integrated military command." Republican Senator Gordon Smith agreed: "It would be a mistake to think of it [NATO] as a really effective war-fighting machine." As Democratic Senator Joseph Biden had asserted to Albright less than a month into the Kosovo operation in a hearing before the Committee on Foreign Relations, "I know there are a number of things the Secretary and the President would like to see done if we were pursuing this war alone."[89] Among other things, the foregoing gives focus to the point at which the neo-conservatives embracing the unadulterated "American supremacy" as the grand strategy best serving U.S. national interests departed from many others in advocating unilateral action.[90] Yet, despite their antipathy toward multilateralism and disenchantment with European allies, the majority of Congress's leading hawks in the 1990s never envisioned the future through such a lens.

THE GENERATIONAL HAND-OFF

When William Kristol created the Project for the New American Century (PNAC) in 1997, it was more than simply an indication that neo-conservatives were active in Washington. It was suddenly apparent that

[88] Interview with Anthony Lake, Georgetown University, Washington, D.C., March 26, 2003.
[89] US Kosovo Diplomacy, Hearing before the Senate Committee on Foreign Relations, United States Senate, 106th Congress, 1st Session, September 28, 1999, and the War in Kosovo, Hearing before the Senate Committee on Foreign Relations, United States Senate, 106th Congress, 1st Session, March 20, 1999, United States Library of Congress.
[90] Tom Barry and Jim Lobe, "The People," in John Feffer, ed., *Power Trip: US Unilateralism and the Global Strategy after September 11* (New York: Seven Stories Press, 2003), p. 49.

somewhere between the fall of the Berlin Wall and the end of the Bosnian war, neo-conservatism had undergone a complete generational transition. By the latter half of the 1990s, Kagan, William Kristol, Muravchik, Perle, Wolfowitz, and others had assumed the leadership roles that had long been held by Nathan Glazer, Irving Kristol, Daniel Patrick Moynihan, and Norman Podhoretz. The younger neo-conservatives had filled a space left by the increasing inability of older neo-conservative views to provide a sufficient interpretive framework for the changing realities of international events in the 1990s. In a glum article in the *Wall Street Journal* in August 1997, Irving Kristol acknowledged defeat, remarking that an American imperium was on its way. This being the Clinton years, however, this was not the celebratory event it would become in the hands of his son, William. He spoke gloomily of the emergence on a global scale of a "dominant secularist-hedonistic ethos" and an "imperium with a minimum of moral substance."[91]

The terms of neo-conservative debate thus shifted. The new genesis had updated neo-conservatism to replace the Soviet threat with a broad idea of "American global leadership" that encompasses the need to "challenge regimes hostile to our interests and values ... increase defense spending significantly ... promote the cause of political and economic freedom abroad ... strengthen our ties to democratic allies," and "accept responsibility for America's unique role in preserving and extending an international order friendly to our security, our prosperity, and our principles." As the PNAC's statement of principles argued in reference to other critics of Clinton, "American foreign and defense policy is adrift. Conservatives have criticized the incoherent policies of the Clinton Administration. They have also resisted isolationist impulses from within their own ranks. But conservatives have not confidently advanced a strategic vision of America's role in the world. They have not set forth guiding principles for American foreign policy. They have allowed differences over tactics to obscure potential agreement on strategic objectives. And they have not fought for a defense budget that would maintain American security and advance American interests in the new century."[92]

Meanwhile, war in the Balkans was an issue on which many older neo-conservatives such as Glazer, Irving Kristol, Moynihan, and Podhoretz had been markedly mute. With the Soviet monolith defeated, they were unable to identify matters of urgent American concern in the sieges of Dubrovnik and

[91] Irving Kristol, "The Emerging American Imperium," *Wall Street Journal*, August 18, 1997, p. A18.
[92] "Statement of Principles," Project for the New American Century, June 1997.

Sarajevo.[93] Many of those who had kept the pressure on Reagan to live up to his ideological promises of supporting and encouraging democratic movements around the world during the Cold War then recoiled from the idea of making the export of democracy a central purpose in American foreign policy after Soviet collapse. Irving Kristol accepted that much of neo-conservatism's ideological campaign against the USSR was essentially defensive, inasmuch as it was responding to an existing threat and that it was required in the circumstances created by the Cold War.[94] As he consequently argued in 1991, "the prospect of American military intervention and occupation to 'make democracy work'... in short... something like an American empire with a purely ideological motive power... is not and cannot be a serious option for American foreign policy."[95]

Kristol's older generation of neo-conservatism aligned itself with the prevailing realism of many in the American foreign policy establishment at the time. What Kagan has called "post–Cold War normalcy" became the favored objective of those such as James Baker, Lawrence Eagleburger, and Brent Scowcroft, who, like Kristol and Glazer, advocated a narrower focus on the national interest.[96] Many of the ideologically committed Cold Warriors of the 1980s became the post–Cold War realists of the 1990s. Across the pages of America's major newspapers, they subsequently countenanced Michael Mandelbaum's well-known thesis that Clinton pursued "foreign policy as social work" in places such as Bosnia and Haiti. In Haiti the administration forced an end to the military regime of Lieutenant-General Raoul Cedras in the hope of restoring democracy. As Mandelbaum argued, Clinton's foreign policy constituted worldwide social work at the expense of protecting American national interests. Many in the American defense establishment who had spent the previous decade fighting the Soviet Union reiterated Mandelbaum's premise that the Clinton administration was preoccupied with "helping the helpless," while it also "alienated vital allies, changed direction repeatedly to repair Clinton's sagging image, and let special interest groups harm U.S. policy towards nations such as Japan and Russia."[97]

The expression of neo-conservatism that emerged in the latter 1990s, therefore, was an entirely new political animal. It was unable to place its

---

[93] John Ehrman, *The Rise of Neoconservatism: Intellectuals and Foreign Affairs 1945–94* (New Haven: Yale University Press, 1995), p. 48.

[94] Ibid.

[95] Kristol, "Defining Our National Interest," p. 62.

[96] Kagan, *Of Paradise*, p. 82.

[97] Michael Mandelbaum, "Foreign Policy as Social Work," *Foreign Affairs*, January–February 1996, p. 28.

intellectual heritage anywhere among the first-generation neo-conservatives, the Reaganite Cold Warriors of the 1980s, or the congressional unilateralists of the 1990s. Their reduced intellectual focus demonstrated this, overlooking many of the issues and debates on metaphysics and social conditions that engaged their forefathers. While it is a considerable challenge to condense into a single definition the vast scope of neo-conservative debate that prevailed in the 1960s and 1970s, its modern expression presents no such difficulty. Across the voluminous amounts of books, articles, and discussion that these neo-conservatives have endlessly generated since the Soviet collapse are four very simple and doctrinaire notions: (1) supporting democratic allies and challenging the evildoers who defy American values, (2) America's total responsibility for global order, (3) the promotion of political and economic freedom everywhere, and (4) increased spending on defense. As the 1990s progressed, the intellectual energy of neo-conservatism became increasingly focused on Iraq as the most important element in U.S. foreign policy debate. William Kristol and his associates published voluminously on the need for regime change in Baghdad with articles, op-ed pieces, and open letters to the president and Congress. Prominent intellectuals in the neo-conservative cause were invited to present their ideas at congressional hearings. What would become their standard discourse after 9/11 of emphasizing an apparently imminent threat from Iraq's supposed weapons of mass destruction was written in its embryonic form during this period. A PNAC letter of May 1998 addressed to the Speaker of the House and the Senate Majority Leader stated, "[T]he only way to protect the United States and its allies from the threat of weapons of mass destruction" was to "put in place policies that would lead to the removal of Saddam and his regime from power."[98] Wolfowitz told the House International Relations Committee in February 1998 that regime change in Iraq was the "only way to rescue the region and the world from the threat that will continue to be posed by Saddam's unrelenting effort to acquire weapons of mass destruction...."[99] He criticized the Clinton administration for having a goal that was "limited merely to getting the U.N. inspectors restored." Foreshadowing what would become the Pentagon's attempted policy of installing a government of friendly exiles in Baghdad five years later, Wolfowitz stressed that Washington should indicate its "willingness to recognize a provisional government of free Iraq." According to Wolfowitz's Senate testimony, "the best place to start is with

---

[98] "Letter to Gingrich and Lott on Iraq," Project for a New American Century, May 29, 1998.

[99] Paul D. Wolfowitz, "Prepared testimony of," House International Relations Committee, United States Congress, February 25, 1998.

the current organization and principles of the Iraqi National Congress" (on this, more below in Chapter 7). Again in a hearing before the House National Security Committee later in the year, Wolfowitz reiterated what had become something of a neo-conservative mantra, namely that it was a mistake to leave Saddam Hussein in power in 1991 and that "the best opportunity to deal with Saddam Hussein was in the immediate aftermath of the U.S. victory...."[100]

Thus, in only a few years since the Soviet collapse, neo-conservatism had refocused itself as an interventionist lobby intent above all else on waging a second Gulf war. A far cry from the schools of Irving Kristol, James Baker, or Joseph Biden, the provocative neo-conservative Michael Ledeen announced in early 2003 a wish list of targets: governments to be changed, including Iran, Iraq, Syria, and Saudi Arabia as the "big four." He also added, "Then there's Libya. There's a North Korean problem too that we'll have to deal with...." Apparently, there is scant intellectual challenge to this remarkable outlook among today's neo-conservatives. In his book on Machiavelli, Ledeen asserts that "the struggle against evil is going to go on forever."[101] At the point when neo-conservatism enjoys more influence in the Oval Office than at any other time since it left the bustling confines of Alcove 1, its thinking has been reduced to this bleak principle.

But as recently as 1994, second-generation neo-conservatism looked nothing like the powerful political force we know today. In November of that year an article in the *New Republic* described William Kristol both as "a one-man Washington think tank" and also as someone who "epitomizes the crisis of the conservative movement: once a genuine intellectual force, it is now engaged in a principle-free politics that is as empty as it is often vicious."[102] As late as 1995, John Judis wrote, "Scattered individuals still see themselves redefining neo-conservatism for the post–Cold War period. Joshua Muravchik and Ben Wattenberg have argued that even with the Cold War over, the United States should continue a crusade for global democracy – what Wattenberg calls a new 'manifest destiny.' But they are largely irrelevant to the policy debate." Judis concluded, "If neo-conservatism exists in the 1990s, it is much the way that the new left survived into the 1980s – as cultural nostalgia rather than distinct politics. Muravchik, Wattenberg, and Gaffney are political anachronisms of the 1990s in the same way

---

[100] Paul D. Wolfowitz, "Prepared testimony of," House National Security Committee, United States Congress, September 16, 1998.
[101] *Panorama* transcript.
[102] Hanna Rosin, "Memo Master," *New Republic*, November 7, 1994, pp. 22–24.

that Noam Chomsky and Richard Barnet became anachronisms a decade before."[103]

Judis may have since refined his thesis. But this underscores the extent to which neo-conservative influence experienced a quantum increase in the late 1990s. One can simply say that 9/11 provided the necessary space for these intellectuals to fill. But this fails to explain what carried them over the considerable distance between being a political anachronism in 1995 and waiting ready at the doorstep of the White House on September 12, 2001. What enabled this kind of thinking to migrate from obscurity in *Foreign Affairs* to the center of policy making in less than two White House terms was largely the emergence of a dynamic shadow defense establishment during the Clinton administration.

THE NEO-CONSERVATIVE NETWORK

In February 1998, a small group of national security thinkers who were outside government sent an open letter to the Clinton White House suggesting "a comprehensive political and military strategy for bringing down Saddam and his regime."[104] Among the signatories were Abrams, Richard Armitage, John R. Bolton, Douglas Feith, Zalmay Khalilzad, Perle, Peter Rodman, Rumsfeld, Wolfowitz, David Wurmser, and Dov Zakheim, who all now hold or held positions in the Bush administration. Other leading figures in Washington to sign the letter were Gaffney, Kagan, Kristol, Muravchik, Martin Peretz, who is editor in chief at the *New Republic*, and Leon Wieseltier, also of the *New Republic*. They called themselves the Committee for Peace and Security in the Gulf. But this was only one player among many. The American Enterprise Institute (AEI), the Heritage Foundation, the Jewish Institute for National Security Affairs (JINSA), the Center for Security Policy (CSP), the Hudson Institute, and the PNAC had also become important elements in a neo-conservative coalition of intellectuals, ex-government officials, political advisers, media figures, and key conservative personalities, all pressing for the era of American supremacy. They spoke at congressional hearings, took an active role in the mainstream media discourse, sent open letters to the White House, published articles regularly in the major newspapers, and produced a stream of books.

From the time of its inauguration in 1997, the PNAC was an essential element of this defense-establishment-to-be. The PNAC signatories were a

[103] Judis, *Trotskyism*.
[104] Stephen Sniegoski, "The War on Iraq," *Last Ditch*, February 19, 2003.

well-connected group of prominent intellectuals and former government officials with strong links to the national security bureaucracy, the defense establishment, the print and cable media industry, dominant sections of the U.S. defense industry, and some of America's wealthiest conservative foundations.[105] A large portion of the signatories, such as Abrams, Gary Bauer, Bennett, Cheney, Eliot Cohen, Aaron Friedberg, Frank Gaffney, Fred Ikle, Zalmay Khalilzad, Kirkpatrick, Dan Quayle, Peter Rodman, Henry Rowen, Rumsfeld, and Wolfowitz had all served in the Reagan or G. H. W. Bush administrations. Others had worked for the CIA, such as Reuel Marc Gerecht and James Woolsey, who was the agency's director from 1993 to 1995.

The list of signatures also included those who would subsequently assume pivotal roles in the foreign policy of George W. Bush's administration, such as Rumsfeld, Cheney, Wolfowitz, and Libby. Later to be Cheney's Chief of Staff and an active neo-conservative in the 1990s, Libby had first begun service in government at the State Department in 1981 as part of the Policy Planning Staff. From 1982 to 1985, he then served as Director of Special Projects in the Bureau of East Asian and Pacific Affairs. From 1989 to 1993, Libby was Deputy Undersecretary of Defense for Policy, and in 1998 served as the Legal Adviser to the U.S. House of Representatives Select Committee on U.S. National Security and Military/Commercial Concerns with the Peoples' Republic of China, which was more commonly known as the Cox Committee. A longtime compatriot of Wolfowitz, Libby also joined the board at the Rand Corporation and became a consultant to Northrop Grumman.

Among the prominent intellectuals to sign up to the PNAC were Francis Fukuyama, Donald Kagan, Norman Podhoretz, and his wife Midge Decter. Other powerful signatories included Jeb Bush, and of course, neo-conservative notable Perle. The PNAC's founders were prominent intellectuals and former Republican administration officials Robert Kagan (son of Donald) and William Kristol. As a pivotal figure in neo-conservative thinking and son of neo-conservative forefathers Irving Kristol and Gertrude Himmelfarb, William Kristol was also founder of the neo-conservative flagship publication the *Weekly Standard*.

Meanwhile, on the three floors above PNAC's headquarters on Washington's 17th Street sits AEI, which also had become a recognized home for the cast of second-generation neo-conservative characters. The institution has long been well connected politically and has a tradition of extensive associations with the top echelons of government. A half-century of direct

[105] Feffer, ed., *Power Trip*, Appendix B, pp. 205–9.

interaction with government circles has included such notables as George H. W. Bush, Gerald Ford, and former Israeli Prime Minister Yitzak Shamir. It was after the Cold War, however, that AEI became the institutional home of modern neo-conservatism. Periodic early-morning meetings at AEI have become known as "black coffee briefings," during which the neo-conservatives and others congregate to expound their views on America's role in the world. These briefings frequently draw in hefty numbers of journalists and diplomats who fully appreciate the influence that these thinkers are having on policy making: George W. Bush reminded an audience of AEI scholars in February 2003 of how they "do such good work that my administration has borrowed twenty such minds."[106] Kirkpatrick, Ledeen, Muravchik, Perle, Wattenberg, and Wurmser are all members.

Perle, in fact, now functions as a link across many of the neo-conservative think tanks, research institutions, and other organizations on the network. At times described as the most influential of neo-conservatives, it was under Reagan that Perle's hard-line anti-Soviet stance and immovable resistance to any kind of arms control brought him the sobriquet "Prince of Darkness."[107] Although not technically part of the Bush administration, he was until his resignation in February 2004 first chairman, then a member of the Defense Policy Board. Although this was once a little-known civilian board intended to offer the Secretary of Defense guidance on military issues, it has now become a pseudo-lobbying group of considerable influence, with close links to the White House and access to classified documents.[108]

Perle is also on the advisory board of JINSA. Throughout the 1990s, other members on the board included Bolton, Cheney, Feith, Kirkpatrick, Ledeen, Muravchik, Rostow, Wolfowitz, and James Woolsey. Established in 1976 with the encouragement of the Pentagon, which welcomed the opportunity to gain support from a voter group that was traditionally suspicious of high defense spending, JINSA gave a voice to those convinced that America should continue to provide Israel with ample support in case of another Arab-Israeli war. It is now committed to explaining the link between American national security and Israel's security, as well as strengthening both. Since the 1970s, JINSA has been transformed from an obscure group to a highly connected and well-funded $1.4-million-a-year operation.[109] A large section of JINSA's annual budget goes toward facilitating contact between Israeli officials and retired U.S. generals and admirals who retain influence in Washington. Some

---

[106] *Panorama* transcript.
[107] Sniegoski, "War on Iraq."
[108] Ibid.
[109] Jason Vest, "The Men from JINSA and CSP," *The Nation*, September 2, 2002, pp. 16–20.

of America's leading figures in military contracting are well represented in JINSA. Advisory board members have worked for Northrop Grumman or its subsidiaries as consultants or board members. JINSA's Flag and General Officers Trips between Israel and the United States have involved more than 250 American officers over twenty years, one of whom was Jay Garner, the Bush administration's first choice for the reconstruction of post-bellum Iraq.[110] Garner also joined a host of retired senior military officials in signing the U.S. Admirals' and Generals' Statement on Palestinian Violence, which stated: "We are appalled by the Palestinian political and military leadership that teaches children the mechanics of war while filling their heads with hate."[111]

JINSA is one of the most visible of links between Israel's supporters in Washington and the neo-conservative network. It also overlaps considerably with the Center for Security Policy (CSP). Kaminsky, Kirkpatrick, and Perle serve on the advisory boards of both. CSP's founder, Frank Gaffney, was a protégé of Perle when they both worked in Jackson's office. Gaffney also worked with Perle at the Pentagon and left shortly after him in 1987.[112] JINSA and CSP are both underwritten to a large extent by Irving Moskowitz, a California entrepreneur. Their membership lists are interchangeable, and these two organizations provided an important point of neo-conservative focus over the Clinton years, as the history of their rosters demonstrates.[113]

Perhaps the most prominent event to come out of the nexus of neo-conservative activity in conjunction with like-minded conservatives within the Israeli body politic was the 1996 research paper published by the Israeli think tank the Institute for Advanced Strategic and Political Studies. Under the title "A Clean Break: A New Strategy for Securing the Realm," it was a policy guideline for the newly elected Israeli Prime Minister, Binyamin Netanyahu.[114] The document argued that Netanyahu's "new set of ideas" provided an opportunity "to make a clean break" with the beleaguered Oslo process. The highlights of this break suggested that Israel "cannot play innocents abroad in a world that is not innocent." The paper berated the "land for peace" initiative and emphasized: "Our claim to the land – to which we

[110] JINSA report no. 321, *Jewish Institute for National Security Affairs*, March 26, 2003, and Vest, "Men from JINSA."
[111] US Admirals' and Generals' Statement on Palestinian Violence, *Jewish Institute for National Security Affairs*, November 6, 2000.
[112] Vest, "Men for JINSA."
[113] Kathleen Christison and Bill Christison, "A Rose by Any Other Name: The Bush Administration's Dual Loyalties," *Counterpunch*, December 13, 2002.
[114] Sniegoski, "War on Iraq," and Vest, "Men from JINSA."

have clung for hope for 2000 years – is legitimate and noble." Netanyahu's clean break also meant reestablishing "the principle of preemption." The study group that contributed to the report included James Colbert (another member of JINSA), Charles Fairbanks, Feith, Perle, Jr., David Wurmser, and his wife Meyrav Wurmser.[115] Perle and Feith had been close associates for some years. Feith had worked on Richard Allen's NSC team in Reagan's first administration and held a position as Middle East specialist from 1981 to 1982. During Reagan's second term, Feith served as Special Counsel to Perle when he was Assistant Secretary of Defense. As ideological compatriots, both men worked together after 1989 in what became the International Advisors, Inc., a group that sought to promote the objectives of industrial and military cooperation between Ankara and Washington. Perle and Feith again worked together as advisers to the Bosnian government in the Dayton Peace talks. A co-signatory of the PNAC statement of principles, Feith remained among the most focused of neo-conservatives on the Arab-Israeli conflict.[116]

Also an author of the "Clean Break" document and a political ally of Perle and Feith was David Wurmser, who is among the more high-profile neo-conservatives. A research fellow on the Middle East at AEI, he become special assistant to John Bolton at the State Department in the Bush administration before moving in early September 2003 to the office of Cheney and Libby. Earlier he had worked at the U.S. Institute of Peace, the Washington Institute for Near East Policy, and the Institute for Advanced Strategic and Political Studies in 1996.

Another member of the neo-conservative family is David Wurmser's wife, Meyrav Wurmser. She represents the Middle East Media Research Institute (MEMRI), and also directs the Center for Middle East Policy at the Hudson Institute, whose trustees also include Perle and Conrad Black at the time the publisher of the *Jerusalem Post, Daily Telegraph, Sunday Telegraph,* and the *Spectator.* Wurmser co-founded MEMRI with Colonel Carmon, for twenty-two years an Israeli military intelligence and later counterterrorism adviser to Israeli Prime Ministers Yitzhak Shamir and Yitzhak Rabin. According to its Web site, MEMRI's purpose is to bridge the language gap between the West – where few speak Arabic – and the Middle East, by providing timely translations of Arabic, Farsi, and Hebrew media. However, opinions on MEMRI's credibility seem as divided as its subject matter. While prominent American journalists, academics, and congressmen have described it

---

[115] "A Clean Break: A New Strategy for Securing the Realm," Strategic Research Publications, *Institute for Advanced Strategic and Political Studies,* June 1996.

[116] Biography of Douglas Feith, *The American-Israeli Cooperative Enterprise,* http://www.us-israel.org/index.html.

as "an invaluable research tool" and the "single most important resource for anyone seriously interested in the Middle East," others have commented that "MEMRI's intent is to find the worst possible quotes from the Muslim world and disseminate them as widely as possible."[117]

Other institutes that became part of the neo-conservative loop include the Washington Institute for Near East Policy and the Middle East Forum (MEF). Both have strong ties to Washington's pro-Israeli lobby and enjoy distinguished membership. Among those on the board of advisers at the Washington Institute are Kirkpatrick, Perle, Wolfowitz, and Woolsey. Its adjunct scholars include Muravchik and Michael Rubin, who is a specialist on Afghanistan, Iran, and Iraq and works with Perle and Wurmser at AEI. Rubin also belongs to MEF, along with William Kristol and Meyrav Wurmser.

THE FINANCIAL NETWORK

But if the rosters on these various neo-conservative think tanks and research institutions seem intertwined, so do the foundations that finance them. Organizations such as the Lynde and Harry Bradley Foundation, the John M. Olin Foundation, the Sarah Scaife Foundation, and the Castle Rock Foundation constitute a core group of conservative bodies that provide the money for research institutions such as AEI, the Heritage Foundation, and the Hoover Institute and for individual scholars, such as Robert Leiken, at institutions such as Harvard University. There is considerable overlap among the benefactors, the members of the major think tanks, and the senior levels of the Bush administration. The Heritage Foundation and the Hoover Institution have been instrumental in connecting policy analysts, Republican Party officials, and conservative scholars for years.

The Hoover Institution at Stanford University has supported research on issues ranging from tax to national security policy and conducted studies addressing problems on every continent. Both Rumsfeld and Condoleezza Rice are Hoover alumni, and several of the institute's fellows sit on the Defense Policy Board.[118] Heritage, AEI, and the Hoover Institution all enjoy patronage from the John M. Olin Foundation, while the Bradley Foundation primarily provides support for AEI and Heritage. AEI has also received extensive funds from the Smith Richardson Foundation. Meanwhile,

---

[117] Brian Whitaker, "Selective MEMRI: Is the 'Independent' Media Institute Quite What It Seems?" *Guardian*, August 12, 2002, and Richard H. Curtiss, "The Secret Life of Meyrav Wurmser," *Arab News*, May 30, 2003.

[118] "The Charge of the Think Tanks," *The Economist*, February 15, 2003, and "The Wealthy Conservative Think Tanks," *Covert Action Quarterly*, winter 1998.

Heritage has close associations with other key neo-conservative financers such as the Castle Rock Foundation. Castle Rock is also a benefactor of AEI and is supported by the conservative Coors family of Coors Brewing Co. Another Heritage trustee, Frank Shakespeare, enjoys similar status at the Bradley Foundation, and former Heritage visiting fellow Alvin Felzenberg now works with Rumsfeld and Wolfowitz at the Department of Defense. On the board of directors at the Bradley Foundation meanwhile is Michael Grebe, who holds a position on the board of overseers of the Hoover Institute. The board's membership also includes Rumsfeld and Richard Mellon Scaife, who is an heir to the Mellon family's industrial fortune. Scaife was on the U.S. Advisory Commission for Public Diplomacy during the administrations of Reagan and George H. W. Bush and helped to found the Heritage Foundation in 1973 along with Joseph Coors and Paul Weyrich. He now runs three out of four Scaife family foundations, the largest being the Sarah Scaife Foundation, which funds, among others, AEI and Heritage.[119]

Confused? One could explore the alleyways of Washington's neo-conservative labyrinth indefinitely. Over the 1990s, Washington's neo-conservative establishment grew into a far-reaching, well-funded, and powerful intellectual-political matrix in the shadow of the Clinton White House. Groups such as the PNAC also forged links with social conservatives such as Gary Bauer and William Bennett. Christian Right groups such as Empower America and the Foundation for the Defense of Democracy (FDOD) became involved in pushing for a conservative internationalism overseas. In building on the biblical foundations for an apocalyptic confrontation in the Middle East, the Christian Right came to support the neo-conservative agenda concerning Israel after having little interest in foreign policy during the 1980s and the early 1990s. Empower America and the FDOD subsequently joined the neo-conservative support of Israel's Likud Party.[120]

However, the efforts of neo-conservatives to build a shadow defense establishment in the 1990s differed from other movements of the political right. For many arch-conservatives, Clinton's failures abroad were something that provided greater fraction for attacking the administration at home. For example, when the Republicans won control of Congress (in November 1994 for the first time since 1952), what made the Republican victory so problematic for Clinton was the fiercely conservative thrust of the incoming Republican majority. The Republican bid to capture Congress was led by the

[119] Jill Junnola, "Perspective: Who Funds Whom?" *Campus Watch in the Media*, October 4, 2002.
[120] Barry and Lobe, "The People."

Speaker of the House of Representatives, Newt Gingrich, who represented a new and emerging political force in the Republican Party. It had survived the collapse of the Reagan era and George H. W. Bush's politically damaging raising of taxes in 1990, to emerge with a distilled and popular conservative ideology. It was decidedly more partisan and directed a particularly sharp rhetoric toward Clinton. Sympathetic to the ideas and values of the Bible Belt, it drew support from disaffected Democrats, including both those who supported a stronger national security policy and those who had been first disaffected by Lyndon Johnson's Voting Rights Act of 1965.[121]

There was, however, a big difference between the Gingrich conservatives and Christian Right, on the one hand, and the neo-conservatives, on the other. The neo-conservatives entertained ambitions for America's global role that went beyond retiring Clinton, beyond returning the Republicans to the White House, and beyond the conservative social agenda of Empower America. Their objective was to seize the political space created by the strategic vacuum of the 1990s to advance a foreign policy agenda that seeks to remake substantial parts of the world in America's image.

A DOCTRINE IN WAITING

This is why, if one wishes to understand the direction of American foreign policy today, one must read what neo-conservatives were writing ten years or more ago. Americans and their overseas allies may believe that they are engaged in a war against terrorism. This is certainly part of what is taking place. But the greater part of the neo-conservative doctrine that was elaborated during the 1990s and that now so heavily influences Washington's priorities had little to do with terror. Instead, the focus was the "emergence of China as a strong, determined, and potentially hostile power; the troubling direction of political developments in Russia; the continuing threat posed by aggressive dictatorships in Iraq, Serbia and North Korea"; and "the increasingly alarming decline in American military capabilities."[122] The mention of Iraq constitutes the only link to today's war on terrorism.

This underscores our contention that the neo-conservative doctrine, conceived during the Alcove 1 days of opposition to the Soviet Union and updated as part of a classic struggle for preeminence among sovereign states, is a questionable model for the threat of terrorism. As shown in Chapter 1,

[121] Jonathan Schoenwald, *A Time for Choosing: The Rise of Modern American Conservatism* (Oxford: Oxford University Press, 2001), p. 7, and Halberstam, *War*, p. 297.
[122] Robert Kagan and William Kristol, eds., *Present Dangers: Crisis and Opportunity in American Foreign and Defense Policy* (San Francisco: Encounter, 2000), p. vii.

President Bush, at one point, described terrorists and the struggle against them as wholly different from the interaction of sovereign states. This is the point we look at in detail below: whether the doctrine, with which the neo-conservatives have landed us, distracts the United States from the pursuit of terrorism and whether it may indeed aggravate the threat.

4

The Neo-Conservative Ascension

With the election of George W. Bush, neo-conservatives sensed a moment of opportunity. During ten years of exile and frustration following what they saw as the premature end of the Gulf War, they had refined their agenda and looked forward to the exercise of power. They knew, however, that they would have to act cautiously. At least one of them, William Kristol, was off the White House dinner list for having supported Bush's primary opponent, Senator John McCain, and telling his Republican colleagues that "getting in bed with Bush was a mistake."[1] Furthermore, George Bush did not approach office with a foreign policy predisposed toward the neo-conservative agenda. During the campaign, nonideological veterans of past Republican administrations, led by the former Deputy National Security Advisor Condoleezza Rice, had taken charge of his foreign policy tutelage.[2] Under their influence, Bush's November 1999 speech, "A Distinctly American Internationalism," presented a balanced approach to international affairs emphasizing a mix of political, economic, military, and cultural elements. In fact, one sentence, that "military power is not the final measure of might," specifically contradicted a central neo-conservative tenet. Far from reaching out to neo-conservatives, the efforts of Bush's advisers were aimed at distinguishing his approach from, on the one hand, Clinton's "dilettantism" and, on the other, nativist Republican isolationism and protectionism. Neo-conservatives such as Richard Perle had to battle for access to Bush and were constantly on the telephone to Austin to reassure themselves that their views were being

---

[1] Hanna Risen and Dana Milbank, "A Political Heretic Is Cast Out," *Washington Post*, March 26, 2000, p. A6.
[2] Ivo H. Daalder and James M. Lindsay, *America Unbound: The Bush Revolution in Foreign Policy* (Washington, D.C.: Brookings Institution, 2003), pp. 17–34.

acted on. "It's almost as though they did not trust Bush," commented one member of the campaign team in Austin. Even after the Bush administration's campaigns in Afghanistan and Iraq, Perle's distrust can also be noted in his concern that, as 2004 began, the "will to win" was ebbing in Washington.[3]

Nonetheless, Bush's emphasis on rebuilding military strength, his America-centric vision of the national interest, and his lack of strong preformed ideas on foreign policy gave the neo-conservatives hope. Before long, a dozen or so neo-conservatives had found their way from think tanks, university campuses, and law firms to Washington's halls of power, taking key positions in the Pentagon, the Vice President's Office, and the National Security Council. From these interconnecting vantage points, they were able to reinforce each other in the agenda painstakingly assembled over the previous decade. And when the opportunity presented itself in the wake of September 11, they were better prepared than anyone in the administration to, as one commentator sympathetic to neo-conservatism observed, "rally the country around their vision of the world"[4] – albeit a vision that was at best barely germane to immediate challenge and, at worst, set the nation on a highly imprudent trajectory of missionary imperialism and international confrontation. This chapter begins with a look at how the neo-conservatives assumed power with Bush's election. It was not a smooth ride.

CONFIRMATION BATTLES

When it became clear in late November 2000 that George Bush would be the president-elect, even though Gore had not yet conceded, Bush bolstered his position by publicly instructing Dick Cheney to request the keys to the transition office and then deliberating over his cabinet appointees – also in public. Former Secretary of State and Bush family friend James A. Baker, a master of that space where law and public opinion intersect, was particularly mindful of the unprecedented and multidimensional contest under way. All statements and initiatives were subject to the closest scrutiny so that Bush's public instructions to Cheney were partly to rally his supporters, partly to demonstrate confidence in his position before the courts, partly to capitalize on public weariness with the seemingly endless process

---

[3] David Frum and Richard Perle, *An End to Evil: How to Win the War on Terror* (New York: Random House, 2003), p. 5.

[4] William Shawcross, *Allies: The U.S., Britain, Europe and the War in Iraq* (New York: Public Affairs, 2004), p. 63.

of chad counting, and partly to begin, in earnest, the process of building an administration.

Even before the Florida primary outcome was decided by the Supreme Court, the transition team was well into the production of a kind of Kabuki theater. At times "candidates" were floated to the press as a "thank you" for campaign support, though they had no chance of being appointed to the suggested position. More often, candidates were floated in the press to gauge reactions, particularly among conservative columnists and Republican lawmakers. Prospective appointees were publicly scheduled for meetings with the president and vice president elect, and eventually a number of established neo-conservatives became top-level nominees for important national security posts.

The neo-conservatives did not, however, assume their new positions without some measure of controversy. Some endured particularly lively confirmation hearings. Among them was John Bolton, now Under-Secretary of State for Arms Control and International Security Affairs. Nominated from his position as senior vice-president for public policy research at AEI, Bolton, who has a remarkable intellect and is former editor of the *Yale Law Review*, had held a variety of posts in both the Reagan and elder Bush administrations at the Department of State, Department of Justice, and the U.S. Agency for International Development (USAID).

Bolton's views, delivered in articles and speeches while an AEI Resident Scholar, stirred controversy on several accounts during the nomination process. With a chilling habit of slicing to the diplomatic nerve, Bolton had become the "enfant terrible" of embassy row. Diplomats and American internationalists alike were seized by his well-documented criticism of the U.N. as bloated, ineffective, and mismanaged. Moreover, his promotion of diplomatic recognition for Taiwan was a source of neuralgia for the State Department's "old China hands" and much of the business community, who feared the consequences of reversing Washington's "one-China policy" maintained since 1978. During the Clinton years, Bolton maintained relations with Baker, in part, by assisting him in peace negotiations in Western Sahara on the Polisario matter. And it was Baker who had recommended Bolton to the Bush inner circle to direct Bush's legal team in Palm Beach County during the Florida recount.[5] Equally, his characterization of Clinton's North Korea policy as "appeasement" portended a change when there was little or no consensus on which alternative policies would be most effective in containing the threat.

[5] Walter Shapiro, "Nominee Skates Past Frozen Dems," *USA Today*, March 30, 2001.

Bolton's nomination distilled the sharp differences between the two parties on the highest profile national security issues and also tested the power of his principal Senate supporter, Jesse Helms, the Republican Chairman of the Senate Foreign Relations Committee. But we return below to Senator Helms, who was of singular importance to the neo-conservatives as a rare supporter in Congress.

Despite much ruffling of feathers, Bolton made it through the hearings. When Secretary of State Powell lays down a policy, Bolton said, "I will adhere to that policy."[6] Bolton did not volunteer opinions on contentious issues, adroitly avoiding a question on the 1972 ABM Treaty by the committee's ranking Democrat, Senator Joseph Biden.[7] Bolton's deft performance was such that it inspired Massachusetts Senator John Kerry to ask whether Mr. Bolton's was a case of "confirmation conversion."[8]

Throughout the hearings, Bolton had a powerful ally in Senator Jesse Helms. Helms had promoted Bolton for the State Department job and introduced him at his hearing as a "brilliant writer and thinker." Helms thought the government, and specifically the State Department, could use someone such as Bolton, "a man with the courage of his convictions . . . who says what he means and means what he says."[9] In the end, Helms got his wish, but the process demonstrated that nominating neo-conservatives to the Bush administration was not a walk in the park. Their eventual primacy was anything but foreordained.

Although filling the top positions at the Pentagon was less controversial than Bolton's State Department nomination, there was no shortage of intrigue. As the process turned to the all-important top Defense post, Republicans were talking about three candidates for Defense Secretary: Senator Sam Nunn, a Democrat from Georgia, Paul Wolfowitz, and Richard Perle.[10] The active consideration of Senator Nunn reflected a politically adroit bow to bipartisanship and healing after an election that pitted quite different world-views and distinct notions of the role of government, not to mention budget and policy priorities. Nunn, a highly regarded former chairman of the Senate Armed Services Committee, was knowledgeable about the Pentagon, tough-minded, and worldly in the ways of global politics.

[6] Skorneck, "State Department."

[7] Shapiro, "Nominee Skates."

[8] Ibid.; Skorneck, "State Department."

[9] Shapiro, "Nominee Skates"; Skorneck, "State Department"; Jane Perlez, "Arms Control Nominee Defends Shifting View," *New York Times*, March 30, 2001.

[10] Mike Allen, "Bush Plays Transition in Low Key; Governor Remains in Background While Considering Nominees for His Cabinet," *Washington Post*, November 28, 2000, p. A10.

Paul Wolfowitz and Richard Perle, also in contention for the top job though different in temperament, had much in common. Perle, with a vacation home in Provence, had been quite a man about town in the 1980s. Reflecting standards *Vanity Fair* called "fairly louche," Perle had a taste for "beluga caviar, imported French bread and cappuccino, Monte Cristo cigars, Gauloise cigarettes ... [and] lives large and is as learned in the offerings of the world's shopping capitals as he is in throw weights,"[11] while Wolfowitz's distilled, academic demeanor reflects more of Wittgenstein than Clausewitz. After a grounding in Wohlstetter's thinking, both were heavily influenced by Senate Armed Services Committee Chairman Henry "Scoop" Jackson, who, as we have seen, gave early political support to the neo-conservatives in the form of aggressive anti-Sovietism combined with relative liberalism on social issues.

As time for a decision drew near, Perle's name was identified less often as a possible secretary and instead mentioned only for "a high-level job."[12] Eventually, Perle's name faded from the radar screen entirely. While no member of the transition team would confirm why Perle was seemingly dropped from consideration, he had apparently offended the Bush inner circle by presuming to speak for the candidate on the hypersensitive issue of Israeli-Palestinian relations and U.S. policy when he had, in fact, no brief to do so. Defense Department sources indicate that Bush felt the need to distance himself from the advice Perle gave to Israeli officials the previous summer. In the days preceding the Camp David Peace Talks, Perle invited Israeli officials Yossi Alper and Yoram Ben-Zeev to dinner at his home and advised them to "accept only a comprehensive peace agreement and to resist any efforts by the Clinton administration to use the summit meeting in the presidential campaign."[13] Bush disassociated himself from Perle, saying he had been "speaking for himself" and not the Bush campaign.[14] Out of the running for a top job at Defense, Perle accepted the position of Chairman of the Defense Policy Board, hitherto a somewhat staid organization designed to provide advice to the Secretary of Defense outside normal bureaucratic channels. He resigned from the chairmanship in 2003 and eventually resigned completely from the board in February 2004.[15]

---

[11] Sam Tanenhaus, "Bush's Brain Trust," *Vanity Fair*, July 2003, p. 141.
[12] Dana Milbank, "White House Gas Up a Think Tank; For Center Right AEI, Bush Means Business," *Washington Post*, December 8, 2000, p. A39.
[13] Alison Mitchell, "The 2000 Campaign: The Texas Governor; Bush Says Aide's Advice to Israel Does Not Reflect His Own Views," *New York Times*, July 13, 2000, p. A24.
[14] Ibid.
[15] Tanenhaus, "Bush's Brain Trust," p. 144.

INTRIGUE AT THE PENTAGON

At the root of the uncertainty about what the administration sought in a Secretary of Defense was George Bush's limited exposure to defense policy, management, and budget and his lack of exposure to the delicate mix of diplomatic and military initiatives required to execute U.S. international obligations. As a result, the short-list for the top job at the Pentagon was constantly changing. By the end of December 2000, however, the finalists were former Senator Daniel R. Coats and Paul D. Wolfowitz, a top Pentagon official in the former Bush administration who was then dean of the School of Advanced International Studies at Johns Hopkins University. Some Republicans worried that Coats's social conservatism, especially on the issue of gays serving openly in the military, would make him a lightning rod for criticism. Still, the inner circle thought him both knowledgeable and manageable and Bush was leaning toward tapping Coats for the job. After a forty-five-minute-long meeting with Coats and Cheney on December 18, 2000, however, Bush seemed to change his mind. Several Bush advisers said the meeting did not go well.[16] The issue of gays in the military was one consideration in this reassessment, but transition "insiders" say it was not the only one. Bush was also said to be concerned that Coats might not be able to stand up to the forceful personalities in the Pentagon and the cabinet.[17]

The Bush team turned to Wolfowitz, but at the same time, they cast an eye to the horizon looking over the field in hopes of finding a candidate with just the right combination of skills and personality. Those close to Cheney pushed hard for Wolfowitz to be nominated – Wolfowitz was Cheney's policy chief at the Pentagon during the Gulf War and had proved himself a first-rate intellectual on military matters. But there was some hesitation. Former officials close to the transition process floated "background" doubts to the press about his managerial skills, while others feared he would be overwhelmed by a military bureaucracy that combined a prodigious old-boy network with the mysteries of Byzantium. No one wanted another Les Aspin.[18] By the end of the month, with the public beginning to sense uncertainty, even confusion, the administration was forced to make a decision. Bush gave the Pentagon's

---

[16] Thomas Ricks, "Pentagon Nomination Delay Becoming an Issue," *New York Times*, December 27, 2000, p. A7.
[17] James Dao and Eric Schmitt, "The 43rd President: The Defense Department; Bush Says He Is Taking His Time on Defense Pick to 'Get It Right,'" *New York Times*, December 23, 2000, p. A14.
[18] Ibid.

top job to Donald H. Rumsfeld, a veteran of the Nixon and Ford administrations and a known bureaucratic infighter from his days as President Ford's Secretary of Defense in the late 1970s.

For those gray heads who remembered Rumsfeld's first tour at the Pentagon, there was some surprise in the appointment, not because he had failed to perform but rather because Rumsfeld and the Bush family had had a long and difficult history. George H. W. Bush, a former congressman, first U.S. envoy to the People's Republic of China, and Chairman of the Republican National Committee in the post-Watergate turmoil, and Don Rumsfeld, a former congressman, Nixon-Ford stalwart, and then White House Chief of Staff, were potent rivals to lead the moderate wing of the Republican party. Certainly, both had presidential ambitions. Rumsfeld was nothing if not an effective political manager. When he made his deputy, Dick Cheney, White House Chief of Staff, moved himself to the Department of Defense, and appointed George H. W. Bush, who had been a possibility for vice president, to the CIA, it was for all intents and purposes the death knell for the distinguished elder Bush's presidential ambitions. The Church Committee, whose vitriolic hearings in 1973 had raised broad questions about the scope and ethics of the agency, had seen to that. One did not have to be a tea-leaf reader to see that Rumsfeld was promoting a rival to oblivion. Thus, far from being thought a friend, Rumsfeld was seen by some members of the Bush family as a treacherous self-promoter, which made his appointment by George W. Bush all the more significant. It signaled an early willingness by the new president to make his own way even if it contravened deeply held family preference.

Meanwhile, Wolfowitz was still under consideration for both the top job at CIA, a position he announced he did not want, and the post at the U.N.[19] that he declined when Secretary of State-designate Colin Powell called to ask him to become the U.S. permanent representative. A *New York Times Magazine* article offered an insightful analysis of the situation: "[G]iven this administration's standoffish relationship with the U.N. and Wolfowitz's own wariness of multilateralism, that [position] could be regarded as a trap rather than an honor." Powell, of course, denies this was the case. He insists that offering the position was a compliment to Wolfowitz's ability to "think big and argue an issue to the ground."[20] Thus, if the chips had fallen just a bit differently, this key neo-conservative would have found himself far removed

[19] David Sanger, "The 43rd President: The Transition; New Picks Firm Up Conservative Cast of Bush's Cabinet," *New York Times*, December 30, 2000, p. A1.
[20] Bill Keller, "Sunshine Warrior," *New York Times Magazine*, September 22, 2002.

from the nexus of U.S. national security policy – instead inhabiting the gauzy world of the U.N. and its myriad agencies, unfathomable to the Bush administration, and separated in time and space from the action in Washington.

As the cabinet posts filled, attention shifted to the key deputies in the national security and foreign policy areas. Prior to Rumsfeld's selection, some expected Richard Armitage to take the Deputy Secretary's position at Defense. Armitage had served the Reagan and Bush administrations in both the Pentagon and the State Department, possessed a powerful intellect, was an accomplished body-builder, and was personally close to Colin Powell and his wife, Alma. Through his relationship with Powell and General Brent Scowcroft, Bush senior's National Security Advisor, he gained access to the campaign's inner circle and was the primary author of Bush's September 1999 "Citadel" speech outlining the candidate's views on the military in the post–Cold War world. He disagreed with Wolfowitz's advocacy of a more aggressive policy toward Iraq, being closer on this issue to Powell, who favored him for the number-two position at Defense.[21] But Rumsfeld's agreement with the White House was that he could select his own senior staff at Defense, and after an hour-long meeting with Armitage on January 4, Shermanesque word leaked out that neither would the Secretary ask Armitage to serve nor would Armitage accept if asked. Ironically, in the light of subsequent developments, it was also felt that Armitage would dominate Rumsfeld, thus entrenching State Department influence over national security policy.[22]

When the dust settled, to no one's great surprise, Wolfowitz found himself in the number-two position at Defense, and Armitage in the number-two position at the State Department. Wolfowitz's nomination to the Defense post underscored Cheney's role in crafting the administration's national security establishment and, more significant, foreshadowed the emerging neo-conservative network. Powell, meanwhile, had supported Armitage for Deputy and Pennsylvania Governor Tom Ridge for Secretary of Defense – with notable lack of success.

As the transition process drew to a close, a number of neo-conservatives had been selected to join Wolfowitz at the Defense Department. Perle had declined the number-three job, Undersecretary for Policy, to accept the Chairmanship of the Defense Policy Board, and so that job went to Douglas J. Feith, a lawyer and neo-conservative stalwart who had worked for Perle in

[21] Thomas Ricks, "Rumsfeld Impresses Armed Services Panel; Wolfowitz, a Cheney Protégé, Is Chosen over Powell Ally for No. 2 Post at the Pentagon," *New York Times*, January 12, 2001, p. A16.
[22] Al Kamen, "Instant Cabinet: Add Clearance Counsel, Sir," *New York Times*, January 5, 2001, p. A19.

the Reagan Defense Department.[23] Joining Wolfowitz and Feith was Dov Zakheim, who had previously served in the Pentagon and the Congressional Budget Office and been a member of the "Vulcans," a volunteer group of foreign policy experts advising candidate Bush on international affairs. Zakheim became Comptroller and Undersecretary of Defense. Rounding out the roster of neo-conservative sympathizers at the top of the Pentagon was then Director of National Security Programs at the Nixon Center, Peter Rodman, who accepted the position of Assistant Secretary of Defense for International Security Affairs.

Neo-conservatives also found themselves in positions of great power beyond the State and Defense Departments. I. Lewis "Scooter" Libby, mentioned above, a Wolfowitz protégé, went from prior positions on Capital Hill, the State Department, and, most recently, the Department of Defense, to become the vice president's Chief of Staff. From early on in the administration, the vice president's office was a formidable presence, little short of a mini-National Security Council. To complement Cheney's own vast experience in foreign and national security policy, Libby assembled a team of unusually accomplished and experienced advisers.[24] With various and many military experts, specialists on foreign and national security matters, seasoned veterans of the Pentagon, political allies and like-minded legislative aides from Congress, as well as veteran lobbyists and speech writers, the vice president's office was equipped to play a significant role in shaping the executive agenda. William Kristol (who had himself been Chief of Staff to Vice President Dan Quayle) commented that it was clear that "Cheney's going to be a real influence." As he noted, "they're serious, experienced people."[25] Douglas Brinkley, a presidential historian at the University of New Orleans, agreed: "Cheney is unique in American history. . . . He is the vortex in the White House on foreign policymaking. Everything comes through him."[26] Whereas previous vice presidential offices had often included maybe one dominant national security aide and policy experts on loan from other federal agencies, Cheney introduced into his team permanent staff experts and full-time specialists on areas such as the Middle East and military affairs.[27] With prominent government lawyer David Addington as his counsel, former chief

---

[23] Bill Keller, "The Sunshine Warrior," *New York Times Magazine*, September 22, 2002.
[24] Eric Schmitt, "Cheney Assembles Formidable Team," *New York Times*, February 2, 2001, p. A1, and Eric Schmitt, "Public Lives: Cheney Aide Will Eat Horse Guts Before He'll Spill Beans," *New York Times*, April 30, 2001, p. A10.
[25] Quoted in Schmitt, "Cheney Assembles."
[26] Quoted in Barbara Slavin and Susan Page, "Cheney Is Power Hitter in White House Lineup," *USA Today*, August 28, 2002.
[27] Schmitt, "Cheney Assembles."

of staff for House Representative Christopher Cox and aide to the Cox panel Dean McGrath as Libby's deputy, neo-conservative ally, former Foreign Service officer, Russia Expert, and U.S. ambassador to Finland Eric Edleman, Middle East specialist John Hannah, Wohlstetter-enthusiast William Luti, and others, such as Heritage Foundation analyst Nina Shokraii, Cheney had a formidable staff able to generate its own ideas in the Washington policy debate.[28] This team had the wherewithal to operate independently of other arms of government, such as the National Security Council (NSC). As Libby and his staff participated in White House foreign policy meetings it is possible to argue that the vice president's small staff became more influential than the larger staff of the NSC itself.[29]

Many of those meetings were held at the NSC where Elliott Abrams, best known as an Iran-Contra figure pardoned by former President Bush, first served as Senior Director for Near East and North African affairs, the position responsible for policy toward Israel and the Palestinians. Though Abram's job title has changed, he remains focused on the region, with responsibility for Arab-Israeli relations and the management of the U.S. involvement in the Middle East peace process.[30]

THE EARLY UNILATERALISM

The well-placed neo-conservative network delivered some important bureaucratic victories early in the administration. Within six months, the administration announced its intention to reject six international agreements, thus attracting charges of "unilateralism" from the international community. Reflecting an important tenet in neo-conservative thinking, Washington had early demonstrated its aversion to new international agreements and organizations on. The issue landed on the front pages when President Clinton, with a last-minute signature, forced the Bush administration to declare its position on cooperation with the International Criminal Court (ICC) on assuming office. On December 31, 2000 (the last day nations could sign the treaty without first having ratified it), the United States signed the treaty to create the first permanent international court designed to try cases of crimes against humanity. Not legally binding without ratification by the Senate, the U.S. signature, according to Clinton, was meant to "reaffirm our strong support

---

[28] Thomas Ricks, "Iraq War Planner Downplays Role," *Washington Post*, October 22, 2003, p. A27, and Schmitt, "Cheney Assembles."

[29] Slavin and Page, "Cheney Is Power Hitter," and Schmitt, "Cheney Assembles."

[30] For more information, see http://www.weeklystandard.com/Content/Public/Articles/000/000/001/998zbrfl.asp.

for international accountability" and to keep the United States "engaged in making the ICC an instrument of impartial and effective justice."[31] Defense Secretary William S. Cohen, on behalf of both the Pentagon's civilian and military bureaucracies, immediately registered his disapproval.

He was not alone, of course. Incoming Republicans also condemned the treaty. Before his appointment to the State Department, John Bolton had emerged as one of the treaty's most outspoken critics writing in publications that ranged from *Mother Jones* to the *Wall Street Journal* to Singapore's *Straits Times*.[32] In a *Washington Post* op-ed entitled "Unsign That Treaty," he argued that "the ICC's problems are inherent in its concept, not minor details to be worked out over time." Creation of the ICC would not, he said, deter "the truly hard men of history from committing war crimes or crimes against humanity." Furthermore, Bolton wrote that support for the ICC was a thinly veiled "desire to assert the primacy of international institutions over nation-states," an objective he did not share.[33]

While John Bolton was a leading opponent of the ICC, he certainly was not the only one. When the Rome Statute giving life to the ICC was initialed in 1998, the United States abstained with the then Defense Secretary William Cohen rejecting the principle of universal jurisdiction over U.S. military personnel.[34] There was bipartisan condemnation of Clinton for changing his mind and signing the treaty in the dying days of his presidency. Senator Jesse Helms said, "I will make reversing this decision, and protecting America's fighting men and women from the jurisdiction of this international kangaroo court, one of my highest priorities in the new Congress."[35] Even before Clinton signed the treaty, Rumsfeld had joined eleven other prominent retired policy makers in signing a letter to Congress that warned that "American leadership in the world could be the first casualty" of the tribunal.[36]

For the court to function, sixty nations were required to ratify the treaty that created the ICC. As states signed on one by one, the ICC began taking shape. Thirty nations had signed on by May 2, 2001. Concerned by the

---

[31] Thomas Ricks, "US Signs Treaty on War Crimes Tribunal," *Washington Post*, January 1, 2001, p. A1.
[32] Caroline Daniel, "Hard Man Who Sits at the Heart of US Foreign Policy," *Financial Times*, December 19, 2002, p. 20.
[33] Ricks, "US Signs Treaty on War Crimes Tribunal."
[34] Geoffrey Robertson, *Crimes against Humanity: The Struggle for Global Justice* (New York: New Press, 2000), p. 328.
[35] Ricks, "US Signs Treaty."
[36] Steven Lee Myers, "US Signs Treaty for World Court to Try Atrocities," *New York Times*, December 31, 2000, p. A1.

steady progress, members of the new administration worked to remove the U.S. signature from the treaty, and some pressed other capitals not to ratify it. The House passed a bill that required America to cut off military aid to most countries ratifying the treaty, unless they pledged never to surrender an American to the court.[37] In a May 2002 statement, Rumsfeld summarized the numerous U.S. grievances with the ICC: "the lack of adequate checks and balances on powers of the ICC prosecutor and judges; the dilution of the U.N. Security Council's authority over international criminal prosecutions; and the lack of any effective mechanism to prevent politicized prosecutions of American service members and officials."[38]

By the following April, the ICC had received more than the required sixty government ratifications, and the court was launched over U.S. objections. In response, the Bush administration restated its opposition to the treaty, adding that the treaty would not proceed to the Senate for ratification.[39] Bolton sent a one-paragraph note to U.N. Secretary General Kofi Annan stating that the United States "does not intend to become a party to the treaty."[40] Clinton's earlier signature of the treaty had, in effect, been nullified. The United States joined Russia and China, who also chose not to ratify the treaty.

On the substance of the matter – as we see below on the Kyoto treaty – the U.S. position may have struck the U.S.'s friends as rigid, but it was not without merit. The ICC's advocates clearly saw the court as a means to apply constraints on U.S. freedom of action that would not otherwise have applied. They were dismissive of American concerns for legal safeguards for the U.S. military, describing these as "obsessive."[41] But it was not just the substance of the U.S. position that generated resentment among friends and allies around the world; it was the way in which it had been handled. The optics were not good – the State Department's new office of Public Diplomacy, in its first of many disasters, had been absent from the process of explaining the U.S. position and unable to blunt the vitriolic response across Europe, in particular. The ICC soon took on a life of its own, becoming part of the litany of complaints about the new administration's unilateralism.

---

[37] Editorial desk, "Attack on the International Court," *New York Times*, May 21, 2001, p. A16.
[38] Statement by Secretary of Defense Donald H. Rumsfeld, issued May 6, 2002, as reproduced on Web site for U.S. Mission to the E.U.: http://www.useu.be.
[39] Colum Lynch, "War Crimes Court Created over Fierce US Objection," *Washington Post*, April 12, 2002, p. A20.
[40] "Letter on the ICC to UN Secretary-General Kofi Annan from Under Secretary of State for Arms Control and International Security John R. Bolton," Department of State, May 6, 2002.
[41] Robertson, *Crimes*, p. 366.

Not only was Washington the target of invective from a determined international community of human rights and legal organizations, but rejecting the ICC accelerated rising anti-Americanism in Britain, Canada, France, and Germany, each of whom would soon become critical to American plans in the U.N. and to forging an anti-Saddam coalition.[42]

The troubles George Bush inherited from his predecessor did not end with the ICC. He was also confronted with the Kyoto Protocol, designed to address global warming, which was even more sensitive politically and clearly carried as much potential to alienate opinion around the world. The treaty, negotiated in 1997 and signed by over 100 countries, had yet to be ratified by any industrialized country. It proposed to commit the United States and thirty-seven other industrialized countries to large cuts in greenhouse gases – specifically, it would have required industrialized countries to cut emissions of greenhouse gases by 2012 from 5 to 7 percent below their 1990 levels. Proponents argued that the United States held only 5 percent of the world's population, but produced one-quarter of the world's emissions; treaty advocates wanted the United States to take the lead in making the protocol binding.

As a candidate, Bush opposed the Kyoto Protocol, charging that it was "unfair to the United States which would be most dramatically impacted by the agreement."[43] He asserted that acceptance of the treaty would reduce U.S. economic growth by two-tenths of a percent just when growth was at its lowest levels in a decade and U.S. economic growth was critical to global economic recovery. Furthermore, the president thought it unfair that the treaty excluded large developing countries such as China and India – clearly future competitors – from the requirement to reduce their emissions. During the campaign, the media used the treaty to depict the differences between the Gore-Lieberman ticket – internationalist and environmentally sensitive – and the Bush-Cheney ticket – national security and business-oriented; Condoleezza Rice bluntly asserted that the treaty was not in the national interest of the United States.

The campaign established the direction on environmental policy, although with the assumption of office on January 20, 2001, the new government's positions had not yet been set in stone. Negotiations on the Kyoto Protocol were scheduled to resume in May at The Hague, but Washington seemed content to drift, did not attend the talks to shape a final agreement, and asked that the next round be pushed back to July. President Bush, seeking

---

[42] Lynch, "War Crimes Court."

[43] Bob Herbert, "Warm and Warmer," *New York Times*, October 30, 2000, p. A23.

to accommodate his new Director of the Environmental Protection Agency, former New Jersey Governor Christine Todd Whitman, and, at the time, a rising star in the GOP, seemed momentarily to address the emissions issue in March when he reiterated his campaign promise to regulate carbon dioxide emissions and endorsed legislation that would do that.[44] Some even thought this boded well for the future of the Kyoto Protocol. Within a week Bush reversed his pledge, and said the administration would not seek to regulate power plants' emissions of carbon dioxide.[45] This move amounted to an effective abandonment of the Kyoto Protocol and seriously compromised international efforts to complete it.

There were, of course, some potentially persuasive arguments against the treaty. Even committed advocates conceded that it contained some substantial shortcomings, for example, that its short-term goals were unrealistic for both the United States *and* the E.U. and that it should take into account carbon dioxide "sinks" such as forests. But the administration did not bother articulating these. Instead, as Josef Joffe put it, the message from Washington was simply "curt and dismissive."[46]

The nail was driven into the coffin later that month, when the administration confirmed, one day before the Meeting of Environmental Ministers of the Americas was to begin in Montreal, that it would not submit the Kyoto Protocol for Senate ratification.[47] Then White House Spokesman Ari Fleischer said Bush's opposition was "unequivocal." David Sandalow, a former Clinton official who helped to negotiate the 1997 accord, said the new administration's stance was a "textbook case of unilateral diplomacy, which rarely works and always brings resentment."[48] Of course, he was making a partisan point, but he was right about the outcome in terms of European resentment. The European Parliament issued severe condemnations of American unilateralism and stated in its resolution that it was "appalled that the long-term interests of most of the world's population were being sacrificed for short-term corporate greed in the U.S." German, French, British, and other European newspapers berated the White House's

---

44 Andrew Revkin, "Despite Opposition in Party, Bush Seeks Emissions Cuts," *New York Times*, March 10, 2001, p. A1.

45 Douglas Jehl, "Bush, in Reversal, Won't Seek Out Emissions of Carbon Dioxide," *New York Times*, March 14, 2001, p. A1.

46 Josef Joffe, "A Short History of American Indifference," *New York Times*, April 15, 2001, p. 4.

47 Douglas Jehl, "US Going Empty-Handed to Meeting on Global Warming," *New York Times*, March 28, 2001, p. A22.

48 Ibid.

course of treaty abrogation. In Washington, meanwhile, Congressmen held debates on the dangers of unilateralism, while op-ed articles questioned the merits of a foreign policy that was undermining relations across the Atlantic as the administration was handling diplomatic skirmishes with China.[49] Liberal Democratic Representative Barney Frank entered into the congressional Registar on May 16 an article by the managing editor of *The Hill*, David Silverberg, which was titled "America's Course toward Splendid Isolation." The piece argued that "a form of isolation appears to be taking shape on a day-to-day basis" and that "the world is not accepting American unilateralism passively."[50] Once again, the optics were poor, the State Department Office of Public Diplomacy was absent from the fray when most needed, and the Kyoto Accord joined the ICC, taking on a life of its own as an icon of U.S. intransigence and seeming disdain for global sensitivities.

Dismissing the bitterness building in world councils and the likely costs going forward, U.S. policy makers proceeded, as if "diplomatically challenged," to reject bluntly a third international agreement, the 1972 Anti-Ballistic Missile Treaty with Russia. Though Vladimir Putin's government saw the agreement as the linchpin of arms control, the United States saw it as an obstacle to the development of an effective missile defense, a top priority for both Bush and Rumsfeld. The administration's announcement of U.S. withdrawal on December 13, 2001, marked the first time in the nuclear era that the United States had unilaterally abandoned a major arms-control pact. "I have concluded that the ABM Treaty hinders our government's ability to develop ways to protect our people from future terrorist or rogue-state missile attacks," Bush said.[51]

Although his language suggests that this decision was a response to September 11, there was little doubt that the die had been cast in the months before the attacks and that the administration had previously decided to withdraw from the treaty. Both parties, in fact, had a legal right to withdraw from the agreement after giving six months' notice. The question was whether the United States would do it with the cooperation of Russia and the European allies or without.

On assuming office, U.S. officials had hoped to convince Russia to replace what they believed was an obsolete agreement with a new strategic

[49] "Climate Change Causes Atlantic Rift," BBC News, April 6, 2001.
[50] David Silverberg, "America's Course toward Splendid Isolation," *The Hill*, May 9, 2001; "The Dangers of Unilateralism," Congressional Record, May 16, 2001; United States Congress, pp. E813–E814.
[51] "America Withdraws from ABM Treaty," BBC News.co.uk, December 13, 2001.

arrangement.⁵² When, by summer's end, this approach failed, the administration made it clear that it would not delay developing or testing new antimissile missile systems. In a late-August interview on Russian radio, John Bolton, who was settling somewhat uneasily into the State Department, announced that the United States had given Russia an unofficial deadline of November to agree to changes in the Antiballistic Missile Treaty or face a unilateral American withdrawal from the accord.⁵³ Bolton then, reflecting an apparent glitch in White House-State Department communications, denied that he had delivered an ultimatum, saying that "a vast open space" still exists for an agreement with Russia on joint development of a limited defense against ballistic missiles.⁵⁴

It turned out, however, his denial was unnecessary. Before a Crawford, Texas, classroom the next day, Bush made U.S. intentions clear: "We will withdraw from the ABM Treaty on our timetable at a time convenient to America."⁵⁵ The schoolchildren may have been a bit perplexed by what Bush had just said, but the message was clear. The announcement should not have surprised the careful political observer; as a candidate, Bush had adhered to the long-standing Republican preference for an ambitious missile defense system and for opposition to treaty-imposed constraints. The treaty's fate was further sealed by the composition of the administration's arms-control team: It named Bolton, who had written and spoken extensively of the Treaty's deficiencies to lead the delegation and made Feith, another critic, in effect number two.⁵⁶

At a heated meeting in Moscow on November 3, Rumsfeld (with Bolton by his side) and Russian President Vladimir Putin failed to agree on U.S. missile defense testing within the terms of the treaty. When Putin said that the U.S. interpretation was not acceptable to Moscow, Rumsfeld told him, "Well, then we will be giving you notification of unilateral withdrawal from the treaty."⁵⁷ Any remaining hopes for reaching an accord after Bush's August

---

⁵² Manuel Perez-Rivas, "US Quits ABM Treaty," CNN.com, December 14, 2001.
⁵³ Patrick Tyler, "US Sets Deadline for an Agreement on ABM Proposal," *New York Times*, August 22, 2001, p. A1.
⁵⁴ Michael Wines, "Still Time to Negotiate Missile Defenses, US Envoy Says," *New York Times*, August 23, 2001, p. A8.
⁵⁵ "Bush Says He'll Leave ABM Treaty," NewsMax.com Wires, August 24, 2001, http://www.newsmax.com, and David Sanger, "Bush Flatly States U.S. Will Pull Out of Missile Treaty," *New York Times*, August 24, 2001, p. A6.
⁵⁶ Caroline Daniel, "Hard Man Who Sits at the Heart of US Foreign Policy," *Financial Times*, December 19, 2002, p. 20.
⁵⁷ David Sanger and Patrick Tyler, "Officials Recount Road to Deadlock over Missile Talks," *New York Times*, August 13, 2001, p. A1.

announcement were dashed in the opening hours of Putin's visit to the White House on November 13. Neither leader came to the meeting with any new ideas, and the fate of the ABM Treaty was all but sealed.[58]

Responses to the unilateral U.S. withdrawal were somewhat muted, perhaps because terrorism was the defining feature of the international agenda and many allies had just pledged to join a U.S.-led coalition to fight it. Moreover, the world watched Moscow, the other party to the treaty, react rather calmly. Speaking in Russia, Bush's tentative new friend, Putin, avoided any hint of being slighted and made clear that he did not feel that the move threatened Russia. He called the U.S. decision simply "an erroneous one" and stated that Russia's commitment to the treaty was the principled course.[59] The world community, however, noted the unilateral character of Washington's move. China was particularly distressed because it believed the U.S. missile defense shield would be used to protect Taiwan.[60] The French, Italians, and Germans saw the U.S. move as worrisome not so much for its arms control implications but rather because it confirmed for them an unprecedented willingness on the administration's part to dismiss, in cavalier fashion, inconvenient international obligations.[61] A number of European leaders thought the administration's disposal of the treaty "a prime example of a worrisome move toward unilateralism" symbolizing a willingness to move away from half a century of painstakingly constructed international agreements.[62]

According to one senior foreign policy adviser, while Bush was mindful of former Secretary of State George Shultz's advice to cultivate and maintain alliances as you would tend the flowers in your garden, six months into his presidency his garden was looking more than just neglected.[63] The rough edges of the administration's foreign relations had become a staple in news headlines across the nation rather than the underlying reasons for difference

[58] Ibid.

[59] Michael Wines, "Facing Pact's End, Putin Decides to Grimace and Bear It," *New York Times*, December 14, 2001, p. A14.

[60] Elisabeth Rosenthal, "China Voices Muted Distress at US Blow to ABM Pact," *New York Times*, December 13, 2001, p. A13.

[61] Steven Erlanger, "Bush's Move on ABM Pact Gives Pause to Europeans," *New York Times*, December 13, 2001, p. A19.

[62] David Sanger and Elisabeth Bumiller, "US to Pull Out of ABM Treaty, Clearing Path for Antimissile Tests," *New York Times*, December 12, 2001, p. A1. For more on the foreign perception of the new Bush administration, see Judy Dempsey and Richard Wolffe, "Differences of Style: Bush's Decision to Opt Out of Treaties Projects a Unilateralist Image That Belies His Desire to Work More Closely with His European Allies," *Financial Times*, July 27, 2001, p. 16.

[63] Dempsey and Wolffe, "Differences of Style," p. 16.

on the treaties that were often argued with greater subtlety. In any case, Washington's cognoscenti took the opportunity to sprout bumper stickers distilling the administration's foreign policy: "My Way or the Highway."[64]

Taken together, these early, unilateral rejections of international agreements reflected the deeply held neo-conservative belief that many international agreements, and institutions as well, limited rather than secured American power and therefore should be approached with caution. Moreover, neo-conservatives, including John Bolton, Doug Feith, Richard Perle, and Paul Wolfowitz, all senior administration officials in the State and Defense Departments, played important roles in defeating these agreements. Bolton had also encouraged U.S. opposition to the now largely dysfunctional "sunshine policy" favored by the then South Korean president Kim Daejung. Thus, the neo-conservatives had significant influence in establishing the direction and priorities of U.S. foreign relations from the early months of the new administration.

It would be a mistake, however, to conclude that the neo-conservatives were *the* decisive force behind the administration's decisions on these matters. President Bush, Vice President Dick Cheney, Secretary of Defense Donald Rumsfeld, Republican senators, and a variety of interest groups all had important, often dispositive, roles in shaping the administration's opposition to these agreements. So, while the early renunciations of these international agreements can rightly be placed in the "win" column by neo-conservatives, they were certainly not victories achieved solely by neo-conservative efforts.

Indeed, just as they had done under Reagan, neo-conservatives soon started to complain. Immediately after Bush's inaugural address, the *Weekly Standard* criticized his "unfortunate and garbled account of missile defense."[65] Throughout the period leading up to September 11, writers in the magazine chastised the president's commitment to rebuilding and reforming the military as "less than anticipated or advertised" and argued that it had "turned its back on increases for defense," which had been "subordinated to tax cuts." In June 2001, Kagan and Kristol further emphasized their disappointment with the administration's failure to increase the defense budget by suggesting that Bush "may go down in history as the man who let American military power atrophy and America's post–Cold War preeminence slip away."[66] Meanwhile, as co-signatory of the PNAC, former CIA

---

[64] Anthony Lewis, "The Feeling of a Coup," *New York Times*, March 31, 2001, p. A15. For a related brief discussion of new presidents enraging foreign leaders in their first hundred days, see Joffe, "A Short History of American Indifference."

[65] William Kristol, "Enter Bush," *Weekly Standard*, January 29, 2001, p. 9.

[66] Robert Kagan and William Kristol, "No Defense," *Weekly Standard*, July 23, 2001, p. 13.

analyst, and Middle East scholar at AEI, Marc Gerecht wrote the following July, "The Bush administration has continued and actually surpassed its predecessor's display of timidity in the Middle East." Under the title "A Cowering Superpower," Gerecht cited examples of how the Pentagon had withdrawn U.S. Marines from military exercises in Jordan and moved anchored ships in Bahrain because of the possibility of terrorist attacks.[67] That same summer, Gerecht also published his article "Liberate Iraq: Is the Bush Administration Serious about Toppling Saddam Hussein?" In it he contended that Powell's early trip to the Middle East to make appeals for renewed U.N. weapons inspections "sent a signal that the Bush administration was retreating" and "dissipated the tougher-than-Clinton aura of George Bush II."[68]

In general terms, neo-conservatives writing for magazines like the *Weekly Standard* were complementary on certain issues such as treaty abrogation, but they were critical of the gap between campaign promises and the programs that resulted when the administration assumed office. The moderation of Powell and his State Department was negatively affecting the course of U.S. foreign policy while the Pentagon was failing to step up to the plate in terms of redefining and rebuilding the military. In this sense, it is possible to see how neo-conservatives again saw themselves as potentially disappointed by another presidency – a fear that has continued to be expressed by Richard Perle in 2004.

The most acute expression of neo-conservative displeasure with the Bush administration in this period came over U.S. relations with China. On April 1, a Chinese F-8 fighter jet intercepted a U.S. EP-3 reconnaissance plane over the South China Sea, forcing it to land on China's Hainan Island with its twenty-four-man crew taken prisoner by the Chinese government. After initial harsh demands for the immediate return of the crew and the sophisticated $80 million aircraft, including all of its intelligence equipment, the administration soon adopted a quieter tone. After intense negotiations between U.S. and Chinese diplomats, which included a letter from U.S. Ambassador to China Joseph Prueher, the crew was released on April 12.[69]

For Kagan and Kristol, this episode was nothing short of what they titled "a national humiliation." They berated the administration's use of the word

---

[67] Reuel Marc Gerecht, "A Cowering Superpower: It's Time to Fight Back Terrorism," *Weekly Standard*, July 30, 2001, p. 26.

[68] Reuel Marc Gerecht, "Liberate Iraq: Is the Bush Administration Serious about Toppling Saddam Hussein?" *Weekly Standard*, May 14, 2001, p. 23.

[69] "Damaged US Spy Plane Arrives in Georgia," CNN.com, July 5, 2001, and "China: Talks on Plane Costs Under Way," *Washington Post*, July 20, 2001, p. A32.

"regret" in the course of its diplomacy and asserted that Powell's statements "represented a partial capitulation, with real-world consequences." As the two intellectuals argued, "in the face of continued Chinese pressure, President Bush showed signs of cracking." This incident was apparently representative of how "the United States is on the path to humiliation."[70] This piece became part of an emerging and disapproving neo-conservative critique of Bush's approach to China during this period. An article in the *Weekly Standard* published weeks later on the subject argued, "It is difficult to escape the conclusion that something crucial has all along been missing in America's response: appropriate and palpable persistence, intensity, and determination at the highest levels of our government."[71] In late June, William Kristol wrote an article entitled "Democracy in China: How about Promoting Democracy Instead of Engaging with Dictators?" In it he argued, "Certain forms of American engagement with Beijing may well be justified. But surely the goal of American foreign policy should be to help bring about the peaceful transformation of Beijing's dictatorship into a democracy like Taipei's."[72]

THE WHITE HOUSE AND FOREIGN AFFAIRS

One of the aspects that allowed the neo-conservatives to step forward in the immediate aftermath of 9/11 was that, unlike previous Republican presidents such as Nixon or Reagan, Bush did not enter the White House with a fully scripted playbook. As noted earlier, when campaigning, Bush did not articulate a foreign policy that reflected the neo-conservatives' view of America's role in the world. It was no secret that his international experience was limited. Aside from a number of short foreign trips and a somewhat more substantial immersion in relations with Mexico, he had shown little interest in international issues. His difficulties in the November 1999 infamous pop quiz on world leaders allowed a moment of media triumphalism.[73] To address this, he was immersed in rigorous, daily briefing sessions each morning led by a select cadre of foreign policy and national security advisers. They provided a structured world-view and a clear concept of American

---

[70] Robert Kagan and William Kristol, "A National Humiliation," *Weekly Standard*, April 16, 2001, pp. 12–14.

[71] David Till, "Dear Mr. President," *Weekly Standard*, June 18, 2001, p. 12.

[72] William Kristol, "Democracy in China: How about Promoting Democracy Instead of Engaging with Dictators?" *Weekly Standard*, June 25, 2001, p. 11.

[73] "Bush Fails Reporter's Pop Quiz on International Leaders," CNN.com, November 5, 1999.

"responsibilities and capabilities." Even so, political opponents accused him of having "almost a principled provincialism."[74]

During the campaign, Bush and his advisers asserted that his experience was adequate.[75] "Each of us had different experiences," he said. "There's a foreign policy component to being governor of Texas and that's dealing with Mexico and Central America and South America."[76] Bush recognized, of course, that he had little experience in foreign policy – and that he was perceived as such – so he made attempts to redress this deficiency immediately after taking office. An "eager student with much to learn" about the world outside America's borders, Bush called nineteen world leaders on the phone in his first two weeks in office.[77] Making contact with the leaders of Mexico, Argentina, Chile, South Africa, Japan, Britain, Russia, South Korea, Egypt, Germany, Israel, Saudi Arabia, and others, Bush made a substantial effort to familiarize himself with important international issues. Unlike Clinton, who often canceled daily CIA briefings, Bush valued his briefings. This effort paid dividends. British Prime Minister Tony Blair emerged from their first meeting at Camp David impressed with Bush's emerging grasp of international affairs and sent personal messages to his European colleagues in which he highlighted his favorable impressions. As then British Ambassador to the United States Christopher Meyer remarked, the relationship between Blair and Bush "got off to a very good start, almost from the very first syllable uttered."[78] The two leaders discussed a number of issues from Western policy on Iraq to the planned U.S. missile defense system and a prospective European rapid reaction force. Blair returned from his trip with positive impressions: "I found him really impressive, really on the ball with a very clear vision of what he wants to achieve, and also very direct." As Blair remarked, "He just tells you what he thinks."[79]

Bush was not the first U.S. president to enter office with relatively little foreign policy experience. When President Harry Truman entered office in April 1945 after serving as a senator from Missouri, and later vice president, he was profoundly inexperienced in foreign affairs. Truman, for

---

[74] James Traub, "The Bush Years: W's World," *New York Times Magazine*, January 14, 2001, p. 28.

[75] Richard Brookhiser, "The Mind of George W. Bush," *Atlantic Monthly*, April 2003, p. 63.

[76] Kevin Lanrdigan, "Bush Refrains from Attacking 'Good Guy' McCain," *Nashua* (N.H.) *Telegraph*, November 11, 1999.

[77] Mike Allen and Vernon Loeb, "On Foreign Policy, Bush Makes the Call," *Washington Post*, February 4, 2001, p. A5.

[78] Interview with Christopher Meyer, "Blair's War," *Frontline*, PBS, March 18, 2003.

[79] Quoted in "Britain Is 'Bridge' across the Atlantic," BBC News, February 25, 2001.

example, was unfamiliar with the Manhattan Project designed to produce the atomic bomb and was broadly unprepared for the job having, in the course of his vice presidency, spent only half an hour alone with President Franklin Roosevelt before the latter's death. Called "the little haberdasher," Truman was thought incorrigibly provincial and was largely excluded from the conduct of the war. Leaders of both parties, perhaps too often, expressed fears for the nation's ability to navigate the treacherous waters following Japan's surrender in 1945. Truman's instincts proved remarkable, however, especially in his assessment of Josef Stalin and the nature of Soviet rule, and Europe's capacity to resist communist advances in France, Greece, and Italy. He surrounded himself with advisers, eventually including George F. Kennan and Paul Nitze, who advanced a coldly realistic policy that came to be known as "containment."[80]

During the campaign, Bush emphasized the need for America to conduct a humble foreign policy. Rejecting President Clinton's seemingly endless humanitarian interventions.[81] Bush embraced an interest-driven foreign policy, repeatedly emphasizing that he would be more hesitant than Clinton (and Gore) to commit troops abroad. At the Ronald Reagan Presidential Library in Simi, California, Bush delivered a much-anticipated first speech setting out foreign policy views on November 19, 1999. Having established that he did not see military intervention as the answer to every problem America faced beyond its borders, Bush closed with, "Let us reject the blinders of isolationism, just as we refuse the crown of empire. Let us not dominate others with our power.... And let us have an American foreign policy that reflects American character. The modesty of true strength. The *humility* of real greatness" (emphasis added).[82] According to his closest adviser on international affairs, Condoleezza Rice, the original draft of this speech had "quite a long section on the need to be humble with power."[83]

Although Bush took many of his cues on international affairs from the cadre of senior foreign policy experts surrounding him, this point, according to Condoleezza Rice, was his own and one that he believed in strongly. Rice

[80] This point is addressed by Arnold Offner, *Another Such Victory: President Truman and the Cold War, 1945–1953* (Stanford, Calif.: Stanford University Press, 2002); see also John Lewis Gaddis, *Strategies of Containment* (New York: Oxford University Press, 1982), pp. 125–26.

[81] Notably, Michael Mandelbaum, "Foreign Policy as Social Work," *Foreign Affairs*, January–February 1996, pp. 16–32.

[82] George W. Bush, "A Distinctly American Internationalism," November 19, 1999, Ronald Reagan Presidential Library, Simi Valley, Calif.

[83] Transcript of *Charlie Rose Show*, "Condoleezza Rice on Governor George W. Bush's Foreign Policy, with Condoleezza Rice," October 12, 2000.

makes the point that this was evident in their earliest discussions and that he felt "very strongly that a country that wields as much power and influence as the United States could easily be perceived as arrogant in the world."[84] Bush expanded on this in his October 11, 2000, debate against Gore at Wake Forest University. When moderator Jim Lehrer brought the debate around to international issues and asked, "How would you project us around the world, as president?" Bush said, "It really depends upon how our nation conducts itself in foreign policy. If we're an arrogant nation, they'll resent us. If we're a humble nation but strong, they'll welcome us. And our nation stands alone right now in the world in terms of power, and that's why we've got to be humble and yet project strength."[85]

Bush was speaking both to a public suffering from intervention fatigue where the cost had been considerable and the results modest and to the foreign policy community where a debate had been raging about the appropriate use of American resources and the best ways in which the nation's interests could be secured. The Republican candidate was rejecting grand notions of remaking whole societies – as mentioned above, we did not then or now understand the intricacies of nation building – and many were hesitant to support military operations in areas not of vital strategic concern to the United States. Early in the election year, Rice had foreshadowed this general policy in her January/February *Foreign Affairs* article entitled "Campaign 2000: Promoting the National Interest."[86] And so it was no surprise that throughout the campaign Bush repeatedly came out against nation building. At the October 3, 2000, debate against Gore in Boston, Bush responded to the question, "How would you go about, as president, deciding when it was in the national interest to use U.S. force, generally?" by saying "Well, if it's in our vital national interests, and that means whether or not our territory – our territory is threatened, our people could be harmed, whether or not our alliances are – defense alliances are threatened. Whether or not our friends in the Middle East are threatened. That would be a time to seriously consider the use of force.... I would take the use of force very seriously. I would be guarded in my approach." This statement, which emphasized American "interests," was meant to distinguish a prospective Bush administration from an "idea-driven" Clinton/Gore foreign policy. "He believes in nation-building,"

[84] Ibid.
[85] "Election 2000 Presidential Debate II with George W. Bush and Al Gore," moderated by Jim Lehrer, October 11, 2000, transcript reproduced on http://www.c-span.org/campaign 2000/transcript/ debate_101100.asp.
[86] Condoleezza Rice, "Campaign 2000: Promoting the National Interest," *Foreign Affairs*, January/February 2000, p. 53.

Bush said of Gore. "I would be very careful about using our troops as nation-builders."[87]

In the following week's debate, Bush went even further on this issue. Bush started by commenting that the U.S. humanitarian mission in Somalia "went wrong" after it "changed into a nation-building mission." Referring to the deaths of eighteen U.S. Army Rangers killed in a Mogadishu gun battle on October 3–4, 1993, Bush said that "our nation paid a price" for trying to fulfill this latter mission. Based on the previous administration's failed attempt at nation building in this case and its inconclusive efforts in Haiti, Bush said, "I don't think our troops ought to be used for what's called nation-building. I think our troops ought to be used to fight and win war." Bristling at the thought of converting the U.S. military into a "nation-building corps," Bush said his administration would "absolutely not" let this happen.[88]

On the campaign trail, Bush continued to hammer home this point. Just one day before the November 7 election, Bush told an enthusiastic crowd in Chattanooga, Tennessee: "Let me tell you what else I'm worried about: *I'm worried about an opponent who uses nation-building and the military in the same sentence* [emphasis added]. See, our view of the military is for our military to be properly prepared to fight and win war and, therefore, prevent war from happening in the first place."[89] While this language served multiple political objectives during the campaign, when viewed retrospectively through the lens of Bush's first two years in office, it indisputably reveals that, when Bush turned to the neo-conservatives after 9/11, he came as a convert, based on intuition and personality rather than deep conviction.

THE DEPARTMENT OF DEFENSE

Reports emanating from the Pentagon in the first months of the administration offer a mirror image of this sense of ad hoc policy making. Rumsfeld had entered office seemingly unprepared for the changes that had taken place since his experience there twenty-five years earlier. He was heard complaining about the confirmation process, the difficulty in filling policy slots, the time-consuming and personnel-intense nature of filing 902 annual reports to Congress and responding to 2,000 congressional requests per week, a defense authorization bill that had grown from fifty pages (during his earlier

[87] "Election 2000 Presidential Debate with George W. Bush and Al Gore," moderated by Jim Lehrer, October 3, 2000, transcript reproduced on http://www.c-span.org/campaign2000/transcript/ debate_100300.asp.
[88] "Election 2000 Presidential Debate II."
[89] Terry M. Neal, "Bush Backs into Nation Building," *Washington Post*, February 26, 2003.

incumbency) to 900 pages, and his general lack of control over many parts of the Pentagon's activities. Those who attended meetings with the secretary were bombarded with words such as "paralyzed," "amazing," "unbelievable," "tangled in our underwear," "hair knot," "cooked like a frog," "wrapped around our anchor chain," with which he described the problems of his department.

A more serious problem, however, was that it appeared that he was operating without any clear understanding of the White House's strategic assumptions or about the preferred level of the defense budget. Rumsfeld was heard to complain that disarray at the Pentagon was putting him in a poor light as compared with the State Department, NSC, and the U.S. Trade Representative.

In the light of this, there is little surprise that Washington was alive with rumors that Rumsfeld would conclude that the damage to his reputation as a successful businessman and public servant was unacceptable and that he would engineer his departure before summer's end. Was it Washington silly season gossip or a straw in the wind? Maybe a bit of both.

SUMMER 2001: QUIET BEFORE THE STORM

As August wore on, the front pages drifted away from the administration's settling-in process. Senior positions across the administration were slowly filled and the confirmation process inched forward. Deepening concern about the economy, job losses, and falling stock market indices emerged, however, to cast a mildly unsettling pallor over the country. Internationally, American allies in Europe and Asia (already alienated by the unilateralism described above) were beginning to grumble that the "grown up" professionalism they had been promised was lacking. Confusion over Korean policy and short tempers about the Balkans together with growing trade tensions were symptomatic of unexpectedly rising concerns about the administration's basic competence.

A summer heat wave settled in, blanketing vacationers from Boston to the Deep South. Glancing at the newspapers in the days just preceding 9/11 – which today seems a world away – one might well read about one of some eight shark attacks that month along the Eastern Seaboard. Though neither the sharks in the ocean nor those in Wall Street were unimportant, their front page coverage suggests the public was paying scant attention to national security issues in the summer of Bush's first year.

Any foreign policy expert keeping the score would have noted determined reversals in Clinton's commitments to Kyoto, the ABM treaty, and the ICC.

But this owed at least as much to the anything-but-Clinton syndrome as to any doctrinal revolution.[90] Unilateralism was certainly on the rise, but this led as much in the direction of withdrawal – for example, from the Balkans, as suggested by Rumsfeld – as of assertion. There were few hints that anyone other than the neo-conservatives had in mind the PNAC template for activist and unashamed American interventionism. This template was, however, ready for operational deployment.

SEPTEMBER 11, 2001

The photos of Bush's face on first hearing of the terrorist attacks in New York and Washington – interrupted by Chief of Staff Andrew Card while reading to a second-grade classroom in Sarasota, Florida – are not easily forgotten. His immediate reactions are now well known: On the Air Force One phone with Vice President Cheney, who had been hurriedly moved to the emergency bunker beneath the White House, Bush said, "We're at war." Hanging up the phone, he turned to his staff who had heard the call and told them, "That's what we're paid for boys. We're going to take care of this. And when we find out who did this, they're not going to like me as president. Somebody is going to pay."[91]

The public gained another enduring image of the president on September 13 when he visited "ground zero," the site of the destroyed Twin Towers. Standing atop a wrecked fire truck with his arm around retired firefighter Bill Beckwith, Bush used a bullhorn to talk briefly to the rescue workers there. He said that "the whole nation is praying for you" and said to a worker who said he could not hear the president: "I can hear you. The rest of the world hears you. And the people who knocked down these buildings will hear all of us soon."[92] Reporters, columnists, and people in the street, themselves grappling with the event, sensed Bush had been transformed, as a person and as a leader.[93] The most significant transformation, however, had only just begun.

The months after the terrorist attacks revealed a profoundly changed George Bush. The duty-bound, born-again, can-do Texan morphed into a man who drew on those qualities and the intensity of those early days to

[90] Charles Krauthammer, "The Bush Doctrine: ABM, Kyoto, and the New American Unilateralism," *Weekly Standard*, June 4, 2001, pp. 21–25.

[91] Bob Woodward, *Bush at War* (London: Simon and Schuster, 2002), p. 17.

[92] David Frum, *The Right Man* (New York: Random House, 2003), p. 140.

[93] For one good account of how Bush responded, see Brookhiser, "The Mind of George W. Bush," pp. 68–69.

focus a searing rage. He was determined to rally the nation and the civilized world to crush al-Qaeda and the diabolical future it represented. The dynamic forged by the moment distilled the many shades of gray reflecting relations among nations into a black and white Manichean "either you are with us or against us" position. To say that American national security priorities were transformed is an understatement. His declaration of the "war on terror" redefined the strategic landscape. Most significant in terms of the shift was the transition from a "humble" candidate Bush to a president whose administration policy was based on unilateral preemption and millenarian nation building.

ENTER THE NEO-CONSERVATIVES

If the events of 9/11 represented a personal inflection point for Bush, they were also immensely empowering for the neo-conservatives. In the tumultuous days following 9/11, the neo-conservatives were ready with a detailed, plausible blueprint for the nation's response. They were not troubled that their plan had been in preparation for over a decade for different reasons, in a different context, and in relation to different countries and, as such, did not in any way represent a direct response to the events themselves. They were motivated only to ensure its adoption. The key to their success was that, unlike other decision makers, they did not have to stop to debate and analyze the best course of action. As Perle notes, the neo-conservatives enjoyed an advantage over those who wished to reflect on the best course of action, specifically, "we have offered concrete recommendations."[94] This advanced state of preparation enabled them to short-circuit the discussion about the impending war on terrorism by inserting into the president's response a commitment to "bring to justice" not only the perpetrators of the events in New York and Washington but those who harbored them.

This may sound like a self-evident proposition, but the operational effect was to turn policy away from the political and intelligence-based mechanisms that have established themselves as relatively successful antiterrorism models in places such as Northern Ireland and the Basque country. Instead, the neo-conservatives propelled the nation toward the much riskier, much more expensive, and historically less promising model of state-on-state conflict, especially with Iraq, rather than analyzing and reviewing the causes of dysfunction that had produced the 9/11 attacks. In place of Northern

[94] Frum and Perle, *An End to Evil*, p. 9.

Ireland, the body count–based methods used in Colombia, Sri Lanka, and Kashmir were adopted together with an open-ended and hugely expensive commitment in the Middle East – precisely the "mission without end" Bush had so decried in his November 1999 speech.

Thus, unlike Pearl Harbor in 1941 or the 1948 collapse of British power in the eastern Mediterranean (still memorialized on the walls in the *Washington Post*'s entry lobby as the seminal post–World War II event), the nation was not provided a policy that responded directly to the crisis at hand. Instead, the neo-conservatives succeeded in having their preexisting agenda adopted – one that, as we show below in terms of its terrorism fighting qualities, leaves the nation more dangerously exposed to terrorism and brings numerous deleterious consequences in other fields. The neo-conservative agenda that was adopted so readily after 9/11 is a far cry from the balanced conservatism that formed the core of Bush's November 1999 speech where he spoke of "idealism, without illusions. Confidence, without conceit. Realism, in the service of American ideals." Hijack may be a harsh word, but there is no better description for what occurred. America and the world will have to live with the consequences long after the neo-conservatives themselves are but a distant memory.

What did the hijack consist of? In the neo-conservative case the vital components were early moves to capture the language of the debate to choke off options they did not like. We discuss this dimension in Chapter 7. This was followed by advancing the long-cherished objective of an almost exclusive focus on the Middle East and the use of military force not simply for defensive purposes but for preemptive reasons.

THE STATE OF THE UNION ADDRESS: ENTER PREEMPTION

The evolution toward a policy of preemption can be seen in a series of speeches Bush delivered in the year after the terrorist attacks. The clearest foreshadowing of future American policy was Bush's State of the Union address on January 29, 2002, terming Iran, Iraq, and North Korea the "axis of evil." This rhetorically self-indulgent phrase (claimed by or credited to speechwriter David Frum) has been the subject of much controversy. It suggests a classic case of unschooled speechwriters imposing policy conundrums that lock administrations into positions that impose severe constraints. The speech focused, as might be expected, primarily on 9/11 and the resulting war in Afghanistan. After acknowledging that some governments would be "timid in the face of terror," the president said, "And make no mistake about it: If they do not act, America will." The tone of Bush's rhetoric was forceful as he outlined a future of *active* U.S. pursuit of terrorists. After invoking the urgency of the situation and saying that America "will do what is necessary to ensure our nation's security," he offered the first glimpse of a preemptive policy. "I will not wait on events," he warned, "as dangers gather. I will not stand by as peril draws closer." With this statement he did not alter America's foreign policy, but he did hint that a more proactive policy was in the works.

Speaking to a special session of the German Parliament on May 23, 2002, Bush again gave an inkling of the policy to come. He first thanked the Germans for their support in the war on terror, emphasized the close relationship between America and Europe, and then outlined the next steps for together meeting "the challenges of the larger world" and "build[ing] the house of freedom." He alleged that "the authors of terror" were seeking nuclear, chemical, and biological weapons. "If these regimes and their terrorist allies were to perfect these capabilities," he warned, "no inner voice of reason, no hint of conscience would prevent their use." This suggested that the United States had to take action *before* the weapons were acquired. Without acknowledging that the United States would engage in preemptive attacks, Bush left no doubt that the United States would and should take action: "[W]e will and we must confront this conspiracy against our liberty and against our lives." In closing, he told the members of the Bundestag that the United States and Germany were joined in purpose to protect the safety of their people and the fate of their freedom. To accomplish this purpose, it was necessary to adopt a more proactive defense policy: "We build a world of justice," Bush said, "or we will live in a world of coercion."

The evolving U.S. strategy was further defined in Bush's remarks at the West Point graduation ceremonies on June 1, 2002, this time in a more direct way. With the war in Afghanistan winding down, Bush shifted the focus to a strategic framework for the post-9/11 world that went beyond the task of destroying al-Qaeda. Referencing a world newly characterized by global terror, he told the cadets that they faced global challenges where the "gravest danger to freedom lies at the perilous crossroads of radicalism and technology." In this world, Bush said, "even weak states and small groups could attain a catastrophic power to strike great nations." Although the Cold War strategies of deterrence and containment seemed to still apply in selected instances, the president emphasized that "new threats also require new thinking." Offering a circuitous reference to the American policy of preemption, he said that when faced with this strategic situation, "If we wait for threats to fully materialize, we will have waited too long." The crowd cheered. Bush then hammered home precisely the point to which he alluded in his State of the Union address, saying that the "war on terror will not be won on the defensive" and reiterating that "this nation will act."

Bush's only direct reference to preemptive action in that speech was couched in a list of what American security would require. After a brief mention of the requirements for the intelligence and military services, Bush said that U.S. security depended on all Americans "be[ing] ready for preemptive action when necessary to defend our liberty and to defend our lives." The crowd, sensing that they were witnessing the making of history, applauded again at what was clearly the unveiling of America's new foreign policy.

Three months later, Bush returned to his theme in an address to the U.N. General Assembly on September 12, 2002. He focused on the case against Iraq, briefly referencing the new American policy. This time, however, he cast it in negative terms, saying, "We cannot stand by and do nothing while dangers gather." While he had not yet issued a new doctrine for national strategy, the president's year-long series of speeches had rendered the "humility" professed at the Reagan Library in 1999 a distant memory.

THE 2002 NATIONAL SECURITY STRATEGY

The administration's emerging policy of preemption achieved formal status when it was included in the *National Security Strategy* published on September 17, 2002. Such a sweeping, proactive strategy statement has few parallels in modern American foreign policy and is certainly not in keeping with the public diplomacy employed by Bush's immediate predecessors. One neo-conservative has described the NSS as a "quintessentially neo-conservative document."[95] Some past presidents have, indeed, contemplated and taken preemptive actions. Secretary of State John Quincy Adams defended Andrew Jackson's punitive invasion of Spanish Florida in 1818 by informing the Spanish government that the laws of "neutrality and war," "prudence and humanity" warranted such anticipatory action.[96] President Lyndon Johnson considered a preemptive strike against China to prevent it from deploying nuclear weapons. President John F. Kennedy decided not to launch a direct preemptive attack on the Soviet missile sites in Cuba in 1962, but his quarantine during the missile crisis comes close to preemptive military action. More recently, American military actions in Panama, Grenada, and Haiti, depending on how one defines the term, contained many of the

---

[95] Max Boot, "Think Again: Neocons," *Foreign Policy*, January/February 2004, p. 18.
[96] Philip Zelikow, "The Transformation of National Security," *National Interest*, spring 2003, p. 26.

characteristics of military preemption.[97] Never before, though, had any president set out a formal national strategy *doctrine* that included preemption. Never had an administration sought to marry the assertion of American interests in a kind of global Monroe Doctrine to the Wilsonian promise to "bring the hope of democracy, development, free markets and free trade to every corner of the world."[98]

All of this begs the question of why, if the arrow was in the quiver, the administration chose to take this highly public and provocative step. Among the immediate results was alarm among allied governments who had to defend their common cause with America before skeptical parliaments and hostile publics. It became an issue, for example, in the 2002 German elections and roiled British politics. Moreover, it was a powerful talking point for opponents throughout Europe and Russia where massive public demonstrations protested U.S. policy on Iraq and the Middle East. And finally, beyond alarming American adversaries, the decision to formalize preemption made it very much more difficult to make progress in key international fora – the U.N. Security Council and NATO – where Washington sought support.

The *National Security Strategy* (NSS) was the first document of its kind released by the new administration and the first since the terrorist attacks. Times were, of course, different from when the Clinton administration published its last *NSS* in December 1999.[99] As such, the two consecutive *NSS* documents differ fundamentally. Whereas President Clinton's strategy statement assumed peace, Bush's did not. The September 17, 2002, document opens with a quotation from Bush's West Point speech about "defend[ing]," "preserv[ing]," and "extend[ing]" the peace. When these goals are compared with the three that Clinton laid out in his December 1999 document – to enhance America's security, bolster economic prosperity, and promote democracy and human rights abroad – it is possible to see how different the administrations' world-views are and how these differences are reflected in the two *NSS* documents.[100]

---

[97] For a review of the historical record regarding the uses of U.S. military force in a "preemptive" manner, see Richard F. Grimmett, "Congressional Research Service Report for Congress" (Washington, D.C.: Library of Congress, 2003), http://www.usembassy.it/policy/crs.htm.

[98] Jackson Diehl, "Bush's Foreign Policy First, but No One Seems to Notice – Even at the White House," *Washington Post*, September 30, 2002, p. A19.

[99] "A National Security Strategy for a New Century," White House, Washington, D.C., December 1999.

[100] This comparison of the Bush and Clinton *NSS* documents largely comes from John Lewis Gaddis, "A Grand Strategy of Transformation," *Foreign Policy*, November–December 2002.

Just what was the nature of this changed security environment, and what was the best response to it? Outlining the post-9/11 international situation, the 2002 *NSS* equated terrorists with tyrants as sources of danger. It argued that given these dangers, the Cold War strategies of containment and deterrence were obsolete, overtaken by events. The White House said, "Given the goals of rogue states and terrorists the United States can no longer solely rely on a reactive posture as we have in the past. The inability to deter a potential attacker, the immediacy of today's threats, and the magnitude of potential harm that could be caused by our adversaries' choice of weapons, do not permit that option. We cannot let our enemies strike first."[101]

To the strategies of containment and deterrence the administration added preemption. It announced:

Traditional concepts of deterrence will not work against a terrorist enemy whose avowed tactics are wanton destruction and the targeting of innocents; whose so-called soldiers seek martyrdom in death and whose most potent protection is statelessness.... The United States has long maintained the option of preemptive action to counter a sufficient threat to our national security. The greater the threat, the greater is the risk of inaction – and the more compelling the case for taking anticipatory action to defend ourselves, even if uncertainty remains as to the time and place of the enemy's attack. To forestall or prevent such hostile acts by our adversaries, the United States will, if necessary, act preemptively.[102]

Thus, while preferring to act multilaterally, the administration asserted its willingness to employ unilateral action.

The Implications of Preemption

Such a policy of (potentially unilateral) preemption required a greatly enabled and reconfigured U.S. military. The document outlined how America would retain its preeminent position: "[O]ur forces will be strong enough to dissuade potential adversaries from pursuing a military build-up in hopes of surpassing, or equaling, the power of the United States." In sum, the doctrine laid out by the *NSS* was exactly what Bush had warned against in his campaign speeches and debates – but it was entirely consistent with the approach advocated by the neo-conservatives for over a decade.

The formal adoption of a radical policy option is significant. Our criticism is that while it accepted the benefits of cooperation among the great powers, the *NSS* set aside the many tools of diplomacy. As the emerging option of choice, it advanced a concept – "the right of preemption" – designed to transform, and indeed deconstruct, those organizations, states, and

---

[101] *NSS*, 15.
[102] Ibid.

regions deemed a threat, in place of a policy that, while implicitly retaining the option of preemption, avoided the burden of international opprobrium. It neglected the full range of possibilities – containment, economic sanctions, denial of military and developmental assistance, and legal action. More to the point, the international "cooperation" envisioned would proceed, if at all, on a basis unprecedented in recent international practice. Important allies, including Britain, objected, maintaining that it violated international convention and invited a world where military strength trumped law as the determining factor in resolving disputes.

Underlying the Bush foreign policy is the assumption that the use of military force to overthrow noncooperative governments in troubled areas, if that can be accomplished, is the remedy for terrorism and tyranny. This is classic neo-conservative philosophy, set out at full length in Perle's book *An End to Evil*.

Terror Transforms Policy

While the terror delivered on 9/11 was a defining moment that would determine the course of George Bush's presidency and the nature of U.S. foreign policy going forward, for professionals in the counterterrorism field it was simply the next step in the evolution of terrorism as an extension of politics. Global terrorism, a new species of the familiar genus, had made a dramatic and horrible entrance. Despite the fact that this point was underscored by British intelligence in conversations with their American counterparts, the psychological dimensions of the event and its devastating impact on the American people – the inflexion point it imposed on the Bush presidency – suspended the flow of events. After emergency procedures to safeguard the country and protect its senior leaders were put in place, the response fell to the White House, where political and security considerations were combined. It was at this unique moment, as Bush sought to link the event with a strategic response, that the neo-conservatives through Vice President Cheney and Defense Secretary Rumsfeld moved to center court. As the days unfolded they built on both raw emotion and policy support, in some quarters, for military and national security initiatives consistent with their long-held objectives. As the work crews dug through the smoldering rubble exposing scores of dead, motorists emblazoned their cars with American flags and neighbors joined together to support one another. The whole country seemed to display bravery and, at the same time, to be bracing itself for whatever might come next. The unanimous fear of and disgust with the violent attacks created an American public that was ready to support a forceful response by its leaders.

When envelopes sprinkled with anthrax started arriving at media outlets and in government offices, the public fear reached a fever pitch. The U.S. public was frightened. And, as such, the administration had almost carte blanche to respond as it liked.

The Defense Planning Guidance

Long before the speech at West Point and the publication of the *NSS*, neo-conservatives had advocated a U.S. policy of preemption. In 1992, aides to Secretary of Defense Cheney, supervised by Paul Wolfowitz and I. Lewis "Scooter" Libby (now the vice president's chief of staff), prepared a document known as the *Defense Planning Guidance (DPG)*. This document was the military's blueprint for planning, building, and deploying forces in fiscal years 1994 through 1999. While never officially finalized, in fact, it was a completed document, and a working draft of the *DPG* was leaked to the *Washington Post* and the *New York Times*. The full text was not reproduced, but the content is well known and appears to line up closely with the principles put forth in the 2002 *NSS*.[103]

The first objective advanced by the DPG was to "prevent the reemergence of a new rival." This required the United States to prevent any hostile power from dominating a region whose resources would be sufficient to generate global power. The authors of the draft argued that "beyond deterring attack on the United States," the United States should be prepared to use force to "preclude threats" and to prevent the spread of nuclear weapons. In addition, the draft advised that the United States should be "postured to act independently when collective action cannot be orchestrated."[104] The language of the draft was significant. According to Barton Gellman, the *Washington Post* reporter who received the leak, the document contained the word "preempt."[105] The broad suggestion that the military should be reconfigured to support the United States as a benevolent global hegemon, however, was poorly received by many in Washington. West Virginia Senator Robert C. Byrd called the Pentagon strategy "myopic, shallow and disappointing."[106] In response to widespread criticism, the administration issued a revised, less provocative version. Regardless, the earlier draft, guided by Wolfowitz and

---

[103] "Pentagon's New World View," *Washington Post*, May 24, 1992.
[104] Steven Weisman, "Pre-emption: An Idea with a Lineage Whose Time Has Come," *New York Times*, March 23, 2003, and "Pentagon's New World View," *Washington Post*, May 24, 1992.
[105] "The War behind Closed Doors: Transcript," *Frontline*, PBS, February 20, 2003.
[106] Barton Gellman, "Keeping the US First, Pentagon Would Preclude a Rival Superpower," *Washington Post*, March 11, 1992, p. A1.

Libby, detailed the nature and scope of threats faced by the United States in 1992 in a manner consistent with the September 17, 2002, *NSS*.

It is debatable as to whether the *NSS* is an extension of the *DPG*. One of the drafters of the *NSS*, member of the Defense Policy Board and Executive Director of the 9/11 Commission Philip Zelikow, denies a connection, saying they were written by different people proceeding from different theories of the problems at hand.[107] Another person guiding the *DPG*, however, was Paul Wolfowitz, who had a hand in the *NSS*. Moreover, there is little question that the latter document reflects a strategic world-view that was first expressed in substantially similar terms in 1992.[108] The muscular idealism revealed in September 2002 was an unabashed manifestation of well-documented neo-conservative thought.

NEO-CONSERVATIVES: ECHOES OF THE 1990S

The foundation and evolution of these ideas has been extensively examined above but it is useful to remember that the mid-1990s were a particularly fertile time for the neo-conservatives. The media and an array of Washington think tanks were bubbling with critiques of the Clinton foreign policy. Publishing in the prestigious journal *Foreign Affairs* in 1996, Robert Kagan and William Kristol's "Toward a Neo-Reaganite Foreign Policy" refused to accept the common assumption that a decline in U.S. power was inevitable. It dismissed warnings of imperial overstretch as "misguided." The authors argued that other nations perceived the United States as a hegemonic presence and, making the now common neo-conservative claim to the Reagan legacy, that the United States should pursue a vision of benevolent hegemony as bold as Reagan's in the 1980s.

The authors advanced a strategy in which "preemptive" action was an enabling element servicing the mechanical requirements of hegemony. Asking, "where is the threat?" in the post–Cold War world, the authors argued, the "main threat the United States faces now and in the future is its own weakness. American hegemony is the only reliable defense against a breakdown of peace and international order."[109]

The concept of "preemption" was again advanced in a 1998 public letter to President Clinton by several well-known neo-conservative thinkers with

---

[107] "Interview with Barton Gellman," *Frontline*, PBS.org, http://www.pbs.org/wgbh/pages/frontline/shows/iraq/interviews/gellman.html.

[108] Ibid.

[109] Robert Kagan and William Kristol, "Toward a Neo-Reaganite Foreign Policy," *Foreign Affairs*, July–August 1996, pp. 22–23.

the Project for the New American Century. They urged President Clinton to use his upcoming State of the Union address to chart a more aggressive course toward Iraq – that is, removal of Saddam Hussein's regime from power. The policy of "containment" of Hussein, the authors wrote, "has been steadily eroding" and was therefore "dangerously inadequate." The letter urged military action against Iraq, stating specifically, "We urge you to articulate this aim and to turn your Administration's attention to implementing a strategy for removing Saddam's regime from power." The signatories included a number of people who found themselves in a position to make U.S. foreign policy a few short years later: Elliott Abrams, John Bolton, Paula Dobriansky, Richard Perle, Peter Rodman, Donald Rumsfeld, Paul Wolfowitz, and Robert Zoellick.[110]

If one enduring neo-conservative objective was to inject U.S. policy with a proactive element, to include preemption, the second was to use force against Hussein's Iraq. Wolfowitz's analysis was central to this notion of a more aggressive stance toward Hussein. As a young Pentagon analyst, he had focused on Iraq in the 1970s. Filling in a gap in the administration's knowledge about Iraq, he directed a secret 1979 assessment of Persian Gulf threats that identified Iraq as a menace to its neighbors and to American interests.[111] To be sure, he did not advocate attacking Iraq a dozen years before the Gulf War, but the assessment shows that he has long been inclined to view Iraq as a country against whom the United States must take an aggressive stance.

Richard Perle, also pinpointed Iraq "long before" the first Gulf War. Interviewed on the PBS program "Think Tank with Ben Wattenberg," Perle said he was "rather uncomfortable with the support that we gave Saddam during the war between Iraq and Iran." In his view, the right course immediately following that war would have been to say to Saddam, "Now we've had enough of you, too, and we're not going to tolerate it." When the United States didn't do that, Perle and many others, including Wolfowitz, urged the first Bush administration to remove him at the end of the 1991 war.[112]

---

[110] "Letter to the Hon. William J. Clinton on Iraq," January 26, 1998, Project for the New American Century. Other signatories were Armitage, Bennett, Bergner, Fukuyama, Robert Kagan, Khalilzad, Bill Kristol, Donald Rumsfeld, William Schneider, Jr., James Weber, and James Woolsey.

[111] Keller, "Sunshine Warrior," p. 48.

[112] These quotations from Perle are taken from PBS, "Think Tank with Ben Wattenberg: Interview with Richard Perle," PBS.org, http://www.pbs.org/thinktank/transcript1017.html. Ben Wattenberg is a scholar at the American Enterprise Institute.

The neo-conservative preoccupation with Iraq continued apace through-out the Clinton administration. In a 1998 article for the *New Republic*, Wolfowitz wrote, "Toppling Saddam is the only outcome that can satisfy the vital U.S. interest in a stable and secure Gulf region, because, to a de-gree unique among contemporary tyrannies, the Iraqi regime is Saddam Hussein.... The vast majority of Iraqis want him out, though only those with a death wish say so openly. We must help them." Wolfowitz again made clear his position on Iraq in 2000 when he was being considered for a post at the Pentagon. At his confirmation hearings, Wolfowitz underscored his Iraq views, saying that sanctions were only part of the solution and that should there be a "real option" to overthrow Hussein: "I would certainly think it was worthwhile."[113]

Why had the neo-conservatives insisted so long on this course of action? According to Perle's interview with Wattenberg, there were two sets of rea-sons. First, Perle was offended by the dimensions of the human rights catas-trophe that befell Iraq, the thousands of people, mostly Hussein's own citi-zens, who died at his hands. Second, Perle believed that Hussein was devel-oping weapons of mass destruction that could threaten American interests. Both sets of concerns were widely publicized in the lead-up to the 2003 invasion of Iraq.

Perle's argument importantly reflected a broad aspiration later apparent in the 2002 State of the Union address when President Bush said that U.S. policy would be steered by a clear set of values: "non-negotiable demands" of human dignity. Focusing on the Middle East, Perle said in this interview that Iraq represented perhaps the best hope for the democratic experiment in an Arab country. "I think there is a potential civic culture in Arab coun-tries that can lead to democratic institutions," he said, "and I think Iraq is probably the best place to put that proposition to the test because it's a sophisticated educated population that has suffered horribly under totalitar-ian rule, and there's a yearning for freedom that, you know, I think we find everywhere in the world but especially in subject populations." While this aspect of the neo-conservative argument was given less prominence in the de-bate preceding the March 2003 war, the intention to spread democracy, and specifically to remake the Arab "neighborhood" beginning with the easiest case, runs through Perle's comments and was clearly an important part of the neo-conservative rationale for the Iraq war.

[113] Jane Perlez, "Capitol Hawks Seek Tougher Line on Iraq," *New York Times*, March 7, 2001, p. A10.

It restates the obvious to say that this proactive agenda, embracing pre-emption and "regime change" in Iraq, became an integral part of the admin-istration's foreign policy in the wake of the terrorist attacks. To prove that the neo-conservatives dominated the creation of U.S. foreign policy post-9/11, however, it is not enough to say that certain long-held neo-conservative de-sires articulated before that date lined up with U.S. strategy after that date. This merely *suggests* that neo-cons played a key role in shaping U.S. foreign policy. To demonstrate conclusively that the neo-cons *drove* the U.S. shift in policy, there must be evidence that they acted on the opportunity presented by 9/11.

The precise sequence of events showing how the neo-conservatives secured the adoption of their agenda is set out below in our case study of Iraq. In summary, the crucial meeting took place on September 15 in the Laurel Lodge at Camp David, at which Wolfowitz made the case for action against Iraq.[114] Five days later, a large group of neo-conservatives outside the government sent an open letter to the White House outlining how the war on terror should be conducted. In fact, it was more an ultimatum than a suggestion. They told Bush that to retain the signers' support, the United States had to pressure Syria and Lebanon to sever ties with Hezbollah, an organization on the State Department's terrorist list. They demanded that Bush bring bin Laden to justice, but also they demanded that he attack Iraq and overthrow Hussein "even if evidence does not link Iraq directly to the [September 11] attack." Among the signers of this letter were Midge Decter, Charles Krauthammer, William Kristol, Norman Podhoretz, and Defense Policy Board members Eliot Cohen and Perle. As we show, this approach reflected a long-standing agenda deriving from the end of the first Gulf war and developed throughout the 1990s.

The neo-conservatives' – and the Pentagon's – immediate focus on Iraq after 9/11 catalyzed the growing rift between the State and Defense De-partments. The early battles for who would fill which positions in the new administration offered a glimpse of the differences between Powell, on the one hand, and Rumsfeld and Wolfowitz, on the other. Now these differ-ences were hardening. On September 12, when Rumsfeld mentioned the possibility of going to Iraq, Powell immediately countered. He said that the administration's actions needed to take into account what the American public would support, and the public was then focused on al-Qaeda. After

---

[114] Bob Woodward, *Bush at War* (London: Simon and Schuster, 2002), pp. 83–84; see also Keller, "Sunshine Warrior," for alternative descriptions of this meeting.

Wolfowitz mentioned in a September 13 Pentagon press briefing that the administration would make "ending states who sponsor terrorism" a priority, Powell publicly dissociated himself from this approach, saying, "Ending terrorism is where I would like to leave it...and let Mr. Wolfowitz speak for himself."[115] In private, Powell is said not to have been so even-keeled about the Pentagon's obsession with Iraq. Talking with Joint Chiefs of Staff General Shelton, Powell asked, "What the hell, what are these guys thinking about? Can't you get these guys back in the box?"[116] That weekend, right after Wolfowitz intervened in the Laurel Lodge meeting, Powell objected. He said that going straight after Iraq would irreparably damage the tremendous coalition the United States enjoyed in the aftermath of 9/11.[117] Thus, the chasm between State and Defense was widening.

This rift was nothing new. The conflict between the two central figures in each department stretches back to the first Gulf war. At the close of that war in 1992, Wolfowitz, then a senior Pentagon official, supposedly clashed with Powell, then chairman of the Joint Chiefs of Staff, over the failure of President G. H. W. Bush to go after Saddam. Powell, who had been reluctant to commit American troops to the Gulf in the first place, was instrumental in stopping the war. According to a 1995 interview with Powell, he went to the White House on February 27, 1992, to brief the president on the situation on the ground and told the president that within the next twenty-four hours he would be bringing a recommendation on the cessation of hostilities. President Bush then asked, "Why not end it now?"[118] The question was rhetorical, but the neo-conservatives had what they thought was a good answer: The administration underestimated Saddam's ability and determination to retain power. Thus, they were less than enthusiastic about Powell's counsel and Bush's decision to end the war at that juncture.

Eight years later, we saw the State Department split with the Pentagon over high-level foreign policy appointments, especially those of Wolfowitz, Armitage, and John Klink, head of the State Department's refugee bureau,[119] during the transition period. Moreover, a number of foreign policy issues arising early in the administration served to heighten suspicions that Powell and Rumsfeld did not often see eye to eye. On an eight-day trip to Africa and Europe in early summer, Rumsfeld frequently spoke about ending military

---

[115] Woodward, *Bush at War*, pp. 60–61.
[116] Ibid., p. 61.
[117] Ibid., p. 84.
[118] "The War behind Closed Doors: Transcript."
[119] Jane Perlez, "White House Rejects Powell's Choice to Run Refugee Bureau," *New York Times*, May 24, 2001, p. A6.

training programs for African peacekeeping forces. This view did not align with Powell's championing of such programs. During the debates over the ABM Treaty, Powell often took pains to emphasize the U.S. desire for consultations with other countries as it proceeded with development of the defense system. Rumsfeld took a more direct, unilateral approach. They did not directly confront each other on the ABM Treaty, as Powell let Rumsfeld take control of the issue, but their difference in approach was noticeable. Again, the two did not clash directly, but neither did they agree on policy toward China. During a late July trip to Beijing, Powell repeatedly called China a "friend." Rumsfeld did not rebuke this characterization, but refused to repeat it, instead referring to China as an authoritarian system and a communist dictatorship.[120] The two men tried to play down the rift between them. Appearing together at a news conference in Australia after talks with their counterparts in late July, the two faced questions about their differences. At one point a reporter asked, "Do you agree on everything?" Rumsfeld paused, then said, "Everything except those few cases where Colin is still learning."[121] Soon before 9/11 Powell admitted that he and Rumsfeld had some arguments but insisted that is how bureaucracies work and maintained that theirs was a good relationship.[122]

As the immediate aftermath of 9/11 showed, such jocular denials did not tell the whole story. In the wake of Bush's September 20 assertion that the United States would pursue global terrorist groups and any nation that harbors or supports terrorism, the two departments engaged in an internal tug-of-war over the scope and breadth of the antiterrorism campaign. On the morning of September 11, Wolfowitz thought to himself that "the old approach to terrorism is not acceptable any longer."[123] He, along with many others from Defense, pushed hard for a broad range of military targets. The extreme violence of the attacks, key Pentagon officials said, could make a previously inconceivable hard-line military strategy politically feasible.[124]

In contrast, Powell consistently urged the administration to utilize the full range of initiatives available – for example, political, financial, legal, and diplomatic – to "dry up the swamp" of international terrorism. Far from Wolfowitz's notion of a broad military response, Powell argued for the military component to be limited, saying in late September only that

[120] "Rumsfeld Denies US Foreign Policy Split," BBCNews, July 30, 2001.
[121] Ibid.
[122] Perlez, "White House Rejects."
[123] Tanenhaus, "Bush's Brain Trust," p. 91.
[124] Mike Allen and Alan Sipress, "High Stakes, Tension Magnify Differences among Members of Bush's War Cabinet," *Washington Post*, September 26, 2001, p. A3.

"there may also be a military component."[125] Both departments agreed that the United States should go to Afghanistan, but they disagreed about the objectives: Defense wanted to make overthrowing the Taliban an explicit objective, while State urged Bush to be cautious and focus on bin Laden and his al-Qaeda network. If the military component were not limited, State felt, the campaign against terrorism might appear to be a war against Islam. According to a senior official, the State Department was highly concerned with the collateral damage a broad military campaign would doubtless entail. If this were not limited, some members of the State Department felt, the U.S. campaign could quickly become a holy war.[126] The distance separating the two sides of the Potomac seemed to be widening as the campaign against terrorism unfolded. In December, Powell and Rumsfeld disagreed about the ending of the campaign in Afghanistan. Playing their respective roles faithfully, Powell said on December 17, 2001, that al-Qaeda had been destroyed in Afghanistan (wrongly, it turns out) and that the country was no longer a haven for terrorists, while Rumsfeld refused to back up this comment, insisting instead on further use of military force in that country.[127]

With the American campaign in Afghanistan coming to a close, Washington focused its attention on other potentially dangerous states. Rumsfeld maintained his aggressive stance and lumped Syria in the "axis of evil." The Pentagon regarded Syria as a terrorist sponsor and emerging producer of weapons of mass destruction. The State Department, however, saw Syria as a stabilizing force in Lebanon and an important player in the Middle East peace process. As such, Powell encouraged U.S. relations with Syria.[128] This sort of divide was one of many cases where the president was forced to choose one department's world-view over another's. Amidst these disagreements, the Pentagon seemed to be making an effort to usurp some of the State Department's power to affect foreign policy. The *Washington Post* reported on April 8, 2002, that the Pentagon "is seeking authority to spend tens of millions of dollars on military assistance to unspecified foreign countries or 'indigenous forces' authority that traditionally has rested with the State Department."[129] This initiative sparked concern among some senior

[125] Ibid.

[126] Patrick Tyler and Blaire Sciolino, "Bush's Advisers Split on Scope of Retaliation," *New York Times*, September 20, 2001, p. A1.

[127] "Rumsfeld and Powell Fight over the Meaning of Victory," *The Guardian*, December 18, 2001.

[128] "Rumsfeld, Powell at Odds over Threat Posed by Syria, Libya," WorldTribune.com, May 1, 2002.

[129] Bradley Graham, "Pentagon Seeks Own Foreign Aid Power," *Washington Post*, April 8, 2002, p. A1.

State Department officials who saw the Pentagon as crossing a line and trying to establish a parallel foreign security assistance program. Armitage wrote a letter to Office of Management and Budget director Mitchell E. Daniels, Jr., requesting clarification of the intent of the Pentagon initiative.

As this divide continued to grow, it could no longer be considered merely a *symptom* of bureaucratic or departmental squabbles, as Powell's earlier dismissal might have led us to believe. It became a distinctive dimension in the foreign and defense policy process. According to some State Department officials, this divide paralyzed U.S. policy in the Middle East as Powell's efforts to break the deadlock were repeatedly undercut during his trip in the spring of 2002.[130] The administration seemed to be unwilling to support Powell in seeking a withdrawal of Israeli forces from West Bank cities and accelerating talks with the Palestinians. Many in the State Department cited resistance to these diplomatic efforts coming directly from Rumsfeld.[131]

In previous years the Middle East conflict largely fell within the ambit of the State Department and White House. In the Bush administration, Rumsfeld, along with Wolfowitz and Feith, was granted a seat at inter-agency discussions on the Middle East.[132] The "battle royal" between State and Defense delayed adoption of a plan on how to proceed in the turbulent region. Just before leaving Jerusalem, Powell told reporters that a cease-fire and political negotiations would go forward only if the Israeli military offensive ceased. The following day, though, Powell and the State Department suffered a major blow as Bush called the Israeli Prime Minister Ariel Sharon a man of peace and credited him with taking satisfactory steps to end the three-week-old invasion.[133] We return to the Middle East conflict in the Conclusion.

The major prize in the State-Defense face-off was policy toward Iraq. After the immediate post-9/11 debate over whether to turn U.S. attention toward Iraq was resolved, the question now was how exactly to deal with Saddam. In the past, Powell had said that Saddam was like a "toothache" that you just had to live with or a "kidney stone that will eventually pass."[134] Never did he prescribe operating to remove the kidney stone, however. In a September 1, 2002, interview with the BBC, Powell said weapons inspectors should return to Iraq as a first step in dealing with Saddam. This contradicted

---

[130] Alan Sipress, "Policy Divide Thwarts Powell in Mideast Effort; Defense Dept's Influence Frustrates State Dept," *Washington Post*, April 26, 2002, p. A1.
[131] Ibid.
[132] Ibid.
[133] Ibid.
[134] "The War behind Closed Doors: Transcript."

the Defense point of view, which Cheney shared, that inspectors would not be of great use. Powell and Rumsfeld were destined to come to loggerheads over Iraq. Powell came into office favoring a policy of "smarter sanctions" that would contain Iraq's development of weapons of mass destruction, but would ease the humanitarian crisis there, whereas Rumsfeld supported a forward-leaning plan to oust Saddam even before the attacks of 9/11. The rift between State and Defense would persist through the prelude to the war, with each department often locking horns over how to deal with the U.N. and the sometimes prickly European allies.[135]

Since the time he joined the administration, Rumsfeld had been inundating Washington with a torrent of memos regarding foreign policy. He would send what came to be known as "Rummygrams" to the State Department, offering unsolicited advice and comments on U.S. foreign policy, often in "pointed terms" (those sent throughout the Pentagon were called "snowflakes").[136] During the run-up to the war on Iraq, throughout the war, and in its aftermath, the volume of "Rummygrams" hit its peak. "There are literally thousands of them," said one frequent recipient of Rumsfeld's unsolicited advice.[137] State Department officials carped that these memos would land on their desks at least once a week, occasionally with newspaper clippings attached.[138] One "Rummygram" questioned whether Powell should engage in a dialogue with Arafat, whom Rumsfeld distrusted. Another expressed concern that the State Department was trying to rehabilitate Libyan leader Moammar Gadhafi. The injection by Rumsfeld of his views into the mid-levels of the State Department and especially the increase in "Rummygrams" in an administration known for its discipline testified to the friction between the two camps as they battled for the president's favor.

Although former Treasury Secretary Paul O'Neill records that, at the first meeting of Bush's incoming national security team on January 30, 2001, an attack on Iraq was discussed,[139] in December 2001 and throughout much of 2002, it was not at all clear which way Bush would go on Iraq. If anything, it was looking as if U.S. pressure might cause Saddam to comply with inspection and disclosure demands without shots being fired. With Cheney signed up in the hawks' camp, however, Bush received advice throughout the summer of 2002 to forget the U.N., forget inspections, and focus instead

[135] "Powell Furious at Rumsfeld's Europe Insults," TheAge.com.au, March 16, 2003.
[136] "Rumsfeld's War," *Newsweek*, September 16, 2002.
[137] "Rumsfeld Proposals Criticized as Off-Base," *Star-Telegram*, May 30, 2003.
[138] "Rivalry Can Make US Policy Look Shaky," *USA Today*, June 13, 2002.
[139] Ron Suskind, *The Price of Loyalty: George W. Bush, the White House, and the Education of Paul O'Neill* (New York: Simon and Schuster, 2004), pp. 70–75.

on taking aggressive action against Iraq.[140] By the end of the summer, it was clear that the neo-conservatives had won the president's favor as he chose to side with the more aggressive approach toward Iraq. As the administration's position became clear, several moderate Republicans publicly associated with President George H. W. Bush's administration added their voices to the debate. In an article in the *Wall Street Journal*, Scowcroft reminded Bush that an important set of Republicans had not been convinced that an aggressive approach was best.[141] While these developments temporarily put the administration on the defensive, they unleashed a vituperative backlash from neo-conservative war hawks, with Kristol calling Scowcroft's arguments "laughably weak."[142]

The reasons Bush now put forth for embracing an aggressive approach were unclear. Indeed, as we show in greater detail below, the reasons for the war – weapons of mass destruction, links with al-Qaeda, human rights abuses – covered a wide and ever-changing kaleidoscope. With the war's conclusion, the "weapons of mass destruction" argument has been largely discredited and is retrospectively seen as a politically convenient pretext.[143]

What, then, was the unstated reason for going to Iraq? According to Wolfowitz, another "almost unnoticed but huge" reason for war was to promote Middle East peace by allowing the United States to take its troops out of Saudi Arabia – ironically, this was precisely Osama bin Laden's agenda. In addition, journalists tried to read between the lines of Wolfowitz's comments to suggest that oil was the main reason for military action against Iraq. Wolfowitz may have given unwanted credence to this in an address at an Asian security summit in Singapore when he said, "The most important difference between North Korea and Iraq is that economically, we just had no choice in Iraq. The country swims on a sea of oil."[144]

These two alternate reasons, even if important, were undoubtedly not the whole story. The real explanation for the war lies elsewhere. Perle's aforementioned comment to Wattenberg about Iraq being the best place to test the proposition that a properly civic culture in Arab countries can lead to democratic institutions, may be the closest thing to an answer. It seems that the neo-conservatives, who were decisively influencing U.S. foreign policy in the prelude to the war, had adopted the notion of remaking the Middle East

---

[140] "The War behind Closed Doors: Transcript."
[141] Brent Scowcroft, "Don't Attack Iraq," *Wall Street Journal*, July 15, 2002.
[142] William Kristol, "The Axis of Appeasement," *Weekly Standard*, August 26, 2002, pp. 7–8.
[143] "WMD Just a Convenient Excuse for War, Admits Wolfowitz," *Independent Digital*, May 30, 2003 (original quote in Tanenhaus, "Bush's Brain Trust").
[144] "Wolfowitz: Iraq War Was about Oil," *The Guardian*, June 4, 2003.

"neighborhood," and Iraq seemed to offer the best prospect for initiating the effort. Before the war, Perle said, "There is tremendous potential to transform the region. If a tyrant like Saddam Hussein can be brought down, others are going to begin to think."[145]

As concerns about the true reasons for the war continued to place the administration on the defensive, National Security Advisor Rice seemed to endorse the neo-conservative position, by comparing the task in Iraq to that of the reconstruction of Europe after World War II.[146] This is at best a strained analogy. In principle the democratization of the Middle East has much to commend it. But the issue in play is the government's credibility. If the neo-conservative desire to transform the Middle East was the decisive reason the United States went to Iraq, then we must ask: Just how deceptive have the neo-conservative representations been? The White House admitted the uranium claims were false and Wolfowitz admitted that in the immediate lead-up to the war the administration settled on weapons of mass destruction only as "a convenient explanation," but the neo-conservatives may have been less than honest with the public even before these instances. In light of these cases of deception, it might be that the *NSS* is not all it seems.

Was the *NSS* merely setting up the preconditions for an attack on Iraq? Perhaps so. Iraq conveniently fit the circumstances outlined in the administration's security strategy document. We return in the Conclusion to a discussion of whether the *NSS* is a wise national strategy, especially whether it is a viable strategy to employ beyond Iraq, but here it is important to note one of the most worrying trends in the neo-conservative hijacking of U.S. foreign policy: the lack of truth in politics.

---

[145] "The War behind Closed Doors: Transcript."
[146] Condoleezza Rice, "Transforming the Middle East," *Washington Post*, August 7, 2003, p. A21.

5

The False History

Having set out the evolution of the neo-conservatives' beliefs and before we move on to see how they operationalized their ideology after September 11, 2001, we can pause briefly to consider how they have also worked hard to place their imprint – a false one, we argue – on the historical record. This was a decision they made consciously. For modern neo-conservatives have drunk deeply of the Leninist theory that to control the future it is necessary to dominate the past. With so many of today's neo-conservatives having careers in the media or academia, they have been able to do this with great skill, creating two "organizing myths": first, that neo-conservatives are somehow unique in wishing to place American values (taking precedence over interests) at center stage in foreign policy; second, that they alone represent the true legacy of President Ronald Reagan and that thereby their brand of policy prescriptions provides only sure bulwark against regression to Clintonian liberalism and mushy multilateralism.[1]

The first aspect is designed to appeal to the country at large, while the second is directed at fellow conservatives and intended to distinguish the neo-conservatives as the true standard-bearers of a values-based conservative foreign policy as opposed to the allegedly valueless, accommodation-oriented realism of Nixon/Kissinger and Bush/Scowcroft or the nativist isolationism of Patrick Buchanan. In this quest for the mantle of the Republican prophet, the neo-conservatives assume many of the characteristics of the fundamentalism they so fervently oppose.

As with all organizing myths, these assertions have enough basis in reality to have some specious plausibility. Both the Nixon and G. H. W. Bush

---

[1] Robert Kagan and William Kristol, "Toward a Neo-Reaganite Foreign Policy," *Foreign Affairs*, July–August 1996, 22–23.

administrations placed a high value on geo-strategic calculation and did not wear their hearts on their sleeves. Did this lead to disaster? Hardly. Nixon's opening to China and the resultant neutralization of China as a hostile element in the US-USSR-China triangle significantly contributed to Reagan's ability to take a hard line on the Soviet Union. The first Bush administration achieved a remarkable advance in American power and values by embracing and then managing the reunification of Germany. This is one of the most undersung accomplishments of recent American diplomatic history. Without doubt it put the capstone on the core value of a Europe "whole and free" that had been at the heart of the Cold War. The achievement is all the more estimable as it was carried out in the teeth of fierce opposition from British Prime Minister Margaret Thatcher, a values-driven Cold War leader who turned decidedly "realist" when confronted by the prospect of a united Germany. Condoleezza Rice, now National Security Advisor, played a key part in this policy and, in some measure, owes her career to it. There is a certain irony, therefore, in the fact that, as the neo-conservative drumbeat intensified in Washington, she appeared reluctant to draw on the lessons of that act of genuine statecraft.[2]

Turning now to Clinton, certainly he did his fair share of dithering (and neither of the authors held back from criticism[3]), but he ended up going into the Balkans and oversaw the expansion of NATO. Perhaps the criticism the neo-conservatives have of him is that he was too forceful in areas, such as Haiti and Somalia, in which they have little interest. Regarding Reagan, the last part of the myth also rings true. Reagan did indeed rewrite the rules of engagement with the Soviet Union in a way that materially hastened its demise. His administration is a high point for all conservatives, including both authors. But just as the neo-conservatives attached a Reagan bumper sticker to their motorcade, they choose to ignore much of the substance: the intense arms control commitment, the summitry, the minimal use of direct American military power, and the rejection of the nuclear doctrine he inherited from neo-conservatives such as Albert Wohlstetter.

VALUES: A CONSTANT IN AMERICAN DIPLOMACY

As we have shown, neo-conservatives certainly draw on a distinguished lineage of emphasizing American values at times when they were at a discount.

---

[2] Philip D. Zelikow and Condoleezza Rice, *Germany Unified and Europe Transformed: A Study in Statecraft* (Cambridge, Mass.: Harvard University Press, 1995).

[3] Jonathan Clarke, "The Intellectual Poverty of American Foreign Policy," *Atlantic Monthly*, August 1995, pp. 54–66.

But their claim today to have a unique relationship with American values goes too far. This is one of the most heavily trodden fields of American diplomatic history, and we pass over it lightly here.[4] From the time when in 1775 Thomas Paine spoke for the revolutionary ethos proclaiming that "we have it in our power to begin the world all over again,"[5] the phenomenon of America's deeply felt "exceptionalism" has been a powerful factor in world politics, alternately inspiring and infuriating America's friends and allies. From the time America emerged as a true great power at the end of the nineteenth century, with the likes of Henry Cabot Lodge and Admiral A. T. Mahan advocating a "large" foreign policy, American leaders have been careful to emphasize the idealist motivations that underlay their international interventions. President McKinley, for example, justified the annexation of the Philippines on the grounds that it would "Christianize" the inhabitants, no doubt to their surprise, as they had been Catholics for almost three centuries. Walt Whitman asserted that it was in mankind's interest that American power and influence should be extended, "the farther the better." This period saw the publication of such books as Josiah Strong's *Our Country*, in which, echoing the poetic champion of imperialism, Rudyard Kipling, he trumpeted the world mission of the Anglo-Saxon race.

And so it went on throughout the twentieth century. Woodrow Wilson came into office denouncing his predecessor's "dollar diplomacy" (which he promptly embraced) and went on to give his name to the idealistic strain in American foreign policy (incurring plenty of hostile comment from overseas for his "ignorant pursuit of impossible ideals").[6] In 1952 Dwight Eisenhower told Americans that, much like today, they were facing the choice between good and evil. Henry Kissinger records that Richard Nixon was motivated by saving America's "honor in distant jungles" and that he wanted the industrial nations to embrace a "moral rededication to common purposes."[7] Jimmy Carter set no store by this and took the country on his version of a moral adventure. Bill Clinton promised to adhere to a higher standard of morality than his predecessor by distancing himself from the "butchers of Beijing," and George W. Bush promised very much the same thing. In fact, in recent history the one American diplomat of distinction openly to reject "the

---

4 Walter A. McDougall, *Promised Land: Crusader State: The American Encounter with the World since 1776* (New York: Houghton Mifflin, 1997); Walter Russell Mead, *Special Providence: American Foreign Policy and How It Changed the World* (New York: Knopf, 2002).

5 Michael H. Hunt, *Ideology and US Foreign Policy* (New Haven, Conn.: Yale University Press, 1987), p. 19.

6 Paul Johnson, *A History of the Modern World* (London: Weidenfeld and Nicolson, 1983), p. 22.

7 Henry Kissinger, *Years of Upheaval 1208–9* (New York: Little, Brown, 1982), pp. 1208–9.

illusions of unique and superior virtue on our part" is also one of its most accomplished exponents: George Kennan, the architect of the post–World War II containment policy that eventually brought down the Soviet Union.[8]

The question, therefore, in American diplomatic practice has never been, as the neo-conservatives argue, *whether* American values should have a place of honor but *how* these values should be accommodated alongside more tangible, interest-driven considerations. This dilemma has presented itself from the early days of the Republic. At that time, statesmen tended to be cautious. Jefferson concluded that America should exert moral authority as a "standing monument and example for the aim and imitation of other countries." In 1821, John Quincy Adams said of America, "She is the well-wisher to the freedom and independence of all. She is the champion and vindicator only of her own."[9] In 1823 then Congressman Daniel Webster, a future secretary of state, argued in favor of moral support for Greek independence from the Ottoman Empire but, inasmuch as the national interest was remote, stopped short of war.[10] As growing American power enabled a more robust emphasis on values, so the liberal Wilsonian strain came to prominence. As we have shown, this is the philosophic approach to which today's neo-conservatives generally adhere, thus aligning themselves in most instances with humanitarian liberalism. The one major difference is that neo-conservatives prefer to act alone and heavily armed rather than work through the often laborious multilateral process.

It is thus clear that the dilemma about how to position values in foreign policy is an age-old debate. The age of international terror has given it new life but not made it any easier to resolve. Where, for example, do Pakistan, Egypt or the central Asian republics stand? They fail every conceivable value test but nonetheless get a free pass from the neo-conservatives inasmuch as these countries, in Daniel Pipes's characteristically blunt phrase, have "thrown in their lot" with the United States on the Middle East, an area to which the neo-conservatives attach greater importance than whether these countries follow democratic norms.[11] The lesson here is that over the years American leaders have been pragmatic on this subject. The neo-conservatives are no different. They drape a heavy veil of values over issues dear to their

---

[8] George F. Kennan, *Around the Cragged Hill: A Personal and Political Philosophy* (New York: W. W. Norton, 1993), p. 182.

[9] Arthur M. Schlesinger, Jr., *The Cycles of American History* (Boston: Houghton Mifflin, 1986), p. 89.

[10] Robert Remini, *Daniel Webster: The Man and His Time* (New York: W. W. Norton, 1997), pp. 216–17.

[11] Daniel Pipes, *Militant Islam Reaches America* (New York: Norton, 2003), p. 21.

agenda but are quite happy to cut corners when it suits them. Although they hold strong views on the subject, they are no more consistent than anyone else.

THE REAGAN LEGACY: LABELING THE UNLABELABLE

The question of the Reagan legacy came to the fore in 1996 in a *Foreign Affairs* article written by William Kristol and Robert Kagan containing a diagnosis of the then current failings of American foreign policy. Their alternative was to advocate "a Neo-Reaganite Foreign Policy." As they explained: "During the Reagan years, the United States pressed for changes in right-wing and left-wing dictatorships alike." Reagan's policy of pressuring authoritarian and totalitarian regimes "had practical aims and, in the end, delivered strategic benefits." For Kagan and Kristol, therefore, a neo-Reaganite foreign policy meant "not just supporting U.S. friends and gently pressuring other nations, but actively pursuing policies – in Iran, Cuba or China for instance – ultimately intended to bring about a change of regime."[12] Perle cites Reagan's legacy as support for his own campaign against the State Department.[13]

Let us concede that, once again, this argument is not without some underlying substance. George Shultz, who saw Reagan's foreign policy from the inside, records that he "changed the national and international agenda on issue after issue," notably by challenging conventional wisdom on the "possibility of movement toward freedom in the Communist-dominated world." But he also records that Reagan was "not a man who would stay labeled."[14] Yet this is exactly what the neo-conservatives have attempted to do: extract from the Reagan record those elements that suit their agenda (the defense buildup, the "evil empire," Central America, Grenada, and Libya), exclude those that do not (arms control, China, arms for Iran, the Daniloff/Zakharov trade, Lebanon, the USS *Stark*), and label the result in their own ideological terms. And then they go on to affix that label over their own purposes that, as we see below, in many cases owe little or nothing to Reagan. And this is true in no case more crucially than in the use of force. This muddying of the historical record is certainly no service to the cause of true conservatism.

---

[12] Robert Kagan and William Kristol, "Toward a Neo-Reaganite Foreign Policy," *Foreign Affairs*, July–August 1996, pp. 4, 18.

[13] David Frum and Richard Perle, *An End to Evil: How to Win the War on Terror* (New York: Random House, 2003), p. 113.

[14] George P. Shultz, *Turmoil and Triumph: My Years as Secretary of State* (New York: Scribner's, 1993), p. 1135.

The Reagan years were never a golden age for neo-conservatism and its dream of uncompromising anticommunist rollback and liberation. Richard Darman, one of Reagan's special assistants, records that "though ideologically committed, President Reagan had understood well that pragmatic compromise was necessary in order to govern."[15] Donald Regan, his chief of staff, records that "Reagan's every action in foreign policy had been carried out with the idea of one day sitting down with the leader of the USSR and banning weapons of mass destruction from the planet."[16] Reagan himself describes the lifting of the grain embargo, his first act in relation to the Soviet Union, as intended to bring about a "meaningful and constructive dialogue which will assist us in fulfilling our joint obligation to find lasting peace."[17]

The neo-Reaganite foreign policy drawn up by Kagan and Kristol is vastly more "neo" than it is "Reaganite." Reagan's approach to the world may, in its basic philosophic instincts, have had something in common with neo-conservatism, but the pragmatism of its execution set it a universe away from today's inflexible neo-conservative designs. The severe neo-conservative critique of Reagan's foreign policy that emerged from the early 1980s made this clear.

THE EARLY REAGAN YEARS: THE NEO-CONSERVATIVE HONEYMOON

At the outset of office, the rhetoric of Reagan's foreign policy sounded like the Cold War fundamentalism for which neo-conservatives had been waiting. He vehemently opposed the concept of communism as something that challenged the very basis of conventional American ideals and conservative truths. The Soviet Union was the "evil empire" and a "sad, bizarre chapter in human history whose last pages are even now being written."[18] He shared the sentiment of neo-conservatives that American power had been allowed to diminish since 1970, while Moscow's had increased, and that the misguided policies of Nixon, Ford, and Carter had allowed the Soviet Union to achieve military superiority over the United States. A run of events in 1979 seemed to underscore that American power and influence were in rapid decline. In

---

[15] Richard Darman, *Who's in Control: Polar Politics and the Invisible Center* (New York: Simon and Schuster, 1996), p. 10.

[16] Donald T. Regan, *For the Record* (New York: Harcourt Brace Jovanovich, 1988), p. 294.

[17] Ronald Reagan, *An American Life* (New York: Simon and Schuster, 1990), p. 273.

[18] Richard Crockatt, *The Fifty Years War: The United States and the Soviet Union in World Politics, 1941–1991* (New York: Routledge, 2000), pp. 305–6, and Robert Dallek, *Ronald Reagan: The Politics of Symbolism* (Cambridge, Mass.: Harvard University Press, 1996), p. 163.

February, an Islamic revolutionary movement that was deeply opposed to America gained power in Iran, overthrowing the Washington-backed shah. Nine months later, fifty-two Americans were taken hostage in Tehran, shortly followed by the Soviet invasion of Afghanistan in December. As *Commentary* suggested in April 1981, Reagan's election demonstrated that "two related arguments which had been raging in the United States for the past decade or so were now finally settled. The first concerned the growth of Soviet power and the second had to do with the decline of American power."[19] The new American president believed that the increasing Soviet adventurism derived from two factors: Moscow was engaged in an aggressive and expansionist policy across the globe, and this was being supported by an enormous military buildup. Accordingly, the basic outline of Reagan's foreign policy was also two-fold: the reestablishment of American economic and military strength and the rollback of Soviet influence across the Third World.

The second of these policies became known as the Reagan doctrine, which sought to provide assistance to anticommunist guerrillas and governments with arms, finance, training, and facilities. To note a few examples, the Reagan administration thus supported the Contras in Nicaragua, the anti-Marxist guerrillas in Angola, the right-wing government in El Salvador, the Mujahiddin in Afghanistan, and the guerrilla coalition in Cambodia.[20] On the question of military strength, Reagan argued that Moscow now enjoyed almost twice the megatonnage in nuclear weapons as the United States, and clear superiority in land-based ballistic missiles. He immediately vowed to close the military gap and undertook America's largest ever peacetime increase in military capacity. Between 1981 and 1986, the annual defense budget grew from $171 billion to $367.5 billion. Over one-fourth of this increase focused on advancing the B-1 bomber program, the MX (Missile Experimental) intercontinental ballistic missile system, and the Trident submarine missile system. The navy was expanded from 456 to 600 ships. Moreover, in the face of concentrated opposition not only in Moscow but across Europe and within the Republican Party itself, Reagan also forged ahead with plans for deploying intermediate-range missiles in Western Europe to counter the increasing force of Soviet SS-20 land-based missiles.[21] In March

---

[19] Norman Podhoretz, "The Future Danger," *Commentary*, April 1981, p. 29.

[20] Fred Halliday, *The Making of the Second Cold War* (London: Verso, 1983), pp. 234–35; Robert J. McMahon, *The Cold War* (Oxford: Oxford University Press, 2003), pp. 150–51.

[21] Crockatt, *Fifty Years War*, pp. 310–12; Halliday, *Making of the Second Cold War*, pp. 234–35; McMahon, *Cold War*, pp. 146–53; Dallek, *Reagan*, pp. 141–43; and Norman Podhoretz, "The First Term: The Reagan Road to Détente," *Foreign Affairs*, America and the World, 1984, pp. 451–52.

1983, the Reagan administration introduced plans for the novel Strategic Defense Initiative (SDI) – a defensive shield based in space and on land that would intercept and destroy incoming missiles. It caused immediate alarm in Moscow over the potential strategic advantage that it offered to Washington.

Hence, Reagan's approach to world affairs seemed a perfect match with the neo-conservative paradigm for American foreign policy. As Podhoretz argued in 1981: "We have, then, a new consensus on the need to respond more firmly and resolutely to the growth of Soviet power and to take extraordinary steps . . . to arrest and reverse the decline of American power." For all the reasons cited in 1983 by Cold War historian John Lewis Gaddis in his *Foreign Affairs* critique on what he regarded as Reagan's heavy-handed approach to foreign policy, neo-conservatives believed that they had found what they had been looking for in Reagan. As Gaddis argued: "The Reagan Administration has rejected détente, with its emphasis on distinctions between interests, on graduations of threat, and on multidimensional responses. Instead we have returned to an earlier form of containment: one that assumes virtually unlimited resources for defense and little real prospect of settling differences through negotiation. . . ."[22]

DISENCHANTMENT

However, if neo-conservatives saw in Reagan a policy maker in their own image, they were to be disappointed. Within four years, Podhoretz had published articles with such titles as "The Reagan Road to Détente," "The Neo-Conservative Anguish over Reagan's Foreign Policy," and "Mistaken Identity." Irving Kristol had written "The Muddle in Foreign Policy," and Robert Tucker had published "The Middle East: Carterism without Carter." These articles made clear that the president had fallen out of favor with the neo-conservatives. The essential causes for the chasm that emerged between Reagan and the strict letter of neo-conservatism were two: the manner in which the president's rhetoric translated into actual policy, and who the real decision makers were in the president's defense establishment. Both were core aspects of the Reagan legacy that Kagan and Kristol failed to account for in their formulation of a neo-Reaganite approach to the post–Cold War era.

[22] John Lewis Gaddis, "The Rise, Fall and Future of Détente," *Foreign Affairs*, 1983–84, pp. 355–77.

Although Reagan introduced to U.S./Soviet relations the most severe expression of anticommunist rhetoric ever used by an American president, there was a disparity between Reaganism as defined in theory and that which became practice. Certainly, his statements of intent to face down the evil empire with the support of a powerful arms buildup were as frightening to the Soviets as they were promising to the neo-conservatives. But as Reagan's term progressed, his pledge to show no compromise with Sovietism the world over gave way to moderation. Shultz commented that "Ronald Reagan was not at the end of his presidency what he was when he started out."[23] While his statements portrayed the all-out desire for intervention, unilaterally, if necessary, to push the Soviets back "right to the gates of the Kremlin itself," they did not transform into real policy, as many neo-conservatives had hoped.[24] Reagan was decidedly unwilling to expend American lives or chance direct conflagration with Moscow. The three interventions conducted by the Reagan administration – deploying troops to Beirut in 1982 and Grenada in 1983 and bombing Libya in 1986 – were limited operations of short duration. Grenada was the only direct use of American troops against a pro-Communist movement.[25] The Reagan administration made efforts to avoid directly confronting Moscow. Consequently, one of the biggest sources of neo-conservative contention with Reagan came over events in Poland.

When Warsaw's Soviet satellite government imposed martial law in December 1981, in response to protests led by the noncommunist labor union *Solidarity*, Alexander Haig, then Secretary of State, records that Reagan came under intense pressure from anticommunist hard-liners to take decisive action. Reagan resisted this pressure.[26] As a limited response, he chose unilateral sanctions on American-made parts for the natural gas pipeline between Siberia and Western Europe. That Reagan failed to heed the hard-line advice in establishing economic embargos against Poland and the Soviet Union, along with a threat to foreclose on the Polish debt, provided "clear evidence" to neo-conservatives that he was timid in his approach to the Soviets.[27] Podhoretz stated in the *New York Times*: "Either this administration does not in fact know what it wishes to do, or what it really wishes to do does not correspond to what the President himself has said."[28] Podhoretz

---

[23] Shultz, *Turmoil and Triumph*, p. 1135.
[24] Quoted in Podhoretz, "Reagan Road," p. 455.
[25] Crockatt, *Fifty Years War*, pp. 303–8, and McMahon, *Cold War*, pp. 147–48.
[26] Alexander Haig, *Caveat: Realism, Reagan, and Foreign Policy* (New York: Macmillan, 1984), pp. 240–41.
[27] McMahon, *Cold War*, pp. 151–52, and Dallek, *Reagan*, p. 182.
[28] Norman Podhoretz, "The Neo-Conservative Anguish over Reagan's Foreign Policy," *New York Times Magazine*, May 2, 1982, p. 32.

believed that "there was a significant non-military response available to the United States" in the cutting of credits, halting the entire construction of the natural gas pipeline, and placing embargos on food and technology. But instead, "like Jimmy Carter in the face of the Soviet invasion of Afghanistan, he [Reagan] announced a program of sanctions." Irving Kristol asked in the *Wall Street Journal*: "Are there no stronger, more meaningful options?" As an alternative, he advocated "moving to destabilize the Castro regime in Cuba as a suitable response to the Soviets stabilizing their puppet regime in Poland."[29] Podhoretz later asked in *Foreign Affairs*, "[W]hy would an administration committed to rollback fail to exploit an event like the Polish crisis of 1981–1982?"[30] As he argued: "[W]hat President Reagan's response to the Polish crisis reveals is that he has in practice been following a strategy of helping the Soviet Union stabilize its empire, rather than a strategy aimed at encouraging the breakdown of that empire from within."[31] Irving Kristol concluded less than a year after Reagan's election victory, "This administration will never get out of the foreign policy muddle it is creating unless it realizes the inadequacy of the intellectual tools with which it is operating."[32] This typical neo-conservative desire for public pyrotechnics led them to miss the more subtle side of Reagan's response: financial assistance delivered to the Solidarity movement via the AFL/CIO and moral suasion through Pope John Paul II.[33]

So Reagan was not the long-awaited neo-conservative man in the White House, after all. Rather, beneath the hard-line rhetoric he was a pragmatist, causing leading neo-conservatives to compare his administration to that of its predecessor. Another area in Reagan's foreign affairs that inspired a similar neo-conservative response was the Middle East. In September 1981, *Commentary* published an article by Princeton professor Robert C. Tucker that argued that Reagan's polices in the region were a disappointment and a tacit endorsement of Carterism.[34] American policy toward the Middle East certainly revealed inconsistencies after Reagan came to office. Deterring Soviet influence in the region as well as resolving the local political conflicts that made it easier for Moscow to fish for influence proved difficult. The thrust of Reagan's policy toward the oil-rich Persian Gulf

[29] Irving Kristol, "The Muddle in Foreign Policy," *Wall Street Journal*, April 29, 1984.
[30] Podhoretz, "Reagan Road," p. 456.
[31] Podhoretz, "Neo-Conservative Anguish," p. 92.
[32] Kristol, "Muddle."
[33] Edwin Meese, *With Reagan: The Inside Story* (Washington, D.C.: Regnery, 1992), p. 170.
[34] Robert Tucker, "The Middle East: Carterism without Carter?" *Commentary*, September 1981.

formulated an anti-Soviet strategic consensus among Israel and those considered to be moderate Arab states. Because of the Iran-Iraq war, the Soviet invasion of Afghanistan and the absence of an Iranian policeman for Western interests in the region following the revolution, Washington sought to forge stronger strategic ties with Saudi Arabia. But when the administration announced plans to sell five early warning radar aircraft (AWACs) to Riyadh, condemnation came not only from Tel Aviv, but also from the ranks of Washington's neo-conservatives.[35] Describing the policy as "Carterism without Carter," Tucker contended: "We are presently engaged in, as we have been for some time, a policy of economic and political appeasement of Saudi Arabia." Calling it a "policy of impotence," Tucker argued that "the only way of assuring access to the oil of the Gulf is through a substantial military policy there of our own."[36] Irving Kristol described it as "an action for which not even a foolish reason can be given." As Podhoretz believed: "in arming the Saudis and depending upon them to police the region on our behalf, the Reagan Administration was resurrecting the Nixon doctrine."[37]

ISRAEL, CHINA, AND CENTRAL AMERICA

Accordingly, neo-conservatives became increasingly concerned over Reagan's policies vis-à-vis Israel. On the one hand, Reagan clearly asserted his commitment to Israel: "The State of Israel is an accomplished fact; it deserves unchallenged legitimacy within the community of nations."[38] However, there continued to be significant points of departure between Reagan's approach to the Middle East and the pro-Israeli perspectives of neo-conservatives. Reagan rejected the Israeli insistence on incorporating the West Bank and the Gaza Strip into Israel. Outlining an Israeli-Palestinian peace initiative in September 1982, Reagan declared that "the United States will not support annexation or permanent control by Israel of the West Bank and Gaza." Along with demanding Arab recognition of Israel, he also insisted on an Israeli settlement freeze on the West Bank: "I will not support the use of any additional land for the purpose of settlements." When Israel approved

---

[35] Crockatt, *Fifty Years War*, pp. 331–32; Dallek, *Reagan*, pp. 170–72; Robert Tucker, "Appeasement and the AWACS," *Commentary*, December 1981, p. 26; and Podhoretz, "Reagan Road," p. 461.

[36] Tucker, "Appeasement," p. 30.

[37] Podhoretz, "Neo-Conservative Anguish," p. 33.

[38] Quoted in *The Reagan Administration's Foreign Policy: Facts and Judgment of the International Tribunal* (Vienna: International Progress Organization, 1984), p. 217.

the de facto annexation of the Golan Heights taken from Syria in the Six-Day War of 1967, Reagan supported the U.N. Security Council in denouncing the act as illegal. The administration subsequently suspended strategic agreements with Tel Aviv.[39]

As events in the Middle East unfolded, the neo-conservatives' critique of Reagan's foreign policy grew more severe. Irving Kristol remarked: "Though this administration came to office with a clear-cut set of attitudes in foreign affairs, it had never thought through the implications of those attitudes for a coherent foreign policy."[40] *Commentary* asserted that the Reagan administration "becomes ever more accustomed to playing the role of supplicant to the rulers of Arabia." Tucker condemned the manner in which "this administration is fast becoming quite as persuaded as was its predecessor that there is an intimate link between 'progress' on the Palestinian issue and the improvement of our position in the Gulf."[41] In the *New York Times Magazine*, Podhoretz criticized "the continuing tilt in American policy towards the enemies of Israel in the Middle East." As he argued: "Does the American reliance on Saudi Arabia mean that we will gradually join in its demand for a Palestinian state on the West Bank ruled by the Palestinian Liberation Organization, even though the PLO is sworn to the destruction of the only democratic nation in the region and is in addition bound by hoops of ideology and arms to the Soviet Union?"[42] By the middle of Reagan's first term, therefore, it was clear that his policies toward Israel and the Middle East were a huge disappointment to neo-conservatives. In Tucker's words: "The promised transformation of America's Middle East policy did not survive the initial weeks of the new administration."[43]

The paths of Reaganism and neo-conservatism diverged yet again over policy toward the People's Republic of China. As president-elect, Reagan had been skeptical about extensive engagement with China's communist government. But as his term progressed, this position softened considerably. The Reagan administration's approach to Beijing moderated after it entered the White House, and June 1981 witnessed Secretary of State Alexander Haig's goodwill trip to Beijing. Reagan's policies toward China bore increasing resemblance to the efforts of the Nixon and Carter administrations to foster improved relations between the two powers. Although the policy was severely undercut by the administration's concurrent sales of arms to Taiwan,

[39] Ibid., and Dallek, *Reagan*, pp. 170–88.
[40] Kristol, "Muddle."
[41] Tucker, "Appeasement," p. 30.
[42] Podhoretz, "Neo-Conservative Anguish," p. 33.
[43] Tucker, "The Middle East," p. 32.

Reagan attempted to pursue a policy of making friends and contacts in China. Though a fierce battle over technology transfer policy raged within the administration, science and technical protocols were signed and high-level visits exchanged. Shultz records that, while Reagan did not mince his words with the Chinese, he did not bear down on them but instead used his meetings with Chinese leaders as a cross-the-ideologies "training ground and confidence builder" for his subsequent, much more intensive, meetings with Soviet leaders.[44] This policy was an anathema to many neo-conservatives and mainstream Republicans alike.[45] Podhoretz exclaimed, "If Mr. Reagan had been as great an ideologue as he was often said to be, he might have taken the position that the loss in clarity of ideological purpose entailed by this policy was greater than any advantage that so economically backward and militarily weak a nation as China could bring to the balance of power." It was obvious to Podhoretz that "Mr. Reagan, while perhaps more swayed by ideological conviction than most professional politicians, showed in his first term (as he has already demonstrated, when governor of California, to those with eyes to see) that for better or worse he was more politician than ideologue."[46] Ironically in the light of later developments, the improvements in relations with China were overseen and encouraged by Wolfowitz as the responsible State Department official.

Thus, although Kagan and Kristol present Reagan as the ideological model for a robust foreign policy in the post–Cold War era, events after 1980 show that the Reagan administration moved progressively nearer to the assumption that foreign policy could not simply be fitted into a purely ideological framework. That core aspects of Reagan's approach to world affairs transmuted from rhetoric into compromise illustrated how local conditions and realities effected a translation of impulse and ideas into specific and practical policies.[47] One of the first shifts from principle into practice came in April 1981, when the Reagan administration lifted the grain embargo on the Soviet Union that Carter had established in response to Moscow's invasion of Afghanistan. In response, Podhoretz asked, "Why . . . would an administration intent on 'doing the Soviets in' lift a grain embargo which, while not exactly calculated to topple the communist system, was nevertheless helping

44 Shultz, *Turmoil and Triumph*, p. 398.
45 Dallek, *Reagan*, pp. 174–75, and Peter Calvocoressi, *World Politics: 1945–2000* (London: Longman, 2000), p. 140.
46 Podhoretz, "Reagan Road," p. 461.
47 Gillian Peele, *Revival and Reaction: The Right in Contemporary America* (Oxford: Clarendon, 1984), p. 189.

to aggravate the very internal economic difficulties that Mr. Reagan cited as a symptom of instability and decline?"[48]

Nevertheless, the Kagan-Kristol article stated, "Reagan mounted a bold challenge to the tepid consensus" that favored "coexistence with the Soviet Union" and "considered any change in the status quo either too frightening or too expensive." They argued that Reagan "refused to accept the limits on American power" and championed a "controversial vision of ideological and strategic victory over the forces of international communism" that transformed "the country and the world."[49] And yet, as Heritage Foundation scholars Kim Holmes and John Hillen noted in *Foreign Affairs* shortly afterward, this is a critical misreading of the Reagan legacy. Holmes and Hillen agree that the two neo-conservative intellectuals are correct to credit Reagan with courage and resolve. But they also point out that Kagan and Kristol are mistaken to take part of his legacy – the moral crusade against the "evil empire" and his campaign for democracy – and exaggerate this as if it were the entire basis for Reagan's approach. The other fundamental aspect of his legacy was "hard-headed realism."

Reagan's foreign policy was not an open-ended campaign for democracy or wherever an opportunity presented itself. For example, he described the need to recognize the electoral defeat of Philippine President Ferdinand Marcos as "inevitable but not enjoyable."[50] It was a concentrated strategy that utilized a range of moral, military, and economic resources primarily to undermine Moscow with nonviolent means. Although Reagan's approach to the world was undoubtedly based on challenging Soviet expansionism and the decline of American influence, it was never predicated – in the neo-conservative manner – on the unilateral deployment of U.S. military power to the virtual exclusion of all other foreign policy instruments. Certainly, it gave a large priority to military power, but it was also careful to maintain a balanced diplomatic approach in places such as the Middle East, Europe, and China. The giant military buildup forced the Soviets into decisions that were ultimately self-destructive.[51] Reagan's move toward arms control actually predated Mikhail Gorbachev's arrival as leader of the Soviet Union.[52] Reagan employed extensive interaction with multilateral institutions, such as when he sided with the U.N. Security Council over Israel's actions in the

---

[48] Podhoretz, "Reagan Road," p. 456.

[49] Kagan and Kristol, "Toward a Neo-Reaganite Foreign Policy," pp. 19–20.

[50] Reagan, *American Life*, pp. 363–65.

[51] Kim Holmes and John Hillen, "Misreading Reagan's Legacy," *Foreign Affairs*, September–October 1996, p. 164.

[52] Crockatt, *Fifty Years War*, p. 307.

West Bank. As much as the Reagan Doctrine was intended to counter Soviet influence in Latin America, it sought to avoid the direct use of U.S. force in conflict. Beyond the commitment of significant funds, material, and covert intelligence resources to the support of proxy warriors and anticommunist regimes in Nicaragua, El Salvador, Honduras, and Costa Rica, Reagan refused to countenance direct military confrontation with Moscow. The Reagan Doctrine in Central and South America was more an extension of the Monroe Doctrine than it was a neo-conservative stance against détente and containment.[53] Grenada was the only country in the region where American troops were deployed, when the administration used 7,000 troops to overpower a 600-man army. The legal basis for the intervention was plausible rather than watertight, and most British Commonwealth governments, including Britain where Prime Minister Margaret Thatcher was enraged at what she saw – completely mistakenly – as American interference in a British territory, considered it an illegal and unnecessary act. But the maneuver was not aimed at inviting a quantum increase in superpower tension; it was a low-risk, limited operation of short duration and fully compatible with the Monroe Doctrine – and the only one of its kind during the Reagan administration.[54]

Accordingly, prominent neo-conservatives of the time did not share the retrospective interpretations of Kagan and Kristol. As Podhoretz argued, "the President's warmest friends and his most virulent enemies imagined that they had found in him a champion of the old conservative dream of going beyond containment of Communism to the 'rollback' of Communist influence and power and the 'liberation' of the Soviet empire. The truth, however, is that Mr. Reagan as President has never shown the slightest inclination to pursue such an ambitious strategy."[55] Podhoretz declared disappointedly that "in Ronald Reagan we thought we had found a political force capable of turning things around." Instead, many neo-conservatives felt that Reagan's first term brought "all the old ideas and policies against which Ronald Reagan himself has stood for so many years."[56] As many neo-conservatives regrettably admitted, Reagan was not a neo-conservative.

---

[53] Established under the administration of President James Monroe in December 1823, the Monroe Doctrine had sought to limit outside influence in the Western Hemisphere – then namely from the Great Powers of Europe – and declared the United States as effective guardian of independent nations in the Americas.

[54] International Progress Organization, Papers, pp. 91–97; McMahon, *Cold War*, pp. 148–50; Calvocoressi, *World Politics*, p. 842; and Crockatt, *Fifty Years War*, p. 307.

[55] Norman Podhoretz, "Mistaken Identity," *Commentary*, July 1984, p. 56.

[56] Podhoretz, "Neo-Conservative Anguish," p. 97.

Instead, he carefully weighed his foreign policy options and acted cautiously.[57] By the middle of Reagan's first term, the editors at *Commentary* and their intellectual allies were "sinking into a state of near political despair."[58]

That neo-conservatism never found clear expression in the policies of Reagan's administration owed a great deal to a second aspect of his legacy: whom he chose for the top cabinet positions. Reagan's cabinet was not dominated by the ideologically pure. Rather, the president chose pragmatists and officials from previous Republican administrations for the highest levels of his administration. It was certainly the case that all whom Reagan appointed were committed, hard-line, anti-Soviet Cold Warriors. He included thirty-two members from the Committee on the Present Danger in staff and advisory positions across his administration. But Reagan did not choose the right-wing ideologues for the highest foreign policy positions. In their stead he appointed mainstream Republicans such as Alexander Haig and Casper Weinberger to the positions of Secretary of State and Secretary of Defense. These men brought pragmatic moderates into subcabinet posts. Lawrence Eagleberger (a career Foreign Service officer) was appointed Undersecretary for Political Affairs at the State Department, while Frank Carlucci took the position of Deputy Secretary of Defense.[59] Although Haig and Weinberger were known for their hard-line convictions and differed over matters such as Israel, they did not share the apocalyptic vision of the Soviet threat articulated by ideologues who joined the administration lower down. Rather, as the men at the top of Washington's strategic triad, Reagan, Weinberger, and Haig agreed that Soviet Communism was a system whose days were numbered and that a decisive military buildup, the checking of Soviet adventurism, and strong support to anticommunist governments and guerrillas would undermine the Soviet Union at a time when it was vulnerable. Accordingly, Podhoretz decided of Haig, "what Mr. Haig wanted to do was return to a policy of détente." As he argued in *Commentary*, "The notion that Mr. Haig was or is a 'super hawk,' a believer in global confrontation or in the 'miniaturization' of American foreign policy, was and is a case of mistaken identity."[60]

[57] John Ehrman, *The Rise of Neoconservatism: Intellectuals and Foreign Affairs 1945–94* (New Haven: Yale University Press, 1995), p. 138.

[58] Podhoretz, "Neo-Conservative Anguish," p. 30.

[59] "Thunderers on the Right," *Time*, March 16, 1981, p. 22, and Ronald Brownstein and Nina Easton, *Reagan's Ruling Class: Portraits of the President's Top One Hundred Officials* (Washington: Pantheon, 1982), pp. 532–34.

[60] Podhoretz, "Mistaken Identity," p. 58.

Of course, Reagan's administration did include neo-conservatives. A number of individuals from the Committee on the Present Danger received appointments, such as Perle, who joined the Department of Defense as Assistant Secretary of Defense for International Security Policy. Kirkpatrick became U.S. Ambassador to the U.N. and Max Kampelman remained chairman of the U.S. Delegation to the Conference on Security and Cooperation in Europe. Moynihan's former political assistant, Elliott Abrams, was made Assistant Secretary of State for International Organizations. Paul Wolfowitz (then more a mainstream official than the activist ideological he was later to become) was Head of Policy Planning at the State Department and subsequently Assistant Secretary for East Asian and Pacific Affairs. Hardliners such as Richard V. Allen became Assistant to the President for National Security Affairs, while Fred Ikle was made Under Secretary for Defense for Policy and Richard Pipes joined the NSC staff.[61]

But although Reagan put a number of Cold War fundamentalists into sub-cabinet positions, those who had hoped that his administration would now be dominated from the top by true-blue archconservatives and uncompromising hawks were disappointed. Right-wing ideologues such as Republican Senator Jesse Helms complained that Reagan was leaving his true supporters out in the cold while he put together a cabinet of moderates. As he personally warned the president in the *Conservative Digest*, "Your mandate for change is in danger of being subverted."[62] Moreover, the influence of moderate pragmatists increased as Reagan's term wore on. Allen was replaced in 1982 with William Clark, who was not from among those in the Committee on the Present Danger. An old ally from Reagan's former days as governor of California, Clark had virtually no experience in foreign affairs. While he was known for being a staunch conservative and an old Reagan ally, he was not a super hawk in foreign affairs by any means. Two of the administration's most avid hawks, Pipes and Perle, also left the government in 1984 and 1987, respectively. The resignation of Haig in June 1982 momentarily raised hopes among the members of Washington's ideological right who had "passionately wanted to get Haig."[63] But any suggestion that his departure might open the way for a candidate able to mollify neo- and archconservative grievances was short-lived. As a former member of the Nixon administration, George Shultz was another pragmatist known for his

---

[61] Ehrman, *Rise of Neoconservatism*, pp. 148–50, and Brownstein, and Easton, *Reagan's Ruling Class*, pp. 533–34.
[62] Crockatt, *Fifty Years War*, p. 365; "Thunderers on the Right."
[63] Podhoretz, "Mistaken Identity," p. 59.

ability to reconcile conflicting positions. His associations with the Nixon-Kissinger establishment along with a recognized ability for compromise marked him as a détentist to many neo-conservatives.[64] As undersecretaries, assistant secretaries, and ambassadors, the neo-conservatives and hard-line ideologues could therefore make only mid-level contributions to the Reagan administration.[65]

This is not to say that the neo-conservatives were of no consequence to American foreign policy under Reagan. Kirkpatrick and Abrams remained high-profile individuals while they were in office. Gifted and confrontational, Kirkpatrick represented a dramatic shift in approach to the U.N. During her tenure as ambassador, she criticized the organization extensively for inducing polarization and exacerbating conflict. She was also highly critical of the foreign policies of previous administrations, especially toward Latin America. As she argued, "The deterioration of the U.S. position in the hemisphere has already created serious vulnerabilities where none previously existed."[66] She showed no tolerance toward anti-American sentiments from the non-aligned countries and did not see the U.N. as a forum for arriving at peaceful solutions. She refrained from cultivating the African representatives as previous U.S. ambassadors had done and articulated Reagan's position on maintaining friendly relations with then apartheid South Africa. She also believed that the U.N. encouraged the formation of geographic blocs and subgroups across Afro-Asian, Latin American, Eastern European, and Western European member states that consistently excluded America and Israel. Aside from the notable exception of when she condemned Israel's bombing of an Iraqi nuclear reactor in July 1981, Kirkpatrick remained a staunch supporter of Israel at the Security Council. She argued that Israel was repeatedly treated unfairly because of the strong Arab influence in the nonaligned movement as well as Soviet opportunism and European ambivalence. But although Kirkpatrick was a high-profile figure in the administration, she remained an ambassador, not a policy maker. Even though she was the administration's intellectual specialist on foreign policy, Reagan did not promote her to the position of NSC Advisor after William Clark transferred in 1983. It was an indication that the president still prioritized the traditional foreign policy

[64] Dallek, *Reagan*, pp. 136–37.

[65] Crockatt, *Fifty Years War*, pp. 356–57.

[66] Jeane Kirkpatrick, "US Security and Latin America," *Commentary*, January 1981, p. 29, and Seymour Maxwell Finger, "The Reagan-Kirkpatrick Policies and the United Nations," *Foreign Affairs*, Winter 1983–84, pp. 436–37.

elites in Washington above the ideological conviction of neo-conservatives such as Kirkpatrick.[67]

Abrams was initially appointed Assistant Secretary of State for International Organization Affairs, then became Assistant Secretary of State for Human Rights and Humanitarian Affairs a year later, and in 1985, he was made Assistant Secretary of State for Inter-American Affairs. Like Kirkpatrick, he was deeply critical of previous policies that were contradictory in their discrimination against Latin American countries while showing indifference to violations by Moscow and its Soviet allies. He shared Kirkpatrick's ideological commitment to encouraging the expansion of democracy and firmly supported the sometimes controversial policies toward the government in El Salvador and the rebels in Nicaragua. However, although both Abrams and Kirkpatrick became the most influential neo-conservative voices in the Reagan administration, even they differed from the Podhoretz-style Cold War fundamentalism. Their objectives in putting policy on the ground were more limited than the ideals of liberation and rollback advocated in *Commentary*. Both shared the conviction that spreading democracy was a gradual process. As Abrams told the editor of *Foreign Policy*, "the task of believers in democracy is not to impose democracy on a world bitterly opposed to it, but rather to help fulfill the expectations that every people acknowledges for itself."[68] This perspective was in keeping with the statements of senior cabinet moderates such as Shultz. When the administration established Project Democracy in 1983 as a pseudo-governmental agency meant to aid foreign democratic institutions through training, funding, and technical assistance, Shultz declared in a state department bulletin, "We do not seek destabilization. Change must come from within, not be imposed from outside. It must follow a path dictated by national and local traditions."[69] In this sense the Reagan administration pursued a pragmatic policy of promoting democracy through the development of civil society, reflected, for example, in Project Democracy, rather than through the neo-conservative template of conquest and occupation, as is the case in Iraq. Thus, even with the presence of high-profile neo-conservatives such as Kirkpatrick and Abrams, the Reagan administration failed to pursue a neo-conservative agenda. Neither Kirkpatrick nor Abrams considered Soviet rollback as a requisite for claiming success in foreign policy, as Podhoretz did.

[67] Peele, *Revival and Reaction*, p. 48, and Finger, "Reagan-Kirkpatrick Policies," pp. 439–50.
[68] Ehrman, *Rise of Neoconservatism*, pp. 155–60.
[69] Ibid., pp. 162–63.

ARMS CONTROL, TERRORISM, AND THE USE OF FORCE

To hear the neo-conservatives (and their fellow-travelers, such as Dinesh D'Souza) tell the story, Reagan's foreign policy consisted of an uninterrupted series of confrontational exhibitions of American power.[70] With the exception of Lebanon in 1983, however, where U.S. troops were deployed in what turned out to be a disastrous and aborted attempt to bring stability in the wake of the Israeli invasion, an exercise that, in fact, marked a turning point underscoring Reagan's unwillingness to use troops where force could not be deployed to decisive effect, the invasion of Grenada and the bombing of Libya were the only times American troops were in action. For the rest, and certainly for 1983 onward, Reagan devoted more of his foreign policy time to arms control than to any other subject. His immediate staff was on notice that his purpose in accelerating the Carter defense buildup was "to position the United States for successful negotiations with the Soviet Union."[71] The negotiations comprised both strategic and intermediate-range missiles, with a treaty being reached on the latter. The intricacies of these negotiations – the zero and double zero options, the trade-off between SS-20s and Pershing IIs, and so on – are beyond the scope of this chapter, but suffice it to say that neither in style nor substance do they conform to the neo-conservative "smackdown" interpretation. They were tough and designed to extract maximum American leverage at the appropriate moment but had no flavor of the "hegemony" claimed by neo-conservatives as Reagan's legacy. At least one of today's neo-conservatives, Richard Perle, could attest to this fact as he was noted as "floating in a cloud over the success of the Geneva summit" between Reagan and Mikhail Gorbachev held in December 1985.[72]

The nexus between the response to terrorism and the use of force produced fierce controversy throughout the Reagan administration. Once again, today's neo-conservatives have drawn much broader lessons than the facts allow. The multiple acts of terrorism in 1985 (TWA flight 847, the *Achille Lauro*, the Berlin discotheque bombing) prompted discussions of preemptive action that foreshadow similar themes today. Yet only in the case of the Berlin attack where irrefutable evidence of Libyan complicity was established did a military response take place – and one which was strictly controlled by Reagan "to avoid any casualties or danger to civilians."[73]

70 Dinesh D'Souza, *Ronald Reagan: How an Ordinary Man Became an Extraordinary Leader* (New York: Free Press, 1997), pp. 129–48.

71 Jack F. Matlock, Jr., *Autopsy of an Empire* (New York: Random House, 1995), p. 77.

72 Shultz, *Turmoil and Triumph*, p. 689.

73 Caspar Weinberger, *Fighting for Peace: Seven Critical Years in the Pentagon* (New York: Warner, 1990), p. 190.

Otherwise Reagan tended to side with the cautious approach of Defense Secretary Caspar Weinberger, who believed that the State Department and National Security Council were forever devising "ever more wild adventures for our troops."[74] The legacy from the Reagan years on force was encapsulated in Weinberger's "six tests":

First, the United States should not commit forces to combat overseas unless the particular engagement or occasion is deemed vital to our national interest or that of our allies.

Second, if we decide it is necessary to put combat troops into a given situation we should do so wholeheartedly and with the clear intention of winning.

Third, if we do decide to commit forces to combat overseas, we should have clearly defined political and military objectives. . . .

Fourth, the relationship between our objectives and the forces we have committed . . . must be continually reassessed and adjusted if necessary.

Fifth, before the United States commits combat forces abroad, there must be some reasonable assurance we will have the support of the American people and their elected representatives in Congress. . . .

Finally, the commitment of United States forces to combat should be a last resort.[75]

These tests are a far cry from the force-friendly *National Security Strategy* published with much neo-conservative input and fanfare in September 2002 when Wolfowitz and Perle had assumed positions of power at the Pentagon. The doctrine they put into place did not derive from Reagan. In fact, their obsession with firepower had more in common with Madeleine Albright's approach to the Balkans. She records National Security Advisor Sandy Berger's objections to her position when he said, "[T]he way you people at the State Department talk about bombing, you sound like lunatics."[76] Rather than confirming current neo-conservative enthusiasm for the use of force, the Reagan legacy points in the opposite direction. The times are, of course, different in a number of ways: The threat of terrorism is more grievous but state sponsorship has declined. If the neo-conservatives wish to make the case for force, they should do so on its own merits, not through the crutch of a false history.

OPTIMISM VERSUS PESSIMISM

When the more technical analysis of Reagan's foreign policy philosophy and execution is laid aside, perhaps the more fundamental difference between him and today's neo-conservatives is one of temperament. As Shultz

---

[74] Ibid., p. 159.
[75] Ibid., pp. 433–45.
[76] Madeleine Albright, *Madame Secretary: A Memoir* (New York: Miramax, 2003), p. 383.

records, Reagan was optimistic; he "appealed to people's best hopes, not their fears."[77] His was a confidence that America itself was attractive in and of itself and that American ideals had an intrinsic appeal. By contrast, the neo-conservative vision is one of fear. Gliding past a long-established body of international relations thinkers and practitioners, their philosophy is centered around Hobbes's doomsday vision of man in his primitive state. They reject the notion – implicit in Reagan's striving for accord with the Soviet Union – that civilized nations can progress beyond the brutish state.[78]

As we have noted earlier, Leo Strauss had set the early neo-conservative tone of extreme pessimism about the future of American culture. The same pattern endures today. Within the country they look with horror at American society, which, in their view, has never recovered from the assault of Woodstock. They decry "lax multiculturalism" as the bane of society.[79] When they look at American youth, they do not see a hopeful future. Instead, they see "an adolescent plugged into a Walkman playing gangsta rap [who] represents a revolutionary and social phenomenon hardwired to the most extreme and corrupting influences."[80] Internationally, they do not see America walking tall and confident. Instead, they see the nation under siege from a coalition of *jihadists* shouting, "Let's conquer America."[81] Their views reflect deeply held beliefs. But, let it be noted, these dark thoughts are different in every way from the vision of America held by Ronald Reagan. It is thus hardly surprising that their conclusions deviate so radically from his.

A NEW POLITICAL ANIMAL

Thus, the neo-conservative assertion of a line of descent from Reagan's foreign policy is far-fetched. Reagan was a conservative but never a neo-conservative – either in content or in personality. As Carol Bell wrote of Reaganism in *Foreign Affairs* in 1984, "the hot soup of declaratory policy, as it emerges from the kitchen of the ideological cooks who prepare it, is always cooled a little by pragmatism before it is served up in the real world."[82] Reagan had presented the conflicts of international politics in essentially moral terms, and for this reason he looked like the president whom neo-conservatives had waited for. But as his declaratory policies gradually moved

---

[77] Shultz, *Turmoil and Triumph*, p. 1135.

[78] Hedley Bull, *The Anarchical Society: A Study of Order in World Politics* (London: Macmillan, 1977), pp. 46–51.

[79] Frum and Perle, *An End to Evil*, p. 97.

[80] Charles Krauthammer, "A Social Conservatives' Credo," *Public Interest*, fall 1995, p. 17.

[81] Pipes, *Militant Islam*, pp. 111–25.

[82] Carol Bell, "From Carter to Reagan," *Foreign Affairs*, America and the World, 1984, p. 490.

toward pragmatism, those events that seemed to be disasters in foreign policy to neo-conservatives appeared as major achievements to the moderates who were making the key decisions in the administration. Furthermore, the Reagan defense establishment remained dominated by these moderates – to the utter disappointment of the hard-line ideologues. By Reagan's second term, many neo-conservatives were disenchanted with the direction of American foreign policy. Despite the presence of individuals such as Kirkpatrick, Perle, and Abrams, Reagan had failed to fulfill neo-conservative hopes.

It was from this point that the neo-conservative movement began to witness its generational transition and, along with it, a characteristic change in nature. The younger neo-conservatives found themselves in a space left by the increasing difficulties of older neo-conservative views to provide a sufficient interpretive framework for the changing realities of international events. As Mikhail Gorbachev became leader of the Soviet Union in March 1985 and began to implement a series of domestic reforms alongside a more conciliatory approach toward the West, so neo-conservatism seemed to enter a state of confusion. Kirkpatrick's departure from the U.N. in the same year deprived the neo-conservatives of their most influential and highest level voice. Increasing congressional opposition to the administration's policy in Latin America and an absence of public support undermined neo-conservative hopes for a sustained campaign of backing the Nicaraguan Contras, despite Abrams's responsibility for handling the administration's Latin American affairs. The Iran-Contra scandal in 1986 made this certain. Meanwhile, the credibility of *Commentary*'s opposition to the concept of arms control agreements between Washington and Moscow was being undermined considerably by the progress of diplomacy between the two superpowers.[83]

As the Soviet bloc crumbled, so did Podhoretz's authority as a foreign policy commentator. The severity of *Commentary*'s line on the Soviet Union turned to inflexibility in the face of international events, and the journal lost both credibility and contributors. At decade's end, the era in which an article in *Commentary* might establish the basis for a policy initiative or lead to an appointment in government was gone.[84] Younger neo-conservatives began to assume the leadership roles that had long been held by Kirkpatrick, Irving Kristol, and Podhoretz. Accordingly, the terms of debate shifted. The new generation now embodied in those such as Charles Krauthammer, William Kristol, Muravchik, and Ben Wattenberg became engaged in updating neo-conservatism. The primacy given to opposing the Soviet threat gave way

---

[83] Ehrman, *Rise of Neoconservatism*, pp. 171–74.
[84] Ibid., pp. 170–71.

to confronting Iraq-style aggressive nationalisms.[85] Saddam Hussein's invasion of Kuwait in August 1990 was a reminder for these neo-conservatives that Western security was still dependent on Washington. Europe's failure to control the collapse of Yugoslavia into war and its inability to defy the aggression of the immensely inferior Bosnian Serb Army was yet another example. Concurrently, the return of war to the Balkans was an issue on which many older neo-conservatives such as Irving Kristol and Podhoretz were markedly mute. Now that the Soviet monolith was defeated, they were unable to identify any matter of urgent American concern in the sieges of Dubrovnik and Sarajevo.[86]

The difference in reaction of some of the older and younger neo-conservatives reflected both a changing of the guard and an acute realignment in perspective. Much of the older neo-conservative discourse on the brutal repressive and degenerate nature of communist regimes had been vindicated by their collapse. Yet though they had maintained a rigid defense of liberal democracy throughout the Cold War, these intellectuals subsequently recoiled from the idea of a democratic crusade following Soviet disintegration. Irving Kristol accepted that much of the neo-conservative ideological offensive against the USSR was essentially defensive. He argued that it was required in the circumstances created by the Cold War. Ehrman has observed that Moynihan spoke of supporting democratic states and forces but not of creating them and that Kirkpatrick offered a firm defense of liberal democracy, but only a defense, and not a call to begin movements to construct new ones.[87] Alternatively, the younger neo-conservative generation considered that even with the Cold War over, Washington should make an armed, preemptive crusade for global democracy the organizing principle of its foreign policy.[88] The bloodline for this model (which has the neo-conservative editorialists of the *Wall Street Journal* waxing enthusiastic about using taxpayer money for electricity and water services in Iraq) may be traced from Wilson via FDR, Kennedy, and Johnson to the "democratic enlargement" of the Clinton administration on which the same editorialists poured so much scorn.[89] This is not an ignoble lineage. If the neo-conservatives wish to claim

---

[85] Judis, p. 128.

[86] Ehrman, *Rise of Neoconservatism*, pp. 183–84.

[87] Ibid., pp. 184–90.

[88] John B. Judis, "Trotskyism to Anachronism: The Neoconservative Revolution," *Foreign Affairs*, July–August 1995, p. 128.

[89] Anthony Lake, "From Containment to Enlargement," remarks at Johns Hopkins University, School of Advanced International Studies, September 21, 1993, U.S. Department of State, *Dispatch* 4, no. 39 (September 27, 1993): pp. 658–64; "What $87 Billion Buys," *Wall Street Journal*, September 11, 2003, p. A18.

it, it would be more becoming and would make for better public policy if they did so openly and honestly, rather than deceptively calling on Reagan's name. Neo-conservatism is not updated Reaganism. It is a new political animal born of an unlikely mating of humanitarian liberalism and brute force.

6

Outreach to the Media and Evangelicals

"Soft power," as Joseph Nye explains, is "getting people to want what you want."[1] While the neo-conservatives spent the 1990s advocating the employment of "hard power" abroad, they made every effort to increase their soft power at home by forming relations with other political forces within the U.S. body politic. We have discussed above how the neo-conservatives' soft-power strategies involved building a shadow defense establishment across a number of think tanks and policy institutes, from which they were able to promote and disseminate their intellectual alternative for American foreign policy. These think tanks were supported by powerful sponsors. They published policy papers, sent open letters to the president, and hosted conferences and symposia attended by political notables of Washington, many of whom would subsequently move into senior policy-making positions.

This chapter looks at how neo-conservatives sought to establish support for their ideas by forging connections with the emerging cable news and political talk radio formats, the most popular of which, unlike the national TV networks, catered to a conservative-leaning listenership. These gave the neo-conservatives a point of purchase for their arguments in an otherwise generally liberal media environment. We also look at how they formed alliances with like-minded political groups within the Christian evangelical community.

If the neo-conservative case for war against Iraq was based on a strategy that aimed at dominating the political discourse, this strategy needed sympathetic news outlets in order to establish the case for war within the general

[1] Quoted in Noy Thurpkaew, "Culture: The Policies," in John Feffer, ed., *Power Trip: US Unilateralism and Global Strategy after September 11* (New York: Seven Stories Press, 2003), p. 108.

182

consciousness of the American public. Information collected by a number of polling firms between January and September of 2003 demonstrate that this effort was extremely successful. The polling data supported three significant conclusions: that a large majority of Americans held at least one fundamentally mistaken impression about the war in Iraq, that these misperceptions held by the public contributed to much of the popular support for the conflict, and that these false impressions derived largely from certain media outlets.[2]

NEO-CONSERVATIVES AND THE MEDIA POST–COLD WAR

The neo-conservatives long strived for the influence that they now enjoy. As we have argued, they were like a coiled spring before 9/11 and simply needed the right moment to translate the attacks into their frame of reference. The preceding decade had been a vital period for neo-conservatives, who had worked hard to capture and redirect what they believed had been a vacuous national debate.

The end of the Cold War saw America's interest in foreign affairs decline. Not only did newspapers run fewer stories about events overseas, but the topic had less and less salience in political debate. In 1996, only 7 percent of Americans had passports – and when talk of foreign lands was heard, it usually concerned a two-week idyll in sunny climes near clear waters. With the passing of the bipolar era and the Soviet threat, the outside world seemed dominated by little more than convulsive political and ethnic fragmentation in faraway regions that did not affect the daily life of Americans. Acclaimed writer and journalist David Halberstam subtitled the 1990s "when America napped." There seemed little reason not to. The strength of Clinton's presidential campaign, which sought to concentrate on domestic issues, such as the economy and welfare, ("It's the economy, stupid") encapsulated a return to the normal American focus on domestic affairs. Although Clinton's presidency saw increased expenditure in welfare programs and a record budget surplus, his foreign policies moved uncertainly across the uncharted terrain of the post–Cold War international order. As Chapter 3 discussed, questions about America's role in this new environment went largely unanswered. The neo-conservatives consequently endeavored to occupy this emerging conceptual and political space within the American media and public discourse. But this was not achieved through the strength of their ideas alone. They

---

[2] Frank Davies, "Polls: Most in U.S. Believe Key War Fallacies," *Miami Herald*, October 3, 2003, p. 3A.

received crucial help from three sources within the media: the cable news talk shows, talk radio, and a well-cultivated alliance with conservative populism – namely Protestant evangelical groups.

Political talk radio has been a feature of American political life since at least the 1930s, but in the late 1980s and throughout the 1990s it started to build significant audiences.[3] Some of these outlets – in parallel with the emerging cable news formats – started to offer a new and useful forum in which neo-conservatives could assert their idea of a world remade. Although by no means ideologically monolithic, these outlets offered a measure of conservative counterbalance to the major metropolitan newspapers, TV networks, and publicly supported broadcasters that are generally perceived as having a liberal leaning and that continue to be the sources from which most Americans obtain their news. Thus, although conservatives were working against an unfavorable mass background, the emerging news formats allowed them to achieve notable penetration among policy-making and politically active circles. Surveys by the American National Election Studies show that listeners to political talk radio identify themselves as 40 percent liberal and 57 percent conservative and tend to be "more knowledgeable about civics and current affairs than non-listeners."[4] Today, media outlets such as the *Wall Street Journal, Washington Times, New York Post, American Spectator, National Review, New York Sun, Weekly Standard*, Clear Channel radio, and the Fox News Channel ensure that conservatives are able to compete with the mass media. The latter two – both owned by media entrepreneur Rupert Murdoch, who has on a number of occasions given crucial support to the neo-conservative cause – became, in the decade after Soviet collapse, focal points in a conservative media phenomenon that served and continues to serve neo-conservatism well.

The Changing Face of the American Media

In the first decades of television, networks were heavily regulated by the government and felt obliged to demonstrate qualities of good citizenship and public service.[5] The major networks sought to emulate the high standards that had been established by BBC World Service radio programs. Although

---

[3] Richard Davis and Diana Owen, *New Media and American Politics* (New York: Oxford University Press, 1998), pp. 28–47.

[4] David C. Barker, *Rushed to Judgment* (New York: Columbia University Press, 2002), pp. 19–20.

[5] Leonard Downie, Jr., and Robert G. Kaiser, *The News about the News* (New York: Vintage, 2003), p. 142.

there were certainly many exceptions – and evidence of liberal bias – evening news programs sought an objective presentation of events like the war in Vietnam, which would have been a distant and largely invisible conflict only a decade earlier. But by the late 1970s and the early 1980s, TV news coverage had begun to change. With corporate mergers and acquisitions within the industry, television became a business that needed to show profits rather than a public information service. This emphasis and new Federal Communication Commission (FCC) regulations in the 1980s, which ended many public service requirements for broadcasters, significantly changed the industry.[6] Moreover, with the creation of CNN in 1980 and other cable networks, such as MSNBC and Fox News, another dimension was suddenly available to the viewing audience. Americans could now obtain news on demand through cable – a phenomenon that continues today. Continuing attempts at corporate consolidation brought a reaction from the Senate in September 2003, however, when a resolution was approved limiting further mergers that might limit variety and local points of view in the news. Among those impacted was Fox News. Fox was ratings-driven, widely popular, and at the forefront of a new kind of opinion news, placing it at the center of these developments.

The Fox News Channel, founded in 1996, hosted the most widely viewed programs on cable. In the 1990s the significance of the Fox network may be seen in its dramatic transformation of the news format. Its talk shows differed substantially from the classic network television seen during the 1950s and 1960s. Fox News was designed as something to be sold to subscribers. Ratings were everything. As one Fox presenter commented, "How do I know if I'm doing a good job? . . . I use my ratings."[7] Thus, its style was not so much informative, but rather opportunistic, often emotional, and based on providing entertainment. The host, though inquisitive, was also combative, interrogative, and not hesitant to show disdain or disapproval. The views of the guest were often not as important as that of the presenter and his editorial staff. Such an example is found in the first week of October 2003, when the American public, journalists, and politicians across the nation were riveted by the revelation that the administration had leaked the name of a covert CIA officer to journalists. The officer in question was the wife of Ambassador Joseph Wilson, who had poured cold water on the administration's contention that Saddam Hussein had sought "yellowcake" from Niger for

---

[6] Ibid., p. 142.
[7] Greta Van Susteren, *My Turn at the Bully Pulpit: Straight Talk about the Things That Drive Me Nuts* (New York: Crown, 2003), p. 21.

his nuclear program. Although the Justice Department opened a formal investigation and later appointed a special prosecutor, significantly, the story did not appear among the top twenty on the Fox News Web site. In contrast to all other news agencies, an issue that was of central interest to the public had less priority than stories about levels of homework for students and a legal case over the name of a baseball team.

What is important to our discussion is that when the neo-conservatives advanced their carefully crafted political discourse designed to meld the "War on Terrorism" into a case for war against Iraq, this media culture was invaluable, as was its partisan support.

The involvement of several senior Fox executives in Republican Party activities raises the question of whether the network sought to shape the news environment around its political preferences and, particularly, whether it has purposefully sought to present White House policy in the best possible light. This was certainly the effect after September 11, not only by providing a neo-conservative interpretation of events, but also by reporting the news within the context of a continual and ongoing crisis – for months – and well after life had generally returned to normal. At a time when many Americans turned to the television for clarification and information, Fox implied terror was always just around the corner.[8] The Fox "Terror Alerts" took place with a frequency that, by any reasonable calculation, went beyond the facts. Americans now watched Fox in fear of an impending catastrophe as much as for informative coverage. The network thus evolved into an electronic tabloid, continuously engaging people's emotions of fear, dread, anger, and revenge. Fox's newscasts became strangely different from the other outlets; more important, Fox's breathless hyper-developments and the neo-conservative "discourse" went hand in hand.

MURDOCH AND THE NEO-CONSERVATIVES

It not surprising that the paths of Murdoch and the neo-conservatives converged in the 1990s. Murdoch asserted his strong personal and business attachments with Israel, and, like many neo-conservatives, he has received recognition in the United States for his support of Israel. The American Jewish Congress of New York voted Murdoch "Communications Man of the Year" in 1982. Moreover, his position on Israel has been enough to force correspondents to resign when their stories did not conform to the approved

---

[8] Douglas Kellner, *From 9/11 to Terror War: The Dangers of the Bush Legacy* (Lanham, Md.: Rowman and Littlefield, 2003), p. 69.

line. A former correspondent for the *London Times*, Sam Kiley, provides a case in point. He resigned after a disagreement over a story involving an incident on the West Bank. Kiley said, "No pro-Israel lobbyist ever dreamed of having such power over a great national newspaper."[9]

With Murdoch's financial assistance, the modern neo-conservative voice came to be heard in magazines, newspapers, and TV news networks.[10] The Murdoch empire grew over the 1990s to include Fox Broadcasting Network; Fox Television Stations (consisting of more than twenty U.S. TV stations and the largest American station group, with coverage of 40 percent of U.S. TV households); and Fox News Channel; a major share in other U.S. and global cable networks, including Sky Television, Star TV, and DirecTV; major shares in the National Geographic Channel, Fox Kids Worldwide, and the Fox Family Channel; more than 130 newspapers, including the *London Times* and *New York Post*; some twenty-five magazines, including the *Weekly Standard* and *TV Guide*; and the publishing companies HarperCollins and Regan Books.[11] As of March 31, 2003, Murdoch's News Corporation had reported total assets of approximately $42 billion and total revenues at $17 billion.[12] Thus as a neo-conservative ally, projecting and conveying its perspectives through the lens of U.S. media, he added a critical dimension to the neo-conservative effort.

Since its founding in 1995, William Kristol has remained editor of the *Weekly Standard*. As mentioned in previous chapters, this is the neo-conservative flagship publication. Unlike other journals and magazines for which neo-conservatives write, it is entirely a creation of the neo-conservative movement. In his lengthy discussion of Murdoch and his media empire, *Atlantic Monthly* journalist James Fallows comments that he "found only one illustration of Murdoch's using his money and power for blatantly political ends: his funding of the *Weekly Standard*."[13] As Howard Kurtz of the *Washington Post* notes, the *Weekly Standard* has operated at a financial loss ever since it was founded. The magazine has achieved no significant increase in its circulation from the original 60,000, of which many are gratis mailings. But it has, however, succeeded in a main purpose, namely to provide legitimacy for Kristol and other staffers in their role as "experts" on Fox

---

[9] Richard Curtiss, "Rupert Murdoch and William Kristol: Using the Press to Advance Israel's Interests," *Washington Report on Middle East Affairs*, June 2003, pp. 24–26.

[10] Joe Hagan, "President Bush's Neo-Conservatives Were Spawned in New York," *New York Observer*, April 28, 2003, p. 6.

[11] Eric Alterman, *What Liberal Media?* (New York: Basic Books, 2003), p. 235.

[12] http://corp.com/investor/index.html.

[13] James Fallows, "The Age of Murdoch," *Atlantic Monthly*, September 2003, p. 90.

and MSNBC television where *Weekly Standard* contributors have become recognized faces. These platforms have, in turn, allowed neo-conservatives to establish themselves as experts providing an important perspective on the major networks' Sunday talk shows. David Brooks, Kristol, and Perle, for example, have often appeared as writers of the *Weekly Standard* and thus apparent notables in Washington's media-political scene, as have Wolfowitz, Krauthammer, Kagan, Fred Barnes, and Morton Kondrake.

NEO-CONSERVATIVES EXPAND ACROSS THE PRINT MEDIA

In Kristol's own words during the Second Iraq War: "Many people at Fox News have been supportive of Bush's foreign policy. They deserve a bit of mention. And Murdoch personally."[14] But Murdoch was never the sole sponsor of neo-conservatism in the media. As mentioned in Chapter 2, several Washington think tanks received funding from conservative foundations, such as the Bradley Foundation, the Olin Foundation, Scaife, and the Smith Richardson Foundation. These institutions similarly provided the financial basis for a conservative print media that served neo-conservatism well. By the end of the 1990s, neo-conservatives had receptive editors across a range of publications, including the *New York Post*, the *New Republic, Commentary*, the *National Review*, the *New York Sun*, the *American Spectator,* the *New Yorker,* the *Washington Times,* the *Wall Street Journal,* and, of course, the *Weekly Standard*.

As Mark Gerson notes, financing for neo-conservatism in the media has also come from New York entrepreneurs such as Bruce Kovner, chairman of the Caxton Corporation, and Roger Hertog, the vice chairman of Alliance Capital management. Both men helped to fund the *New York Sun* and also joined Martin Peretz as co-owners of the *New Republic*, which became, in the decade before September 11, another focal point for neo-conservative opinion. As neo-conservative business intellectuals, both Kovner and Hertog sit on the board of the Manhattan Institute, where Gerson and Kristol are trustees, as well as on the roster of AEI (Hagan, "Spawned in New York").

Backed by sympathetic and powerful sponsors as the 1990s progressed, neo-conservatives were able to publish increasing amounts of material in the U.S. print media. The *New York Post* became a forum for intellectuals such as John Podhoretz, whom Murdoch moved from the *Weekly Standard* to supervise the newspaper's editorial page.

---

[14] Joe Hagan, "Spawned in New York," *New York Observer*, April 28, 2003, p. 6.

As indicated above, the conservative media complex grew as many of those writing for the conservative publications became regulars on the cable talk show circuit dominated by MSNBC and the Murdoch derivatives. Rich Lowry, editor of the conservative publication the *National Review*, became a well-known figure on Fox News, as did a number of the magazine's contributors, such as neo-conservative intellectual Michael Ledeen, and other notables, such as David Frum, Jonah Goldberg, and John Podhoretz. The *National Review* shared its sponsors with other conservative publications, such as the *American Spectator*, *Commentary*, and the *New Criterion*.

But the significance of such neo-conservative links to a broadly conservative media empire that grew over the 1990s lies not simply in the fact that these intellectuals raised their public profiles over time. The crucial aspect of this discussion is that when the time came to define the events of 9/11 and sell a new policy, the media infrastructure was already in place to carry the discourse. If the state of U.S. TV networks was conducive to the dissemination of neo-conservative ideology after the terrorist attacks, American radio was waiting ready with a near conservative monopoly on the airwaves.

THE PRIMACY OF CONSERVATIVE RADIO

In March 2003, Clear Channel Radio Stations sponsored rallies in Atlanta, Cleveland, and San Antonio, replete with country music and tailgate parties, supporting the administration's stance against Saddam Hussein. Attendance was reported to be near 20,000 at each. Called "Rally for America," the events were criticized by some, such as *Chicago Tribune* national correspondent Tim Jones, who pointed out that "while labor unions and special interest groups have organized and hosted rallies for decades, the involvement of a big publicly regulated broadcasting company breaks new ground in public demonstrations."[15] It is unusual for a publicly regulated broadcast company to become involved in this type of demonstration. Former FCC Commissioner Glen Robinson said, "I can't say this violates any of a broadcaster's obligations, but it sounds like borderline manufacturing of the news."[16] This was reflective of the remarkable role that conservative radio had achieved.

In a Senate committee meeting of May of 2002, the topic of discussion was the impending FCC regulations that would allow mergers to take place in both the print and broadcast media, effectively relaxing the controls on

---

[15] Tim Jones, "Media Giant's Rally Sponsorship Raises Questions," *Chicago Tribune*, March 19, 2003, p. 6.
[16] Ibid.

how many outlets a company or individual could own.[17] Murdoch would have much to gain by a change in these regulations, enabling him to buy additional TV stations. The networks would be able to own stations reaching 45 percent of the market, up from 35 percent. When Murdoch was questioned by Democratic Senator Byron regarding a bias in the media, he quoted the Fox News slogan that "his news organizations always strove to be fair and balanced." The senator then asked Murdoch to explain the fact that his radio networks had 300-plus hours of nationally syndicated conservative talk each week, versus five hours of liberal talk.[18] If there is a debate over whether Fox *is or is not* the voice of conservative opinion, talk radio certainly *is*. As Eric Alterman says in his book *What Liberal Media?*, even the "usual suspects" would not dispute the dominance of conservative talk radio, as its coverage is so extensive.[19] The limited amount of liberal talk without high-profile liberal personalities put conservative radio hosts and their viewpoints in the majority. Some of the better known conservative hosts include Sean Hannity, Don Imus, Laura Ingraham, G. Gordon Liddy, Rush Limbaugh, Oliver North, Laura Schlessinger, and Armstrong Williams, to name a few.[20] There is nothing illegitimate about this. It is the market speaking. As former congressman J. C. Watts, now a director of Clear Channel, puts it, "the dogs ain't eating the dog food" offered by liberals.[21] The powerful partisan forces behind talk radio were another important plank in the media infrastructure that carried the neo-conservative discourse after 9/11.

Rush Limbaugh has become a leading conservative radio talk voice, with the largest market share on radio. His show is reported to have between fifteen and twenty million listeners, and the number of stations airing his show has been as high as 650.[22] Listeners have stayed loyal even after his acknowledged problems with drugs. Espousing a combination of partisan straight-talk and blue-collar truisms, he has garnered respect in the media community and is a powerful conservative voice. He has been a White House guest and was honored by sitting next to Barbara Bush at a State of the

[17] These changes would have taken effect on September 4, 2003, but were blocked by an appeals court. The present stay preserves current regulations while the court conducts a review.

[18] Jones, "Media Giant's Rally." p. 84.

[19] Alterman, *What Liberal Media?*, p. 70.

[20] Report by Scarborough Research, a joint venture between Arbitron, Inc., and VNU Media Measurement & Information, May 15, 2002. Cf. ibid., p. 70.

[21] Jeff Sharlet, "Big World: How Clear Channel Programs America," *Harper's Magazine*, December 2003, p. 43.

[22] Jim Rutenberg, "Despite Other Voices, Limbaugh's Is Still Strong," *New York Times*, April 24, 2000, p. C1; Howard Kurtz, "Limbaugh, Post-Clinton: Dining Happily on What's Left," *Washington Post*, May 7, 2001, p. C1.

Union address. Limbaugh was, after Newt Gingrich, credited with helping Republicans to take back the House in 1994. In October of 2001, Tony Blankley, former Press Secretary to Speaker of the House Newt Gingrich and now editor of the *Washington Times* editorial page, said:

After Newt, Rush was the single most important person in securing a Republican majority in the House of Representatives after 40 years of Democratic rule. Rush's powerful voice was the indispensable factor, not only in winning 1994, but in holding the House for the next three election cycles. At a time when almost the entire establishment media ignored or distorted our message of renewal, Rush carried (and often improved) the message to the heartland. And where Rush led, the other voices of talk radio followed.[23]

Rush Limbaugh's broadcasts have also had an impact on George Bush's presidency. He is a conservative force that delivers his message with great effect. Limbaugh is credited with generating support for Bush when he opposed Senator John McCain in the 2000 presidential primaries. William Kristol, a McCain supporter, said of Limbaugh: "He helped make it the orthodox conservative position that McCain was utterly unacceptable and also that Bush was fine, neither of which were intuitively obvious if you're a conservative."[24] Blankley summed up the powerful effect of Limbaugh on George W. Bush's win of the presidency in 2000: "Given the closeness of the election, but for Rush Limbaugh's broadcasts, we would now be led by President Al Gore."[25] As E. J. Dionne points out in the *Washington Post* about Limbaugh:

Limbaugh's new respectability is the surest sight that the conservative talk network is now bleeding into what passes for the mainstream media, just as the unapologetic conservatism of the Fox News Channel is now affecting programming on the other cable networks. The shift to the right is occurring as cable becomes a steadily more important source of news.[26]

Clear Channel's radio station ownership has enjoyed phenomenal growth in the United States. With only forty-five stations in 1995, it now has over 1,200 and claims 110 million listeners across the country – in all states and the District of Columbia. Their growth coincided with the point at which the FCC rules were changed regarding ownership regulations (the Telecommunications Act) in 1996, enabling the company to expand rapidly.

Clear Channel also owns 26 percent – the largest share – of the Hispanic Broadcasting Corporation (HBC), the leader in Spanish language radio

---

[23] Tony Blankley, "Rush's Show Goes On," *Washington Times*, October 10, 2001.
[24] Alterman, *What Liberal Media?*, p. 75.
[25] Blankley, "Rush's Show Goes On."
[26] E. J. Dionne, "The Rightward Press," *Washington Post*, December 6, 2002, p. A45.

stations in the United States. Like Fox News, Clear Channel is hopeful that the FCC will relax the regulations regarding media ownership so that it can consolidate HBC with Univision Communications, the market leader in Spanish-language television, cable, and music. The $2.4 billion deal would create a new company that would effectively control almost "70 percent of Spanish-language advertising revenue in the United States."[27] Should the merger proceed, it would be of clear benefit in expanding the presentation of neo-conservative views. Unlike Fox News, Clear Channel openly claims to be conservative and supportive of the administration – which seeks to court the Hispanic voter. In addition to Clear Channel's phenomenal radio reach, it owns some 750,000 outdoor advertising displays, including billboards, and transit panels around the world. According to their Web site, "no one else can even begin to match our strength in numbers," which enables them to "reach over half of the entire U.S. population and over 75% of the entire U.S. Hispanic population." And that, Clear Channel says, has not only a tremendous reach but also a "tremendous amount of presence power." Clear Channel also owns thirty-nine TV stations.[28]

Clear Channel joined other like-minded outlets in forming a powerful information infrastructure supportive of the administration's objectives in the post-9/11 period. Neo-conservatives had, for all intents and purposes, an ideological monopoly on talk radio both because of the celebrity of conservative hosts and because of the sheer number of stations that projected their assumptions and policy proscriptions nation-wide.

PUBLIC MISPERCEPTIONS, THE U.S. MEDIA, AND THE IRAQ WAR

As will be explained in the following chapter, the case for war against Iraq was built through discursive strategies and practices that caused the American public to perceive an (as yet) unproven link between 9/11 and Iraq.[29] Empirical evidence shows that the media outlets were fundamental in this process. From January to September 2003, seven different polls were conducted jointly by two polling networks that analyzed the perceptions of the American public toward the war with Iraq. The data demonstrated that in the lead-up to the war and during the postwar period, a large section of the American public held a number of misperceptions that played a vital

---

[27] Eric Boehlert, salon.com, April 24, 2003.
[28] This information comes from the company's own publicity materials.
[29] The title of this section and much of the data are taken from the survey "Misperceptions, the Media and the Iraq War," conducted by the Program on International Policy Attitudes and Knowledge Networks Poll, October 2, 2003.

role in creating and sustaining support for the decision to go to war. For example: Significant numbers of the U.S. electorate believed Iraq to have been directly involved in the attacks of 9/11; that Iraq and al-Qaeda were linked; that weapons of mass destruction were found in Iraq after the war; that Iraq actually used weapons of mass destruction during the war; and that world opinion generally approved of America's going to war. The polls show that these data are derived, to a great extent, from how certain media outlets portrayed events. The results of the seven polls, which were fielded using a nation-wide panel of some 10,000 randomly selected respondents, revealed that these misperceptions did not originate from a failure to pay attention, but rather from paying greater attention to particular news networks.

Analysis of the respondents illustrated that the frequency of misperceptions varied significantly according to the respondent's primary source of news, and that those who principally watched Fox News were far more likely to have these misperceptions than those who did not. In testing the frequency of three specific mistaken impressions – that evidence of links between Iraq and al-Qaeda had been found, that weapons of mass destruction had been discovered in Iraq, and that world public opinion approved of America's going to war – results showed that Fox News watchers were by far the most likely to hold these views and were three times more likely to hold all three. The audiences of NPR/PBS, however, consistently demonstrated a majority who did not hold any of the three views. Some 80 percent of Fox viewers and 71 percent of CBS viewers held one or more of the three perceptions, while the equivalent percentage of viewers for NBC and CNN was 55 percent in both instances. Although the percentage of viewers who held all three misperceptions in the case of NBC and CNN was 13 percent and 12 percent, respectively, the portion of Fox viewers who held all three was 45 percent. The percentage of viewers for CNN and NBC who did not hold any of the three misconceptions was 45 percent in both cases, while the amount of Fox viewers who were without misperception was 20 percent.

These data are decidedly significant to the discussion on how the neoconservatives were able to influence the decision in favor of war with Iraq for two reasons: First, they significantly contributed to the platform of American support for the decision to go to war, and second, Fox consistently commanded among the higher audience ratings in the United States.

It is important to note that these variations in misperceptions according to news source cannot be explained merely in terms of political preference or the characteristics of each audience. It is certainly the case that audiences reflect differing demographics including socio-economic, ethnic, age, education, and party preference. But the polling study revealed, by examining misperceptions within the specific demographic groups such as political affiliation, that the variations in level of misperception across a specific demographic category remained consistent in accordance with the news source. Put another way, while the level of misperception differed to a limited degree in accordance with political positions, within the groups that supported or opposed the administration, the level of misperception still depended crucially on the news source.

A natural assumption when looking at the public's interpretation of international events would be that misperceptions in foreign policy derive from a failure to pay attention to news and that those with greater exposure to news would have fewer mistaken impressions. But in the case of Fox News, the polling data demonstrated clearly that the more attention viewers paid to that network, the greater the likelihood that they would hold serious misperceptions such as the proven existence of weapons of mass destruction in Iraq or Saddam Hussein's links to 9/11. That those with higher exposure to Fox News and CBS News were more likely to misperceive and support the war in Iraq is a telling commentary on how little these networks concentrated on the objective provision of information. A remark by a senior CBS journalist gives the game away: "Covering the war was the great, pure authentic experience of my career. . . . I was in the enchanted forest."[30]

Building an Echo Chamber into the U.S. Media

Shortly before the bombing campaign began in Afghanistan, an anonymous military officer told the *Washington Post*, "This is the most information-intensive war you can imagine . . . we are going to lie about things."[31] Regardless, there was a grain of truth in what he said. The administration seemed intent, from the early stages of the war, to sell a policy that relied as much on the media as on the official statements of government officials. In waging a war of words to provide the basis for a war of weapons, the media was of paramount significance, and the extent to which the media outlets underpinned the successful formulation of a neo-conservative foreign policy was of great importance. They amplified the administration's discursive rationale, broadly advancing the public neo-conservative policy agenda. Beyond the presentation of policy objectives, this process had the effect of diminishing and marginalizing dissenting voices arising from other

[30] Bill Katovsky and Timothy Lyons, *Embedded: The Media at War in Iraq* (Guilford, Conn.: Lyons, 2003), p. 23.
[31] Quoted in Thurpkaew, "Culture," p. 113.

sections of the policy community. It had created, in effect, an echo chamber, in which the administration's rationale was repeated and sustained in primary and secondary circumstances, such that opinion was formed and then reinforced through the endless repetition of neo-conservative themes.

With 9/11, TV and cable networks, American talk radio, and Internet sites were an extensive media complex that quite simply sprang into operation in the days and weeks that followed. Fox News presented leading conservative foreign policy authorities such as Jeane Kirkpatrick and Newt Gingrich on television almost at once with their theories about how the West was now effectively at war with Islam, how Saddam Hussein was quite possibly involved in the attack, and how he must be removed. This sort of analysis became standard fare across the networks, as neo-conservatives seemingly appeared from all directions to interpret and define this historical moment. The various and many conservative TV and radio stations immediately began a sustained bombardment of aggressive rhetoric forging a national consensus around the need for broad military action. As the administration defined the abstract discourse of a war on terror, the American public endured endless slogans, such as "War on America" and "America at War," which saturated the many conservative-sponsored fora of public debate. Talk Radio went so far as to call for general violence against Arabs and Muslims and even nuclear retaliation and global war. Radio shows became hyperdramatic, featuring patriotic war music for days. Neo-conservatives and their allies were now able to infuse the TV networks and radio programs with their views, which they duly did.[32]

Thus, by the time that speechwriters and neo-conservative officials within the administration began to construct the notional discourse, half of the task had already been completed by the overwhelming and sensational coverage from much of the America media. As one experienced CNN correspondent observed, "to a certain extent, my station was intimidated by the administration."[33] The period after the terrorist attacks is testimony to how the echo chamber effect became even more invasive as ideas first presented on television and on the radio talk shows were repeated in conversations among family and friends, thus gaining acceptance as valid and eventually as conventional wisdom. The impact of this process on the national policy debate, where public concerns about and knowledge of international issues are essential, has been insidious and negative. In the sense that accurate public information on international issues, and the policies that address them, is

---

[32] Kellner, *From 9/11*, pp. 60–65.
[33] Paul Krugman, "Lessons in Civility," *New York Times*, October 10, 2003, p. A31.

essential to put tension in the dialogue to create rational decisions, the echo chamber as described disabled a fundamental aspect of democratic governance. This media environment would become crucial in turning a terrorist attack into a justification to remove Saddam Hussein.

NEO-CONSERVATIVES AND CHRISTIAN CONSERVATIVES

If the neo-conservative media discourse after 9/11 presented a binary interpretation of the event casting it as an apocalyptic contest between good and evil, it found support and common ground among domestic Christian conservative groups. Commentators such as Jerry Falwell and Christian Broadcast Network President Pat Robertson offered similarly Messianic accounts of the event. Falwell and Robertson agreed with other conservative segments of opinion that American liberals, such as Bill Clinton, had paved the way for this event. While the Christian media figures argued that this was because of the manner in which the "liberals, feminists, gays and the ACLU" had enraged God, Fox News commentators suggested that it derived from Clinton's lapses in security.[34] But this was by no means the first time that neo-conservatism and Christian conservatives had converged.

As first-generation neo-conservative Peter Berger noted, the religious right had often found itself fighting from the same corner as the neo-conservatives, if for slightly different reasons. Just as neo-conservative intellectuals reacted to the counterculture and its effect on American society in the latter 1960s and early 1970s, so the evangelicals considered that the cultural revolution flew in the face of important American values. Both groups placed a high value on the role of religion in daily life and saw the emergence of an increasingly secular society as a threat to this role. An early battleground for Christian conservative groups became education. As the impact of the counterculture found its way into public schools, the religious right became engaged in political battles over curricula and textbooks. Again a few years later, just as the neo-conservatives reacted strongly to Carter, so did the religious right. When, as Democratic Party nominee, Carter had declared himself "born again," evangelicals pinned great hopes on the Carter presidency. But any positive support from the religious right rapidly soured as Carter failed to live up to expectations. The White House Conference on the Family in 1980 sealed the evangelical disenchantment with the Democratic president. To accommodate the so-called alternative life-styles heralded by the changing culture, the name of the conference was, in a fit of

---

[34] Kellner, *From 9/11*, pp. 57–60.

what is now called "political correctness," changed to the White House Conference on *Families*. The religious right promptly reacted by sponsoring a variety of profamily networks and political organizations to mobilize sentiment.[35]

This cycle of hope and disappointment, which characterized much of the evangelical relationship with mainstream American politics from the 1960s onward, once again put Christian conservatives and the neo-conservatives into a position of shared disenchantment after Reagan captured the White House in 1980. In a manner similar to that of the neo-conservatives, evangelicals had mobilized support for Reagan in the 1980 campaign under the tutelage of conservative Christian figures such as Falwell. Both neo-conservatives and the religious right were enticed by the firm rhetoric of Reagan's election campaign. As he subsequently softened certain of his early foreign policy positions and statements and moderated his approach, he disappointed many neo-conservatives. Similarly, he modified positions he had earlier taken on abortion, prayer in schools, and other issues dear to the hearts of evangelicals. Once more, there was common ground in the views of neo-conservatism and the religious right.[36]

As previously noted, the disappointment among evangelicals galvanized into renewed political effort and greater levels of organization, which built to a climax in 1988 with the presidential campaign of Pat Robertson. This event also marked a significant turning point at which evangelicals rejected the traditional notion that Christian morality implied a nonpartisan approach to politics. It signified recognition that the Democratic Party was feckless in the "culture wars" and unreliable in battling for the values of the Christian right. Hence, the movement determined to exercise influence by building close political ties to the Republican Party. Neo-conservatism and the religious right both emerged in the 1990s as essentially Republican forces. Led by Ralph Reed, a talented political strategist, Robertson's Christian Coalition played a decisive role in the midterm elections of 1990 and 1994. Like neo-conservatism, the religious right became a strong force for criticism in the media against the Clinton White House. It may be noted, therefore, that although neo-conservatism and the evangelical political movement started from very different points, they both experienced some of the same hopes and disappointments during the Carter and Reagan administrations, and by the Clinton administration, their paths were tending to converge along essentially parallel courses of development, namely of discontent with an

---

[35] Peter Berger, "Democracy and the Religious Right," *Commentary*, January 1997, p. 54.
[36] Ibid.

increasingly secular society and the unwillingness of the political class to do anything about it.[37]

Under the auspices of its second generation in the 1990s, neo-conservatism extended its links with evangelical groups to include foreign and defense policy. The Project for the New American Century (PNAC) forged links with social conservatives such as Gary Bauer. Christian conservative groups such as Empower America and the Foundation for the Defense of Democracy (FDOD) came to support the neo-conservative ambition of a conservative internationalism overseas. Former Education Secretary and co-signatory of PNAC statement of principles William Bennett helped to bridge the gap between neo-conservatism and social conservatism. With Jack Kemp, Bennett founded Empower America in 1999 as a conservative policy group designed to encourage conservative moral values. Kristol and Bennett also teamed up with prolife leaders, such as Bauer, executive director of Christian Legal Society, Samuel Casey, president of the Christian Coalition, Roberta Combs, chairman of the Religious Freedom Coalition, and William Murray, in sending open letters to the White House on issues such as human cloning, while urging Congress to pass legislation banning certain types of cloning and abortion. After 9/11, Empower America and the FDOD helped to carry the administration's message across the media. Neo-conservative figures such as National Security Council official Elliott Abrams (who has a long-standing interest in religious affairs (on which he has published extensively) were also instrumental in helping to promote the links between Washington's neo-conservatives and Christian evangelicals, sometimes serving as advocates for issues of importance to religious groups such as sex trafficking and AIDS.[38]

The support of conservative religious media figures and their outlets provided momentum for the neo-conservative discourse. A survey released by a fundamentalist Christian group in 2002 reported that 69 percent of conservative Christians favored military action against Baghdad, some ten points more than the U.S. adult population in general.[39] The links in ideology between neo-conservatives and evangelicals grew more obvious after 9/11. Robertson was now able to join those such as Ledeen in taking quotations from the Koran as evidence that Islam "is not a peaceful religion."[40]

---

[37] Ibid., pp. 54–55.

[38] Elizabeth Bumiller, "Evangelicals Sway White House on Human Rights Issues Abroad," *New York Times*, October 26, 2003, p. A1.

[39] Jim Lobe, "Conservative Christians Biggest Backers of Iraq War," *Inter-Press Service*, October 10, 2002.

[40] Pat Robertson, "The Roots of Terrorism and a Strategy for Victory," Address to the Economic Club of Detroit, March 25, 2002.

Robertson cited events from the year 632 as evidence that a permanent jihad against those who were not part of the Islamic tradition was inherent in Islam. He could now link terrorism directly to the demand for greater support of Israel, by claiming that America had been at war for thirty years with fanatical terrorists from the Middle East. Like Ledeen and other neo-conservatives, Robertson advocated supporting democratic insurgencies in the region and spoke of Iraq as "a source of terror and deadly terror with biological, nuclear and chemical warfare."[41] Franklin Graham, the son of Billy Graham and head of Samaritan's Purse, a Christian relief organization, spoke in a similar vein. Together they found common ground with neo-conservative figures such as Daniel Pipes and Michael Ledeen in helping to project an ever more hostile backdrop of commentary toward Arab and Islamic culture in the mainstream TV and print media.

In parallel with hostility toward Islam, scriptural considerations based on the evangelical view of Israel as the site for the second coming of Christ tended to fuel support for Israel in general and for the Likud Party in particular. As Middle East tensions rose after the failure of the Camp David initiative, Ralph Reed joined together with Rabbi Yechiel Eckstein to found the Stand for Israel, designed to mobilize political support among the grassroots Christian Community for the state of Israel and later the war on terror. The group was created out of the International Fellowship of Christians and Jews (IFCJ), which has been a central forum for promoting the relationship between evangelical Christians and American Jews since 1983. A survey conducted after 9/11 showed that 56 percent of evangelical Christians, when asked to cite the most important reasons why they supported Israel, referred to its alliance with America in the war against terrorism. Neo-conservative Daniel Pipes remarked in July 2003, "To those who wonder why Washington follows policies so different from the European states, a large part of the answer these days has to do with the clout of Christian Zionists."[42]

Thus, neo-conservatives had built up a range of media outlets and national fora that enabled them to underpin their policy interpretations to the many constituents of the American public. The cable networks, the conservative talk radio shows, and the conservative print outlets were all in place to carry the abstract war into the governing philosophy of American foreign policy by inundating people with the discursive reality created by neo-conservatives. The neo-conservatives, both in and out of the administration, inserted

---

[41] Ibid.
[42] Daniel Pipes, "Israel's Best Weapon?" *New York Post*, July 15, 2003.

themselves into this environment before 9/11 and benefited from it afterward. It was the arm with which they represented their views to the larger segments of the American body politic. It was the machinery that synthesized the popular mindset that proved so critical in making war with Saddam Hussein.

7

Iraq

The False Pretenses

> Ladies and Gentlemen, these are not assertions. These are *facts*. . . .
>
> > Secretary of State Colin Powell,
> > Presentation to the U.N. Security Council,
> > February 6, 2003

> The open question is how many stocks they had, if any, and if they had any, where did they go? And if they didn't have any, then why wasn't that known beforehand?
>
> > Colin Powell, January 24, 2004

Days before the second anniversary of 9/11, a *Washington Post* poll revealed that seven in ten Americans thought Saddam Hussein had played a direct part in the terrorist attacks.[1] There were many reasons to indict Saddam and to welcome his removal, but this was not one of them. That the American people two years after 9/11 entertained such demonstrable misperceptions about who was responsible for the most significant event in the nation's recent history should not be a matter of pride for any of us. An uninformed democracy is a vulnerable democracy. But these misperceptions should surprise no one. They arose as the result of deliberate government action.

This is the theme of this chapter, rather than the merits of the Iraq undertaking and whether it is likely to be successful. In a region as ancient and complex as the Middle East, success or failure will emerge over a long period. After World War I, the British spent some forty years in Iraq, only to be taken by surprise by the 1958 revolution that put an end to the

---

[1] Dana Milbank and Claudia Deane, "Hussein Link to 9/11 Lingers in Many Minds," *Washington Post*, September 6, 2003, p. A1.

pro-British monarchy.[2] So any judgment at this time is likely to be speculative and subjective. It makes little sense to measure success, as neo-conservatives tend to do, in terms of electricity produced or schools painted.[3] The evidence is already at hand that the prime advocates of the Iraq war – notably the neo-conservatives who had been advocating this course since the end of the first Gulf war – did not level with the American people. They offered the image of a "cakewalk," keeping quiet about the true dimensions of their objectives, which involved a vast project for reengineering the political, cultural, economic, and religious face of the Middle East: Iraq at the beginning, with Syria, Iran, and Saudi Arabia to follow.[4] Instead of putting this case to the American people and seeking their support, they spun a web of deception with a reason "du jour" being offered other than the truth. Wolfowitz would later acknowledge that Iraq's supposed supply of WMD had never been the most compelling case for war: "For bureaucratic reasons we settled on one issue, weapons of mass destruction, because it was the one reason everyone could agree on."[5]

Our theme in this chapter addresses this great conjuring trick. We show how the trick was used to fashion a "political discourse" that hard-wired the public mind to link a global assault on al-Qaeda with a territorial assault on Iraq. We call this process the "discursive representation of reality."[6] Among others, Kathleen Hall Jamieson, Dean of the Annenberg School of Communication at Columbia University, has described the phenomenon as the creation of "frames." She notes that presidential power lies in the ability to "develop and disseminate frames or interpretations that are accepted by the press and the public and as a result become the lenses of which they are unaware but nonetheless shape how we think about political affairs."[7] Harvard professor Pippa Norris uses the frame analysis to look at the media's treatment of terrorism.[8]

[2] John Keay, *Sowing the Wind* (New York: W. W. Norton, 2003), pp. 346–49.

[3] David Frum and Richard Perle, *An End to Evil: How to Win the War on Terror* (New York: Random House, 2003), p. 39.

[4] Kenneth Adelman, "Cakewalk in Iraq," *Washington Post*, February 13, 2002, p. A27.

[5] Sam Tanenhaus, "Bush's Brain Trust," *Vanity Fair*, July 2003, p. 145.

[6] The subject of the language underpinning American foreign policy after September 11, 2001, is fully addressed in Sol Garcia Estrada, "Linguistic Foundations of US Foreign Policy after 9/11," M. Phil. thesis, Centre of International Studies, Cambridge University, July 2003. Our treatment is indebted to the ideas set out in this thesis.

[7] Kathleen Hall Jamieson and Paul Waldman, *The Press Effect: Politicians, Journalists and the Stories That Shape the Political World* (New York: Oxford University Press, 2003), pp. 151–52.

[8] Pippa Norris, Montague Kern, and Marion Just, eds., *Framing Terrorism: The News Media, the Government and the Public* (New York: Routledge, 2003).

Regardless of which term is used to describe it, the neo-conservative "discourse" was remarkably effective. Seemingly out of nowhere, Iraq was represented as an immediate danger to America. Of course, a government is entitled to sell its policy. Every politician, diplomat, and journalist is aware that the artful presentation of policy is essential to gain public support. Roosevelt gets high marks from historians for his lack of full disclosure in relation to U.S. help for Britain before the U.S. entry into World War II.[9] But when artfulness shades into outright untruth, for example over the secret bombing of Cambodia in the 1970s, criticism is appropriate – and has been voiced even by those untroubled by the Iraq deceptions.[10] We argue that the case for war against Saddam Hussein as presented to the American people went well beyond artfulness. The neo-conservatives in Washington linked their preexisting agenda (an attack on Iraq) to a separate event (9/11) and thus created an entirely new reality. It was like attaching a line of railroad cars to a locomotive of which they were the secret drivers. This process had the effect of co-opting important allies and entire government agencies in a pattern of deceit. It suspended ordinary judgment across the American polity. They manipulated the institutional power of their own positions to draw the American public into what can best be described as a synthetic neurosis that supported their template for regime change in the Middle East. With the American people so acutely sensitive to any threat to national security after 9/11, the agenda of the possible was thus transformed.

Misleading the American people by advancing, as public policy, a vague and shifting rationale for the attack on Iraq, irrespective of the desirability of bringing about change, has brought about a broken public trust. Already we can detect the substantial damage accruing to both core American political institutions and to American international legitimacy through this subterfuge. The bonds of our civil society are also under strain. Allied governments are in difficulty. This makes it important to understand how the discourse that led to war was fashioned. Our objective is not to play a tiresome game of catching the nation's elected leaders in minor inconsistencies but to examine the power possessed by governments – and special interests within governments – to mislead. We look at the techniques of persuasion. With major media influence tending to consolidate itself within ever smaller circles, this power contains within it troubling implications for our democratic governance.

---

[9] Doris Kearns Goodwin, *FDR: No Ordinary Life* (New York: Simon and Schuster, 1994), pp. 210–15.
[10] Christopher Hitchens, *The Trial of Henry Kissinger* (London: Verso, 2001).

WHY IRAQ, WHY NOW: THE NEO-CONSERVATIVES
CAPTURE THE DISCOURSE

Before 9/11, foreign policy observers were in agreement on the heinous nature of Saddam Hussein's regime, but few outside neo-conservative circles
saw Iraq as a direct threat to American security, let alone were privy to
their millenarian objectives of forceful regional transformation linked to the
Middle East peace process. As presidential candidate, Bush told an inter-
viewer that the most realistic way to deal with Saddam and his kind was to
"keep them isolated in the world of public opinion and to work with our
alliances to keep them isolated."[11] This, of course, changed abruptly after
the terrorist attacks. Within the week, members of the war cabinet proposed
including Iraq in the first round of military targets. At Camp David's Laurel
Lodge on September 15, 2001, Wolfowitz presented the argument that the
United States should attack not Afghanistan, but rather Saddam Hussein.
Although the intelligence services had no evidence linking Saddam Hussein
to the attacks, Wolfowitz had already made headlines in a Pentagon press
briefing two days earlier by advocating not just pursuit of al-Qaeda but a
"broad and sustained campaign" that would involve "removing" and "ending states."[12] James Woolsey was even quicker off the mark, saying that
Iraq should be the target, "no matter who should be responsible" for the attacks.[13] Laurie Mylroie, to whom Wolfowitz, Libby, and Richard Perle had
given intellectual and administrative support in her articles and book seeking to link Saddam with the 1993 World Trade Center attacks, and Richard
Perle matched Woolsey's speed out of the blocks.[14] On September 12, she
published an article in the *Wall Street Journal* linking Iraq to 9/11.[15] On the
same day, Perle pointed the finger at Iraq under the codeword of a "large
government."[16] Four days later on September 15, the president's national
security team met at Camp David's Laurel Lodge to discuss the next steps.
Written and oral accounts of this meeting after 9/11 must be treated with

[11] *NewsHour with Jim Lehrer*, transcript, February 16, 2000, http://www.pbs.org/newshour/bb/
election/jan-june00/bush_2-16.html.
[12] Department of Defense News Briefing, September 13, 2001, http://www.defenselink.mil/
transcripts/2001/t09132001_t0913dsd.html.
[13] James Fallows, "Blind into Baghdad," *Atlantic Monthly*, January/February 2004, pp. 54–56.
[14] Laurie Mylroie, *Study of Revenge: Saddam Hussein's Unfinished War against America*
(Washington, D.C.: American Enterprise Institute, 2000); Laurie Mylroie, "The World
Trade Center Bomb: Who Is Ramzi Yousef? And Why It Matters," *National Interest*, Winter
1995/96.
[15] Laurie Mylroie, "Bin Laden Isn't the Only One to Blame," *Wall Street Journal*, September 13,
2001.
[16] Steven Mufson, "U.S. Urged to Target Nations That Aid Terrorism," *Washington Post*,
September 12, 2001, p. A 12.

a modicum of skepticism, but the consensus is that, first, no evidence was presented implicating Iraq and, second, Wolfowitz argued forcefully for an attack on Iraq.[17] The two conclusions apparently emerging from the meeting were that the decision was taken to attack Afghanistan immediately in a debate that centered on timing and that Iraq was a central element in a larger strategy.[18]

The days after 9/11 were the critical space in which the requirement of top policy makers to devise a concrete response to a national emergency coincided with the perspectives of neo-conservative thinking that had spent some twelve years in the making. Suddenly, the neo-conservatives' long-desired goal of regime change in Baghdad coincided with the president's political need for a powerful response. Drawing on his experience of similar debates within the Clinton administration on the Balkans, General Wesley Clark commented that the focus on Iraq "was the old idea of state sponsorship – even though there was no evidence of Iraqi sponsorship whatsoever – and the opportunity to 'roll it all up.' I could imagine the arguments. War to unseat Saddam promised concrete, visible action."[19]

Years before, these ideas had been reduced to paper by those around the president's cabinet table. As early as 1992, Cheney, Wolfowitz, and Libby had established the intellectual basis for driving American tanks up the streets of Baghdad.[20] They and Rumsfeld had all been signatories on the PNAC's founding statement of principles in 1997. Rumsfeld, Wolfowitz, and Libby had each signed the open letter to Clinton in January 1998, entitled "Remove Saddam's Regime from Power," along with seven other signatories[21] who had also become members of the Bush administration.[22] The case for war against Iraq as discussed on September 15, 2001, was thus the operational roll-out of the neo-conservative template. Earlier, Daniel Bell, himself a neo-conservative, had observed: "being ideological you have prefabricated ideas."[23] He might have been writing of this moment.

---

[17] Todd S. Purdham, *A Time of Our Choosing: America's War in Iraq* (New York: Henry Holt, 2003), p. 10, and Bob Woodward, *Bush at War* (New York: Simon and Schuster, 2002), p. 83.

[18] Interview with a White House official, September 6, 2003, and Tanenhaus, "Bush's Brain Trust," p. 145.

[19] Gen. Wesley Clark, "The Clark Critique," *Newsweek Magazine*, September 29, 2003, p. 31.

[20] For a full discussion of then-Defense Secretary Dick Cheney's Defense Planning Guide, see Chapter 4.

[21] These were Elliot Abrams, John Bolton, Paula Dobriansky, Zalmay Khalilzad, Richard Perle, Peter Rodman, and Robert Zoellick.

[22] Project for the New American Century, "An Open Letter to President Clinton: Remove Saddam from Power," January 26, 1998.

[23] Joseph Dorman, *Arguing the World: The New York Intellectuals in Their Own Words* (New York: Free Press, 2000), p. 158.

As war seemed a forgone conclusion in early 2003, the neo-conservatives became more forthcoming about their objectives. Kaplan and Kristol wrote that the strategy was "so clearly about more than Iraq...more even than the future of the Middle East." It would represent "what sort of role the United States intends to play in the world in the twenty-first century."[24] In neo-conservative eyes, the Iraq war was not about terrorism; it was about the pivotal relationship between Saddam Hussein and the assertion of American power. Hussein provided, in effect, the opportunity to clarify America's global objectives and moral obligations. His continued survival in power was a metaphor for all that had gone wrong with American foreign policy since the Soviet collapse in the sense that the first Bush administration's Realpolitik and Clinton's wishful liberalism had left the Iraqi dictator in power.[25] Iraq was now the arena in which to demonstrate the crucial tenets of neo-conservative doctrine: military preemption, regime change, the merits of exporting democracy, and a vision of American power that is "fully engaged and never apologetic."[26]

In the discussions on September 15, 2001, the signatories of the PNAC were able to elevate their ideas from the pages of the *Weekly Standard* into the highest levels of U.S. policy making. Saddam Hussein was back in American cross-hairs. But if the neo-conservative idea had captured the imagination of the president and his war cabinet, the American public was more cautious. The administration could not simply add its signature to the PNAC declaration on the merits of a bold doctrine for U.S. supremacy in a world order of Washington's making. It would have to convince a domestic electorate and an international court of opinion about why such a strategy was justified. In short, a casus belli was needed. The challenge for the neo-conservatives was to frame the administration objectives in terms that justified war. It needed something more than a list of reasons why the world would be better off without someone.[27] Enter the "discursive representation of reality."

THE DISCURSIVE MANIPULATION OF 9/11

The notion of the "discursive construction of reality" asserts that one of the principal functions of language is to provide an intelligible conceptual

---

[24] Lawrence Kaplan and William Kristol, *The War over Iraq: Saddam's Tyranny and America's Mission* (San Francisco: Encounter, 2003), pp. vii–viii.

[25] Ibid.

[26] Ibid., ix.

[27] Fergal Keane, "The Road to War," in Sara Beck and Malcolm Downing, eds., *The Battle for Iraq: BBC News Correspondents on the War against Saddam and a New World Agenda* (London: BBC, 2003), p. 39.

framework. Social reality and the relations, entities, and beliefs within it are regarded not as predetermined and fixed but as created in and through language. Our perceptions of something, the meaning or significance it holds in our lives and the value that we ascribe to it, is discursively constructed – that is, defined by words – and changes with the way that we speak about it. How reality is discussed and represented greatly influences our responses and judgments.

Having said this, it is important to bear in mind the difficulties faced by governments in acting in a coordinated and focused manner. For that reason and because the administration consists of sets of competing elites, it is virtually impossible for the government to proceed with one voice, much less as a conspiracy. Nonetheless, with the knowledge that the neo-conservatives held sway in the White House and could not be easily overwritten or dislodged, the various departments, wishing to retain White House favor, reflected the White House linguistic line as it unfolded over time.

The neo-conservatives responded with skill and speed to fashion and sustain a domestic and international environment filled with insecurity. They championed the logical solution as a new world order where the United States would lead other nations toward the ultimate ideal of freedom and security. This discourse, reflecting the authority of the highest reaches of government, enshrined a referential framework in which official interpretations, however far-fetched, received the benefit of the doubt to the exclusion of other more moderate responses.[28]

In the days and weeks after 9/11, the attacks were transformed into an abstract conflict. The president's "declaration of war" was a metaphorical construction phrased in a manner that supported the larger strategy outlined above. Had language been used such as "War has been declared on us by nineteen young men," by "a group of terrorists," or even by both, the larger strategy would have been difficult to sustain. Rather, the administration said war had been "declared on America." It had been brought "on us." It had been waged "against us." Although naming the then little known group called al-Qaeda as bearing the main responsibility, the administration progressively broadened the language to establish the argument that the American way of life was under attack.[29] Was it craft on Bush's part, in which case he was purposeful, or was it inexperience and lack of perspective, in which case he failed to understand where his words would lead the nation and its allies? If the significance of the president's phraseology was not

[28] Garcia Estrada, "Linguistic Foundations," pp. 6–21, 29, 55, 57, 62, 64, 89.
[29] Ibid., pp. 19–20, 27–29.

immediately apparent, the world was left in little doubt after his first State of the Union address of January 2002, where the elasticity of the notional war was stretched to the concept of defeating all things evil. This meant not only terrorist organizations but also states.[30] These images cascaded through the media.

Underpinning this discursive strategy was the administration's clear understanding that security is not an objective concept. Government officials decide when a development constitutes a security threat. They decide when such a threat is over and when their citizens are more secure. As professor of international politics at the University of Newcastle, David Campbell has asserted that danger has no necessary relation to the action from which it is said to derive; nothing is more dangerous than anything else except when interpreted as such. How Saddam Hussein was presented as a threat of transcendental levels, above all other possible security threats to America, is an example of such interpretation.[31] But this is not simply a question of how an interpretation of reality had the manifest power to change it. The influence of discourse also depends on the forum in which it is used and the entity that articulates it. The institutional power behind discourse is highly significant because it acts to render certain versions of reality more credible or authoritative than others, both through its privileged access to media audiences and by the authority invested in the institution.[32] The link between power and discourse is critical in analyzing how the administration built support for its war plans. Global power, in this sense, is more than a physical manifestation. It is also the ability to define the terms of one's surrounding environment, the capacity to impress one's definition of reality and to make it prevail. It is the ability to transform a certain set of subjective interpretations into something perceived as the only valid objective interpretation. After 9/11, the neo-conservatives possessed this capability.[33] The "axis of evil" speech marked the beginning of a discursive crescendo.

BUILDING A CLIMATE OF FEAR

Later, John Le Carré, a man with deep experience of the connection between words and the world of shadows, commented that the American public was

---

[30] For a discussion of George W. Bush's 2002 State of the Union address, see Chapter 4.

[31] David Campbell, *Writing Security: United States Foreign Policy and the Politics of Identity* (Manchester: Manchester University Press, 1996), and Garcia Estrada, "Linguistic Foundations," pp. 57–58.

[32] Garcia Estrada, "Linguistic Foundations," pp. 6–7, and Norman Fairclough, *Language and Power* (London: Longman, 1989).

[33] Garcia Estrada, "Linguistic Foundations," pp. 6–10.

not just being misled; it was being ushered into a state of ignorance and fear under the pressure of a carefully constructed neurosis.[34] Fear of terrorism provided the necessary glue to meld otherwise uncorroborated statements, assumptions, predictions, and ideas into a case for war. Official discourse turned the assessment of a hypothetical danger into the absolute proof of a real danger. The administration gradually built an assumption into the critical consciousness of the American polity, namely that the war on terror and war in Iraq were joined at the hip.[35]

The American public was barraged with a litany of doomsday scenarios. Perle predicted on behalf of the Pentagon's Defense Policy Board that should the United States fail to carry through with its Iraq policy, "it will open the floodgates to terror against us."[36] Bush told an audience in the Rose Garden in late September 2002, "The danger to our country is grave. The danger to our country is growing."[37] Although Iraq had just accepted the unconditional return of inspectors, whose aim was to account for weapons as yet undiscovered, Bush seemed already certain of their actual existence when he declared, "The Iraqi regime possesses biological and chemical weapons.... The Iraqi regime is building facilities necessary to make more biological and chemical weapons.... The regime is seeking a nuclear bomb." A month later he repeated the nuclear claim: "The evidence indicates that Iraq is reconstituting its nuclear weapons program," and "it could have a nuclear weapon in less than a year." As he urged, "we've experienced the threat of September 11," and "America must not ignore the threat gathering against us."[38] He promised an audience at AEI, the neo-conservative stronghold, that "we will lead in carrying out the urgent and dangerous work of destroying chemical and biological weapons."[39] In Kentucky, Bush spoke of a preemptive conflict with Iraq in terms of "how to make our country a safer country."[40] He warned his audience about "al-Qaeda, Iraq and other places," as if the terrorist organization and the Iraqi dictatorship were

---

[34] John Le Carré, "The United States Has Gone Completely Mad," *London Times*, January 15, 2003.
[35] Garcia Estrada, "Linguistic Foundations," pp. 64–65.
[36] Interview with Richard Perle, "The War behind Closed Doors," *Frontline*, PBS, January 25, 2003.
[37] Remarks by the President on Iraq, September 24, 2002, http://www.whitehouse.gov/news/releases/2002/09/print/20020926-1.html.
[38] Remarks by the President on Iraq, Cincinnati Museum Center, July 10, 2002, http://www.whitehouse.gov/news/releases/2002/10/print/20021007-8.html.
[39] President Bush at the annual dinner of the American Enterprise Institute, February 26, 2003.
[40] Remarks by the President at Louisville, Kentucky, September 5, 2002,. http://www.whitehouse.gov/news/releases/2002/09/print/20020905-1.html.

abstract locations in the same war. A fifty-page British intelligence dossier provided further grist for the mill; the president told journalists in the Rose Garden that "according to the British government, the Iraqi regime could launch a biological or chemical attack in as little as 45 minutes after the order is given."[41] In making these charges about Iraq's weapons of mass destruction, the administration made no distinction between nuclear, biological, or chemical capabilities, thus allowing a climate of undifferentiated fear to arise and making a cost/benefit analysis of war almost impossible to undertake.[42]

THE CONDITIONALITY OF THE NEO-CONSERVATIVE DOOMSDAY

Thus, the process of establishing a logic in people's minds that led from the terrorist attacks through the war on terror to destination Saddam Hussein was relentless. Al-Qaeda and Saddam Hussein were morphed into the same enemy. But the scare mongering was highly selective in terms of the wider strategic environment. The administration's discourse largely ignored Iran's nuclear weapons program. The threat from North Korea was made light of, even when Kim Jong-Il publicly and with evident pride announced that his country was enriching uranium for weapons purposes.[43] The same pattern can be observed regarding Pakistan. Agencies within the latter's government supported both al-Qaeda and the Taliban. The military coup that brought General Pervez Musharraf to power had raised considerable concerns in the West about the stability of an embryonic nuclear power struggling to contain numerous and popular anti-Western forces within its society, including its intelligence service, which was decidedly sympathetic to the Taliban. If one of the many political forces of Islamic militancy in Pakistan were to overthrow Musharraf's unstable regime, then it would have nuclear weapons to target U.S. regional locations and other places within hours. Clearly, the scenario put forward by senior officials for the transfer of weapons of mass destruction technology to terrorist groups was at least as plausible in Pakistan, where senior military officers are known to harbor great sympathy for Kashmiri militants and other extremist Islamic movements, as in Iraq. These officers *could have* decided to provide the militants with weapons or

---

41 Remarks by the President on Iraq in the Rose Garden, September 26, 2002, http://www. whitehouse.gov/news/releases/2002/09/print/ 20020926-1.html.

42 Jessica Mathews, George Perkovich, and Joseph Cirincione, *WMD in Iraq: Evidence and Implications* (Washington, D.C.: Carnegie Endowment for International Peace), 2004.

43 John Newhouse, *Imperial America: The Bush Assault on the World Order* (New York: Knopf, 2003), pp. 129–37.

technology.[44] But such worst-case scenarios were excised from a discourse that focused on Iraq. Iran, North Korea, and Pakistan all provide instructive examples of how the government's ability to manage the "discursive reality" can be used in the *opposite* direction, namely to calm rather than inflame anxieties. A crisis is not a crisis unless the government anoints it as such.

Instead of these palpable dangers, a hypothetical and unproven state of affairs in Iraq was placed at the center of U.S. national security strategy. Kagan and Kristol laid out the "indisputable" evidence on the pages of the *Weekly Standard* in January 2002. When U.N. inspectors left Iraq at the end of 1998, apparently "they believed" Iraq possessed enough precursor chemicals for 200 tons of poison. Kagan and Kristol asked, Who knows how many of those factories are operational? They declared, "We can only imagine" how much anthrax Saddam Hussein "may" have at his disposal. Further, they asked, "What if" Saddam provides some of his anthrax to a terrorist group such as al-Qaeda? They quoted an official as declaring, "There may well have been" interaction between Saddam Hussein and Osama bin Laden.[45] And so a list of unfounded hypotheticals informed the best case the neo-conservative brain trust could muster in its flagship publication.

THE DISCOURSE PRESENTED TO THE U.N. SECURITY COUNCIL

In February 2003 Secretary of State Colin Powell put a disparate collection of unanswered questions, suggestions, and documented events on the table at the Security Council as the firm case for regime change. He would later admit to being uncomfortable with various aspects of his presentation, but as he told his audience, "What you will see is an accumulation of *facts* and disturbing patterns of behavior." He said "the *facts* and Iraq's behavior show that Saddam Hussein and his regime are concealing their efforts to produce more weapons of mass destruction." Although the world waited for Powell's PowerPoint presentation to clarify what had heretofore been mixed messages and allusive justifications for a war that seemed to have no one single reason, he declared, "I cannot tell you everything. But what I can share with you, when combined with what all of us have learned over the years, is deeply troubling." So the climax of the U.S. case for war began with an immediate disclaimer. The iron spine of the argument was an inserted proviso that

---

[44] Michael Klare, "Deciphering the Bush Administration's Motives," *Foreign Policy in Focus*, January 16, 2003.
[45] Robert Kagan and William Kristol, "What to Do about Iraq," *Weekly Standard*, January 21, 2002.

even if we remained unconvinced by the collective anthology of "additional information" from a "variety of sources," the administration still had a case that it could not tell us about. To omit relevant intelligence was strange practice for an argument founded on relevant intelligence.[46]

In his own words, Powell's casus belli was based on the sense that events in Iraq were "deeply troubling." He put forward reams of circumstantial evidence that would not have passed muster in a court of law, let alone commit a country to war and long-term military occupation in the Middle East. He included telephone conversations with vaguely incriminating statements, such as "You don't have one of those do you?" and "I have one." He asked questions about computer hard drives, such as "Who took the hard drives?" and "Where did they go? What's being hidden?" His evidence relied on assertions such as "Numerous human sources *tell us* that Iraqis are moving, not just documents and hard drives, but weapons of mass destruction" (emphasis added). Powell appealed to his global audience, saying, "You know the facts" and "There can be no doubt that Saddam Hussein has biological weapons and capability to rapidly produce many, many more." Asserting that Saddam was going to keep what the inspectors had not, in fact, proved that he possessed, he said: "We know that Saddam Hussein is determined to *keep* his weapons of mass destruction" (emphasis added).[47]

BRIDGING THE SPACE BETWEEN AL-QAEDA AND IRAQ

The administration's case as set out on the Security Council floor also rested, in part, on the "sinister nexus between Iraq and the al Qaeda terrorist network." This essentially came down to the movements of one man, Abu Musab Al-Zarqawi. The "sinister nexus" relied on two factors: Zarqawi's two-month stay for medical treatment in Baghdad and his links to Ansar-al-Islam, a localized terrorist organization operating in the northern Kurdish areas outside Baghdad's control. Powell's assertion of the "sinister nexus," which was not shared by the CIA, provided no detail of the nature of the relationship between Zarqawi and Ansar-al-Islam and, significantly, ran contrary to the accepted fact that Saddam Hussein was a life-long secular enemy of militant Islamists such as bin Laden, who viewed him in equally antagonistic terms.[48] These details were simply added to the conditional argument that branded Iraq a clear and present danger.

[46] Secretary of State Colin Powell, "Presentation to the UN Security Council: A Threat to International Peace and Security," in Micah Sifry and Christopher Cerf, eds., *The Iraq Reader: History, Documents and Opinions* (New York: Simon and Schuster, 2003), pp. 465–78.
[47] Ibid.
[48] Klare, "Deciphering."

A month after Powell's speech, *New York Times* columnist Maureen Dowd remarked that it was no wonder Americans were confused; the United States was about to go to war against a country that did not attack it on September 11, as did al-Qaeda; that did not intercept its planes, as did North Korea; that did not finance al-Qaeda, as did Saudi Arabia; that was not home to Osama bin Laden's lieutenants, as was Pakistan; and was not a host body for terrorists, as were Iran and Syria.[49] While Dowd's cynical appraisal underscored the difficulties of the administration's case, Brent Scowcroft, National Security Advisor to Gerald Ford and George H. W. Bush, challenged the structure of the administration's argument. He commented in the *Wall Street Journal* that there was scant evidence to tie Saddam Hussein to al-Qaeda and even less to 9/11. He reminded readers that the Iraqi dictator's goals had little in common with terrorists and gave him little incentive to make common cause with them. Scowcroft argued that Saddam Hussein was unlikely to risk investment in weapons of mass destruction, nor tempt an attack on Iraq, by handing such weapons to terrorists who could use them for their own purposes, leaving Baghdad as the return address. Besides, it was clear to Saddam Hussein, as a power-hungry survivor, that threatening to use weapons even for blackmail – much less actually using them – would open him and his regime to an immediate and devastating response from an unflinching United States.[50] But he was dismissed by the administration, which said: "Ambition and hatred are enough to bring Iraq and Al-Qaeda together."

The Credibility Gap

It would soon emerge on both sides of the Atlantic that both the U.S. and British governments had given in to the temptation to include uncorroborated or questionable intelligence in speeches and statements to bolster the case for war. Neo-conservative fellow-travelers labeled it "The Phony Scandal" in the *Weekly Standard* when it subsequently emerged that a sixteen-word sentence in the State of the Union address quoting British intelligence on Saddam Hussein's apparent pursuit of uranium from Africa was uncorroborated. The article argued that the administration had nothing to apologize for, since the phrase had been included by the president's speechwriters, "who accumulated evidence about Saddam and weapons of mass destruction to strengthen the case against him." Further, the article said, the CIA had

---

[49] Maureen Dowd, quoted in Sifry and Cerf, eds., *Iraq Reader*, p. 385.
[50] Brent Scowcroft, "Don't Attack Saddam," *Wall Street Journal*, July 15, 2002.

not warned the speechwriters to be wary of the intelligence.[51] This would turn out to be incorrect, but of this more below.

While various officials in the administration and writers in the *Weekly Standard* casually dismissed the scandal as a lot of fuss and partisan sniping about nothing, the issue would not go away. The uranium claim was a central part of the case made by the administration in asserting that Saddam Hussein was a serious threat because of his nuclear ambitions.[52] In fact, when both houses of Congress passed the resolution authorizing the use of force against Iraq in October 2002, more than 180 members cited the possible Iraqi nuclear threat as a reason for supporting the resolution, and a number of senators specifically cited the British report of Iraqi efforts to purchase uranium yellowcake.[53] Moreover, when Iraq released the 12,200-page weapons declaration to the U.N. on December 7, 2002, the administration included in its eight essential omissions and deceptions the assertion: "The declaration ignores efforts to procure uranium from Niger." Condoleezza Rice cited it prominently.[54] Further, when the International Atomic Energy Agency (IAEA) asked the administration for proof of the Niger case to investigate the claim because it was such a significant charge, Washington provided nothing for over six weeks while it continued to build the case for war. Regardless, the administration's adroitly crafted discourse was effective. In a *Time* magazine poll taken four weeks before coalition forces entered Iraq, 72 percent of Americans thought war was justified because it would help to eliminate Saddam Hussein's weapons of mass destruction.[55]

FAULTY EVIDENCE AND DYSPEPTIC SPIES

The administration's Iraqi discourse was fundamentally challenged in February 2003 by an extraordinary rebellion among British intelligence officials against their prime minister. In an unprecedented leak, a Defense Intelligence Staff (DIS) document was released to the press. This indicated the level of dissatisfaction that British intelligence officers felt over having their

---

51 Fred Barnes, "The Phony Scandal," *Weekly Standard*, July 26, 2003, p. 22.
52 Dana Milbank and Walter Pincus, "Bush Aides Disclose Warnings from CIA," *Washington Post*, July 23, 2003, P. A1.
53 Mitch Frank, "Tale of the Cake," *Time*, July 21, 2003, p. 22, and William Kristol, "Bush Suckers the Democrats," *Weekly Standard*, July 28, 2003, p. 9.
54 Condoleezza Rice, "Why We Know Iraq Is Lying," *New York Times*, January 23, 2003, p. A25.
55 Michael Duffy and James Carney, "A Question of Trust," *Time*, January 28, 2003, p. 23.

work politicized. The presumption is that, since DIS documents are highly secret, their publication would have required approval at a senior level. The document indicated that British intelligence believed there were no current links between Saddam Hussein and al-Qaeda and that any contact between officials in the Iraqi regime and the al-Qaeda network yielded nothing due to reciprocal mistrust and incompatible ideologies. One intelligence officer was quoted in the *Independent* as saying, "You cannot just cherry-pick evidence that suits your case and ignore the rest. It is a cardinal rule of intelligence." A U.S. intelligence source in Washington corroborated this by saying that, "partisan material is being officially attributed to these agencies."[56]

The day after Powell's presentation, a Cambridge University analyst revealed that the British government's dossier on Iraq, referred to in Powell's speech as "the fine paper that the United Kingdom distributed yesterday, which describes in exquisite detail Iraqi deception activities," was lifted from a ten-year-old article in *Middle East Review of International Affairs* and two articles in Jane's *Intelligence Review*, including spelling mistakes.[57] The implication that a case for war was being copied and pasted from the Internet was made somewhat worse by the manner in which the plagiarized evidence had apparently received a minor facelift. The Downing Street team, headed by Alistair Campbell's personal assistant, Alison Black, had modified the language to heighten the drama.[58]

SELLING WAR AND IGNORING THE CIA

As the American public became increasingly convulsed by the prospect of an Iraqi war, sustaining a discourse supportive of the neo-conservative agenda assumed paramount importance. If there were doubts about the strength of intelligence publicized in London, the sentiment was increasingly shared in Washington. Powell himself omitted from his U.N. presentation the claim made in the State of the Union address about Iraqi attempts to acquire uranium yellowcake from Africa, since he did not consider the assertion strong enough "to present to the world."[59] Let us take a moment to review the

---

[56] Paul Lashmar and Raymond Whitaker, "MI6 and CIA: The New Enemy Within," *The Independent*, September 2, 2003.
[57] "UK Dossier Lifted Evidence," *The Guardian*, February 7, 2003, and Lashmar and Whitaker, "MI6 and CIA."
[58] Quoted in Lashmar and Whitaker, "MI6 and CIA."
[59] For full details, see Michael Duffy and James Carney, "A Question of Trust," *Time*, January 28, 2003, p. 23.

Niger file, because it is not simply a matter of inconsistency. It exemplifies how the repeated warnings of intelligence officials and government experts were ignored because they did not match the climate of the discourse and the momentum toward war.

The journey along the yellowcake road began in late 2001, when the Italian government obtained half a dozen letters and other documents allegedly indicating that Iraqi agents had attempted to buy uranium yellowcake from government officials in Niger. This evidence was then shared with both British and U.S. intelligence services. In February 2002, the CIA sent a former State Department official Joseph Wilson to investigate. On his return he stated in an oral report to both CIA and State Department officials that he could not confirm the allegations. This was nine days after the State Department's Bureau of Intelligence and Research had sent a memo directly to Powell that refuted the Italian intelligence.[60]

The matter should have ended there, but six months later, the allegation came back to life as intelligence. The Blair government's dossier published on September 24, 2002, claimed, "Iraq had sought significant quantities of uranium from Africa." The then White House spokesman Ari Fleischer suddenly asserted, "We agree with their findings." Six months later, it was in the president's most important speech of the year. But although it was good enough for the State of the Union address, it was not good enough for Powell when he went to the U.N. Nor was it good enough for CIA Director George Tenet six days later, when he testified before a Senate panel.

This was not a realization that had suddenly dawned on senior administration officials after the State of the Union address. Importantly, Tenet's views had been conveyed to the White House National Security Council before the State of the Union address. Tenet had advised Deputy NSC Advisor Stephen Hadley personally by telephone in October 2002 to remove a line referring to the uranium claim from a speech that Bush was about to give in Cincinnati. That same month, CIA officials had referred to the uranium claim in the classified ninety-page National Intelligence Estimate on Iraqi weapons programs. Counter to the neo-conservative defense that White House speechwriters had been unaware, the CIA had included as a footnote to the assessment that the uranium allegations were "highly dubious." Six months after the State of the Union address, it emerged that chief White House speechwriter Michael Gerson, along with Hadley and others, had received a CIA memo dated October 5, 2002, which objected to the uranium claim in a White House speech draft. The architects of

---

[60] Seymour M. Hersh, "The Stovepipe," *The New Yorker*, October 27, 2003, pp. 77–87.

the discourse knew of the doubts among the intelligence services. But these doubts were marginalized in the face of political imperatives.[61]

Rice defended the administration by arguing that "if the CIA, the Director of Central Intelligence, had said 'Take this out of the speech,' it would have been gone, without question."[62] But a second memo also emerged dated October 6, 2002, and addressed personally to Rice and Hadley. It again included clear objections to the uranium charge, emphasizing a "weakness in evidence."[63] As Hadley told reporters, "I should have recalled . . . that there was controversy associated with the uranium issue." Strangely, Hadley then forgot about the warning when it came to drafting the president's State of the Union speech less than two months later.[64]

The case for war against Iraq was an argument of disconnected claims and images, such as the uranium claim, many of which turned out to be false or uncorroborated. Where Bush asserted, "We know that Iraq in the late 1990s had several mobile biological-weapons labs," the CIA and State Department intelligence analysts could not agree on whether or not they were labs. Where Bush stated, "Our intelligence sources tell us that he [Saddam Hussein] has attempted to purchase high-strength aluminum tubes suitable for nuclear weapons production," it turned out this derived from the fact that an Iraqi scientist had buried centrifuge blueprints in his garden twelve years earlier, in 1991. But no evidence of a recent nuclear program had been found. It was thus sentence by sentence that the administration was able to translate Iraq into the essential vocabulary of "terror." This served not only to legitimize military force, but also to deflect approaches that might have employed nonmilitary solutions as legitimate policy.

A TIME FOR TRUE BELIEVERS

By fighting in the name of moral absolutes, the administration made its policies less controversial. The classification of Saddam Hussein as a belligerent in the "war on terror" rendered the suggestion of responses other than armed force obsolete and open to challenges of appeasement. Americans were already growing used to living in a dangerous world defined by the polarized identities of "us" and "them" that precluded any dialogue about or between what had become completely incompatible entities. The grounds for discussion were limited. Anyone who might wish to question the policy was now

---

[61] Milbank and Pincus, "Bush Aides."
[62] Evan Thomas and Tamara Lipper, "Condi in the Hot Seat," *Newsweek*, July 4, 2003, p. 17.
[63] Milbank and Pincus, "Bush Aides."
[64] Thomas and Lipper, "Condi," p. 17.

on the wrong side of rationality, morality, and patriotism.[65] In defining the goals of U.S. foreign policy as the "defense of freedom" and the "search for security," the administration had been able to build the environment surrounding the terrorist attacks of September 2001 into a wide moral platform from which to launch a preemptive strike.[66]

This is perhaps the most dangerous aspect of the neo-conservative influence deriving from 9/11. The environment in which the administration proceeded to war obstructed the systemic checks and balances that would have produced necessary questions requiring answers before military boots hit Iraqi soil. Important questions were not asked because the administration's policy-making culture had become highly politicized in support of the neo-conservative agenda. Either policy makers were "with the program" or they were consigned to outer darkness, as happened to advisers on the economic side, such as Lawrence Lindsey, and on the military side, such as General Eric Shinseki. This was a major institutional failure, notably on the part of agencies such as the National Security Council. The NSC, in particular, failed to fulfill its responsibility to integrate the competing claims on national resources, to rationalize the differing perspectives of the State and Defense Departments, and to contain special interest agendas such as those of the neo-conservatives. Given the intensity of the competing views and the seniority of those who held them, this was no easy task. Nonetheless, its non-accomplishment created a weakness in the policy chain where one should not have existed. We return to this in the Conclusion.

THE HUMANITARIAN CLOAK

While the creation of a peaceful market-democratic Iraqi citizenry was featured in the administration's discourse, it was only a part of the broader ambition – to remake the Middle East – that drove the administration after 9/11. As Kagan and Kristol argued, "a devastating knockout blow against Saddam Hussein, followed by an American-sponsored effort to rebuild Iraq and put it on a path toward democratic governance would have a seismic impact on the Arab world – for the better.... Once Iraq and Turkey – two of the most important Middle Eastern powers – are both in the pro-Western camp, there is reasonable chance that smaller powers might decide to jump on the bandwagon."[67]

---

[65] Lawrence F. Kaplan and William Kristol, *The War over Iraq: Saddam's Tyranny and America's Mission* (San Francisco: Encounter Books, 2003), pp. 40–49, 80–88.

[66] Ibid., p. 88.

[67] Kagan and Kristol, "What to Do about Iraq."

The democratizing sympathies of Kristol, Perle, Wolfowitz, and other neo-conservatives referred only to the Middle East – and for specific reasons. Kaplan and Kristol write that the administration's "national security strategy commits the United States to champion the cause of human dignity . . . by creating a balance of power that favors human freedom."[68] But the architects of the PNAC were perfectly aware that the United States does not have the resources to occupy every country deserving of regime change.[69] Nor was that their cause. When discussing the spread of democracy, they were not referring to the increased authoritarianism and severe political repression in Central Asia or Zimbabwe. In their book about "America's mission," Kaplan and Kristol do not mean Cuba or North Korea.[70] Widespread torture, severe restrictions on the media, arbitrary imprisonment of citizens, harassment and incarceration of opposition leaders, closure of opposition newspapers, and elections that are neither free nor fair are not an issue to neo-conservatives when they take place in Uzbekistan or Kyrgyzstan. Kristol's case for "human dignity" and "human freedom" is not related to the forcible relocation of civilians and the widespread use of forced child-labor camps in Myanmar or to the Bhutanese government's atrocities involving village raids, gang rapes, torture, and forced evictions against its southern Nepali-speaking population. The infamously despotic regime of Equatorial Guinea and the President of Turkmenistan who granted himself presidency for life in a country known for its arbitrary imprisonment and torture of citizens is not referred to in the "great moral cause" and the "great strategic goal" of the Bush doctrine.[71] Moreover, this selective focus on humanitarian transgressions contains a troubling strategic liability. U.S. acquiescence to tyrannical excess in Central Asia could well bring the same dysfunctionality that neo-conservatives have decried in the Middle East, where U.S. policy has largely enabled autocratic governments to pursue antidemocratic policies that have generated support for Islamic fundamentalism.

CHALABI AND THE GRAND NEO-CONSERVATIVE TEMPLATE FOR MIDDLE EASTERN HARMONY

After Saddam Hussein had been defeated, installing a "decent and democratic government in Baghdad" would be "a manageable task for the United States," according to Kaplan and Kristol. In the estimate cited in their book,

---

[68] Kaplan and Kristol, *War over Iraq*, pp. 95–99.
[69] Ibid.
[70] Klare, "Deciphering."
[71] Kaplan and Kristol, *War over Iraq*, pp. 95–99.

only 75,000 troops would be required to police the war's aftermath, at only $16 billion a year. As Iraq rebuilt its economy and political system, that force could be drawn back to "several thousand soldiers after a year or two." But neo-conservative predictions were unfortunately based on the rosiest of rosy scenarios and completely ignored Arab perceptions of the United States.

As Wolfowitz claimed, the vista that the first Arab democracy could open up would be stunning. Kaplan and Kristol quoted Kanan Makiya as saying that it *could* be as large as anything that has happened in the Middle East since the fall of the Ottoman Empire. Iraq's experience of liberal democratic rule "*could* increase the pressure already being felt by Tehran's mullahs to open that society"; Iraq "*could* replace Saudi Arabia as the key American ally and source of oil in the region" (emphasis added). And after that, a "democratic Iraq would also encourage the region's already liberalizing regimes – such as those in Qatar, Morocco and Jordan – to continue on their paths toward democracy." Kaplan and Kristol proclaimed, "Indeed, the exile umbrella group, the Iraqi National Congress (INC), is already working on the shape of Baghdad's postwar government."[72]

If they meant people such as the INC's leader, Ahmed Chalabi, they were talking about a man who had spent more than four decades in exile, whose power base inside the country was untested, and who was entirely dependent on Western patronage.[73]

Chalabi was an established neo-conservative ally of some two decades. He met Wohlstetter while studying mathematics at the University of Chicago, who introduced him to Perle in 1985. Described by someone at the Hudson Institute as being both "deep in the Arab world" and "fundamentally a man of the West," he subsequently established key supporters among those who would occupy the Pentagon's Middle East policy offices, most prominently Wolfowitz but also including other prominent officials such as Douglas Feith, Peter Rodman, and David Wurmser.[74] In the 1990s, Chalabi gained political favor with Washington's staunch pro-Israeli think tanks, the Washington Institute for Near East Policy (WINEP) and JINSA. He became a frequent guest at their symposia and drew wide support from key figures with neo-conservative connections, such as Cheney, Rumsfeld, Wolfowitz, and Woolsey.

---

[72] Ibid.
[73] Alan Little, "Promise and Fear – Iraq's Future in the Balance," in Beck and Downing, eds., *Battle for Iraq*, p. 198.
[74] David Ignatius, "The War of Choice, and One Who Chose It," *Washington Post*, November 2, 2003, p. B1.

Born in 1945, Chalabi was of a wealthy Shi'a family with links to the Hashemite monarchy that had fled in 1958 when a coalition of army officers overthrew King Faisal.[75] Chalabi spent most of his years in the United States and Britain. The 1990s were not a period of success for him. In 1992, he was convicted of embezzlement and sentenced in absentia to twenty-two years' imprisonment by a Jordanian court after a private bank that he had established in the 1980s collapsed. Three years later, he attempted to organize an uprising in Kurdish-controlled northern Iraq, which failed and left hundreds dead.[76] Although Chalabi established the INC in the 1990s as a wide coalition of opposition forces committed to democracy in Iraq, almost no one in the opposition movement – not even in the INC itself – considered him to have an established domestic power base within Iraq. As Entifadh Qanbar, the INC's head of office in Washington, contended when questioned over whether people in Baghdad had ever heard of Chalabi, "[t]hey may not know the man. But he represents their views."[77]

Despite widespread apprehension over Chalabi's absent power base in Iraq before the war, however, he was embraced by neo-conservatives and the Defense Department as the man for the job. Kagan and Kristol urged, "The United States should support Ahmed Chalabi and the Iraqi National Congress."[78] Rumsfeld rejected charges from other Iraqi groups that the administration was giving preferential treatment to Chalabi. But when the twenty-five-person Iraqi Governing Council was established on July 13, 2003, it had within it nine members who were subsequently chosen to serve as presidents of the council on a rotating basis. This group of nine was almost identical to the Leadership Council of Exiles that had formed the previous February at the encouragement of the Pentagon. So the template for democracy set out by Kagan, Kaplan, and Kristol essentially meant a process of hoisting their favorite Iraqis straight onto center-stage of the nation's political system.[79]

THE NEO-CONSERVATIVE PARADIGM: A REALITY CHECK

Misplaced optimism from sources such as Chalabi coupled with the assertions that Iraq would be a "cakewalk" greatly complicated the job of the first

[75] Robert Dreyfuss, "Tinker, Banker, Neocon, Spy," *American Prospect*, November 18, 2002.
[76] "Ahmed Chalabi: Pentagon Placeman?" BBC News, May 9, 2003.
[77] Peter Finn, "Exile Group's Militia to Move into Baghdad to Help U.S.," *Washington Post*, April 14, 2003, p. A28.
[78] Kagan and Kristol, "What to Do about Iraq."
[79] Fareed Zakaria, "Beware the Puppet Masters," *Newsweek*, August 11, 2003.

American officials to arrive in Iraq to run the civil administration. Looting was rampant. The destruction of former government buildings demolished seventeen out of the twenty-one ministry buildings that Washington had planned to use. Millions of dollars' worth of equipment and materials were stolen or obliterated.[80]

Moreover, the decision to enter Iraq with a "war lite" policy had not been supported across the U.S. defense establishment. There had been public disagreement between the civilian analysts and top military professionals. U.S. Army Chief of Staff General Eric Shinseki told the Senate Armed Services Committee on February 25, 2003, that several hundred thousand troops would be needed to sustain security in Iraq in the period after the war. Shinseki echoed the views of other defense analysts developed some eighteen months earlier.[81] But Rumsfeld and Wolfowitz immediately criticized Shinseki and played down the estimate. At a congressional hearing two days later, Wolfowitz described Shinseki's figure as "widely off the mark."[82] This reaction owed a great deal to the manner in which the general's statement ran counter to the desire among the Pentagon's neo-conservative leadership to demonstrate that this project could be done at minimal cost with high levels of technology. As senators on the Senate Armed Services Committee noted, the administration could not proceed with a war that required the troop levels after combat, as described by Shinseki, unless it gained support from the U.N. Security Council.[83] But strict adherence to the neo-conservative ideals of acting unilaterally and without the support of multilateral organizations was a central plank of the Iraq policy. So Shinseki simply had to be wrong.

The pressure among neo-conservatives to keep their mission consistent with the appearance of being doable also led them to ignore crucial advice from within government over financing postwar Iraq. As Wolfowitz told Congress during the early stages of the war, "we are dealing with a country that can really finance its own reconstruction, and relatively soon." Cheney asserted on the day that Baghdad fell that Iraq's oil production could hit 3 million barrels a day by the end of 2003. But these optimistic statements suggesting that Iraq's oil wealth would underwrite

[80] Romesh Ratnesar and Simon Robinson, "Life under Fire," *Time*, July 14, 2003.

[81] Philip H. Gordon and Michael E. O'Hanlon, "A Tougher Target," *Washington Post*, December 26, 2001, p. A31.

[82] Eric Schmitt, "Pentagon Contradicts General on Iraq Occupation Force's Size," *New York Times*, February 28, 2003, p. A1.

[83] "Army Chief Says 200,000 Troops Needed to Keep the Peace," *Los Angeles Times*, March 27, 2003.

the rebuilding of Iraq, rather than American taxpayers, ran counter to the assessment of a government task force that had been established months before the war in order to study Iraq's oil industry. Again, it was the case that detailed research was ignored by neo-conservatives because it did not fit their template for intervention. The government task force had been part of the planning for the war and produced a book-length report that described how the Iraqi oil industry was so damaged after a decade of trade embargoes that its production capacity had been severely limited.[84]

As Paul Bremer, who soon became the top civilian administrator in Iraq after the war, told a Senate hearing in late 2003, "The oil infrastructure was severely run down over the last 20 years, and partly because of sanctions over the last decade." But this should not have been a surprise to anyone who was driving the Iraq policy in Washington. The civilian leadership at the Pentagon had been made well aware before the war that Iraqi oil was not a ready source for reconstruction. As an expert who had been consulted by the government before war, Amy Myers Jaffe was head of the energy program at the James Baker III Institute for Public Policy at Rice University, Houston. Her group had concluded in the previous December that oil revenues would certainly not be sufficient to cover the cost of reconstruction. Furthermore, reports produced by the U.N. over the previous half-decade made clear documentation of the fact that Iraq's oil system had deteriorated greatly. U.N. reports from 1998 to 2001 stated that a huge investment would be necessary for Iraq's oil industry, which was running well under production capacity.

However, Wolfowitz duly assured the House Appropriations Committee on March 27 that reconstruction would largely be covered by proceeds from Iraqi oil. Congress was told that oil revenues in Iraq could yield between $50 billion to $100 billion over the following two to three years. Wolfowitz argued, "There's a lot of money to pay for this. It doesn't have to be U.S. taxpayer money." This turned out to be incorrect, but as Director of the U.S. Agency for International Development, Andrew Natsios, told ABC's *Nightline*, "the American part of this will be $1.7 billion. We have no plans for any further-on funding on this." Natsios argued that the remaining costs would be paid for with international contributions and from Iraq's oil wealth.[85]

---

[84] Jeff Gerth, "Report Offered Bleak Outlook about Iraqi Oil," *New York Times*, October 5, 2003, p. A1.

[85] Pamela Hess, "Dems Charge 'Bait and Switch' on Iraq," *Washington Times*, October 3, 2003.

In September 2002, the president's chief economic adviser, Lawrence Lindsay, estimated that the costs of war with Iraq could be as high as $100 billion to $200 billion. The administration was quick to dismiss Lindsay's estimates. Mitch Daniels, Director of the Office of Management and Budget, discounted Lindsay's statement as "very likely very high." Instead, administration officials spoke of figures in the region of $50 billion. Soon after the war started, the administration's budget office provided Congress and journalists with a paper claiming that Iraq would not require massive and sustained aid because of its abundant resources, namely in oil. Rumsfeld told the Senate that reconstruction would be financed by the resources of the Iraqi government and not by American taxpayers. But just as the advice and information available to policy makers before the war had made clear, this turned out to be false.[86]

THE OSP AND THE NEO-CONSERVATIVE TAKEOVER OF DECISION MAKING

The many troubles of postwar Iraq were not, however, simply due to lack of foresight. Led by senior civilian officials at the Pentagon and supported by the vice president's office and certain NSC officials, the neo-conservatives were able to dominate the Iraq policy process and moved the country to war while largely excluding and marginalizing professionals with dissenting views – including significant numbers of senior officers assigned to the Joint Chiefs of Staff. As noted by David Phillips, deputy director of the Center for Preventive Action at the Council on Foreign Relations and a participant in prewar preparatory study groups, it was wrong to say that the administration had no plan for postwar Iraq. The previous year, the State Department and seventeen other federal agencies had embarked on an enormous effort called the Future of Iraq Project, which involved hundreds of Iraqis from the country's many ethnic and religious factions and working groups on topics ranging from the economy and agriculture to government structures. Eventually, a thirteen-volume report emerged.[87] Anticipating many of the problems that eventually beset post-conflict Iraq, the participants worked on plans for filling the security vacuum, restoring services, and making the transition to democracy. The project devised strategies for winning hearts and minds of the average Iraqis by improving and securing living conditions

---

[86] Pamela Hess and Elizabeth Bumiller, "Threats and Responses: The Cost; White House Cuts Estimate of Cost of War with Iraq," *New York Times*, December 31, 2002, p. A1.

[87] Fallows, "Blind into Baghdad," pp. 56–57.

and emphasized cooperation with Iraq's existing technocracy to ensure the uninterrupted flow of water and electricity. Phillips, who was adviser to the project's democratic principles working group, stated that while civil servants were mostly Baath Party members, the working group contended that not all Baathists were war criminals and that these people were a necessary part of the nation-building process.[88]

But instead, the civilian leadership at the Pentagon was more interested in the advice of Chalabi and the INC. Undersecretary of Defense for Policy at the Pentagon, Douglas Feith and his staff deliberately ignored the year-long State Department plan on postwar Iraq and prevented the State Department's planning chief, Thomas Warrick, from being allowed to go to Iraq. Warrick had recruited some 240 Iraqi exiles in Europe and the United States who had professional experience in a multitude of areas, such as criminal justice, economics, and oil. They had drawn up blueprints for every aspect of reconstruction, but the neo-conservative leadership at the Pentagon simply cut them out of the loop.[89] As former CIA analyst Judith Yaphe told journalists in the summer of 2003, "Feith along with other Pentagon hawks did not want State to be involved."[90]

While the detailed work of the Future of Iraq project was brushed aside, Chalabi's people at the INC assured the administration that they controlled a vast underground network that would rise up in support of coalition forces and support the enforcement of security. They were adamant that the whole of the Iraqi army must be immediately disbanded and that most Baath Party members were probably war criminals and should be excised from the process. The Pentagon accepted the INC position while ignoring the advice and expertise collected by other U.S. federal agencies that had planned for postwar Iraq. As Phillips remarked, Chalabi's promised network failed to materialize, and the resulting power vacuum contributed directly to the sabotage and looting that paralyzed the Iraqi infrastructure. On the INC's recommendation, the Baath Party was banned and party members were dismissed from their jobs, thus helping to leave millions of Iraqis without electricity and fresh water. Meanwhile, the State Department Working Group asserted that exiles alone could not speak for all Iraqis and that discussions both inside and outside Iraq must form the basis of a legitimate and representative transitional structure. Nevertheless, Chalabi's neo-conservative supporters

[88] David Phillips, "Listening to the Wrong Iraqi," *New York Times*, September 20, 2003, p. A13.
[89] Eric Schmitt and Joel Brinkley, "State Department Study Foresaw Trouble Now Plaguing Iraq," *New York Times*, October 19, 2003, p. A1.
[90] Richard Sale, "Pentagon Hawk Dodges a Bullet," *Washington Times*, September 4, 2003.

at the Pentagon succeeded in establishing him and his associates as Iraq's "interim government in waiting," duly airlifting him and his U.S.-trained 700-man paramilitary force to Nasyria halfway through the war.[91]

Feith had become instrumental in the post-9/11 period. The Office of Special Plans (OSP), which began as an ad hoc office under Feith, emerged as the center of an informal neo-conservative network of political appointees that circumvented the usual interagency channels in order to push the country into war.[92] The OSP was initially created by Rumsfeld and Wolfowitz after September 11 in order to investigate possible links between Saddam Hussein and al-Qaeda. But along with the Pentagon's Near East and South Asia bureau (NESA), it evolved into a point of coordination for a broader network of neo-conservative officials committed to regime change in Iraq.[93]

The heads of NESA and OSP were Deputy Undersecretary William Luti and Abram Shulsky, respectively. Luti was a protégé of Newt Gingrich, former Republican Speaker of the House of Representatives and now a member of the Defense Policy Board. Other appointees in the two offices included Michael Rubin, previously with AEI, and David Schenker, previously with the Washington Institute for Near East Policy. Under Feith, the OSP worked closely with those in the Defense Policy Board, such as Adelman, Gingrich, and Woolsey, in disseminating the analysis they developed to sympathetic media outlets such as the Fox News Network and the *Weekly Standard*. It was a process of carefully crafting the Iraq discourse for the American public.[94]

In interagency discussions, Feith and the two offices communicated largely with compatible allies in other agencies, rather than with those who were their official counterparts. They seldom had communication with the CIA and instead left such activities to senior political figures such as Gingrich and Cheney, whose visits, according to CIA congressional testimony, had the effect of exerting pressure on analysts to support political objectives. Several retired officials from the State Department, the CIA, and the Defense Intelligence Agency have maintained that both OSP and NESA manipulated and exaggerated intelligence over Iraq before delivering it to the White House and the media outlets.[95]

[91] Ibid.
[92] Eric Schmitt, "Aide Denies Shaping Data to Justify War," *New York Times*, June 5, 2003, p. A20.
[93] David Rieff, "Blueprint for a Mess," *New York Times Magazine*, November 2, 2003, p. 31.
[94] Stephen F. Hayes, "Case Closed," *Weekly Standard*, November 24, 2003 This included actual wording from allegedly classified documents.
[95] Schmitt, "Aide Denies Shaping Data to Justify War."

THE HARMFUL INFLUENCE OF IRAQ ON THE REAL WAR
ON TERROR

By September 2002, bin Laden had been on the run for a year in isolated parts of Afghanistan and eastern Pakistan, remaining out of sight and depending on the support of local tribes.[96] As the planning of an Iraq invasion began, Washington moved many of the Special Operations Forces that had been hunting bin Laden to the Gulf area. A senior U.S. official told *Time*, "They all basically packed up and moved." The A-team members left with much of their high-tech equipment and were replaced with fresh troops who were mostly reservists, with regional training not in Islamic affairs but in Russian- and Spanish-speaking countries. Although the administration was warned that a changing of the guard would undoubtedly ease the pressure on those being sought, the war with Iraq took precedence over all other issues.[97] Both U.S. and British officials believed that the change allowed bin Laden to slip away from the Afghan-Pakistan border area with many of his associates who had survived the initial period of months on the run.[98]

Retired General Brent Scowcroft, widely respected in Washington for his service in the Nixon, Ford, and G. H. W. Bush administrations, wrote in the *Wall Street Journal* before the war that an attack on Iraq would jeopardize the global counterterrorist campaign. He argued that in simple economic terms, the administration's go-it-alone strategy would incur enormous financial cost that would impose unacceptable restrictions on the resources available for the campaign against global terrorism. Scowcroft also stressed that the consequences in the region would be dire. While Iraq was the Middle Eastern obsession of the United States, the region itself was obsessed with the Israeli-Palestinian conflict. If America was perceived – rightly or wrongly – to be making an all-out effort to subdue Iraq while making lukewarm or indiscernible efforts to solve that bitter conflict, the region would explode in outrage. Washington would essentially be seen as ignoring a key interest of the Muslim world in order to satisfy what was considered in the region to be a narrow American interest. The level of terrorism Americans might experience could thus greatly increase.[99]

Scowcroft also urged that an equally significant cost would be the serious degradation in international cooperation with America against terrorism.

---

[96] Michael Duffy and Massimo Calabresi, "Letting Up on Osama," *Time*, July 11, 2003, p. 13.
[97] Ibid.
[98] Ibid.
[99] Scowcroft, "Don't Attack Saddam."

Effective means of pooling intelligence and information across international borders is, of course, a key element in any campaign to control international terrorism, which requires open lines of communication and good diplomacy among governments at every level of the bureaucratic chain.

THE LOST CAUSE OF DIPLOMACY

Regardless of concern about sustaining international cooperation, the Iraq war revealed that diplomacy was out of fashion in Washington. American power, reversing half a century of consensus-driven diplomacy, apparently needed little support. International cooperation over the Iraq war remained largely unattainable, since the neo-conservative agenda was inflexible. The administration boasted before the Iraq war that a coalition of some fifty countries supported it, including minute Pacific states such as Micronesia and the Solomon Islands. The brutal reality was that America and Britain were almost entirely alone, absent a small amount of support from Australia.[100] Although there has been much mud-slinging across the Atlantic over events at the U.N. Security Council in the six months preceding the war, diplomacy essentially broke down in essence because other powers concluded that Washington would wage war regardless of their views. The first Security Council resolution of November 8, 2002, reached a consensus because it obscured two irreconcilable positions and because the protracted debate at the U.N. did not upset the Pentagon's military timetable for deployments that were occurring simultaneously and in isolation from diplomatic efforts. For France, Germany, and Russia, the idea behind Resolution 1441 was to get inspectors back into Iraq to search for forbidden weapons. For the administration, it was acceptable, if it succeeded, but otherwise provided an opportunity to wait quietly while military preparations continued, in hopes that Saddam Hussein would miscalculate in a way that invited the legitimacy of international support.

Washington's case for war stood largely apart from the conclusions contained in the reports proffered by Chief Weapons Inspector, Dr. Hans Blix, in which the U.N. process would determine the context within which war would be waged. But this was not the case for other members of the international community.[101] As Blix's January report failed to deliver the casus belli that the administration had hoped for, many sections of world opinion simply began to doubt whether Iraq was an immediate threat and whether

---

[100] Bridget Kendall, "Showdown at the UN," in Beck and Downing, eds., *Battle for Iraq*, p. 65.
[101] Ibid., pp. 52–59.

there were any banned weapons to discover. Meanwhile, Washington and London announced that the "material breach," which arguably triggered war, had occurred on the basis of intelligence already discussed in this chapter and the dictator's history of not cooperating with U.N. resolutions. In diplomatic skirmish after skirmish, the positions of both sides seemed to harden, more so after French Foreign Minister Dominique de Villepin and German Foreign Minister Joshka Fischer summoned Powell to a meeting (which Powell later characterized as an ambush) at the U.N. in January 2003.

In reality, the entire diplomatic process at the U.N. was flawed from conception because it was not born out of a genuine multilateral process designed to make an objective assessment of whether Saddam Hussein was a clear and present danger. Administration officials made it clear from the start that they were not abandoning the doctrine of preemption, and were prepared to proceed within the ambiguities contained in Resolution 1441. The administration had its own evidence and its own justification and would pursue, if forced to do so, its own foreign policy. The U.N. exercise was, as much as anything, an attempt to garner international support for war with Iraq, if possible, to satisfy moderate voices in the administration and among the public, and, as one American diplomat disingenuously expressed it, "to help out friend Tony."

Any help that Americans offered to Blair, however, was temporary and largely ineffective. Blair had, unfortunately, made the wrong mistake. As Le Carré wrote, "the most charitable interpretation of Tony Blair's part in all this is that he believed that, by riding the tiger, he could steer it." Unfortunately, all he could do was to give it "a phony legitimacy and a smooth voice."[102] Blair's tribulations were best expressed in the resignation of his Leader of the House of Commons, Robin Cook, who stated that the European Union was divided, that the U.N. Security Council was in stalemate, that the British people were not persuaded that Saddam Hussein was a clear and present danger to Britain, that they wanted inspections to be given a chance, that they suspected that they were being pushed too quickly into conflict by a U.S. administration with an agenda of its own, and that they were uneasy at Britain's "going out on a limb on a military adventure without a broader international coalition and against the hostility of many of Britain's traditional allies."[103]

---

[102] Le Carré, "The United States."
[103] Quoted in Martha Kearney, "Blair's Gamble," in Beck and Downing, eds., *Battle for Iraq*, p. 90.

DECEPTION'S LEGACY

As Paul Chilton, director of research at Aston University's School of Languages and European Studies, has contended, "the foreign policy of a nation addresses itself not to the external world, but to the image of the external world that is in the minds of those who make foreign policy."[104] Indeed, the Iraq war was the physical manifestation of the image of the external world that had evolved over the previous decade in the minds of neo-conservatives. There may have been a rhetorical determination to solve the Iraq issue for years among the architects of this war, but it was 9/11 that provided the political context in which the thinking of neo-conservatives could be turned into operational policy. The Iraq war was the point at which neo-conservative ideology became fully operational. It no longer depended on the lifeblood of academic symposia at Washington think tanks. It had the full might of history's most powerful military force at its disposal. The administration's intervention in Iraq, the mistakes made, and the costs yielded in dollars, blood, and international legitimacy are emblematic of the systemic weaknesses that expanded across the American policy-making machinery with the ascendancy of neo-conservative influence.

But this war also sets a unique precedent in the relationship between a government's objectives and its ability to synthesize a favorable climate for them through the discursive creation of reality. To modify Chilton's point, this war was not just an extension of the image of the external held in the minds of the policy makers. It was also an extension of the image of the external world that had been created in the minds of the American public. The use of an abstract enemy in a notional war had been used to justify the removal of Saddam Hussein under the terms of national security, which left open the possibility of such interventions elsewhere in the future. The contrived neurosis of the post-9/11 era, where abstract terror abounds, constituted the basis on which disparate and uncorroborated fragments of information about Iraq formed into a mosaic of specific threats and dangers. Estrada remarks that the official discourse of the U.S. government after 9/11 laid the foundations for restructuring the international system and creating a new world order in the twenty-first century.[105] It was the template that had been laid out in the PNAC's 1997 statement of principles. But the neo-conservatives had been unable to convince the American people of such naked ambitions without recourse to a discursive fabrication that hid their true objectives.

[104] Paul Chilton, *Security Metaphors: Cold War Discourse from Containment to Common House* (New York: Peter Lang, 1996), p. 27.
[105] Garcia Estrada, "Linguistic Foundations," pp. 97–101.

A slew of administration opponents have used strong, harsh words about the administration's arguments in favor of going to war.[106] This is not the camp from which we come. Our concern is with the manner in which major decisions of state are arrived. Our starting point is that Americans are entitled to the truth and that decisions drawing on truth-based presentations by governments – any government – are more likely to endure than those based on deception. Our view is that, on Iraq, deception had the upper hand – perhaps quite unnecessarily, as the American people might well have supported the case had it been properly stated. This is at least one lesson to be drawn from this episode: If there is a case to be made, the government and advocates within governments should make it truthfully rather than using the techniques of mass persuasion we thought we were banning from the world when we broke down the Berlin Wall.

---

[106] David Korn, *The Lies of George W. Bush: Mastering the Politics of Deception* (New York: Crown, 2003).

8

America: Perception and Counterperception

To properly understand America's increasing isolation within the international community, this chapter steps back to explore the foundations of today's anti-Americanism. Acknowledging the complexity of this syndrome, we have emphasized that contemporary reservations about American policy, while arising, in part, from specific initiatives of the current administration, are rooted in a 200-year experience in which social, economic, and political-military developments and philosophical distinctions have caused global perceptions of America to be, in some important respect, quite different from the way in which American perceive themselves. In this sense the reader will find this chapter to be different from those above.

While acknowledging the strength and attraction of American ideals and culture, it provides additional historical perspective on the nature and evolution of anti-Americanism in Europe and Britain to better allow an understanding of today's events. It frames the phenomenon in several ways using selected historical examples and contemporary references to provide the reader with both an anecdotal and an evolutionary understanding of what has become a significant factor in today's international policy environment.

This chapter contends that today's neo-conservative policies, which embrace preemption and reject the international consensus on a variety of legal, environmental, and security arrangements, act in an uncanny fashion to exacerbate certain reservations about American society held by elites in continental Europe and the United Kingdom. The authors further observe that these opinions, which had once been the province of these elite intellectual and social circles, have become increasingly commonplace, forming a block of domestic opinion in many countries that has restrained the support of allied governments and others and that in critical areas has brought opposition to American initiatives in a range of international settings.

> The more the elites here and in Europe holler, the solider the Bush support gets.
>
> Richard Perle, New York City, February 13, 2003[1]

This is not an untypical neo-conservative reaction to international opinion. Just as they dismissed dissent from fellow Americans, neo-conservatives have placed little value on external opinion, unless it is slavishly favorable. Indeed, they seem perversely to have drawn strength from foreign opposition. Accordingly, this chapter is written for those who, whether or not they are aware of the full dimensions of the phenomenon, sense that a sea-change in international attitudes toward America is taking place and, unlike the neo-conservatives, conclude that this is not necessary, welcome, nor supportive of the national interest.

A passive distaste for things American is hardly new and certainly cannot be laid entirely at the neo-conservative door. It has been in existence since the first days of the American colonies when upstart "Americanism" first blew some fresh air through the stale drawing rooms of old Europe. Today, we see words such as "predator" and "rogue nation" attached to the United States.[2] The French have described the United States as the "hyperpower," and even the friendly British have held anxious-sounding conferences devoted to "Living with the Megapower."[3] Harsh though these words sound, they belong to a well-understood tradition, spanning the spectrum from the polite America-skeptic snobbishness encountered at Oxbridge "high tables" to the "Yankee go home" graffiti on barrio walls. They may well reflect as much on the user (more often than not a European seeking to compensate for his or her country's reduced circumstances) as on the United States itself. The French philosopher Jean-François Revel observed that "if you remove anti-Americanism, nothing remains of French political thought today, either on the left or right."[4] Successive administrations, including the Bush administration, have, at times, poured substantial resources into

---

[1] Richard Perle, public speech in New York City, February 13, 2003; William Safire, "Nixon on Bush," *New York Times,* July 7, 2003, p. A17.

[2] Emmanuel Todd, *Après l'Empire: Essai sur la décomposition du systéme américain* (Paris: Gallimard, 2002), and Clyde Prestowitz, *Rogue Nation: American Unilateralism and the Failure of Good Intentions* (New York: Basic Books, 2003).

[3] "Living with the Megapower: Implications of the War on Terrorism," Royal Institute of International Affairs, London, July 2002.

[4] Jean-François Revel quoted in James W. Ceaser, "A Genealogy of Anti-Americanism," *Public Interest,* summer 2003, p. 4.

"public diplomacy" designed to moderate these negative images. Even the CIA got into the act, providing covert funding in the 1950s for the London-based *Encounter* where Irving Kristol, then more a Trotskyite than the neoconservative titan he would later become, served as the first editor. Such efforts, in retrospect, have had little impact, and, were the situation normal, their limited utility (leaving aside the ethical questions that caused the CIA to discontinue media programs of this type) might generate only mild concern.

The situation today, however, is not normal. In a crucial shift, the Cold War's end relaxed the sense whereby most Western Europeans believed that their increasing prosperity and stability were a function of NATO's ongoing commitment to Europe. During the Cold War, American cultural expression, management expertise, and investment were widely embraced, seen as essential elements in a progressively brighter future. Expectations of American fair play, predictable government, and idealism were high, perhaps too high, setting an unrealistic standard. It is not surprising, therefore, that intellectual and political elites were quick to complain when they believed that America had not lived up to its promise. Disappointment in Europe was accelerated from time to time by mini-crises such as the Pershing Missile controversy and Ronald Reagan's comments on "limited nuclear war" and "wiping the Soviet Union out of the book of history as the incarnation of evil."[5] And Americans took those disappointments seriously: Dr. Barbara Bodenhorn, a fellow of Pembroke College, Cambridge, remembers reading *The Ugly American* in high school and the general concern it raised. She adds: "Today, I suspect, it would be dismissed by a lot of folks."

Yet the frightening reality of the Cold War and the Soviet threat framed the way Western Europe viewed the United States. Anti-Americanism was balanced by "anti-Soviet Unionism," by "anticommunism," and by the imminent threat posed by its Eastern satellites. Thus while America's deepening involvement in Vietnam, the Watergate imbroglio, and other major and minor political scandals contributed to Europe's skepticism about the United States and its global role, on balance favorable attitudes reflecting the tremendous appeal of American culture, Americans, and America as a tourist destination among Europe's publics prevailed. Anti-Americanism amounted to little more than a venting of steam from Europe's elite circles, who knew that, in the final analysis, the Soviet threat was the only game in town. In West Germany especially, opinion polls taken since 1957 showed that the

5 Ibid.

number of those who expressed a negative opinion about America never exceeded 25 percent – and this was, in part, a function of the U.S. troop presence.[6] Additionally, even though a fairly strong minority among West Germans from 1954 until 1979 harbored doubts about the quality of American leadership and disapproved of "excessive" American influence in world affairs, public opinion as a whole did not seek to distance the Federal Republic from the United States. In 1954, some 62 percent of those polled favored a good relationship with America, whereas only 10 percent preferred the Soviet Union. Similarly in 1979, some 63 percent favored the United States, while only 12 percent supported Russia.[7] By the early 1980s, however, the disappointments had begun to take a toll.

Attitudes were not very different in France, where polls taken during the Cold War reflected rising pro-American feeling. Though these views were not expressed by a majority, they were, nevertheless, stronger than the anti-American sentiment. On the eve of American elections in November 1984, for example, 44 percent of French respondents expressed pro-American sentiments, as opposed to 15 percent who declared themselves anti-American.[8]

ENTER: UNIPOLARITY

The neo-conservative emphasis in 2000 on turning the "unipolar moment into a unipolar era," in which relations with allies are subordinated to American policy priorities, has arisen under very different circumstances and after commitment to a shared fate with the United States had largely passed.[9] University of Virginia professor James W. Ceasar (who has close neo-conservative links) recently underscored this, noting that "according to the most developed views of anti-Americanism, there is no community of interest between the two sides of the Atlantic, because America is a different and alien place."[10] Looking at Europe from America, Ceasar's neo-conservative colleague Robert Kagan endorses the thesis that American and

---

[6] Schweigler cited in Friedrich Ebert Stiftung, *America's Image in Germany and Europe* (papers of a Seminar in Washington, D.C., March 31, 1985).

[7] Ibid., table 13.

[8] Jacques Rupnik and Muriel Humbertjean, "Images of the United States in Public Opinion," in Denis Lacorne, Jacques Rupnik, and Marie-France Toinet, eds., *Rise and Fall of Anti-Americanism: A Century of French Perception*, trans. Gerry Turner (New York: Macmillan, 1990), p. 79.

[9] Robert Kagan and Bill Kristol, "The Present Danger," *National Interest*, spring 2000, pp. 57–69.

[10] Ceasar, "A Genealogy," p. 16.

European values are diverging, memorializing this change with the phrase "Americans are from Mars, and Europeans are from Venus."[11] He has subsequently warned that "a mutual antagonism threatens to debilitate both sides of the trans-Atlantic community."[12] The result is that just when it is essential to reinforce Atlantic community ties, leading neo-conservatives have signaled they have lost confidence in Europe. Some advocate reversing the American fifty-year commitment to a more closely integrated Europe.[13] Among the many examples of this are serious differences in perceptions of the function of international law. Projecting a very narrow view of sovereignty, neo-conservatives see the law not as a means of codifying best American practices on a global scale but "in the context of other countries' attempting to constrain the United States."[14]

These attitudes encourage and exacerbate anti-American resentment, particularly among European elites. As the polling data below shows, international perceptions of the United States are today in flux – all to the negative. Anti-Americanism has become something more than a mere venting of steam by frustrated foreign officials. Without the glue of the shared Soviet threat, the potential damage from a deepening in the rift between the United States and our natural friends and allies is all the greater. Today, the United States has a massive and complex global agenda: terrorism and the menace of nuclear proliferation, the vulnerabilities in the world economy and in the environment, and the distress of the underdeveloped world and the menace of "failed states." To have any hope of handling this agenda with even moderate success, the United States will need the closest possible international cooperation – and not just from minor states that the United States can browbeat or bribe into cooperation. Nearly all counterterrorism experts acknowledge that the intelligence flow from friendly foreign services is the lifeblood of success. Nearly all American executives confirm that a well-disposed attitude of, for example, China and India, to American investment is vital to the future of corporate America. Nearly all economists can demonstrate how even a marginal shift of the vast Asian and European reserves from dollars to euros could have a substantial and negative longer-term impact on the American economy.

[11] Robert Kagan, *Of Paradise and Power: America and Europe in the New World Order* (New York: Knopf, 2003), p. 3.
[12] Robert Kagan, "A Tougher War for the U.S. Is One of Legitimacy," *New York Times*, January 24, 2004, p. A17.
[13] David Frum and Richard Perle, *An End to Evil: How to Win the War on Terror* (New York: Random House, 2003), p. 247.
[14] R. James Woolsey, ed., *The National Interest on International Law and Order* (New Brunswick, N.J.: Transaction, 2003), p. viii.

At the present time, when neo-conservatives believe that the chief instrument for preserving American leadership consists of "maintaining the preeminence of American military force," their disregard for international opinion is particularly pernicious.[15] It risks turning garden-variety anti-Americanism into something more insidious, specifically an activist phenomenon that we call "counter-Americanism." By this we mean a movement in which influential segments of the international community actively seek to frustrate American objectives. How might this manifest itself? The European opposition to genetically modified foods, though reflecting a range of motivations, has some of the hallmarks of counter-Americanism. The determined resistance to U.S./U.K. initiatives in the U.N. Security Council by Germany, Russia, and particularly France in the course of the Iraq debate would be another example. A third would be instructions from governments in Brazil and Germany for their federal agencies to switch their computers away from Microsoft Windows to open-source operating systems.[16] If these and other forms of opposition entrench themselves, it would represent a drastic change from the preceding half-century when America was, generally, pushing through an open door. For a variety of purposes – diplomatic, commercial, educational, cultural, touristic – this was a priceless asset. Neo-conservatives are not solely responsible for the emergence of counter-Americanism, but the war-fighting policies they have imposed on the nation, their confrontational approach (which, as we have noted, is their stock in trade), and their aggressively America-centric norms of analysis are feeding the beast. If American business people find their products more difficult to sell, if American negotiators find agreements harder to reach, if American movie stars and athletes receive the cold shoulder, if American tourists find their welcome overseas less cordial today, they are entitled to look, in part, to the neo-conservatives.

POLL DATA

Most Americans are today utterly unaware of the skepticism with which the United States is often viewed internationally, even in Britain. Here are some figures. According to a Pew Research Center poll conducted in August 2001 – before the September 11 attacks and the announcement of the "Bush Doctrine" – respondents in Britain, France, and Germany "highly disapproved of [Bush's] handling of the international situation." Over 70 percent

---

[15] Donald Kagan, Gary Schmitt, and Tom Donnelly, "Rebuilding America's Defenses" (Washington, D.C.: Project for the New American Century, 2000), p. iv.

[16] Jonathan Karp, "A Brazilian Challenge for Microsoft," *Wall Street Journal*, September 8, 2003, p. A16.

expressed the opinion that President Bush "makes decisions based entirely on American interests and understands less about Europe than previous American presidents."[17]

This changed markedly with September 11, however. The attacks brought an outpouring of sympathy for America and clear support, outside the Muslim world, for the war in Afghanistan (73% in Britain, 64% in France, and 61% in Germany).[18] It was a remarkable moment, offering a unique opportunity to strengthen relations with non-Muslim nations worldwide. But the opportunity was cut short by the "axis of evil" phrase (which was celebrated in neo-conservative circles as introducing a new American policy based on morality, preemption, and unilateralism) used in the January 2002 State of the Union address.[19] Taken together, these events generated strong disapproval in Europe, effectively, if momentarily, disabling alliances carefully nurtured over half a century.

In a survey called "What the World Thinks in 2002," the Pew Research Center for the People and the Press reported the following:

Opinion of the US varies greatly around the world. Negative opinion of the US is most prevalent in the Middle East (75% negative in Jordan, which is among the largest recipients of US aid; in Egypt and Pakistan 69% negative, and over 50% "strongly negative") but is by no means confined to those countries. Positive opinion about the United States declined in 7 of 8 Latin American countries in 2002 with the two largest countries tending negative: Barely half of Brazilians hold the US in good stead and only 34% of Argentines hold favorable opinons of the US, down from 50% in 2000.[20]

Public perceptions of the United States in Turkey, a NATO ally, have declined sharply in the last few years. In 1999, a slim majority of Turks felt favorably toward the United States, but now just three in ten do. The intensity of negative opinion is strong: 42 percent of Turks have a very unfavorable view of the United States. The same pattern is evident in Lebanon, where 59 percent have a poor opinion of the United States.[21]

In Western Europe, America's image among its closest allies remains largely positive, although it has declined over the past two years. At least seven in ten in Great Britain (75%), Canada (72%), and Italy (70%), and

---

[17] Pew Research Center for the People and the Press, *Bush Unpopular in Europe, Seen as Unilateralist*, August 15, 2001, http://people-press.org/reports/print.php3?PageID=36.

[18] Pew Research Center for the People and the Press, *What the World Thinks in 2002*, http://people-press.org/reports/display.php3?ReportID=165.

[19] Charles Krauthammer, "Axis of Petulance," *Washington Post*, March 1. 2002, p. A25.

[20] Pew Research Center for the People and the Press, *What the World Thinks in 2002*.

[21] Ibid.

roughly six in ten in France (63%) and Germany (61%), still retain a favorable opinion of the United States. Yet relatively few people in these countries have strongly positive feelings toward the United States, and favorable opinion has diminished among three of four major U.S. allies in Western Europe (16% in Britain, 23% in Italy, 34% in France, and 35% in Germany hold unfavorable views of the United States).

In four of the six Eastern European countries, surveyed opinion of the United States has declined since 2000 (19% in Ukraine, 11% in Poland, 18% in Bulgaria, 27% in the Czech Republic, and 33% in Russia dislike the United States).

In Asia, there is a strong support for the United States in Japan and the Philippines, both longtime U.S. allies. Yet South Koreans are much more skeptical despite that country's close military and economic ties with the United States. More than four in ten South Koreans (44%) have an unfavorable opinion of the United States.

These trends continued in 2003. Favorable opinion in Poland and Ireland, two nations with close ties to the United States that had resisted the broader negative trend, slipped sharply. Opinion in Indonesia, a Muslim country, showed perhaps the most dramatic shift. Five years earlier, 90 percent of respondents had positive feelings toward the United States, while in 2003 opinion was 90 percent negative.

Referring to European attitudes, the June 2003 poll revealed a particular desire for greater independence from U.S. diplomatic and security policy. It was felt that Europe and Britain had become overly dependent on an unpredictable Washington and that the American "with us or against us mentality" placed unacceptable burdens on friendly governments balancing fractious domestic polities, not to mention the complex international environment.[22] On the eve of President Bush's visit to the United Kingdom in November 2003, a poll undertaken for the European Commission indicated that Europeans regarded the United States on a par with North Korea as a threat to world peace.[23]

Having referred to today's declining international approval of the United States, measured by the Pew polls, this chapter places this disturbing phenomenon in perspective by reflecting briefly on Europe's eighteenth- and nineteenth-century discomfort with America and how these historical images and conclusions informed the evolution of anti-Americanism. For

[22] Ibid.
[23] Alan Cowell, "Bush Visit Spurs Protests against U.S. in Europe," *New York Times*, November 16, 2003, p. A15.

readers more focused on contemporary transatlantic issues, this excur-
sion into the historical record may seem something of a diversion. But
we do this with a purpose. In setting this historical context, we touch on
the political, cultural, and economic arguments often used against things
American to provide the reader a flavor of the multiple dimensions within
which Europeans – particularly the British and French – have nursed their
differences with the new nation. Clearly, attitudes toward America and the
"idea of America" remain mixed, often revealing intense love/hate sentiments
in which American freedoms and optimism clash with disdain for American
conformity and provincialism. Our discussion then turns to the impact of
neo-conservative policies on America's image abroad and shows how those
policies have shaped today's anti-Americanism, especially among Europe's
decision-making elite. We address an unusual phenomenon, namely criticism
of America by Americans, that has been adopted by Europeans and is now a
standard part of Europe's anti-American rhetoric. For a vivid contemporary
vignette, we touch on the iconic case of McDonald's. We conclude with a
look at the cost of anti-Americanism, how the British have fared in all of
this, and what the future holds.

WHAT IS AMERICANISM?

For a better understanding of the character and dimensions of anti-
Americanism, it may be worth looking first at Americanism, the phenomenon
on which it is based. At the end of World War 1 there was much discussion in
the United States about the notion of Americanism, what it was, and how it
distinguished Americans from the rest of the world. It was a time of intense
activity in the United States. The Wilson administration was deeply involved
in structuring the war's end and fashioning the international arrangements
that would succeed it. As men returned home from the European War and the
United States realized the role it had played in forging the future, Americans
reflected an increasingly coherent notion of who they were and what distinguished them from the Europeans. Much of this was due to the experience
of living and fighting abroad, seeing another culture, perhaps falling in love,
and certainly becoming aware that the world was a large and varied place –
and that America had a role in it. A sense of this awakening is captured
by David Hill, who in 1918 published *Americanism, What Is It?* Though his
book remains little known, his words still ring true:

We have developed here in America a new estimate of human values, and this has led
to a new understanding of life. . . . We long ago abandoned a great deal of what Europe
still holds sacred. If we had a dynasty of hereditary rulers; if we had a state religion;

if we had formed a habit, and it became hereditary, of giving ourselves up, body and soul to the exigencies of the state; if we were surrounded by powerful enemies; then we might understand many things that happen in Europe which now seem to us unreasonable and almost insensate.... We sometimes forget that our earliest traditions ... were an open, heroic and a bloody revolt against all of that.[24]

To Hill, Americanism is an idea:

Americanism is what is most original and distinctive in American political conceptions and most characteristic of the American spirit and the American Way of Life. Americanism is a positive, constructive force and it starts with the idea that the human individual has an intrinsic value.... Each person's value lies not in what he has but in what he is and mostly in what he may become. And he may become anything his capacities and his achievements may enable him to be.[25]

Franklin Roosevelt said that "Americanism signifies the virtues of courage, justice, sincerity and strength – the virtues that made America."[26] Further defining the term "Americanism," British historian Richard Crockatt says, "Americanism can be better explained as an expression of nationalism which is both a product of the United States and of the image that other nations have of the United States together with their expectations from it."[27]

THE NOTION OF UN-AMERICANISM

Related to Americanism is the notion of un-Americanism. Crockatt defines un-Americanism as "a form of heresy ... to be un-American is to denounce some of the elements of Americanism." He goes on to say that "there is a close relationship between un- and anti-Americanism, the distinction between them being that the former is generally applied to Americans, while the latter generally, though not exclusively, refers to non-Americans."[28] Un-Americanism is vague, having achieved its highest profile during the McCarthy era when the House Un-American Activities Committee held hearings to uncover possible communist agents in the Department of State and in the Department of Defense, and it refers to a rejection of ideas that are central

[24] David Jayne Hill, *Americanism: What Is It?* (New York: D. Appleton, 1918), p. viii.
[25] Ibid., pp.vii–ix.
[26] Marie-France Toinet, "Does Anti-Americanism Exist?" in Lacorne et al., eds., *Rise and Fall*, p. 219.
[27] Richard Crockatt, *America Embattled: September 11, Anti-Americanism, and the Global Order* (London: Routledge, 2003), p. 47.
[28] Ibid., p. 50.

to the American political culture. The concept, unlike anti-Americanism, is not linked to a particular critique of America and lacks the dynamic quality of the latter.

David Strauss provides yet another perspective on anti-Americanism. He calls it a "sharp criticism of American policies, frequently resulting in violent demonstrations against the symbols of American power abroad." He adds that anti-Americanism might refer to "a philosophy, ideology or institutional framework based on assumptions and principles which run counter to the Americanist position."[29]

Anti-Americanism is not exclusively a foreign phenomenon. While there have often been intense and legitimate differences among patriotic citizens about how the nation might realize its greatest potential, some, reflecting a distinct but identifiable tradition, blamed the United States for the attacks in New York and Washington. Following 9/11, for example, Noam Chomsky (whom Professor Paul Hollander calls one of the "usual suspects") demonstrated a reflexive 1960s era radicalism, using the event to trot out a litany of complaints about the nature of the American political process and the nation's global role. Chomsky, among others, impelled Hollander to comment on the 9/11 attacks as a most "intense and irrational manifestation of anti-Americanism."[30] Here Hollander discusses aspects of anti-Americanism, defining it as "a hostile predisposition":

The term has been employed to denote a particular mindset, an attitude of distaste, aversion or intense hostility the roots of which may be found in matters unrelated to the actual qualities or attributes of American society or the foreign policies of the United States. . . . [A]nti-Americanism refers to a negative predisposition, a type of bias which is to varying degrees unfounded. . . . I regard it as an attitude similar to its far more thoroughly explored counterparts, hostile predispositions such as racism, sexism and anti-Semitism.[31]

Hollander distinguishes critiques of American policies from anti-Americanism. He argues that anti-Americanism is irrational per se and "is born of a scapegoating impulse fuelled by a variety of frustrations and grievances."[32] However, once one unpacks the word and sees its deeper meaning, it is much more complicated. In Crockatt's view, anti-Americanism assumes many forms in different contexts and should be thought of as "a family

[29] David Strauss, *Menace in the West: The Rise of French Anti-Americanism in Modern Times* (London: Greenwood, 1978), p. 6.

[30] Paul Hollander, "Anti-Americanism Revisited," *Weekly Standard*, October 22, 2001.

[31] Paul Hollander, *Anti-Americanism: Critiques at Home and Abroad, 1965–1990* (Oxford: Oxford University Press, 1992), p. viii.

[32] Ibid., pp. 334–35.

of related attitudes rather as a single entity."[33] Thus, depending on differing historical, socio-economic, and policy contexts, anti-Americanism is manifested differently in each political culture.

Anti-Americanism may begin as what Moises Naim, the current editor of *Foreign Policy*, terms "lite anti-Americanism," referring to simple criticism of American policies or of American society, and can evolve under certain circumstances into what has been described as an allergic reaction to anything American.[34] Extreme and violent expressions of anti-Americanism, such as the one we all experienced on September 11, are often drawn from more widely accepted critiques of the United States. But anti-Americanism should not be viewed as an ideology, in the sense of a science of ideas that legitimizes the power of a dominant class or group of people. Rather, anti-Americanism is more accurately a sentiment, a set of opinions about America, its people, and its policies, which adopts different forms and expressions and arises from different experiences.

ANTI-AMERICANISM: THE EARLY ROOTS

Contemporary polling data can tell only so much of the story. The historical foundations go deeper and, to understand how modern elite opinion builds on these foundations, we look at some of the images, travel logs, literary descriptions, and, of course, the philosophical challenge of equality, that have over the centuries formed a point of departure – often not a positive one – for Europeans and others thinking about America. The reason for understanding this history lies in the fact that neo-conservative policy today has in a most cavalier manner played into this matrix, exacerbating latent feelings of hostility and focusing resistance to American initiatives. We begin with precolonial America.

As early as the mid-eighteenth century, respected "scientific authorities"– the Count of Buffon and Cornelius de Pauw, in particular – proposed a thesis of degeneracy that was meant to prove that all forms of life in the New World were subject to hostile atmospheric conditions – especially a debilitating humidity.[35] The adverse conditions in the New World were thought to have rendered all forms of life there not only inferior to their equivalents in Europe but in a state of decline. Pauw insisted, "No sooner did the Europeans debark from their ships than they began the process of decline,

---

[33] Crockatt, *America Embattled*, p. 44.
[34] Moises Naim, "The Costs of Lite Anti-Americanism," *New Perspectives Quarterly*, spring 2003.
[35] Ceaser, "A Genealogy," p. 6.

physical and mental." America, accordingly, would never be able to produce a political system or culture of any merit. Reflecting these views, the encyclopedist Abbé Raynal opined: "America has not yet produced a good poet, an able mathematician, one man of genius in a single art or a single science." So prevalent were these beliefs that Alexander Hamilton, Thomas Jefferson and Benjamin Franklin each, in turn, sought to refute the assertions. Hamilton writing in the Federalist Papers as Publius said: "Men admired as profound philosophers gravely asserted that all animals, and with them the human species, degenerate in America" – that "even dogs cease to bark after breathed a while in our atmosphere." Franklin and Jefferson, joined the argument for reasons that extended beyond pure science. Their concern was practical politics. After all, "Who in Europe would be willing to invest in and support the United States if America if it were regarded as a dying continent?"[36]

REVOLUTIONARY AMERICA

These early impressions of America, conveyed through letters and books depicting the manners, esthetics, dinner table conversation, and values of Americans, have been refined over the past two hundred years, forging some of the impressions that resonate today. Britain provided a prime point of reference, indeed a foil for an early America where the lack of aristocracy, a different view of the land, the embrace of specific freedoms, and demand for "equality" formed a cultural ideal peculiar to the colonies. British society, emphasizing formal relations among its classes with little or no mobility, reflected profoundly different values from those in America's newly forming culture.

Early attitudes in Great Britain were mixed. Though the Crown and most in London's surprisingly political society disapproved in varying degrees of the seeming reckless egalitarianism evident in the colonies and of the growing self-confidence of the emerging merchant classes, some believed America could be made to remain a colony. Speaking in the House of Commons in 1775 before the outbreak of the Revolutionary War (called the War of Independence in Britain), Edmund Burke urged a better understanding of the Americans:

In this character of the Americans a love of freedom is the predominating feature, which marks and distinguishes the whole; ... your colonies become suspicious, restive, and intractable, whenever they see the least attempt to wrest them by force,

---

[36] Ibid., pp. 6–7.

or shuffle them by chicane, what they think the only advantage worth living for. This fierce spirit of liberty is stronger in the English colonies, probably than in any people of the earth.[37]

Such views were, however, short-lived. In 1776, *Common Sense*, by Tom Paine (by birth an Englishman), captured the emotion of the moment by speaking of Britain as a "vile impostor, an old abandoned prostitute, a robber, a murderer ... a Jezebel."[38] Paine's pamphlet provided a dynamic definition of the events of the time, injecting the debate with "radical Republican" values and offering independence as a solution. Though most of London's self-absorbed society displayed little interest, for the Crown and for many in parliament, Paine was a horror.

American refusal to accept British "protection" and control over foreign and defense matters was particularly frustrating. Even so, many in parliament believed that Britain could and should manage the colonies with a loose hand, bringing the aspiring republic along, even allowing considerable self-government. But the Americans demurred. The Revolutionary War was often fought in what the British thought was a "savage and ungentlemanly" manner, fueling a certain stereotype of the Americans. Guerrilla tactics taken from the Indians were employed to great advantage; though there were many set battles, all too often lines of redcoats in formation were met with hit-and-run tactics.[39] Thus the American Revolution unceremoniously ended the British imperium in America and ushered in the American "experiment in democracy."

The "Idea" of Nineteenth-Century America

With the nineteenth century there were innumerable novels and travel logs depicting a rude and uncouth America. A body of literature had begun to develop often conveying negative impressions of the Americans as a people and a culture. Much of this revolved around esthetics and manners and how very different America was from Britain. Paul Langford says:

In the American eyes British society was incorrigibly aristocratic, bound by rigid upper-class rules, preserved by cringing lower-class servility and served by

[37] Edmund Burke, H. J. Carmen, H. C. Syrett, and B. W. Wishy, *A History of the American People* (New York, 1961), vol. 1, p. 175, quoted in Isaac Kramnick, introduction to Thomas Paine, *Common Sense* (New York: Penguin, 1976), pp. 21–22.

[38] Pauline Maier, *From Resistance to Revolution: Colonial Radicals and the Development of American Opposition to Britain, 1765–1776* (New York: Knopf, 1974), p. 270.

[39] John Keegan, *A History of Warfare* (New York: Knopf, 1993), pp. 345–46.

institutional conservatism. In British eyes American society was dangerously egal-
itarian, conducted according to barbaric ideas, governed by unprincipled democrats
and bereft of decorum and order.[40]

Frances Trollope's book *The Domestic Manners of Americans* caused quite
a scandal when it was published in 1832. Trollope was an Englishwoman
who lived in various places west of the Appalachian Mountains in the late
1820s. Traveling on the Mississippi River to Ohio and then to Pennsylvania,
Washington, and New York as well as other places, Trollope paints a re-
pellent picture of the cities – mud-filled streets, flowerless gardens, rabble-
rousing town meetings – and of her exchanges with the Americans. It was
their habits, described as vulgar, that she found so disturbing: "I hardly
know any annoyance so deeply repugnant to English feelings, as the incessant remorseless spitting of Americans."[41] A descendant, Joanna Trollope,
wrote in 1984 about the book's impact: "Reaction was explosive. Americans
were outraged, English radicals were loud in protest and English Tories were
jubilant."[42]

As Trollope so vividly demonstrates, the first expressions of anti-
Americanism in Europe were apparent in the field of culture, rendering
anti-Americanism largely a phenomenon of the elites, as continues to be
the case today. However, what was initially a comfortable feeling of cultural superiority soon gave way to the need for European elites to defend their values from troublesome American notions of social equality and
mobility.

In a refreshing change, Alexis de Tocqueville's personal diaries provide a
fascinating and optimistic glimpse of America in 1831 and 1832, as shown
in this talk with a Mr. Livingstone at Greenbrugh on the Hudson. What is
interesting are the distinctly American views of class and heredity:

T: How do the wealthy classes put up with such a state of affairs?
Mr. L: They put up with it as something inevitable since there is nothing whatsoever
to be done about it.
T: But is there none the less some resentment between them and the common people?
Mr. L: None. All classes joined together in the Revolution. Afterwards the strength
of Democracy was so paramount that no one attempted to struggle against it.

---

[40] Paul Langford, "Manners and Character in Anglo-American Perceptions, 1750–1850," in
Fred M. Leventhal and Roland Quinault, eds., *Anglo-American Attitudes: From Revolution of
Partnership* (Aldershot: Ashgate, 2000), p. 76.
[41] Frances Trollope, *Domestic Manners of the Americans* (London: Century, 1984), p. 12.
[42] Joanna Trollope, foreword to ibid., p. viii.

T: It seems to me that American society suffers from taking too little account of intellectual questions.
Mr. L: I agree, far from improving, we get daily worse in this respect.[43]

As the century proceeded, English immigration continued apace through the 1870s and early 1880s, but by the mid-1880s, it had slowed significantly. Growing immigration from Southern and Eastern Europe brought fundamental changes to the U.S. population. Reacting in part to reduced Anglo-Saxon immigration to America in the 1890s, elites on both sides of the Atlantic urged a greater unity of America with the "English speaking peoples."[44] In 1898, U.S. Secretary of State Richard Olney wrote that an "Anglo-American close community based on origin, speech, thought, literature, institutions, ideals would obviate any future conflict between the two countries and would indeed cause them to stand together against common enemies."[45] This notion would influence Winston Churchill some years later and continues to resonate today with various Anglo-American initiatives, such as the Atlantic Studies Programme at Cambridge (administered by one of the authors) and the Rothermere Institute at Oxford, not to mention the Donner and Rhodes scholarship programs and the American Enterprise Institute's "New Atlantic Initiative."

With the turn of the twentieth century, it was not difficult to assemble the elements composing a European view of the new American republic. British images brought forward over four or five generations depicted a wild land that succumbed to radical notions of man and society and employed savage guerrilla-type warfare to gain its independence. Horrific manners, questionable habits, galloping commercialism, and an emerging "blue water navy" were thought to pose both a social and a political challenge to Europe's refined societies and the imperial systems they administered. Clearly, if in 1905, you were to ask the average man on a street corner in New York or London whether he thought the United States and Britain would be closest allies with a "special relationship" in the coming century, he would say you were mad.

43 J. P. Mayer, ed., *Alexis de Tocqueville: Journey to America*, trans. George Lawrence (London: Faber and Faber, 1959), p. 19.

44 John Dumbrell, *A Special Relationship: Anglo-American Relations in the Cold War and After* (London: Macmillan, 2001), p. 4.

45 C. S. Campbell, *From Revolution to Rapprochement: The United States and Great Britain, 1783–1900* (New York: Wiley, 1974), p. 201; Dumbrell, *A Special Relationship*, p. 4.

ANTI-AMERICANISM IN THE TWENTIETH CENTURY

Turn-of-the-century European elites became increasingly aware of the United States, which had suddenly emerged as both a military and a commercial power. Just as Britain found itself locked in a competition with Germany to produce the fastest, most powerful warships, Whitehall was startled by President Teddy Roosevelt's "Great White Fleet" then displaying American sea power in an around-the-world tour. Moreover, social and cultural changes in the United States complicated perceptions of America in Britain as well as in Continental Europe, where elites believed that modernity was running rampant in an America where there was no traditional *ancien régime* to oppose it. In 1901, the British journalist William Thomas Stead published a study, *The Americanization of the World or the Trend of the 20th Century*, in which the author saw "Americanization" as a metaphor for the modern industrial age, creating "a term that evoked [the] nightmare of an emerging mass society where the rule of misanthropic rationalization and a trivial mass culture destroy[ed] all individuality."[46] In most cases the process of "Americanization" referred to a modern mass society and the subsequent alienation of the individual. America was all too often suspected of employing a variety of means to influence European cultures and to undermine European individualism – and the degree of Americanization implied an equal degree of de-Europeanization.

Reflections of these concerns about the American emphasis on "action," commercialism, and efficiency are certainly found on the Continent. The writings of German philosopher Friedrich Nietzsche, initially known in avant-garde intellectual and literary circles in the late nineteenth century provide an early hint to these themes more widely circulated, by Max Weber in the 1930s. In Nietzsche's view, a peculiar America mentality had pioneered certain dehumanizing techniques of mass production. All had been reduced to those things that were "calculable" in the effort to generate wealth: "The breathless haste with which they [the Americans] work – the distinctive vice of the new world – is already beginning ferociously to infect old Europe and is spreading spiritual emptiness over the continent."[47]

In *The Protestant Ethic and the Spirit of Capitalism*, Weber, known as one of the "fathers of modern sociology" and writing in the 1930s, criticizes then contemporary American capitalism and Ben Franklin's contribution to it in the early days of the Republic. Referring to Franklin's "idea of a duty of the

---

[46] Stead cited in Dan Diner, *America in the Eyes of the Germans: An Essay on Anti-Americanism*, trans. Allison Brown (Princeton, N.J.: Markus Wiener, 1996), p. 48.
[47] Nietzsche cited in Ceasar, "A Genealogy," p. 12.

individual toward the increase of his capital, which is assumed to be an end in itself," he says that "what is preached here is not only a way of making one's way in the world, but a peculiar ethic." He continues: "all Franklin's moral attitudes are colored with utilitarianism. Honesty is useful, because it assures credit; so are punctuality, industry, frugality, and that is the reason they are virtues.... According to Franklin, these virtues, like all others, are only in so far virtues as they are actually useful to the individual, and the surrogate of mere appearance is always sufficient when it accomplishes the end in view." He continues, "The impression of many Germans that the virtues professed by Americans are pure hypocrisy seems to have been confirmed."[48]

Weber proceeds to underscore his objection to the utilitarian employment of virtue he detects in Franklin's writing, saying, "[That] state of mind ... which called forth the applause of a whole people, would both in ancient times and in the Middle Ages have been proscribed as the lowest sort of avarice and as an attitude entirely lacking in self-respect.... The ideal type of the capitalistic entrepreneur, as it is represented even here in Germany by occasional outstanding examples, has no relation to such more or less refined climbers. He avoids ostentation and unnecessary expenditure, as well as conspicuous enjoyment of his power, and is embarrassed by the outward signs of social recognition he receives.... It is, namely, by no means exceptional but rather a rule, for him to have a sort of modesty which is essentially more modest than the reserve Franklin so shrewdly recommends."[49] Thus Weber revealed important distinctions about how Europeans and Americans viewed daily life and morality differently – particularly issues such as wealth and work.

In the world of diplomacy and world affairs, the end of World War I had brought new political tensions. President Woodrow Wilson's Fourteen Points, meant as a statement of principles to guide the peace, reflected a clear American predisposition against the imperial systems then administered by both Britain and France. American notions of "the self determination of peoples," a demand to end the "secret diplomacy" that Washington felt had poisoned European relations and cost millions of lives, including over 100,000 Americans, and the imposition of American notions of egalitarianism on European affairs were greeted without enthusiasm. Following World War I, with America's new global status, productive relations between the United States and France masked a revival of negative views of America. The

[48] Max Weber, *The Protestant Ethic and the Spirit of Capitalism* (London: George Allen and Unwin, 1930), p. 52.
[49] Ibid., p. 56.

late 1920s saw a return of French anti-Americanism with the publication of three studies on the United States by Lucien Romier, André Sigfried, and André Tardieu, and later writers such as Georges Duhamel. Though they mentioned the dangers of rising American power and of American imperialism, the focus of their criticism was on the threat from American mass culture, the implications of mass production, and the new consumer society.[50] For example, Duhamel's book, *Scènes de la vie future*, published in the 1930s, targeted America as "a leveling conformist and exclusively materialistic society of miserable creatures all reduced to the same level of uniformity."[51] Reflecting this theme in Germany, the philosopher Martin Heidegger joined in the tradition of Nietzsche and Weber excoriating American "soullessness," which he coupled with a concern that the emphasis in American culture of quantity over quality would lead to growing economic power, if not domination.[52]

Similar attitudes were expressed among elites during the interwar years in Britain, where both a sense of cultural superiority and a fear of subordination to America's mass culture were obvious. In 1928, the British philosopher C. E. M. Joad asked, "Does England dislike America?"[53] What distinguished English anti-American sentiments from those of France and Germany, however, is the fact that these sentiments in England arose in the context of a "special relationship." British interests were often well served by interpreting Europe to America and vice versa, while moderating the potentially offensive initiatives of each.

While the Allies were and remain deeply grateful for America's sacrifice in defeating Nazi Germany, the war itself and its immediate aftermath were not without their anti-American moments. Roosevelt and Churchill had strong differences over the time and effort devoted by senior management in Washington to the war in the Pacific – Churchill complained that every hour Roosevelt spent on Japan was an hour not spent on Europe – and the future of the British empire was seen in fundamentally different terms in London and Washington. British concern about American anti-imperial attitudes flashed to the surface in March 1945 when J. V. Perowne, a senior Foreign Office official, said that "the chief consequence of the war, from our point of view, will be that we will have exchanged a direct threat from Germany for a more or less direct threat from Russia and the USA...."[54]

[50] Strauss, *Menace*, pp. 67–72.
[51] Lacorne et al., eds., *Rise and Fall*, p. 47.
[52] Ceaser, "A Genealogy," p. 12.
[53] Crockatt, *America Embattled*, p. 56.
[54] J. V. Perowne, Minute, March 19, 1945, Foreign Office, 371/45012 AS 1599/176/51.

It was not, however, until after the Second World War that American economic power became obvious – with the result that it stimulated even stronger criticism from the continent.

AMERICA AFTER THE SECOND WORLD WAR

In the years following the end of the Second World War, the glaring economic imbalance between the United States and Europe began to hit home. It was not uncommon for European elites to criticize American "cultural imperialism" as well as politics and foreign policy. De Gaulle's France became the vortex of European denunciation of America. In a press conference on May 18, 1958, de Gaulle presented himself as an alternative to the United States, which he claimed was leading outside powers seeking to impose a solution on the French in their war with Algeria. As de Gaulle wrapped himself in the destiny of France during the election that year, he was inviting the nation to reject America and a world in which American power sought to undermine French interests. De Gaulle's behavior at the time confirmed for many in both France and the United States his position at the apex of the most obstinate and virulent kind of anti-Americanism.

Cultural anti-Americanism during the 1950s was most vigorously expressed by elite intellectuals such as Jean-Paul Sartre and Simone de Beauvoir. Sartre's opinion on America can be summarized in the following statement: "Don't be surprised if from one end of Europe to the other we are shouting: watch out, America is a mad dog! Let's cut every tie that binds us to her lest she bites us and we go mad too."[55] Similarly, de Beauvoir noted that "with the exception of certain individuals, the Americans had become a nation of sheep, they were entirely conformist and bereft of any critical spirit."[56]

Though Europe's elites rejected a perceived vulgar mass American culture, anti-Americanism after World War II turned more fundamentally on resentment over the loss of imperial power and being replaced by a nation with different views of the relationship between the "developed" and the "underdeveloped world," as it was then coming to be known. Unlike America, which emerged from the war stronger than before, European economic, political, and social structures were in crisis. In these circumstances, America's dynamic growth was viewed with both envy and awe. British

---

[55] Sartre cited in Michel Winock, "The Cold War," in Lacorne et al., eds., *Rise and Fall*, p. 70.
[56] Beauvoir cited in Marie Christine Granjon, "Sartre, Beauvoir, Aron: An Ambiguous Affair," in ibid., pp. 122–23.

author Denis Brogan, musing on British feelings toward the United States, said that "it was unjust that America should be so rich, so powerful, so indispensable."[57] Further illustrating his point, Brogan quoted Napoleon: "Why," Napoleon was asked, "do your brothers and sisters whom you have made kings and queens, quarrel with you so much?" "Because they think I have cheated them of their share in their inheritance, from their father, the late king."[58]

In Britain's case, the "special relationship" imposed unique burdens. As mentioned above, London was uncomfortable playing Greece to Washington's Rome. Though there were many benefits, the decline in national stature and military capacity was unmistakable. Britain, particularly in the wake of the 1956 Suez Crisis, felt the need to clear virtually all of its foreign and security policies with Washington. This was further underscored in the Cuban Missile Crisis, when the West found itself on the very cusp of nuclear war with the USSR. While Churchill's words "never to be out of step with the United States" rang down through the decades, it was not surprising that Britain was said by cynics to be "America's fifty-first state."[59]

During this period, Britain and France had somewhat more in common than with their German counterpart. In France, anti-Americanism evolved from a sentiment to a compelling emotion, eventually becoming the virtual lone principle in foreign policy. Jean-François Revel described it as a "constant alibi – a consolation for European failure." Revel says anti-Americanism in France is a "sickness" but then poses the question: "If America is so sick, why are we so worried about its wealth, its technical supremacy and its cultural model?"[60] In another dimension, Revel asserts that the function of anti-Americanism is to allow Europe and leftist movements in Europe to purify themselves of all their moral failures and ideological mistakes.[61] In this sense, anti-Americanism has functioned as a way for France to assure the protection of its own culture.[62]

---

57 Denis Brogan, "From England," in Franz M. Joseph, ed., *As Other See Us: The United States through Foreign Eyes* (Princeton, N.J.: Princeton University Press, 1959), p. 15.

58 Ibid.

59 Richard Pells, *Not like Us: How Europeans Have Loved, Hated, and Transformed American Culture since WWII* (London: Basic Books, 1997), p. 159.

60 Jean-François Revel in "La maladie française," *Times Literary Supplement*, October 1, 2003, p. 3.

61 Jean-François Revel, *L'obsession anti-Américaine: Son fonctionnement, ses causes, ses inconsequences* (Paris: Plon, 2002), p. 271. English translation published as *Anti-Americanism* (New York: Encounter, 2003).

62 Ibid., p. 185.

This period, however, found Germany in a different category. In the years immediately after the war, Germans embraced the United States as a savior; not only was the Marshall Plan rebuilding Europe, but Hitler had been replaced after twelve years by the Allied administration, democratic government, and a return of personal freedoms. German responsibility for plunging Europe into two world wars and its subsequent defeat and humiliation brought resentment mixed with feelings of guilt for its Nazi past. The then divided German nation believed it had paid a high price for Hitler's crimes, however, and wished to get on with the task of reconstruction. The United States, which contributed decisively both to Germany's defeat and to its reconstruction, had been complicit in generating these complex emotions over the years. The United States had, after all, both spearheaded the Nuremberg trials proving German responsibility for the Holocaust and guaranteed German postwar security. These issues lay at the center of a convulsive debate carried on in the newspapers and journals of New York, London, and Paris about Nazi guilt and German ambivalence about accepting responsibility for the actions of a previous generation of leaders. Thus not surprisingly, German opinion toward the United States, though generally positive, was sharply divided.

And so in Britain, France, and Germany a common concern with what are seen as the American obsession with "standardization," excessive emphasis on efficiency, and growing economic and military power combined with certain country-specific issues to complicate views of America. Some were moral questions, such as Weber's charges of hypocrisy and utilitarianism and Revel's critique of his fellow countrymen's fixation on America. Others were political matters as with de Gaulle's allegations of interference with the war in Algeria. In Britain the benefits of the "special relationship" clashed with London's belief that Washington was instrumental in deconstructing the empire and the resulting diminution in world status, while in Germany a love-hate syndrome mixed memories of the war and anger about Holocaust charges with gratitude for the Marshall Plan and NATO's defense of the continent.

All of this contributed to conflicted yet generally positive views of America – with Britain clearly in a separate category. Professional political-military analysts knew, however, that these mixed emotions and experiences provided far less than the firm foundation required to advance a controversial policy. Certain areas, most notably the Middle East, brought sharply diverging perspectives between Washington and the councils of Europe, allowing neo-conservative unilateralism to generate transatlantic tensions not seen in a quarter-century.

POLITICAL ANTI-AMERICANISM TODAY

> Eleven thousand soldiers
> lay beneath the dirt and stone
> all buried on a distant land
> so far away from home.
> And now the shores of Normandy
> are lined with blocks of white
> Americans who didn't turn
> from someone else's plight.
> Eleven thousand reasons
> for the French to take our side,
> but in the moment of our need,
> they chose to run and hide.
>> Don Fichthorn, Major, U.S.
>> Marine Corps (ret.),
>> April 2003

Reflecting the common feeling of betrayal felt by the Americans, the above poem reflects the deep transatlantic breach over the war on Iraq. Americans "dumped French wine in the gutter" and renamed "French fries" as "freedom fries" following "betrayal and abandonment" by their traditional allies and friends. The neo-conservative *Weekly Standard* joined the party with an article entitled "Our Friends the French – Really!"[63] In Germany, waiters in dozens of bars and restaurants intoned: "Sorry, Coca Cola is not available any more due to the current political situation." Even in London, consumers boycotted 330 American products, ranging from Mars bars to Gap jeans and American films. In Zurich, travel agents said that loyal customers who had traveled to the United States for years changed their plans because "they don't like what Bush is doing."[64] A poll by the Pew Research Center showed strong opposition to the war in Western European capitals that was directly linked to widespread anti-American sentiment. The poll further showed that in Great Britain, the war caused favorable views of the United States to decline from 83 percent in 1999–2000 to 48 percent in March 2003.[65] In France, the percentage of respondents holding favorable views of the United States fell from 62 percent in 1999–2000 to 31 percent in 2003, and in Germany favorable views fell from 78 percent to 25 percent. These figures

---

[63] Fred Barnes, "Our Friends the French – Really!" *Daily Standard*, March 12, 2003.
[64] Erik Kirshaum, "EU: Boycott of American Goods over Iraq War Gains Momentum," *Reuters*, March 25, 2003.
[65] Pew Research Center for the People and the Press, "America's Image Further Erodes, Europeans Want Weaker Ties," March 18, 2003.

are directly linked to the Iraq war and reflect majority opinion in all European countries.[66]

In the Arab world, boycotts of American goods due to American support for Israel began earlier. For example, Mecca Cola, a new soft drink launched in France in November 2002, claimed to have sold 800,000 liter bottles there between November and February; 1.5 million liter bottles each in the United Kingdom and in Germany, plus another million bottles in the Middle East and Africa.[67] American businesses operating in Egypt, Lebanon, Jordan, and the Persian Gulf countries have been targeted by scores of boycotts since violence erupted between Palestinians and Israelis in September 2000. Mahmoud El Kaissoumi, an executive at American Foods in Cairo, said that "this is getting very serious. Some chains are experiencing 50% losses in sales. We are just trying to survive."[68]

Some argue that these boycotts are not likely to have a negative impact on the American economy as a whole. "The sound and fury likely signifies nothing," believes Jan Lindermann, global brand–valuation director at Interbrand.[69] "Despite a deluge of images showing outraged protesters and headlines calling for boycotts, the activists are a minority," Lindermann says. He points out that consumers abroad act much like their American counterparts and do not take their political views to the cash register. "There is little historic proof that war and anti-war sentiments have had massive impact.... [T]his anti-American debate is waged by groups that don't reflect most consumers."[70]

Academics and political analysts point out, however, that you do not need large numbers. If only 5 percent of the people in a country are part of the boycott, that can hurt a U.S. company.[71] In the United States, people vote independently; they make independent choices and there is less likelihood of an effective collective action, such as a boycott. But many Asian countries have a more collective culture. In these societies, social sanctions are likely to be greater against the public consumption of a boycotted product.[72]

---

[66] Ibid.

[67] James Cox, "Arab Nations See Boycotts of US Products; West Bank Action Ignites Grassroots Activity in Region," *USA Today*, June 25, 2002, p. B3.

[68] Ibid.

[69] Jan Lindermann cited in *Business Week Online*, April 8, 2003.

[70] Ibid.

[71] Professor Shin-Fen Chen, "On Possible Economic Side Effects of War with Iraq," cited in the *Boston Globe*, March 16, 2003, also see http://www.brandeis.edu/global.news_iten.php?news_item_id=890.

[72] Ibid.

Looking beyond the inconclusive boycott data, one finds a deeper and perhaps more important issue. A new post–Cold War reality has emerged. Neo-conservative policies, as expressed by the U.S. position on the Kyoto Accords, the International Criminal Court, the Anti-Ballistic Missile (ABM) Treaty, and the National Missile Defense (NMD), taken together, are seen by many, including important allies on the U.N. Security Council, as insensitive to the concerns of the global community. Governments, reflecting the views of their citizens, condemn U.S. environmental policy, see the ICC issue as one of fairness in which all governments should be subject to the same set of laws, and see the U.S. position on the ABM and NMD as potentially destabilizing and dangerous. The common denominator in these perceived neo-conservative positions, the pivot on which differences turn, is the notion that if multilateral agreement is not readily forthcoming, unilateral American action is perfectly acceptable – and certainly easier. The neo-conservative inclination to minimize the benefits of multilateral cooperation and of U.N.-sanctioned action is, moreover, an affront to would-be global partners such that the administration's actions on the specific issues cited above have stimulated broad criticism in the international media, massive street demonstrations, and other expressions of anti-American sentiment, including boycotts, unseen in over a decade. But at the heart is a concern that the neo-conservative elixir of the "unipolar moment" has gone to America's collective head and that America no longer feels bound to play by the rules. Commenting on America's unparalleled power, Harvard professor Joe Nye observed:

The world is off balance. . . . Not since Rome has one nation loomed so large above the others. Indeed the word "empire" has come out of the closet. Respected analysts on both the left and the right are beginning to refer to "American empire" approvingly as the dominant narrative of the 21st century. And the military victory in Iraq seems only to have confirmed this new world order.[73]

Reaction to this new distribution of power has elicited a vigorous response from European intellectuals. *Why Do People Hate America?*, by Ziauddin Sardar and Merryl Wyn Davies, is a typical example of this genre of incandescent anti-Americanism. Making the global financial institutions such as the International Monetary Fund and World Trade Organization proxies for American power, they argue that through these institutions, America controls the economic destinies of over two-thirds of the world's

---

[73] Joseph S. Nye, Jr., "American Power and Strategy after Iraq," *Foreign Affairs*, July/August 2003, p. 60.

population.[74] Loans given to developing countries through the IMF are thought to exploit and dominate local economies. In exchange for loans, for example, developing countries are asked to allow foreign banks to own more equity in the local banking sector. Sardar and Davies claim that this has led to U.S. corporations owning banks, financial institutions, and other key sectors in the developing world, depriving local economies of the "benefits" of these institutions. More striking, they claim, is that refusal or unwillingness to accommodate the rules imposed by the IMF and the WTO are met with the threat of retaliation against exports or modification of the loan conditions.[75]

A CONTEMPORARY EXAMPLE: MCDONALDIZATION

As an example of how these antipathies play out in the real world, let us look at the phenomenon of "McDonaldization" as an example of how a concept – fast food – that all Americans find familiar and innocuous can, on the one hand, conquer the world and, on the other, act as the lightning rod for so many of the tensions between the United States and the international community. Where Americans see convenience, Europeans see "American cultural imperialism" and the "McDonaldization of society."

University of Maryland sociologist George Ritzer has summarized the criticism of McDonald's as "the process by which the principles of the fast food restaurant are coming to dominate more and more sectors of American society as well as of the rest of the world."[76] Ritzer mentions a poll of school-age children that showed that 96 percent of them could identify Ronald McDonald, second only to Santa Claus in name recognition.[77]

Though the concept of McDonaldization has been much discussed, the extensive roots that feed its power are little understood. McDonald's has become a "negative symbol" to a number of global social movements concerned about ecological hazards, dietary dangers, the evils of capitalism, and the dangers posed by Americanization. Some of this became evident in the 1997 London trial of Helen Steel and David Morris, whom the McDonald's Corporation charged with libel.[78] Although the tribunal did

[74] Ziauddin Sardar and Merryl Wyn Davies, *Why Do People Hate America?* (Cambridge: Icon, 2002), pp. 63–91.
[75] Ibid.
[76] George Ritzer, *The McDonaldization of Society* (Thousand Oaks, Calif.: Pine Forge Press, 2000), p. 1.
[77] Ibid., p. 7.
[78] Ibid., pp. 214–15.

not find in favor of the activists, the trial widely publicized the alleged hazards of McDonaldization, namely the way the corporation treated animals, the questionable nutritional value of the food it produced, the damage to the cultural environment, and the exploitation of workers. This, of course, fueled the disapproval of those who rejected the U.S. position on the Kyoto Accords, the Rio Pact, and the United Nations Convention of the Rights of the Child and played into the subsequent controversy on genetically modified foods.

In France the symbol of the resistance to McDonaldization is Jose Bové. The forty-seven-year-old sheep farmer became a symbol for antiglobalization activists in France and abroad when he led an attack on a McDonald's restaurant under construction in Millau, in southern France, in August 1999. He argued that the action was a symbolic, nonviolent protest against multinational corporations. His trial turned into a giant antiglobalization festival drawing the participation of over 45,000 people from all over France. The French media portrayed him as the new Vercingetorix, a near mythic hero who led the great Gallic revolt against the Romans in 52 B.C. and was put to death by Julius Caesar. All this illustrated that in France anti-Americanism could in certain important respects be explained as the result of egoism and the search for a scapegoat to rationalize the French decline. Michael Harrison points out that "the US was the most natural object of French hostility because the decline of France was accompanied by the rise of the United States to the point where the United States had to be counted on to save France until finally it (France) had to succumb to becoming a formal part of the American protectorate after 1947."[79]

While commodity prices motivated some activists, the wider French public supported Bové's fight because it went to the heart of their cultural traditions, where the life cycle of food holds a special place. The practice of "cuisine" and the traditional agricultural practices on which it depends are central to the daily life of every French man and woman, regardless of class. Ask anyone in France for his or her opinion of American cuisine, and more often than not the response, a mixture of nationalism and arrogance, is that "Americans have no cuisine!" McDonald's, for Bové and his supporters, is the symbol of a homogenized, mass food production and preparation process they regard as the antithesis to French culinary tradition and that threatens to erode their cultural identity.

In its colloquial sense, McDonaldization is despised by intellectuals and activists as a successful business model that has insidious application to the

[79] Michael Harrison cited in Lacorne et al., eds., *Rise and Fall*, p. 169.

world beyond business. Ritzer draws his analysis and in part his authority from Max Weber. Weber was one of the early critics of bureaucracy, which he regarded as part of a "rationalizing process" embraced by the modern Western world to achieve greater efficiency and predictability.[80] He argued – not unlike Nietzsche before him, and the echoes are heard today through academics such as Ritzer – that capitalism and modernity reflect a rationalizing process imposed on everyday life that has resulted in a loss of individuality.

Just as Herbert Marcuse, the sage of the 1960s whose book *One-Dimensional Man* chronicled the plight of America's entrapped, alienated, and dehumanized corporate man, Ritzer uses Weber's iron cage to describe the effects of McDonaldization in contemporary society.[81] Customers cheerfully enter the iron cage of McDonaldization and lose their individuality in a world of homogeneity.[82] Excoriating criticism is directed toward the impact of McDonaldization on social life. Referring to the disintegration of the family, Ritzer argues that the fast food culture has had a debilitating effect as dinners at home are said to have become McDonaldized. McDonaldization is thus thought to have an inexorable quality, sweeping through seemingly impervious institutions and parts of global human life. "The scale of global 'McAttack' is impressive."[83]

McDonald's, of course, is not the only symbol of an omnipresent American commercialism. Coca-Cola has been the drink of choice for decades, and teens from Malaysia to Morocco are not complete without their Nike shoes; each is a product targeted to a global "mass consumer society." And each has become a symbol overloaded with complex cultural associations demonstrating, among other things, the power and success of American commerce and the appeal of the American way of life. Many feel, for example, when they drink Coke or eat at McDonald's or Burger King, they are participants, if only for a moment, in the American Dream.

This is, perhaps, what makes Americanization so complex. While for elites McDonaldization symbolizes disapproval of homogenization, it meets the requirements of many modern life-styles. It adapts to the needs of people looking for reasonable quality in the minimum amount of time. But perhaps more threatening to European elites is the sense that the appeal

---

[80] Weber argues that "rationalization happens in different times at different places and that Euro-capitalism was dependant on, and proceeds from, the prior existence of rational administration, of rational bookkeeping, laws and rational production."

[81] Ritzer, *McDonaldization*, pp. 22–26.

[82] Herbert Marcuse, *One-Dimensional Man* (Boston: Beacon, 1964), pp. 1–18.

[83] Cited in Douglas Kellner, "Theorizing-Resisting McDonaldization: A Multiperspectivist Approach," in Barry Smart, ed., *Resisting McDonaldization* (London: Sage, 1999), p. 192.

of McDonald's and of other American consumer products to the younger generation is irreversible. The success of these companies (often founded, in fact, on cultural sensitivity and local differentiation – CNN International, for example, is a product completely different from its American parent) suggests to these elites that their own culture cannot compete.

McDonaldization, as a caricature of the international American presence for many elites, presents the United States in a questionable, even negative context that tends to inhibit acceptance of American initiatives in policy areas far removed from cultural conflicts or commercial competition. By fueling the anti-American sentiments of those sensitive to cultural intrusion, it empowers politicians and others to resist ideas that are often productive. As a practical matter, Washington's motives are suspect today. While it is true that European elites in particular ground their objections to McDonaldization in Weber and Marcuse, their skepticism has gained traction among the public. This means that perceptions of American initiatives, whether in the U.N., the Middle East, or the WTO, must be carefully and extensively nurtured to overcome this ubiquitous symbol that has become an integral part of present anti-American rhetoric.

THE COSTS OF ANTI-AMERICANISM

No country can stand idly by while its interests are attacked. This is a core neo-conservative tenant and one with which few if any will disagree. But there is a price to be paid for seeing almost everything in terms of the need for unilateral action, specifically a reduction of "soft power," that is, the power to persuade by example, instead of coercion.[84] Ronald Reagan often referred to "the shining city on the hill" as a metaphor for an America guided by high ethical standards, forthright in its views and willing to work multilaterally if possible to address problems of instability and social progress. Reagan, in fact, saw "soft power," coupled with his admonition to "trust but verify," as the leading edges of U.S. diplomacy. What is remarkable is the speed with which the neo-conservative ascendancy has diminished, perhaps extinguished, this preferred medium of diplomatic exchange. The apparent dismissal of "soft power," together with the effects of globalizing developments and the expansion of U.S. military capability, provide the context for contemporary anti-Americanism.

[84] Joseph S. Nye, Jr., *The Paradox of American Power* (Oxford: Oxford University Press, 2002), pp. 8–12.

As mentioned above, prevailing attitudes toward the United States in Europe and the Middle East, particularly, but including parts of Latin America and many other parts of the world, are characterized by declining approval, especially in the past two years. Terms often used to describe American interaction with others include "imperialist," "condescending," and "arrogant." Unfortunately, these views are sustained, even accelerated, by three important global trends that frame our perceptions of the world around us. Globalizing developments have meant, effectively, that the world is smaller. Travel from New York to London in five hours or to Tokyo in twelve means that virtually any city on the planet is accessible in thirty-six hours. People speak with each other by cell phone as the mood strikes anywhere, anytime; teleconferencing instantly puts voices and faces together across the world; funds move with a click of the mouse; contracts, partnerships, investment – all can proceed in Singapore or in Maryland with nearly equal dispatch. But such a world brings disparate peoples and their cultures close together – often too close for comfort.

Just as international conflict resolution mechanisms such as the U.N. and the ICC are products of an elite transnational culture, so local conflict resolution mechanisms – tribal arbitration councils and "Dutch Uncles," for example – are deeply rooted within local cultures bounded by time and space. Both are generally resistant to change, and the latter have been slow to keep up with the rapid technical advances that characterize the dynamic international environment. Not only do local values increasingly clash with (American-inspired) "metropolitan" values, but corporate, trade, and other value-based grievances proliferate. What is important for our discussion is that the disjunction between metropolitan and local values, as conveyed interpersonally and through the media, has denied legitimacy to both the metropolitan and local mechanisms designated to resolve differences. Among the results has been an acceleration of polarizing social action: street demonstrations, "Intifadas," and the like.

It is into this combustible environment that the neo-conservative obsession with overwhelming and growing American techno-military power, characterized by a preference for unilateral solutions and a perceived arrogance, has played with destructive effect. What is that effect? Anthropologist Ruth Benedict pointed out in 1934 that civilizations and cultures finding themselves in ever closer proximity or threatened by a powerful outside force experience rising social tension, manifest nationalist themes, and often embrace the imagery of racial superiority in their media and political discourse as means of reinforcing social and cultural norms and maintaining equilibrium.[85] Cornell professor Benedict Anderson makes the point more recently that nationalism and challenges to it "arouse deep attachments and command profound emotional legitimacy."[86]

It is in important measure due to these converging trends – a shrinking globe, expanding U.S. military capability, and sharply limited ways of resolving conflict – that cultures, beliefs, and life-styles throughout Europe, the Middle East, and many other places are challenged. America is thought responsible for these unwanted pressures, bringing a rise in anti-American feelings often expressed, as pointed out by Joseph Nye, by a rigorous nationalism.

Leaving aside the question of how and why U.S. military power is projected in the current environment, many whom Washington wish to cultivate in the Middle East and also in Europe, particularly, object to U.S. policies that inject American cultural and economic products into local economies and cultures. Particularly offensive to European and Middle Eastern opinion makers is the assumption of superiority underpinning American policy that uncritically advances market democracy as the formula for progress in those areas that do not yet have it. They perceive their political cultures as subject to a kind of socio-political assault that serves American strategic and commercial interests by assuming that the world will be a better, more peaceful place if local institutions and cultural practices are replaced by those practiced in the metropolitan West.

THE BRITISH DIMENSION

In the coming decades, American global capabilities may be impacted by attitudes in China or India, but for the present moment, Britain is the key country. In Britain's case, attitudes toward America are seen through the lens of the "special relationship." Though banned from British diplomatic discourse by the British Ambassador in Washington in the late 1980s, the concept will not go away. Both sides play it up. Neo-conservatives openly praise Britain as "our key and indispensable ally throughout," and British leaders have nothing but warm words for the United States when they pass through Washington. But beneath this calm surface lurks a less comfortable reality. Over the decades British leaders have constantly had to avoid criticisms that they had become Washington's "poodle." The dilemma they face

---

[85] Ruth Benedict, *Patterns of Culture* (Boston: Houghton Mifflin, 1934), p. 11.
[86] Benedict Anderson, *Imagined Communities: Reflections of the Origin and Spread of Nationalism* (London: Verso, 1991), p. 4.

spans the distance from Churchill's observation that "we must never get out of step with the United States – never"[87] to the comment by Lord Strang, a former Permanent Secretary at the Foreign Office, who said in 1963: "As the weaker power... we ought to continue to work with the United States but not be subservient to them and not be above some exploitation of events in our own national interest."[88]

British attitudes toward the United States vacillate in accordance with the perceived success or failure of the British government to solve that dilemma: Stay close to the United States while at the same time retaining the confidence that Britain remains in sovereign control of its national destiny, particularly in the foreign, defense, economic, and environmental areas. To date, British leaders have more or less successfully answered this challenge. Since World War II, British prime ministers from both right and left have stood shoulder to shoulder with the United States in all the major crises of the day and have generally carried the public with them. The sole exception was Harold Wilson, who resisted Lyndon Johnson's repeated entreaties to send British troops to Vietnam. Tony Blair's instinctive solidarity with the United States after 9/11 was part of this tradition. While he was following a well-trodden path, his courage was palpable, as was his readiness to accept the risks to his premiership from a skeptical British public. His fluent articulation of the coalition's case for war won extensive praise, including from neo-conservatives, who draw a sharp distinction between Britain and its E.U. partners. Some neo-conservatives propose that the United States should take active steps to detach Britain from France. They suggest that "we must do our utmost to preserve our British ally's independence from Europe." Possible incentives for Britain to follow this course include a single defense procurement market for the United States and the United Kingdom.[89]

Courageous though Blair's stance was, however, this was the less complex side of the equation. The more difficult challenge from British leaders – and the more important one in preserving the long-term health of the Anglo-American partnership – lies in answering Strang's requirement that there should be some form of return to the British other than the glow of satisfaction of standing by its closest ally and the *gloire* of cutting a big figure on the world stage. This is where many British analysts find the balance sheet more difficult to assess. They find it easy to identify the legitimacy

---

[87] Quoted in D. R. Thorpe, *Eden: The Life and Times of Anthony Eden, First Earl of Avon, 1897–1977* (London: Chatto and Windus, 2003), p. 541.

[88] Quoted in Anthony Adamthwaite, "Suez Revisited," *International Affairs*, summer 1988, p. 464.

[89] Frum and Perle, *An End to Evil*, pp. 250–53.

conferred on U.S. policies by having Britain in the same camp but not so easy to calculate the direct returns to Britain. Much though they admire Britain, the neo-conservative unilateralists have little sympathy with this dilemma. This is a mistake. This approach has severely complicated Blair's and the British government's task and has thus put at risk one of the enduring assets enjoyed by the United States in its diplomacy. Simply put, unilateral U.S. action severely reduces the appeal of American policy; by contrast, acting in concert with Britain brings an indispensable measure of international legitimacy and acceptance.

British diplomacy in support of the United States post–9/11 was tireless. On September 12 Blair flew to the United States, paying a highly emotional visit to Trinity Church, on Wall Street a short distance from Ground Zero, and endorsing the administration's characterization of the event as an assault on the civilized world and, particularly, on the freedoms held inviolate by the West. In the course of it all Blair emerged center stage in a global drama with the highest approval ratings of his prime ministership. As he addressed the Labour Party conference not a month later on October 4, Blair sought to weld the British agenda for confronting the causes of terrorism – which emphasized a resolute approach to the Israeli-Palestinian conflict and a multilateral approach to the problems of poverty, education, and nutrition in the Third World – to his invigorated partnership with Washington. It was a complex moment and perhaps one in which he failed to appreciate fully the immense power wielded by Britain's widely perceived legitimacy. While he succeeded in causing Washington to act deliberately and in concert with its allies in attacking the Taliban regime in Afghanistan, the process of association placed Britain in a subordinate position, as the weeks unfolded, to the neo-conservative juggernaut then driving Washington's policy process.

And where did this lead? In August 2003 the British saw their prime minister and other ministers called to account for their actions before a senior judge investigating the suicide of Dr. David Kelly, a government scientist who was quoted by the BBC as saying that the government's case for war was "sexed up." While the government was not on trial and was eventually cleared of the charge in January 2004, public trust was further strained.

The turning point had come in President Bush's State of the Union address, delivered in January 2002, when, with neo-conservative input, he used the phrase "axis of evil." The speech was a pivot point both for the neo-conservatives, who took delight in seeing their ambitious agenda for Middle East transformation receive implicit White House blessing, and for the prime minister, who from that point on faced increasing concerns that Britain was being drawn into a program of action that did not correspond to British interests. A less committed supporter of the United States than Blair might have paused for breath at this point, but instead he undertook a high-risk high-gain strategy. To succeed, it required that the rationale for military action be, in the words of the Hutton Report, the official British investigation, "as strong a case as possible in relation to the threat posed by Saddam Hussein's WMD." To this end, as the official report makes clear, 10 Downing Street suggested "changes in the wording of the draft dossier which would strengthen it."[90] This proved to be the Achilles heel of the British effort. The crux of the problem is found in the distinction between the quality of evidence available to the intelligence services and the political needs of the day to stress the immediacy and magnitude of the Iraqi threat. The Hutton report makes it clear, for example, that, following a meeting with intelligence officials on September 9, 2002, the prime minister's office sent them written guidance of what the report was expected to contain for public consumption. Downing Street's expectations were for evidence that "makes us worried he (Saddam) cannot be allowed further to develop these weapons (of WMD)."[91]

To untutored eyes, this may look innocuous, but it represents a lethal combination of politics and intelligence. In effect, the prime minister's office was seeking intelligence not as a contribution to truth but in support of a specific political objective. This placed an enormous strain on the intelligence process. Inasmuch as this process is often less categorical, conclusive, or authoritative than is sometimes imagined or desired, including by ministers, it buckled under the pressure. Predictably, the political imperative won the day, with marginal sources being given credibility and assessments being redrafted, as the Hutton report states, until they came acceptably close to underpinning the public case for war. The raw balance of power within the British government structures made such an outcome inevitable. If Downing Street signals and, as in this case, provides written guidance for the desired outcome, this is likely to be what it receives – no matter whether this guidance is accompanied, as the Hutton report suggests, by emollient wording. At the margin, the intelligence officer in the field will downplay his doubts, the assessment officer at home will upgrade a source's reliability. No system is

---

[90] Lord Brian Hutton, "Investigation into the Circumstances Surrounding the Death of Dr. David Kelly" (London: Department of Constitutional Affairs, January 28, 2004), chapter 6, paragraph 228 (5).

[91] Ibid., chapter 6, paragraph 173.

proof against these human frailties. The longer-term consequences in terms of diminished confidence in the intelligence services was thus not only an American phenomenon. This deeper problem will endure long after the sloppy language of a BBC journalist has been forgotten.

In retrospect, Blair made a Faustian bargain with neo-conservative Washington. Most notably with respect to the Middle East, where he assured his E.U. colleagues that British support over Iraq would lead to a more even-handed U.S. policy, Blair found that his agenda differed substantially from that embraced by the neo-conservatives. This was his mistake. He neglected to see that in the swirl of politics and interest that is today's Washington, Britain became, for all intents and purposes, another "interest group," albeit a very powerful one, lobbying for a shared approach to international diplomacy in a political culture that, under neo-conservative influence, is either tone-deaf or downright hostile to such a notion. While Britain is arguably the most important ally that Washington has, one would not know it from the manner in which British political sensitivities were accommodated. Though the White House agreed reluctantly to act through the U.N., the "with us or against us" body language and expressed willingness to move unilaterally raised continuing and substantial questions among the British public and in Europe about the Britain's embarrassingly subordinate role.

The wider lesson here is not that Americans should make undue compromises to save British face or that the British should feel aggrieved if the United States does not heed its (no doubt sage) advice. The latter have their own reasons for their closeness to the United States. This is a relationship between consenting adults. In an affectionate but acute observation about the British to one of the authors about how to calibrate his dealing with them, the Secretary of State at the time warned him to be cautious "because the British will slit your throat and you will not know it until you turn your head, and it falls off." The real lesson is a double one.

For the Americans, the legitimacy the British bring with them is a real asset. Not only does it signal to the world that the United States is not isolated, but it lends the momentum of inevitability to U.S. plans. War on Iraq? Reform of the U.N., IMF, and World Bank? Defense of international market capitalism? Think how challenging these tasks become without British support. This is an asset for which it is worth paying a price today for benefits tomorrow. But the asset cannot be taken for granted. Today, the forces within the British foreign policy and business establishment who would like to see Britain align itself more exclusively with the E.U. are in check, but the trend is in their favor. Since the 1956 Suez Canal crisis, a central objective of British foreign policy has been to avoid choosing between the United States and the E.U. But the alternative is there, not necessarily to be exercised today, but nevertheless on the table.[92]

For the British, the lesson is that the legitimacy they confer brings both power and responsibility with it. The power is an obvious by-product of the legitimacy. It means that they routinely are seated if not in the throne room of American foreign policy formation, then at least in one of the proximate antechambers. They receive earlier intimation of American thinking than that provided to any other country. This leads to responsibility. If American decision making appears to be falling under the influence of a narrow self-interest, as happened with the neo-conservatives, the British – and perhaps only the British – have the standing to restore balance to the debate. This is the responsibility aspect.

Neither the American nor the British side emerges unscathed from recent events. The neo-conservative–inspired unilateralism has caused the Americans to do too much; British timidity has caused them to do too little. But at a time when the United States is redefining its global posture in terms of, once again, neo-conservative–inspired confrontation, this is a favorable moment for the Anglo-American axis to assert itself as a system-balancing mechanism.

NEO-CONSERVATIVES, THE UNITED STATES, AND THE REST

We now turn the telescope around and look through two conceptual lenses – "knowledgeable ignorance" and "Orientalism" – that may have had some influence on the way in which neo-conservatives perceive the world. In their approach to foreign policy, neo-conservatives have often tended to diminish the importance of regional or country expertise, proposing instead that when possible, the State Department replace such analysts with political appointees.[93] Search their books, articles, interviews, and letters and you will be hard-pressed to find examples of the usual ingredients of foreign policy analysis: in-country expertise, language skills, residence in or travel to the countries concerned. Ideology and commitment to the agenda almost invariably take precedence over these elements. It goes without saying that area specialists can be and sometimes are wrong, losing perspective on their specialties and suffering from what is called "clientitis." When they have offered differing priorities and perspectives, however, neo-conservative

---

[92] Hugo Young, *This Blessed Plot: Britain and Europe from Churchill to Blair* (London: Macmillan, 1998).

[93] Frum and Perle, *An End to Evil*, pp. 226–27.

decision makers have been inclined to diminish their contributions not as factually inaccurate but as "out of sync."[94] It is within this context that neo-conservative policy makers may have been bolstered by the "certainties" provided by "knowledgeable ignorance" and "Orientalism." The result is that policy decisions and direction are reached without a precise understanding of the political cultures with which the United States must find common ground. Specifically, "knowledgeable ignorance" and "orientalism" have served in important ways to distort policy analysis of, and thus solutions to, a range of social and economic problems such that they have tended to evolve into security issues.

Knowledgeable Ignorance

The British historian Norman Daniel introduced the term "knowledgeable ignorance" to describe what medieval Europe thought of Islam and the Muslims more generally.[95] A well-established concept among anthropologists, "knowledgeable ignorance" is defined as "knowing a people, ideas, civilizations, religions, or histories as something they are not, and could not possibly be, and maintaining these ideas even when the means exist to know differently."[96] Of importance to us is that scholarly Orientalism supports the idea that the stereotypical negative characteristics of Muslims are a "natural" consequence of their beliefs.[97]

The problem of knowledge is not, of course, exclusive to America or to the West in general. It is a feature of all civilizations. In this case, however, our concern is that which the West takes for knowledge of the non-West – learned opinion and scholarly evidence – is often itself a problem.[98] London University Professor Mark Hobart points out that the growth of knowledge "concomitantly entails the possibility of increasing ignorance . . . manifested practically in local knowledge being devalued or ignored, in favor of scientific, technical and managerial knowledge" and that as "technical superiority grows so does the growth of ignorance."[99] Knowledge is based on commonly accepted truths and data advanced by intellectuals, politicians, and commentators who, in turn, form public opinion. But how do "truths and

---

[94] Newt Gingrich, "Rogue State Department," *Foreign Policy*, July–August 2003, p. 45.
[95] Norman Daniel, *Islam and the West: The Making of an Image* (1960; Oxford: Oneworld, 1993), p. 12.
[96] Sardar and Davies, *Why Do People Hate America?*, p. 11.
[97] Ibid., p. 52.
[98] Ibid., p. 12.
[99] Mark Hobart, ed., *An Anthropological Critique of Development: The Growth of Ignorance* (London: Routledge, 1993), p. 10.

data" become commonly accepted or become common sense? Why are certain facts and not others selected for use by opinion makers? It is common for cultures to construct what they know about other cultures, in some measure, through a binary format of "like and not like."

"Like and not like" has been the *leitmotif* reflected in the Manichean world of contemporary neo-conservative thought. The selective range of media outlets including Fox Television, the *Weekly Standard*, and others described in Chapter 6 above have advanced notions of the Islamic world, reinforcing the neo-conservative discourse, such that their perception of the Muslim world is largely undifferentiated. The subtle requirements of accommodating the multiple tribal, ethnic, and religious groups in constructing a postconflict polity in Iraq were subsumed under the banner of Saddam's "weapons of mass destruction state" until well past the time such analysis might have been dispositive. Iran, for example, is portrayed as a "terrorist nation" with little attention given to the diverse socio-political developments there indicating change. Libya is seen as an unreconstructed terrorist state, despite its well-identified attempts to rejoin the world community. The assumption among many neo-conservatives has been that they "know" all that is necessary for their sweeping policy purposes – even when, as Daniel points out, "the means exist to know differently." It is here that the insidious and destructive nature of the "echo chamber" effect is seen as administration declarations are repeated and "substantiated" by the neo-conservative network of writers, commentators, and activists. Thus, "knowledgeable ignorance" emerges as a powerful phenomenon in explaining the apparent disconnect between the United States and Islam.

Orientalism

"Knowledgeable ignorance" is an important part of another idea known as "Orientalism" popularized by Edward Said, who was a controversial Columbia University historian highly critical of the way in which the Muslim world is viewed by the West and the relationships that have evolved as a result. Neo-conservatives regard Said as little more than an apologist for terrorism.[100] According to Said, the West invented the idea of the Orient during imperial times to describe the exotic and mysterious Arabic lands of the "Near East." He defines Orientalism as the "corporate institution for dealing with the Orient – dealing with it by making statements about it, authorizing views of it, describing it, by teaching it, settling it, ruling over

---

[100] Stephen Schwartz, *The Two Faces of Islam* (New York: Doubleday, 2002), pp. 218–19.

it: in short, Orientalism is a Western style for dominating, restructuring, and having authority over the Orient."[101] In the flow of today's events, Said believes that Orientalism provides the intellectual substructure that informs significant parts of the European skepticism toward the United States on the subject of the Middle East and that in turn breeds anti-Americanism.

Embedded in the concept of Orientalism are values and conclusions used to create negative stereotypes of Muslims as the norms of analytic discourse. "Arabs" are presented in the imagery of static, almost ideal types, and neither as creatures with a potential in the process of being realized nor as those in the process of making history.[102] Orientalism is thus an intellectual framework, a tool of knowledge about the Arab world that stems from the West's discursive construction of reality. It is a concept that infuses the media and social exchange and that has slowly become a part of American popular culture. The successive, artfully titled books by Princeton professor emeritus Bernard Lewis, who maintains close links with neo-conservative decision makers, fall into this category.[103] The essence of Orientalism is the cultural and sociological distinction between the "Orient" and the "Occident." Apart from being arbitrary, Said believes the distinction is communicated in a way that implies Western superiority. In other words, Orientalism and its distinguishing features are derived from a negative appreciation of the Orient and form the stereotypes that have been reflected by Western popular culture. It is a concept that assumes that the norm is Western domination of the Orient.[104] The assumption of neo-conservatives that they are delivering democracy to a region that would not otherwise attain it precisely draws on this belief that Western culture and, for our purposes, American culture are both superior to non-Western political and cultural systems.

Orientalism embodies the notion of "the other," which is an important element in the construction of self-identity. To define a cultural self-identity, the existence of another different and competing identity, an "alter ego," is required. In the case of Western culture, according to Edward Said, this different identity is the Orient, which assembles all the cultural characteristics the West denies or sees as different from its own. The Orient has therefore been used by the West to provide a boundary that defines its contrasting

---

[101] Edward W. Said, *Orientalism* (London: Penguin, 1995), p. 3.

[102] Ibid., p. 321.

[103] See Bernard Lewis, *The Crisis of Islam: Holy War and Unholy Terror* (New York: Modern Library, 2003) and *What Went Wrong: Western Impact and Middle Eastern Response* (New York: Oxford University Press, 2002).

[104] Said, *Orientalism*, pp. 7–28.

image, ideas, and experience. In this sense it represents one of the West's deepest and most recurring images of "the Other."[105] A failure to comprehend "the Other" on its own terms is a pivotal disconnect in the relationship between America or the West as a whole and the Arab world.

While international relationships are nearly always multidimensional, effective policy demands that peoples and nations be viewed within the context of their own history. Said uses the Iran hostage crisis in 1979–80 when Americans were held prisoner in the U.S. embassy in Tehran to illustrate this point. Christian Bourguet, a French lawyer with connections to Iran, was a negotiator between the United States and Iran.[106] He describes a meeting with President Jimmy Carter at the White House:

Bourguet: at a given moment Carter spoke of the hostages, saying, you understand that these are Americans. These are innocents. I said to him, yes, Mr. President, I understand that you say they are innocent. But I believe you have to understand that for the Iranians they aren't innocent. Even if personally none of them has committed an act, they are not innocent because they are diplomats who represent a country that has done a number of things in Iran. You must understand that it is not against their person that the action is being taken. Of course you can see that. They have not been harmed. They have not been hurt. No attempt has been made to kill them. You must understand that it is a symbol, that it is on the plane of symbols that we have to think about this matter.[107]

This dialogue is, of course, used by Said not to justify hostage taking, but instead to demonstrate that there is in the West a certain tendency to "neglect realities" and act in accord with ideas fashioned by Orientalism. Carter chose not to view the embassy seizure as a symbol of resistance to America's historical involvement in Iran's domestic affairs. For him and for most in the West, the taking of innocent hostages was contrary to law; Iranians should not have seized Americans to demonstrate their grievances against the United States. But over time, the extreme measure employed by the Iranians determined who they were in Western eyes; the extreme became the norm and was presented as such. Thus, these two phenomena, "knowledgeable ignorance" and "Orientalism," provide lenses that have both helped to fashion views about the Muslim world and inhibited the flow of balancing perceptions and judgments. Both have had a role in the neo-conservative discourse, and both have functioned in symbiotic coordination with neo-conservative–influenced media outlets.

---

[105] Ibid., p. 332.
[106] Ibid., p. xxvi.
[107] Ibid.

LOOKING INTO THE FUTURE

With anti-Americanism well into its third century of active duty, it is clear that it is not going to fade from the scene at an early date. Americans are going to have to put up with a full range of negative comments from across the Atlantic and Pacific. Foreigners are also going to have to live with increasingly robust retorts from Americans. To adapt Lady Metroland's withering comment about the Earl of Balcairn in *Vile Bodies*, Americans "feel their full income" when they look foreigners in the eye today. Neo-conservatives have no quarrel with this deterioration in the international discourse. Having, as we have shown, more or less abandoned international cooperation as a means of achieving American objectives, having an almost religious belief in military power, and living by a historically anomalous selfish interpretation of American leadership, neo-conservatives prefer to go it alone.

Our sense is that in the long run this approach will only make America's international burden just that bit heavier – and quite unnecessarily so. For at least fifty years, the United States actively maintained a set of shared values with the rest of the world. In a fit of pique, neo-conservative unilateralism significantly complicates efforts to extend that long and successful period. It is another example of the unhappy legacy that neo-conservatives are leaving behind.

9

The Neo-Conservative "World War IV" and Its Impact on American Society

In his 1998 book *All the Laws but One: Civil Liberties in Wartime*, Chief Justice William H. Rehnquist notes, "Without question, the government's authority to engage in conduct that infringes civil liberty is greatest in the time of declared war."[1] Rehnquist added, "It is neither desirable nor is it remotely likely that civil liberty will occupy as favored a position in wartime as it does in peacetime."[2] There is no gainsaying these succinct formulations. They lay the basis for the somber changes that have come over our lives in America during the past three years – changes that have substantially and perhaps permanently shifted the balance of power between the government authorities and the private individual. Those who welcome these changes, among which group neo-conservatives are prominent, argue that the attack on America leaves no choice. "Security inevitably means restrictions," pronounces Robert H. Bork, as if this were a self-evident, almost welcome proposition.[3] This is the world of the trade-off between security and liberty, where the former has the upper hand and the latter is on the defensive. As Bork's comment shows, the neo-conservative instinct tends to go against liberty. They favor what they call "twenty-first-century surveillance."[4]

To date this argument has carried a majority of the country with it. Opposition on Capitol Hill is absent or hesitant (the USA Patriot Act passed the Senate on a 98–1 vote) and polls consistently show that Americans have accepted this logic, believing that "investigating threats, even if it results in a

[1] William H. Rehnquist, *All the Laws but One* (New York: Vintage, 1998), p. 218.
[2] Ibid., pp. 224–25.
[3] Robert H. Bork, "Civil Liberties after 9/11," *Commentary*, July–August 2003, p. 29.
[4] David Frum and Richard Perle, *An End to Evil* (New York: Random House, 2003), p. 73.

loss of privacy, is more important right now than respect for privacy."[5] The courts have shown a "deferential" approach to government actions in this field. These attitudes universally depend on the logic of war. This chapter examines this logic. It suggests that "war" may not be the best or even a desirable conceptual framework for combating terrorism and, following from this, asks whether the trade-off endorsed by the neo-conservatives is in fact as inevitable as they claim.

In earlier chapters we have made the case that the state of war in which, according to the neo-conservatives, the nation finds itself is highly abnormal. While the Afghanistan war was a direct response to an outside contingency – 9/11 in parallel to earlier attacks such as Pearl Harbor or the sinking of the USS *Maine* – the current state of affairs arises from a deliberate act of choice, conceptualized and promoted preeminently by the neo-conservatives, first by their advocacy of war against Iraq a decade before 9/11 and, second, by their embrace of the concept of an endless, ongoing "World War IV." "We remain a nation at war," pronounced Deputy Secretary of State Paul D. Wolfowitz before the Senate.[6] The endpoint of this vision is a disfigured America, a condition described by Friedrich Nietzsche as: "He who fights too long against dragons becomes a dragon himself; and if you gaze too long into the abyss, the abyss will gaze into you." To use Nietzsche's terminology (incidentally, a philosopher whose intellectual sophistication is anathema to neo-conservatives),[7] the United States runs the risk of resembling the dragons against which it is fighting. A development of this kind would be an appalling tragedy both for Americans and the world, undercutting as it would America's historic capacity to act as a force for good.

The alternative view we put forward will, if it is persuasive, show that the real trade-off America faces is between policies based on neo-conservative radicalism and policies that reflect America's more historically proven values and interests. This is an encouraging diagnosis, for it involves political choices over which Americans have control rather than a national emergency where we have lost control. If policies based on America's core values are allowed to predominate, they will permit the nation to face the challenges posed by our enemies without immolating ourselves on their altars. This is not as difficult as it sounds. For all of its horror, terrorism is not an impenetrable or unfathomable phenomenon. It has been around for centuries,

---

[5] Richard C. Leone and Greg Anrig, Jr., eds., *The War on Our Freedoms: Civil Liberties in an Age of Terrorism* (New York: Public Affairs, 2003), p. 11.

[6] Paul D. Wolfowitz, "Helping Win the War on Terror," testimony before the Senate Armed Services Committee, September 9, 2003.

[7] James W. Ceasar, "The Politics of Evil," *Weekly Standard*, April 1, 2002.

and a great deal is known about it. Certainly, the motivations and modalities of terrorism have changed over the years. But while the emergence of nonstate actors with powerful communications, access to financial resources, and potential possession of weapons of mass destruction are new factors, we reject the idea that we are dealing with a wholly new, postmodern "twenty-first-century" version where the rules of the past do not apply.[8] We set out below some of the evidence showing that it can be effectively combated while retaining the political legitimacy and moral authority to which we have referred before as the priceless ingredient in America's success. In fact, we make the case that terrorism can be better addressed if we resist the temptation to cut constitutional corners. We then draw attention to some of the legal provisions being introduced that may call this legitimacy into question.

Our purpose is to remind ourselves that "the bottom line for democracies is to remember not only whom they are fighting, but also what they are fighting for."[9] An old parable tells of a frog placed in a bowl of cool water as it is slowly heated over a fire. At the point the frog realizes the danger it is in, it is already too weakened to get out. It is boiled alive. Americans today find themselves in water with the temperature rising. To date the political discourse, impregnated as it is with neo-conservative formulations, has led them to acquiesce in the demands of those who are stoking the fire. The danger here is that Americans will awake too late to take corrective action. They will end up with a government equipped with and authorized to use the awesome capabilities of modern electronic data collection, but with no gain to their peace of mind or necessarily to their security.

THE GLOBAL TERRORISM CONTEXT

Reflecting their binary analytic format, neo-conservatives tend to argue that "terrorism is terrorism." They see efforts to understand the "root causes" as illusory or contradictory and as the first steps away from "moral clarity."[10] Prior to 9/11, international terrorism had certainly shown up on the radar screen but, in proportion to other human activities, had claimed very few American lives.[11] To the U.S. audience, therefore, these attacks appeared

---

[8] Walter Laqueur, *No End to War: Terrorism in the 21st Century* (New York: Continuum, 2003).

[9] David Charters, ed., *The Deadly Sin of Terrorism: Its Effects on Democracy and Civil Liberty in Six Countries* (New Brunswick, N.J.: Greenwood, 1994), p. 10.

[10] William J. Bennett, *Why We Fight* (Washington, D.C.: Regnery, 2002), pp. 19–22.

[11] Between 1996 and 1999, seven U.S. citizens died from terrorism, compared with world total of 3,225. U.S. Department of State, *Patterns of Global Terrorism 2001*. In a similar period,

to be the starting point of a terror campaign, representing a completely new phenomenon. To terrorism observers in other states used to the encroachments of terrorism, however, the sense of novelty was less. For example, extrapolation of the casualty figures in Northern Ireland in relation to the population of the United States would in terms of American citizens have cost some 276,000 deaths and 1.5 million injured.[12] This is simply to say that other nations have been there before. And they have lessons to offer.

Terrorism did not start on September 11, 2001, but has evolved and adapted to changing times and situations. The history of terrorism stretches back through the reign of terror in the French Revolution to as far back as the Sicarii sect of the Zealots in A.D. 66–73.[13] Terrorism's very durability suggests that, as Harvard law professor Alan Dershowitz notes, "it works."[14] It is a complicated term. Sometimes it is used in the service of ends of which we might approve. At least one neo-conservative has proposed, for example, that Iraqis be encouraged to maintain order in Iraq through means (assassinations, summary executions, etc.) that in any other context he would call terrorism.[15] In World War II, several of the resistance movements to Nazism acknowledge that they used terrorism.[16] Sometimes, foreign groups start off as terrorists and then lose that designation as U.S. policy moves closer to them. This was the case with the Kosovo Liberation Army in the 1990s.[17] Earlier, Arthur Koestler described the Stern Gang and Irgun (of which he had been a member) as terrorist movements because of their activities in the struggle to achieve the establishment of Israel. None of this is mentioned today.[18] Sometimes the opposite happens, as the Chechen fighters, once regarded as rightfully seeking self-determination, are now viewed as having al-Qaeda and Wahabbi terrorist links.[19] Sometimes Americans give material support (with official acquiescence) to groups that close American allies regard as terrorists. This was the case with the flow of money and arms from

---

70,360 people were murdered in America and 167,190 died in traffic accidents. *Independent Review* 7, no. 1, summer 2002, p. 59.

[12] Paul Wilkinson, ed., *British Perspectives on Terrorism* (London: Allen and Unwin, 1981), p. 1.

[13] Grant Wardlaw, *Political Terrorism* (Cambridge: Cambridge University Press, 1989), p. 18.

[14] Alan M. Dershowitz, *Why Terrorism Works: Understanding the Threat, Responding to the Challenge* (New Haven: Yale University Press, 2002).

[15] Max Boot, "The Lessons of a Quagmire," *New York Times*, November 16, 2003, p. A13.

[16] M. R. D. Foot, *Resistance: European Resistance to Nazism, 1940–45* (London: Eyre Methuen, 1976), pp. 87–92.

[17] Madeleine Albright, *Madam Secretary: A Memoir* (New York: Miramax, 2003), pp. 380–86.

[18] Arthur Koestler, *Promise and Fulfillment* (New York: Macmillan, 1949), pp. 90–98.

[19] Leon Aron, "New Dimensions of an Old Problem," American Enterprise Institute, February 1, 2003.

Irish Americans to the IRA.[20] In the neo-conservative view, analysis of this kind leads to moral relativism and policy paralysis, but the ambiguities implicit in terrorism are worth bearing in mind.

The first contemporary act of international terrorism occurred on July 22, 1968, when the Popular Front for the Liberation of Palestine (PFLP) hijacked an El Al flight from Rome to Tel Aviv. The sequence of attacks on international transportation – the hostage taking, hijackings, and bombings – was confirmed later in 1972 when the Japanese Red Army attacked Lod Airport in Israel and the Black September group seized and murdered Israeli athletes in the Olympic village in Munich. As with the attacks in 2001, the death of civilians at the hands of terrorists played out in front of national and international media. The government response often took the form of setting up dedicated counterterrorism centers inside the intelligence community and within the military.

The year 1979 was an important one in the development of today's terror phenomenon. The Iranian Revolution of 1979 brought to life a new breed of fanatical religious terrorists and the subsequent rise of fundamentalism, which spread rapidly across the Islamic world. The crucible for the pan-Islamic movement, however, was the jihad against the Soviet invasion of Afghanistan in 1979 – where, as is well known, U.S. and British intelligence services were working hand-in-glove with the jihadists, all the while being well aware of the latters' extremist tendencies. By the time that the Soviet Union withdrew from Afghanistan in 1989, a whole generation of religiously inspired terrorists had been produced and subsequently dispersed across the globe. Radicalized by Islamic indoctrination and militarized by training in Afghan and Sudanese academies, religiously motivated terrorists were able to move freely across state borders and to communicate using the products of the information revolution. Unlike the "transcendant" motivations of terror groups focused on achieving specific national goals, the universal cause of religious fundamentalism was not limited by geography to one specific theater of operations.[21]

The direct cause of 9/11 may be traced to the diseased anger of one man, Osama bin Laden. But the attacks took place in a wider context that suggests that anti-American terrorism is not a transient phenomenon. The events of 9/11 rest partly on developments in Iran and Afghanistan as described above but are, perhaps, more directly linked to the upheavals in the international political system that have occurred since the late 1990s. The technological

---

[20] Tim Pat Coogan, *The IRA* (New York: Palgrave, 2002), pp. 524–25.
[21] Jessica Stern, *Terror in the Name of God* (New York: Ecco, 2003), p. 282.

and political changes occurring since the end of the Cold War, the increasing impact of globalization, and the information revolution each had a role. Globalization became synonymous with the advance of U.S. culture and the belief in the developing world that the West "has driven the globalization agenda, ensuring that it garnered a disproportionate share of the benefits, at the expense of the developing world."[22] The attendant frustration was underscored by the overwhelming military dominance of the United States during the 1991 Gulf war. And it was this inability to directly confront U.S. military strength that brought terrorism as the tool of choice in a "surrogate war."[23] In the conflict between "Jihad and McWorld" the use of terror to fight the threatened economic, military, and cultural domination by the United States became the "weapon of the weak."[24] This is what the Pentagon calls "asymmetrical warfare."

During the 1990s the religious terrorists harnessed the accelerating process of globalization, exploiting the advances in information technology of the last decade to morph from the traditional hierarchical organizations into terrorist networks connected by global communications. The most crucial development in this process has, however, been ignored by the neoconservatives, namely that these organizations became independent of states. These global terrorist networks replicated organizational developments in the world's largest business corporations and in transnational criminal networks. And, to further complicate matters, these terrorist networks consist of small, dispersed groups that communicate, coordinate, and conduct their campaigns over the Internet, without precise central command.[25]

While terrorism against the United States reflected the network organizations' ability to capitalize on the information revolution, a similar evolution took place in the methods of terrorist attack. The National Commission on Terror, chaired by L. Paul Bremer and reporting to Congress in 2000, indicated a steady decrease in the quantity of international terrorist attacks during the 1990s but a parallel increase in the destructiveness of these attacks.[26] The reason for the increase in civilian casualties from terrorist attacks is linked to change in motivation for global terrorism. Prior to 9/11, terrorists wanted a lot of people watching, not necessarily a lot of people dead. The

---

[22] Joseph E. Stiglitz, *Globalization and Its Discontents* (New York: W. W. Norton, 2002), p. 7.

[23] Walter Laqueur, *The New Terrorism: Fanaticism and the Arms of Mass Destruction* (London: Phoenix, 1999), p. 243.

[24] Benjamin R. Barber, *Jihad vs. McWorld* (New York: Times Books, 1995), pp. 155–68.

[25] John Arquilla, "Networks, Netwar and the Information Age Terrorism," in Ian O. Lessor, ed., *Countering the New Terrorism* (Santa Monica, Calif.: Rand Corporation, 1999), p. 47.

[26] L. Paul Bremer III, chairman, Report of the National Commission on Terror, *Countering the Changing Threat of International Terrorism* (Washington, D.C.: 105th Congress, 2000).

use of violence by international terrorist groups had a clearly defined upper limit set by the link between terror groups and state sponsors and the desire of nationalist terror groups to gain popular support. The attacks were usually highly discriminate and aimed at a government or military targets. Prior to 9/11, the failure to discriminate between legitimate and illegitimate targets and to protect "innocent" civilians from harm could have a significant detrimental impact on support for the cause of the terrorist. The terrorist incident at Omagh in Northern Ireland, in which twenty-nine shoppers were killed, effectively brought to an end the dissident Republican campaign, after the splintering of the Provisional IRA in 1998. Even the hard-line Marxist terrorists of the 1970s were forced to discriminate in their targeting, so as to avoid killing the working class it was attempting to liberate.

While traditional forms of terrorism aspired to achieve greater discrimination in targeting, the planners of the attack on 9/11 were not limited by such ethical concerns. Compared with secular terrorism, violence inspired by fanaticism, either religious or millenarian, may tend toward more nihilistic justifications and by definition toward higher levels of destruction. The power of religious indoctrination removed the moral restraint on terrorists to cause mass civilian casualties from indiscriminate attacks.

The upward trend in casualties is also the result of the symbiotic relationship between terrorism and the media. Terrorism cannot exist without communication.[27] Now deep into the age of global media coverage and living within dense communications infrastructures, the terrorist message can be transmitted instantly to a waiting global audience. The planners of 9/11 properly anticipated that the violence they delivered would achieve a geometric effect through the media. Osama bin Laden fought against the Soviet Union in Afghanistan for over seven years; the conduct and purpose of his insurgency campaign went largely unnoticed by the general public. Within twenty-four hours of the attacks on September 11, 2001, he had generated a global awareness of his cause and his organization. In the absence of any claim of responsibility for the attacks, it seems clear that its primary purpose was to strike at the preeminent symbols of U.S. economic and political power (though the latter failed) and to demonstrate that U.S. "hyper-power" was vulnerable to the "asymmetrical" warfare – about which the Pentagon had warned. Its secondary purpose, amplified by global media coverage, gained attention for the demand that the West, in general, and the United States, in particular, withdraw from Saudi Arabia and the region. Of course,

[27] Harvey W. Kusner, "Terrorism in the 21st Century," in Kusner, ed., *The Future of Terrorism: Violence in the New Millennium* (Thousand Oaks, Calif.: Sage, 1998).

bin Laden's definition of the attacks, as a strike against American "oppressors" by Islamic "martyrs," was soon overwhelmed by the description of the events given by Washington and London, namely that it was an unprovoked murderous assault on innocents.

The media played a major role both in spreading the psychological dimensions of the attack through repeated broadcasts of the video of the collapsing towers and, in a powerful demonstration of "definition dominance," in establishing Washington and London's view of what had happened. Equally important, the media imagery had become critical to the calculus of such events – which meant, among other things, that to gain similar attention future attacks may require increasing levels of destructiveness.

The events of 9/11 increased the spectrum of the terrorist threat, which now ranges from pseudoterrorist crime to traditional terrorism to the new form of superterrorism that uses unconventional techniques or weapons of mass destruction.[28] The process of globalization will make the task of maintaining total security within the United States more difficult. The increasing flows of people, information, and finance into the United States will offer opportunities to spread the terrorist networks into the heart of U.S. society. The need for increasing interaction in a globalized society will prevent the total isolation of the United States from the terrorists. RAND analyst Bruce Hoffman noted, "We cannot participate and enjoy the increasingly globalized and interconnected world and economy while isolating ourselves and our citizens from the enemies of the system."[29] Even the most stringent forms of border surveillance cannot interdict networks of terrorists, some of which may already be operating from within the United States. There is therefore an upper limit to the effectiveness of security measures to exclude terrorism from entering the United States.

The threat of superterrorism to the United States from transnational networks means that counterterrorism cannot be seen purely as a national security issue. It is also one of foreign policy, indeed one that involves the totality of the U.S. interaction with the rest of the world.[30] At the same time, traditional forms of U.S. diplomacy are becoming less useful in dealing with new threats, which originate from substate or nonstate actors. Deterrence and nuclear diplomacy has little relevance when dealing with fanatical individuals. Unilateral action by the United States will be insufficient to counter a global terror network. The U.S. military with its global reach and precision

---

[28] Lesser, *Countering the New Terrorism*, p. 86.

[29] Bruce Hoffman, *Inside Terrorism* (New York: Columbia University Press, 1998).

[30] Paul R. Pillar, *Terrorism and US Foreign Policy* (Washington, D.C.: Brookings Institution, 2002), p. 9.

strike capability cannot defeat integrated networks alone without the sort of low-level tactical intelligence that originates from national sources. The U.S. action in Afghanistan in 2002 has not eliminated the al-Qaeda network as demonstrated by the Bali bomb, subsequent attacks in Morocco, and the arrest of a senior al-Qaeda coordinator in Iraq some weeks after Saddam Hussein's capture. Indeed, U.S. officials regularly post warnings about al-Qaeda's strength. It must be understood that the United States, despite its military and economic hegemony over other nations, cannot coerce or destroy a global network of individuals. The removal of nodes by unilateral military action will only temporarily weaken the power of the network, which over time can reconstitute and strengthen. The United States cannot fight terrorism alone nor can it dictate that the war will be fought only on other nations' soil.

TERRORISM AND THE MILITARY

As soon as men decide that all means are permitted to fight an evil then their good becomes indistinguishable from the evil that they set out to destroy.[31]

As we have shown in Chapters 1 and 7, the American decision to respond to the 9/11 attacks as an act of state-on-state war rather than as an action by a nonstate actor was heavily conditioned by neo-conservative thinking. Throughout the 1990s they had concentrated on advocating a military buildup against potential "peer-competitor" states, such as China. In his book *While America Sleeps*, Yale professor Donald Kagan makes only one passing reference to nonstate actors.[32] Neo-conservatives argued – and continue to argue – that military force is the preferred option for responding to foreign challenges. The neo-conservatives have actively encouraged the interpretation of counterterrorism as a war, which mobilizes all national resources and legitimizes all available means. This is quite different from the British, for example, who have regarded terrorism as a problem management issue requiring a distilled socio-political response. Moreover, Harvard professor Philip Heymann raises legitimate questions about whether war is the right metaphor for the handling of the terrorism menace.[33]

At first glance the increased lethality and fanaticism of terrorists supports the view that only force can be used to deal with those who would

---

[31] John Locke, *Second Treatise on Civil Government* (Amherst, N.Y.: Prometheus, 1986).
[32] Donald Kagan and Frederick Kagan, *While America Sleeps: Self-Delusion, Military Weakness and the Threat to Peace* (New York: St. Martin's Press, 2000), pp. 2 and 341–66.
[33] Philip B. Heymann, *Terrorism, Freedom and Security: Winning without Fighting* (Cambridge, Mass.: MIT Press, 2003), pp. 19–33.

threaten the established order. The key question, however, is whether the neo-conservative emphasis on the efficacy of force provides the basis for a long-term counterterrorist policy. Historical examples provide some evidence to support the view that force provides some short-term tactical success in deterring state-sponsored terrorism and eliminating key elements of a hierarchical terrorist organizations. The U.S. air attacks against Libya in 1986 in retaliation for the terrorist attack against servicemen in a Berlin disco certainly influenced Libya's decision to suspend its sponsorship of terrorism and provided the background to the contemporary strengthening of Libyan moderates. The Israeli attacks against the PLO in Tunis in 1982 eliminated many of the key terrorist commanders. But in the new conditions, there is reason to believe that, even in the short term, the application of force will be less useful in dealing with global terrorist networks where the Internet rather than a "Great Leader" provides the motivation and resources for terrorist action. These leaderless resistance networks are unlikely to be degraded by the loss of only a single person. The proof of this may become apparent only after the capture or demise of Osama bin Laden.

In the long term, the use of force does nothing to help us come to terms with the political nature of the causes of terrorism. First, it must be understood that terrorism is a method and not an ideology. Terrorism neither occurs in a vacuum nor is it generally the product of outside agitation or imported ideologies.[34] Rather, terrorism can be seen to follow Clausewitz's dictum as politics by other means. Placed in a political context, there can be no military conclusion to a counterterrorist campaign. Even former terrorists agree that the only way to fight terrorism is to address the problems that have motivated their actions. Terrorism is normally self-terminating as the terrorists lose popular support. More important, and contrary to the neo-conservative perspective, is that military dominance does not guarantee victory against terrorism. The British experience in Palestine in 1945 was that despite its military superiority it could never bring its capabilities to bear down on the terrorists without the detailed intelligence that only the local population could provide. This intelligence was not forthcoming, as the British military alienated itself by acts of repression and reprisal. Without accurate intelligence the British military acted indiscriminately, engendering further hostility and creating support for the terrorists. The inability of the military to deal with political problems is well understood. John Adams noted, "Soldiers quartered in a populous town will always occasion

---

[34] Neil C. Livingstone, *The War on Terrorism* (Lexington, Mass.: D.C. Heath, 1976), p. 159.

two mobs where they prevent one. They are wretched conservators of the peace."[35]

The value of the military is that it can be used to buy time in order to achieve a political solution and not the reverse. The neo-conservatives have the sequence back to front. In the absence of a political solution, the military will be left to hold the ring in a conflict without hope of resolution. It is accepted that even a concerted political and military campaign is never likely to destroy a terrorist movement totally. After prolonged and successful counterterrorist campaigns, a hard core will always remain that includes the most extreme elements of disaffected and fanatical individuals. The use of force is legitimate against these fanatical elements who pose a direct threat to U.S. citizens and who will not and cannot be brought to justice. These actions must be considered as exceptional, used only as a last resort where no other means of self-defense exist to protect U.S. citizens. This is exactly the rationale and the cautious caveat used by Reagan to justify the attack on Libya.[36]

The reality is that military and legal prophylactic measures will not in themselves eliminate the causes and symptoms of terrorism in the long term. Counterterrorism will always be a long war in which short-term tactical advantages are generally worthless. The long campaign doctrine has many practical implications for the America's war on terror. Throughout such a long campaign, and because psychological factors are so important, the government should seek consistency in its response to terrorism both at home and abroad. Variations in policy will undermine public confidence and the support of allies essential to conduct a global campaign. With reference to the latter, it is particularly important to avoid quixotic acts of repression even in the response to future terrorist attacks, as they inevitably undermine support for the government both at home and abroad.

A protracted counterterrorism campaign must be fought on two parallel levels: the security war to protect the citizens and eliminate the terrorists and the political and psychological war in order to maintain popular support. Terrorists must also be isolated from their support. The most basic requirement for the retention of popular support from U.S. citizens is the provision of personal security at an acceptable cost. The government must demonstrate the ability to deter and prevent terrorism by use of the law and

[35] Quoted in David G. McCullough, *John Adams* (New York: Simon and Schuster, 2001), p. 67.

[36] Ronald Reagan, *An American Life* (New York: Simon and Schuster, 1999).

legitimate force. By pursuing an aggressive policy of military preemption and lending their support – reluctant or otherwise – to legislation that encroaches on civil liberties, the neo-conservatives are ignoring the methods used by other liberal democracies to conduct their long-term campaigns against terrorism. The key here is to isolate the terrorists by delegitimizing their actions while retaining the legitimacy of the government action. The process of delegitimization is conditional on legitimate conduct by the government. Where the government's legitimacy is beyond question, terrorism delegitimizes itself and is bound to fail.[37] Legitimacy for U.S. action against terror will come only through adherence to the rule of law, both national and international. By their readiness to countenance moves away from the bedrock of the rule of law, the neo-conservatives risk causing the nation to lose the moral high ground in the struggle for legitimacy. This is not to say that legal changes are not necessary. Where the law is inadequate or out-of-date, the United States should enact legislation adequate to meet the new challenge. The difficulty comes when the United States uses international law when it is convenient and discards it when it restricts short-term objectives. The legal ambiguity, for example, both national and international regarding the detainees at Guantánamo Bay has caused many of the United States's closest allies in Britain and Europe, who otherwise support U.S. objectives, to question the legitimacy of the U.S. position.

Failure to abide by the limiting principles of law and human rights has often been excused by the exceptional threat posed by a terrorist attack. Such excuses were used by the British in Northern Ireland in 1972 to introduce internment and effectively to suspend the right of habeas corpus for individuals accused of terrorist activities. The result of this action was the loss of popular support for the government by the Roman Catholic community and the peaking of violence in Northern Ireland immediately after internment was introduced that year. Despite the enactment of antiterrorist legislation in Britain, very similar in its nonjudicial powers to the Patriot Act, the terrorist attacks continued. Limiting civil liberties does not therefore guarantee security. Like Britain during the worst period of Northern Ireland troubles, the neo-conservatives have responded to the threat of terrorism by attempting to ignore or to rewrite certain fundamental principles of law and human rights, and trade freedom for security. In the short-term desire for total security, the long-term and fundamental principles of the U.S. society have been compromised by a range of institutional failures, including the absence of a vigorous

---

[37] Alex Schmid, "Towards Joint Strategies for Delegitimizing the Use of Terrorism," in *Countering Terrorism through International Co-operation* (Milan: ISPAC, 2001), p. 260.

public debate, the muted voices of learned journals, and the immobility of hitherto reliable "checks and balances" in the judicial arena. In this respect, if the United States has turned its back on the experiences of other liberal democracies, much of the responsibility can be laid at the neo-conservative doorstep.

THE LEGAL CONTEXT: TWO VISIONS OF AMERICA

As we come now to discuss the practical legal responses undertaken in response to the events of September 11, two visions of America are competing with each other. Neo-conservatives argue that the country finds itself in a war posture analogous to World War II or earlier wars, with all the legal precedents set during those times available to the government in pursuit of public safety. Their writings reflect few if any qualms about the path of legislation since September 11. They regard opposition as "civil hysteria."[38] Professor Ben Barber has called this version of America the "Fear's Empire."[39] An alternative vision, which we share, is that the highest value at stake here is not the nature of the individuals who are America's enemies but who we are ourselves. It is agreed that, in its wars against al-Qaeda, the Taliban, and Saddam Hussein's Iraq, the United States has been fighting against abhorrent organizations or regimes that deny their people civil liberties and that are implacably opposed to the most basic tenets of American life. This pattern will continue in other struggles against other adversaries. However, as we have argued above, an essential aspect in combating terrorism is to be politically and morally legitimate. This means conducting ourselves according to our rules, not theirs. This section holds up a mirror to some of the legal changes that are being wrought or contemplated under the rubric of war. The danger is not that America's leaders are enthusiastic or insensitive advocates of placing arbitrary limits on civil liberties; it is that in the overheated atmosphere arising from the neo-conservative fanning of the "World War IV" flames, encroachments may be set in place today that will be very hard to reverse in the future – whether or not the legislation is subject to a so-called sunset provision. Following from this, the danger is that these civil liberties may be placed permanently on hold, because, if the neo-conservatives have their way, we may not experience "peacetime" in the foreseeable future. A foreign policy that emphasizes a chronic state of war will inextricably lead to domestic polarization that can be controlled only by

[38] David Tell, "Civil Hysteria," *Weekly Standard*, July 22, 2002.
[39] Benjamin R. Barber, *Fear's Empire: War, Terrorism and Democracy* (New York: Norton, 2003).

intrusive means that have more in common with our enemies' values than our own.

Commentators from across the political spectrum – from the American Civil Liberties Union on the left to the Coalition for Constitutional Liberties founded by the Free Congress Foundation on the right – have presented a rare united front in opposition to the antiterrorism legislation that became law in the immediate aftermath of the terrorist attacks, specifically the USA Patriot Act and its subsequent derivatives. Republicans from core Republican states are on record as saying, "We don't like the government intruding on our constitutional rights."[40] There has even been concern raised by the Justice Department's own officials.[41]

This legislation concentrates increasing levels of governmental power in the hands of the Executive Branch, with the effect of weakening the barriers guaranteed by the Bill of Rights (and, in particular, by the Fourth Amendment) between the intrusive powers of the government and the privacy of individual citizens. The removal of these barriers is all the more worrying because of the rapid advances in surveillance technology that are being made by government laboratories. It may be an exaggeration to comment that the government's surveillance capabilities are taking on the form of an increasingly "bigger monster," but there is little doubt that these technologies have an astonishing range and are gaining strength at an exponential rate.[42]

Statutory Measures: The USA Patriot Act

After the attacks of 9/11, Americans looked to the government in Washington for a strong response. The administration and Congress, supported by the neo-conservatives, generated legislation now on the statute books that probably would not be there in ordinary times. The centerpiece of the antiterrorism legislation is the awkwardly named "Uniting and Strengthening America by Providing Appropriate Tools Required to Intercept and Obstruct Terrorism Act of 2001," popularly known as the USA Patriot Act, which was signed into law on October 26, 2001.

It is likely that the significance of the Patriot Act, which is 342 pages in length and written in dense and technical legalese, will take years to

[40] Dan Eggen and Jim VandeHei, "More Wish to Curb Anti-Terrorism Powers," *Washington Post*, August 29, 2003, p. A1.
[41] Eric Lichtblau, "Treatment of Detained Immigrants Is under Investigation," *New York Times*, June 26, 2003, p. A18.
[42] Jay Stanley and Barry Steinhardt, "Bigger Monster, Weaker Chains: The Growth of an American Surveillance Society," ACLU report, January 2003.

determine. In its key provisions it updates the Foreign Intelligence Surveillance Act (FISA) by removing or loosening constraints on government capabilities to collect intelligence. The debate is whether the act provides the government with necessary methods of combating terrorism or whether it has the potential to allow intelligence and other government agencies to infringe on the privacy and civil liberties of American citizens and weaken judicial checks on such infringements. John Podesta, Bill Clinton's Chief of Staff from 1998 through 2001, has written:

> The events of September 11 convinced . . . overwhelming majorities in Congress that law enforcement and national security officials need new legal tools to fight terrorism. But we should not forget . . . [that] many aspects of the bill increase the opportunity for law enforcement and the intelligence community to return to an era where they monitored and sometimes harassed individuals who were merely exercising their First Amendment rights. Nothing that occurred on September 11 mandates that we return to such an era."[43]

Among the potentially intrusive aspects of the Patriot Act are those that toughened the law in the area of electronic surveillance. Section 216 of the act, for example, expands to the Internet the allowable use of so-called pen register and trap and trace devices, which record outgoing and incoming telephone numbers, respectively. The act now defines a pen register as "a device or process which records or decodes dialing, routing, addressing, or signaling information transmitted by an instrument or facility from which a wire or electronic communication is transmitted" and a trap and trace device as "a device or process which captures the incoming electronic or other impulses which identify the originating number or other dialing, routing, addressing, and signaling information reasonably likely to identify the source or a wire or electronic communication."[44] While the surveillance of the actual content of Internet transmissions is prohibited, the line between transactional information and content is less clear when applied to electronic communications as compared with telephone calls. Internet Web sites and other electronic transactional information provide far more details about an individual's actions and personal life than a simple telephone number or address; for example, a Google search can result in a URL producing highly personal information such as where a person shops, what he or she reads, with whom he or she communicates, and details of sexual orientation.

---

[43] John Podesta, "USA Patriot Act: The Good, the Bad, and the Sunset," American Bar Association, winter 2002.
[44] The USA Patriot Act, Section 216.

Compounding the problem is that the Patriot Act does not require intelligence agencies to demonstrate before a court of law that there is a probable offense in order to obtain a judge's approval. The act simply requires agents to state that the tap would be of some use, however general or ambiguous, in a criminal investigation, rendering judicial oversight of such activities negligible. This change from prior law removes a primary check on the power of the Executive Branch and does much to subvert the system of checks and balances instituted by the Constitution. This is a dangerous precedent to set in the long term, regardless of whether this aspect of the Patriot Act is deliberate or simply accidental. In addition, under the Patriot Act the FBI can now use its controversial "Carnivore" system, which allows it to monitor all subscribers of an Internet service provider, such as America Online, if one user is a target, with few barriers or privacy protections.

Section 206 of the Patriot Act embodies another change in long-standing wiretap law. This section amends the 1978 Foreign Intelligence Surveillance Act, which, in part, required intelligence agents to obtain separate court orders to monitor each telephone, computer, or other communication facility. Section 206 permits "roving wiretaps," which, in the words of Podesta, allows officials to "tap the person rather than the phone." The problem here is that surveillance targets can and do use public communications facilities, such as libraries and cybercafés. "It is conceivable," writes Podesta, "that all the pay phones in an entire neighborhood could be tapped if suspected terrorists happened to be in that neighborhood." The government will be able "incidentally" to intercept the communications of ordinary Americans, without, as the Fourth Amendment requires, a search warrant that "particularly describe[s] the place to be searched."[45] Jeffrey Toobin writes,

What people have to understand is that there is a lower standard to getting FISA taps. You don't have to show probable cause; you basically just have to ask for them. And, unlike a law enforcement tap, the government never has to tell the subject that they've done it. If the government thinks you're under the control of a foreign government, they can wiretap you and never tell you, search your house and never tell you, break into your home, copy your hard drive, and never tell you they've done it.[46]

Section 215 allows business records and computer hard drives of United States citizens and noncitizens alike to be searched in the name of a terrorism investigation and, like the new wiretap law, gags people from informing anyone of such monitoring: "No person shall disclose to any other person

---

45 EPIC analysis of the USA Patriot Act.
46 Jeffrey Toobin, "Should We Be Worried about the New Antiterrorism Legislation?" *The New Yorker*, November 5, 2001.

(other than those persons necessary to produce the tangible things under this section) that the Federal Bureau of Investigation has sought or obtained tangible things under this section." Included as "tangible things" are records held by public libraries. *Time* reports, "Librarians are alerting visitors that their Internet surfing or book borrowing may be monitored by the government."[47] The effect of this provision is that government officials have much easier access to monitoring the legal, First Amendment–protected activities of American citizens. To obtain such records, the government need only certify that the target is part of a foreign intelligence investigation and does not have to submit any sort of proof that the target is in any way a foreign agent. Whether this provision has or has not (as the Department of Justice asserts) been acted on at any particular time is less relevant than that the power now resides with the government.

Section 213 in the Patriot Act also amends the Federal Rules of Criminal Procedure to allow authorities to search and seize the property of a target without notifying the owner. So-called sneak and peek searches are barred by traditional warrants. But these searches now can be conducted if the government argues that notification would engender an ambiguously stated "adverse result."

The Domestic Security Enhancement Act (dubbed "Patriot II") takes these provisions further. Here we are talking about proposals, not enacted legislation. But the danger – and the trendline – is similar to that identified earlier. Those charged with protecting the nation's security take their responsibility seriously and, in a climate characterized as war, will place security ahead of liberty. Among the draft provisions are powers that would allow federal authorities to place a wiretap on any individual for fifteen days without obtaining a court warrant and to arrest and detain terrorist suspects without releasing any information about the person's crimes or whereabouts until charges are filed. The motivation behind these powers are undoubtedly well-intentioned, but the effects on those caught in the legal web come close to the secret arrest regimes well known from Cold War days. The act also creates a massive so-called Terrorist Identification Database that would include the DNA of citizens and noncitizens alike. Individuals would be forced, on penalty of $200,000 and a year in jail, to submit DNA samples to authorities on mere suspicion of an association with some sort of terrorist group.[48]

Section 501 of the act states that any American citizen can be stripped of his or her citizenship "if, with the intent to relinquish his nationality, he

[47] Michelle Orecklin, "Checking What You Check Out," *Time Magazine*, May 12, 2003.
[48] David Sanger, "President Urging Wider U.S. Powers in Terrorism Law," *New York Times*, September 11, 2003.

becomes a member of, or provides support to, a group that the United States has designated as a 'terrorist organization.'" In recent years, an American citizen has had to actively state his intent to give up his citizenship; under Patriot II, a citizen could be involuntarily expatriated if his or her intent is "inferred from conduct." Patriot II would conceivably allow the Department of Justice to summarily remove a natural-born American's citizenship without judicial review if that citizen engages, even unknowingly, in legal activities with a government-defined "terrorist organization."[49]

Of the measures enacted beyond the Patriot Act perhaps the most notable is the designation of individuals – Americans and non-Americans alike – as "enemy combatants" and the use of military tribunals to try detainees in Guantánamo Bay, Cuba. The two cases differ somewhat. The first places a drastic power into the hands of the executive branch. By simple administrative fiat the government may designate anyone, including an American citizen, as an "enemy combatant" and hold him or her indefinitely and incommunicado. No access to a lawyer or family is allowed. Such action implies an erosion of the "due process" protections that in American law adjudicate the balance between individual and state interests. This power is so sweeping that the Supreme Court is reviewing its constitutionality.

The military tribunal procedure involves a cost to political legitimacy, given that military tribunals are, rightly or wrongly, widely perceived as administering a rougher version of justice than civil courts. The unifying thread between the two is that neither process would be in existence were it not for the image, fostered by the neo-conservatives, that the nation is in a state of war. This has dragged even mainstream legal authorities down into the same linguistic ditch, arguing that military tribunals are justified by America's "right to return fire."[50] The legal precedent for the "enemy combatant" designation comes from a 1942 World War II episode, the so-called *Ex parte Quirin* case.[51] Conditions in Guantanamo have led to tensions with Britain, with Prime Minister Tony Blair describing the situation in Guantanamo as "highly unusual and difficult," and the Court of Appeal calling it bluntly a "legal black hole."[52]

[49] Adam Clymer, "Justice Dept. Draft on Wider Powers Draws Quick Criticism," *New York Times*, February 8, 2003, p. A10.

[50] Ruth Wedgwood, "Justice Will Be Done at Guantanamo," *Financial Times*, July 15, 2003.

[51] Jeremy Rabkin, "After Guantanamo: The War over the Geneva Convention," *National Interest*, summer 2002; Michael Dobbs, *Saboteurs: The Nazi Raid on America* (New York: Random House, 2004), pp. 233–52.

[52] Foreign and Commonwealth Office, "Human Rights: Challenges and Progress," chap. 1, p. 19.

This is not the place to rehearse the legal technicalities. Americans are sufficiently familiar with lawyers to know that legal arguments can always be found to underpin the actions of the authorities. Instead, this is a down-to-earth, practical question. If America vacates – or is seen to vacate – the moral high ground in the struggle against its adversaries, will this make these struggles easier or more difficult? Our experience from equally morally charged situations during the Cold War suggests that information flows more easily when the interested parties perceive shared moral values.

Surveillance Technology Advances

In *1984*, George Orwell wrote, "How often, or on what system, the Thought Police plugged in any individual wire was guess work. It was even conceivable that they watched everybody all the time. But at any rate, they could plug in your wire whenever they wanted to." While it is far-fetched to suggest that George Orwell was only twenty years off the mark in his prediction of a surveillance society run amok in *1984*, his prophecy is more a reality today than many Americans realize. Big Brother is increasingly watching – or, at least, is increasingly capable of watching. The combination of an explosion of inexpensive and readily available surveillance technology with the weakening of laws governing the use of such technology (as described in the preceding section) means that privacy, as it has traditionally been understood, is increasingly vulnerable – even quite separate from any consideration of national security. Americans have always assumed that the legal movements and activities of their everyday lives remain known only to them; such an assumption differentiates American life from that of individuals in nondemocratic regimes. However, speedy developments in surveillance capabilities are already at work and have the potential to burrow ever more deeply into every aspect of American life and to produce the deadening and conformist qualities long associated with the totalitarian regimes of the Soviet Union and its Eastern Bloc.

Georgetown University law professor Jonathan Turley notes, "For more than 200 years, our liberties have been protected primarily by practical barriers rather than constitutional barriers to government abuse. Because of the sheer size of the nation and its population, the government could not practically abuse a great number of citizens at any given time. In the last decade, however, these practical barriers have fallen to technology."[53] Video surveillance of public places, for example, is expanding at a fast pace. A recent study

---

[53] Quoted in Nat Hentoff, "We'll All Be under Surveillance," *Village Voice*, December 6, 2002.

concluded that it is now impossible for a person to walk around Manhattan without being recorded at almost every instant.[54] Traceable (radio frequency indicator devices) RFID and GPS (global positioning system) microchips are now implanted in a wide range of household appliances, such as cellular phones, PDAs, and car navigation and highway toll-payment systems, and allow the movements of users to be tracked. Biometric devices can now identify a person from his or her fingerprints, iris pattern, facial structure, and DNA and can even execute brain-wave fingerprinting. A technology such as face recognition can recognize an individual from a distance and without his or her knowledge or consent. Additionally, data surveillance can monitor people's credit card use and other financial transactions, and initiatives such as the FBI's "Carnivore" program can easily tap Internet activity.

We are constantly barraged with news of new technologies that make surveillance cheaper, easier, and more invasive. The September 8, 2003, cover of *U.S. News & World Report* trumpeted, somewhat sensationally, "Careful! Your Phone Is Watching You." The story details the rise of locator technology, which permits microchips to be implanted in a wide range of gadgets such as cell phones to pinpoint the whereabouts of any individual – to "keep you from ever getting lost." While such technology can save lives in determining, for example, the location of 911 callers, they could also conceivably allow authorities to track anyone, whether they like it or not.[55]

Each of these technological advances may seem somewhat trivial when viewed on an individual basis. After all, why should an ordinary American care whether a video camera captures him or her shopping for jeans at the Gap, or whether his or her use of a credit card to purchase the latest Stephen King novel from Amazon.com is recorded? Furthermore, it would not be fair to charge those who are developing these technologies with having intrinsically sinister motivations or being government stooges. Usually, the devices concerned have their primary application in fields such as medical care or traffic safety or for everyday purposes such as time saving while shopping. the concern, however, is the totality of the information-collection systems now available to private corporations and governments. When viewed in concert, various surveillance methods could allow the government's intelligence agencies to reconstruct a complete picture of almost every moment of each American's day-to-day activities. Non-Americans are also exposed to similar surveillance intrusion. It is calculated, for example, that a shopper

54 Stanley and Steinhardt, *Bigger Monster*.
55 David LaGesse, "They Know Where You Are," *US News & World Report*, September 8, 2003, pp. 32–38.

on London's Oxford Street is photographed some seventeen times as he or she walks down the street – and the number increases substantially if the person enters a store. On average, someone living in or visiting London may be photographed some 300 times in single day.[56]

Let's examine, for example, the potential of a technological development such as the placing of sensors in automobile seats designed to monitor driver behavior. The data accumulated from such a seat could be stored in a "black box" within the car (a rental car company has already attempted to use such boxes to monitor potential speeding violations by its customers) or even wirelessly transmitted to a central database via locator technology, such as is currently available in cellular phones. Intelligence agents could then monitor the activities of all drivers or passengers, in an attempt to identify potential criminal or terrorist behavior. Each development of surveillance technology is not isolated, but becomes part of an expanding surveillance network.

The government has already proven itself eager to take advantage of surveillance technology in a similar way. Shortly after September 11, the Pentagon announced its "Total Information Awareness" (TIA – which, in an effort to assuage public concerns, was swiftly renamed as "Terrorist Information Awareness") initiative, to be headed by Admiral John Poindexter under the auspices of the Defense Advanced Research Projects Agency (DARPA). In May 2003, DARPA submitted to Congress an extensive report on its plans.[57] DARPA is dedicated to formulating high-tech, out-of-the-box approaches to tackling security issues, and TIA was announced as a prototype program that would combine every current government and commercial database from across the globe into a single "ultra-large-scale" database capable of allowing the government to detect "patterns of activity" that provide warning signals of possible terrorist activity. This may sound prudent. But TIA's research methods – if they turn out to be technically feasible – represent a new level of secret government data collection on private individuals, involving as it does details of their credit cards, travels, hotel use, household purchases, and other routine aspects of daily life. In the DARPA report's words, the object is to allow "identification of connected items of information from multiple sources and databases whose significance is not known until the connections are made."[58]

---

[56] Fred Guterl and William Underhill, "Taking a Closer Look," *Newsweek International*, March 8, 2004.

[57] John M. Poindexter, "Finding the Face of Terror in Data," *New York Times*, September 10, 2003; DARPA, "Report to Congress Regarding the Terrorism Information Awareness Program," Department of Defense, Washington, D.C., May 2003.

[58] DARPA, "Report," p. 7.

This, of course, is the rub. DARPA is at pains to demonstrate its respect for civil liberties (indeed, there is a hint of a guilty conscience in its repetitive protestations on this point). Poindexter (who has since been replaced) averred that TIA's "research is being conducted on technologies that will keep the identities of subjects hidden from analysts, but still allow the detection of patterns of terrorist activity. If this research proves successful, then we would have the option of conducting surveillance first and asking for identities after sufficient justification was established." This sounds fanciful. As any counterterrorist expert will confirm, the only way that the technology can prove in any way helpful in a counterterrorism context is if it rapidly transitions from the general to the individual. At this point, the routine activities of all American citizens become the subject for secret government investigation. In essence, the government would be able in a matter of seconds to re-create the movements and activities of any individual over any period of time, without any sort of judicial oversight – to say nothing of the potential for incorrect data entries, misidentifications, and access by hackers. Already a number of mistakes have come to light where, in the name of antiterrorism precautions, personal information has leaked into commercial databanks under contract to the government.[59]

A close cousin of TIA is Computer Assisted Passenger Pre-Screening II (CAPPS II) to be administered by the Transportation Security Agency. CAPPS II significantly extends the reach of the existing system introduced after the terrorist destruction of Pan Am 103 by being able to "fuse threat data gathered from State, Federal, and private sector sources."[60] Under this proposed computerized profiling system, each air traveler would be screened via a database that would combine information about his or her travel history, living arrangements, credit card and telephone records, and other data in order to attempt to assess whether that passenger might constitute a terrorist threat.

Both TIA and CAPPS II have attracted substantial opposition, with the Senate voting in September 2003 to cut off funds from TIA. But a variant of CAPPS II is due to go into effect during 2004, and there are reports that research into a successor program to TIA is under way within the Homeland Security Advanced Research Projects Agency (HSARPA).[61] The point here

[59] Philip Shenon, "JetBlue Gave Defense Firm Files on Passengers," *New York Times*, September 20, 2003, p. A1.
[60] "Report to Congress on Enhanced Security Measures," U.S. Department of Transportation, Washington, D.C., 2002, p. 6.
[61] Sara Kehaulani Goo, "U.S. to Push Airlines for Passenger Records," *Washington Post*, January 12, 2004, p. A1.

is, once again, not that the U.S. authorities are ill-intentioned but that a war climate and rapidly advancing surveillance capabilities spell dangers for the sort of open society that Americans have traditionally taken for granted.

RECONCILING THE DEBATE

As with all debates involving neo-conservatives, polarization is never far away. So let us steer in the other direction. The debate over security and civil liberties is not an all-or-nothing affair. Nor has the final word been uttered. But it is as well to state clearly that public safety is the prime government responsibility. Those charged with carrying out this responsibility should be accorded the respect that they are operating in good faith. The same respect is also due to those who raise concerns about legislative trends. Once provisions make their way onto the statute books, the time will come when they will be used, perhaps in the context for which they were intended, but also possibly for a different purpose. The state of Virginia, for example, is using a section of its antiterrorist law to seek the death penalty in a serial murder case. This is not what the legislation intended.

Liberty and vigilance are mutually dependent, and the debate about the dividing line between them is an old one. The path of least resistance is not to pay attention. In the context of today's exponential expansion of data collection and data-mining capabilities, this may also be the most dangerous one, if we are to safeguard America's unique legacy of freedom.

10

The Balance Sheet and Looking Ahead

Lord Robin Renwick, former British Ambassador to Washington, commented during breakfast with one of the authors at the Ritz on July 14, 2003, "Churchill said that the Americans can be generally counted on to do the right thing in the end but will exhaust every possible alternative in the meanwhile. At this point, however, one can not be sure that they will do the right thing in the end."

The administration of U.S. foreign policy is a complex undertaking and has, more often than not, remained the province of an elite community of analysts and diplomats. Usually avoided by political managers because it is remote and complicated and of limited interest to the voting public, foreign policy has, historically, received less public scrutiny than economic policy, education, health, or urban policy. In normal times, this disconnect between the public and the type of foreign policy pursued by the government is unfortunate but not damaging. That is not the case today – and the result has been that, externally, Americans and their nation are at greater risk than at any time since the Cuban Missile Crisis, and, domestically, we approach a polarization not seen since the Vietnam War. It is for this reason that it is worth reviewing the aspects that, in our view, have gone wrong and where Americans and their well-wishers around the world might consider corrective intervention.

The Charges against the Neo-Conservatives

Foreign Policy. In this book, we have sought to analyze how we came to this state of affairs. We have argued that the chief responsibility lies with the neo-conservatives and the special interest ideology they have imposed on the rest of us. At its most basic, their philosophy proceeds from a crucial misinterpretation of the dynamics of the "unipolar" system created by American military predominance.[1] Drawing on a straight-line extrapolation of the preeminence of America's weapons technology and assigning subordinate importance to other factors – such as the asymmetrical military capabilities of adversaries, world opinion, and resource limitations – the neo-conservatives have caused the United States to turn its back on the benefits of half a century of diplomatic partnership and cooperation. Theirs was not the only voice in policy making after 9/11, but their ready-made plans for the Middle East were the ones adopted. We believe that we have shown that, had these plans not already been in existence and had the neo-conservatives not adroitly melded their agenda with other more permanent themes in U.S. national security thinking – the belief in American exceptionalism, a predisposition to act independently, and a commitment to progress through market democracy – thus acquiring a broad and unassailable base within the administration, events might have taken a very different course.

The consequences of this were entirely predictable. The United States now finds itself uncomfortably isolated within the international community; anti-American feelings have risen quickly; and the nation confronts an increasingly dangerous and complex security environment. In a misfocused obsession with the most rigid interpretation of American sovereignty, their policies have narrowed American options and augmented America's human and financial burdens. Most important, their embrace of a coarse-grained unilateralism has tarnished America's moral authority. Under their influence, America has, sadly, lost legitimacy. As we have already noted, Robert Kagan, one of the principal architects of the neo-conservative belligerence that has brought us to this state of affairs, acknowledges this point. "America," he writes, "for the first time since World War II, is suffering a crisis of international legitimacy."[2]

We have documented a further central charge. While the government comprises many sets of competing elites not subject to coordination, much less conspiracy, senior neo-conservative officials have orchestrated a sustained program of deception toward the American people to obscure the implications of their long-standing goals of regime change in the Middle East. In

---

[1] Charles Krauthammer, "An American Foreign Policy for a Unipolar World," Irving Kristol lecture at AEI, February 10, 2004.

[2] Robert Kagan, "A Tougher War for the U.S. Is One of Legitimacy," *New York Times*, January 24, 2004, p. A17.

doing this, they have, at various times, directly and indirectly co-opted certain institutions of government, the media, the academy, and foreign allies, making them complicit in their deceit. Even the letters home from GIs in the field, dictated by a middle-ranking officer trying to win the favor of his superiors, have felt their contaminating breath. Again, the consequence is predictable. Public trust in America's public agencies is less, and the institutions themselves are demoralized. Americans openly question the administration's veracity. For the first time in three decades, the nature of one's patriotism is an issue, and domestic surveillance is a growth industry.

A further charge is that neo-conservatives have mispositioned the nation's response to terrorism. The threat is real, specifically from nonstate actors such as al-Qaeda and their many imitators. Instead of a carefully calibrated approach to these adversaries drawing on a mix of instruments – political, intelligence, police, special forces, and so on – America has gone to war with an idea – "terrorism" – and now finds itself on the cusp of a "clash of civilizations" with the Islamic world.

Finally and perhaps most seriously, to fight this war, all other priorities and distinctions – between state and nonstate actors, and between the various categories of weapons of mass destruction for instance – have been overridden. The neo-conservatives may believe that the rest of the world stops to allow them to complete their agenda. But it does not. Among the most serious strategic developments is that, while American attention has been monopolized by Iraq, the American primacy in Asia is slipping away. China is in the ascendant over North Korea and Taiwan. In December 2003 China successfully made the administration party to a Faustian bargain that undercuts the diplomatic ambiguity that has, for half a century, balanced Taiwan's democratic development, U.S. interests in East Asia, trade and investment in the region, and China's political sensitivities. However much neo-conservatives such as William Kristol accuse the administration of being "soft as marshmallows" over China, this development provides a case in point illustrating the cost of the neo-conservative–driven overextension of American resources in the Middle East and lack of subtlety over North Korea.[3] Both principle and policy were sacrificed in the case of Taiwan, where American support for market democracy was subsumed by the practical reality of China's growing power and America's costly and unproductive involvement half a world away. The irony, of course, is that what Taiwan has achieved is precisely what the neo-conservatives hope to impose in Iraq, and in both Iraq and Taiwan,

---

[3] Robert Kagan and William Kristol, "Stand by Taiwan," *Weekly Standard*, December 30, 2003.

the net result of administration action has been to compromise America's strategic posture.

Elsewhere, there is little senior management time to spare for nuclear proliferation on other continents, for the proper management of relations with the European Union and Russia, for the maintenance and expansion of an open economic order, for the maintenance of space as a demilitarized zone, for the alleviation of destabilizing world poverty and disease. Pakistan – barely governable in the face of religious radicalism, increasingly the unwilling host of a resurgent Taliban, armed with deliverable nuclear weapons, and, by self-confession, a seller of nuclear technology[4] – receives perfunctory attention. Even Afghanistan, marked by a nineteen-fold increase in opium production and reconstruction aid less than one-sixteenth of that for Kosovo, has become peripheral. So recently the center of attention, it is a victim of the reconstruction budget for Iraq, which has sapped resources from other needs. Inattention to these needs, whether in Afghanistan or in Bolivia, may have damning consequences in the form of imploding states and narcotics-financed terrorism, two of the threats underscored in the 2002 National Security Strategy.[5] Economic issues, as we discuss elsewhere, are largely overlooked. There is no time to ponder, let alone to prepare for the more distant challenges destined to emerge once the world reverts to multipolarity.[6] The list of neglected important priorities could go on.

The Changes in America. The damage deriving from neo-conservative policies is not confined to the international arena. The truly enduring priority overlooked since 9/11 has been the health of our society at home. It is here that the continuing impact may be longer-lived. In the nearly three years that have passed since the attacks in New York and Washington, America has become a profoundly different place. Until it became a political liability, we lived for eighteen months on the edge of crisis, locked in a mesmerizing and unintelligible discourse of daily alerts that allowed no rational response but kept us hostage to the next announcement. Hyper-news from the cable news shows that breathlessly bring the latest rumor ("sources indicate" and "breaking news"), flashing interstate signs with 800 numbers to call if terrorists were seen, and color-coded alert levels moved through the spectrum with no discernible effect.

---

4 Mark Landler and David E. Sanger, "Pakistan Chief Says It Appears Scientists Sold Nuclear Data," *New York Times*, January 24, 2004, p. A1.
5 James Dobbins, et al., *America's Role in Nation-Building: From Germany to Iraq* (Santa Monica, Calif: Rand Corporation, 2003), p. 146.
6 Charles Kupchan, *The End of the American Era* (New York: Knopf, 2003).

While the sense of crisis suddenly appears and then disappears, our civil liberties remain under pressure, particularly our Fourth Amendment rights and assumptions of privacy. Our political life drifts toward polarization with critics branded disloyal or defeatist, often subsumed by robotic supporters parroting the official line. The normal decencies of our civil society are measurably in retreat.[7] At any given time, the best-seller lists are full of no-holds-barred attack books. Political debate takes place not on the basis of ideas but by assigning them to one or another ideological pigeonhole. These pressures mean that assumptions regarding traditional civil liberties in America must be reexamined. In a series of steps, obscured from the public by dense technical language and inadequately examined in the Congress, the protections afforded by the grand jury system have been eroded. Of equal concern are tendencies within the Department of Justice to use the 9/11 emergency to undermine some of the constitutionally ensured freedoms it is entrusted to protect.

Just as the use of language by the administration was critical in the run-up to the Iraq war, so it has been critical with respect to the domestic security agenda. In short, Washington has portrayed itself as a government at war and claimed accompanying wartime powers. Chief Justice William Rehnquist warns that "the government's authority to engage in conduct that infringes civil liberties is greatest in wartime," but, we add, this war on an idea is unlike any we have fought before (adversaries in the Cold War had a name and address). Although it had a beginning, how will anyone know when it has ended? Moreover, at what point does the government cease arrogating to itself more and more of the authority that has, until now, resided outside its realm? And will these civil liberties be restored when some future administration declares peace is at hand? There is palpable doubt about a positive answer to this question. As Princeton professor Aaron Friedberg (who in 2003 joined Vice President Cheney's national security staff) has noted, a characteristic of America's separated-powers governance is that "new executive branch agencies, programs and functions that survive immediate post-crisis rollback will tend to become 'locked in' and will be very difficult to abolish."[8] As a democracy we have clear vulnerabilities. We must, however, remember not only whom we are fighting, but also what we are fighting for. Our strengths, ironically, render us vulnerable to terrorism; our

---

[7] Judith Rodin and Stephen P. Steinberg, eds., *Public Discourse in America: Conversation and Community in the Twenty-first Century* (Philadelphia: University of Pennsylvania Press, 2003).

[8] Aaron L. Friedberg, *In the Shadow of the Garrison State* (Princeton, N.J.: Princeton University Press, 2000), p. 32.

various freedoms, including privacy, assembly, and due process, make it harder to prevent attacks and easier for terrorists to manipulate our judicial system. But to surrender these rights in order to more effectively battle terrorism hands victory without a fight to those who would destroy our society.

Advances in surveillance and government intentions to utilize available technology in this area make it imperative that checks and balances instituted by the Constitution be maintained to limit government intrusion into privacy on the Internet, including personal details on where people shop, what they read, their sexual proclivities, and with whom they communicate. The removal of checks and balances in this arena assumes perfect behavior on the part of the prosecutors and police, an assumption not made by the framers of the Constitution. Among the first abuses was reported on September 15, 2003, when a prosecutor in North Carolina charged a suspect in a raid on a methamphetamine lab with possession of weapons of mass destruction. It is encouraging that groups across the political spectrum from the American Civil Liberties Union on the left to the American Conservative Union on the right have risen in opposition and to see that their concerns have been reflected in Congress and in the 2004 presidential campaign.

The concern is that advances in surveillance technology have made the world a smaller place, enabling the authorities to assemble all the electronic information pertaining to an individual in one place that creates an Orwellian reality making it impossible to live "off the grid." The assumption is that the expanded and integrated information network will allow the administration to stop terrorists before they act. But given the myriad, unpredictable, and quirky habits of a population of nearly 300 million people, the prospect of sleuthing out terrorist patterns is remote. While the system may be helpful to investigators following a terrorist incident, preventing one is an entirely different matter. It is quite possible therefore that America will end up with the worst of both worlds: a highly intrusive surveillance infrastructure that contributes little to public safety.

Having said this, it is important to add there is no doubt that the vast majority of those working to protect the nation's security are well-meaning, dedicated public servants. They are not the arbitrary architects of these intrusive measures. The question remains, however, as to whether there is another way to balance the equities at hand. Might we view terrorism as a problem management issue – as the British, Spanish, Italians, and Germans have – rather than restructure our society and our values to address it? The alternative is to see our civil society damaged with little likely advance in security.

The Wider Responsibility

In a moment we turn to some of the specific areas in which the nation has suffered damage from the fallout of neo-conservative policies. But there is another side to the equation in which we are all involved and for which we bear some responsibility as ordinary citizens. We address this to illustrate the importance of an aware and involved public in future international issues.

An Under-informed Citizenry. Some seven years ago the veteran journalist Garrick Utley pointed out a counterintuitive paradox. He wrote that as U.S. global power – military deployments and economic integration – expanded in the 1990s, coverage of international affairs in the nation's press diminished.[9] A further look revealed that with the exception of the principal national newspapers, most major metropolitan papers had little or no staff reporting daily from abroad. The reason, according to the news editors, was that they could not justify the costs of expensive overseas bureaus in the light of their readers' limited interest in foreign affairs. Other press organizations followed this lead; for example, the Freedom Forum, long a force in international journalism, has closed its international bureaus and ceased its international activities. As a result, readers were offered fewer foreign stories and had less context for understanding events overseas. When the president travels overseas, the media goes with him; but when he moves on, so does the media caravan. There is no one left behind to report the aftermath, as, for example, in October 2003, when China's president appeared before the Australian parliament twenty-four hours after his American counterpart and, in place of the grim American "with us or against us" exhortations regarding the impending terrorist threat, offered an interactive, optimistic, trade-based vision of East Asia's future. Who left the deeper impression? It was not until two months later that American readers were given the information needed to decide for themselves.[10]

While the issue of China's gains amidst America's current distractions is a separate question, the lack of timely, in-depth international reporting has meant that Americans are more likely to react to events abroad through the limited prism of their emotions or ethnic backgrounds or in line with their domestic political alignments. The scope for misunderstanding was further broadened during the 1990s when the cable news channels introduced a type

---

[9] Garrick Utley, "The Shrinking of Foreign News: From Broadcast to Narrowcast," *Foreign Affairs*, March–April 1997, pp. 2–10.
[10] Jane Perlez, "With U.S. Busy, China Is Romping with Neighbors," *New York Times*, December 3, 2003, p. A1.

of hyper-tabloid coverage directed at targeted demographies and driven by ratings. The result, discussed in Chapter 6, was a format that saw itself as entertainment. It simplified news developments and hardened viewer attitudes toward what were often nuanced international challenges. A new genre of celebrity, the "talking head," emerged, the main quality of whom were firm, unambiguous opinions rather than grounded knowledge. The situation has not been helped by the fact that only 12 percent of Americans hold passports.

Five years later in 2001, an America largely disinterested and uninformed about foreign affairs was convulsed by terrorism spawned abroad. It was a moment defined by fear, the most basic of human emotions that, more than others, suspends time and thought and renders those in its grip unusually susceptible to demagoguery. This was the moment when a small, largely unknown group of neo-conservatives injected itself decisively into the foreign policy process. In retrospect, one could not know how susceptible an inexperienced president and a less informed polity would be to the policies that have brought the risky position in which the nation now finds itself. Since that time, the major print and electronic media have moved to redress the balance on foreign news. But it is a game of catch-up. Foreign bureaus are still underresourced, and the availability of news, other than on immediate crises, remains limited. As research cited in Chapter 6 shows, the American people still lack a foundation of knowledge that would provide the perspective to dodge, for example, Fox News's frequent disinformation bullets. And perhaps most disturbing, an accurate understanding of the issues we face remains elusive. Just before the second anniversary of 9/11, polls showed that 70 percent of Americans believed that the 9/11 hijackers were Iraqis, that Saddam used chemical weapons against our troops, and that the link between Saddam and al-Qaeda had been proven. The evidence is clear that this lack of context on the part of the American public contributed to the limited debate in the decisive hours after 9/11 when the neo-conservatives moved to steer policy in their direction.

The lesson here is that a lack of accurate information over time rendered an uninformed citizenry vulnerable to being misled by a special interest. In this instance, the neo-conservatives took advantage of their opportunity – and others will be able to do so in the future. The further lesson is that America's disinterest in foreign events, personalities, and cultures haunts American security. Just as we demand effective education for our children or spend hours on the Internet studying health problems so that we can have an intelligent conversation with our doctors, so a similar commitment to familiarization with events abroad and with cultures and countries very different from ours would pay enormous dividends. The alternative is to suffer, as we do now, from narrow, interest-based policies set by a small group of insiders without adequate public discussion of the full range of available options and their implications.

An Underperforming Center. Among the more striking aspects of U.S. response to 9/11 was the unwillingness of the center – there was a time when this would have been called the "Establishment" – the Senate, the House of Representatives, the Judiciary, leaders of the foreign policy institutions, the media leaders – to open a public debate in 2003 on the administration's policy. The problem is found in the network of overlapping interests within the center that made it difficult to break ranks and to ask disquieting questions. Politicians are sensitive to the opinion polls of the moment; journalists need sources so they do not tell all they know; news anchors need prominent guests and thus often foreshadow the issues to be raised in interviews; academics often rely on federal and foundation grants so they are cautious about giving offense; think tanks, as one denizen of this world records, are ever more dependent on partisan fund raising.[11] Regardless, a major national enterprise was allowed to proceed without a full examination of the tenets underlying the White House case, a clear understanding of the costs, or what the end game would look like. There was, for example, little discussion of an "exit" strategy – that is, how and when the vast Middle East project would conclude. Nor was there discussion of whether hostilities might extend to nations surrounding Iraq or, for that matter, of the effect on the region. Administration claims of extensive forthcoming help from allies were taken largely at face value. Senators John Kerry, John Edwards, and Joe Lieberman and Congressman Richard Gephardt all voted in favor of the authorization to proceed to war.

It was not until growing public uncertainty with the scope of the Iraq venture registered in public opinion polls and provided solid ground for the Democratic challengers that a critical debate was opened – and even then, the mainstream candidates were hesitant. Among other things, with troops on the way or in the field, and the nation on a war footing, they faced the charge of being soft on national security, historically a Democratic liability, or, worse, being labeled unpatriotic. Dissent was thus relegated to the periphery.

It would be wrong, however, to conclude that the political process, as relates to this critical issue, failed completely. Though this was not the center's

---

[11] Charles Kupchan, *The End of the American Era* (New York: Knopf, 2003), p. 325.

finest hour, the political process clung to life through 2003 largely through the campaign of an obscure newcomer, Howard Dean, a former governor of Vermont. With less to lose than his Washington-based colleagues, he was able to speak out when those more experienced than him held back. He succeeded in mobilizing a coalition of those who objected to the unilateral, preemptive nature of the attack on Iraq, the assertion that Iraq was the "central front" in the war on terror, the massive expenditures required for the war and reconstruction, and the alienation of America's allies. He captured the emotion – the anger – of those who felt that the expenditures in Iraq were diverting resources needed for education, social and health services, and infrastructure improvement in the United States. Whatever Dean's future trajectory, his focusing of discontent over the war in Iraq showed that, even as the center was underperforming, the intrinsic vitality of the American political process still performed its proper function of providing a check on the central government.

For some six months, the critique advanced by the Democratic left amounted to little more than a lonely vigil on the outpost of the political debate. But the administration's request to Congress in September 2003 for $87 billion for military and reconstruction efforts in Iraq and Afghanistan changed the dynamics. It functioned as a pivot in the national debate, challenging the Democratic presidential field to take a position on the proposal placed before Congress. As is inevitable in circumstances such as these, the White House initiative forced members of Congress, in this case including many Republicans, to establish conditions on how the money would be spent before approving the request. This, in turn, opened the argument, raising broader questions on the rationale for the policy itself. Sensing these changes, White House political advisers assumed a more prominent role. The result is that Iraq policy started to be filtered through the lens of domestic political calculation, rather than on its own merits.

The challenge to their objectives was not lost on the neo-conservatives. Michael Ledeen, writing in the *American Spectator*, said, "We are living through one of the great potential turning points of history.... The whole world now pivots on a Middle Eastern hinge, and its final stopping point will shape the planet for a generation or more to come." He continued, "[W]e can determine the outcome ourselves (of the Middle Eastern drama), through our own strength, wisdom and determination."[12] Robert Kagan and William Kristol, writing in the *Weekly Standard*, were even more pointed. In an article on Iraq entitled "America's Responsibility," they said: "It is the responsibility

[12] Michael Ledeen, "Pivot Point," *American Spectator* 36, no. 3, June/July 2003, p. 38.

of the United States to build in Iraq a *condition of security and stability, moving toward prosperity and democracy*" (emphasis added). They continue: "And if we lose, we will leave behind us not blue helmets but radicalism and chaos, a haven for terrorists, and a perception of American weakness and lack of resolve in the Middle East and reckless blundering around the world. That is the abyss we may be staring into if we do not shift course now."[13]

These commentaries exhibit a sad decline from those of the neo-conservative first-generation pioneers, men and women of great intellectual gifts. Today, we are left with predictable polemicists. What is also note-worthy is that while Kagan and Kristol raise the specter of the abyss, in their statement of America's responsibility the first signs of uncertainty are evident about the enterprise they so ardently embraced post-9/11. Why, if our mission is to democratize the Middle East and to bring stability to Iraq, do the neo-conservative wise men call upon us to bring about conditions that, before the event, they promised would result effortlessly from the invasion?

The answer returns us to our starting point. Military unipolarity is not enough to deliver their objective of transforming the Middle East.

The Neo-Conservative Confidence Trick

The combination of a public starved of international affairs perspective and of an elite center falling down on the job provided the opening for the neo-conservatives to frame the post-9/11 policy process in their terms. The methods used to bring this about bear directly on the question of public trust. Specifically, in order to make the case for the decade-old neo-conservative objective of attacking Iraq, a web of deception was needed: that Saddam Hussein had, and intended to use, weapons of mass destruction; that Saddam Hussein protected and supported al-Qaeda; and that were he not removed the weapons might be provided to al-Qaeda, which could use them against the United States.

These claims, in effect, transformed the issues at hand by turning the possible existence of these threats into "proven" facts. The process, which anthropologists call the "discursive construction of reality," uses language to create a reality different from that which existed prior to the use of the language. In this case, prominent neo-conservatives fashioned a dialogue, a linguistic environment, that caused many to believe that the claims were

---

[13] Robert Kagan and William Kristol, "America's Responsibility," *Weekly Standard*, September 15, 2003, p. 10.

rooted in fact, which was not the case. Thus a set of subjective interpretations, repeated in various fora and presented as fact, emerged as the only valid way to comprehend the choices confronting the nation, rendering the war with Iraq the only rational course of action. Justification for the war was thus created through hypothesis and interpretation.

The administration's case, characterized by hearsay statements and worst-case hypotheticals, was designed to convince the American people that they would suffer further attacks, similar to 9/11, were Saddam not removed from power and the Iraqi regime eliminated. The record is replete with examples of the discourse, including phrases such as: "U.N. inspectors *believe* Iraq maintains," "the U.S. has long *suspected*," "*who knows* how many of these factories," "*we can only imagine* how many anthrax," "*what if* Saddam provides," "Saddam *could help* a terrorist," and "*there may well have been interaction* between Mr. Hussein and various terrorist networks, including that of Osama bin Laden."

What is significant is that the lexical exchange of the concrete terror wrought by the nineteen hijackers for more abstract threats defined in hypothetical and ambiguous language built support for actions that would otherwise have been highly controversial. The shifting focus from 9/11 to Saddam was managed by the administration, which encouraged and sustained a post-9/11 security neurosis. Fear was the adhesive linking the chain of uncorroborated statements, assumptions, and predictions. This phenomenon gave disproportionate emphasis to Saddam, diverting attention from the failure to capture Osama bin Laden, the architect of 9/11, and downplaying other equally plausible threats. For example, the prospect that a coup in Pakistan replacing General Musharraf, who had ascended to power himself by a coup, could place nuclear weapons at the disposal of Islamic radicals within hours was left largely unaddressed. Given Pakistan's possession of medium-range missiles, this would be an immediate threat to American allies in the region and in Europe. Moreover, it was a distinct possibility given Musharraf's narrow base of support and the divided loyalty of his intelligence service.

Thus, knowingly or not, the administration used language to form a reality for the nation that defined the situation brought by 9/11 as leading logically to war with Iraq. In so doing, it solidified opinion and political support in a manner that muffled dissent. The academy was muted, and institutions, including the intelligence community and the press, whose vitality are essential to the nation's political well being, suffered substantial damage. The power of any administration to create and shape a discourse compatible with its interests should not be taken lightly. That in this case one faction, the neo-conservatives, was able to exercise so decisive an influence over the totality of foreign policy should disturb all of us. For among the casualties is the trust so essential to democratic government, which will not be restored easily or soon.

Public Trust: The Policy Damage

The deception practiced by the neo-conservatives has left a disturbing legacy. A fundamental quality of democratic government is in play, namely the public's trust. While the administration embraces the lofty objective of providing democratic government and markets to those laboring under authoritarian regimes, while lathering the argument with the "war on terrorism," its true objectives, focused by the neo-conservative agenda, are much more specific. If the administration is committed to the spread of market democracy, why has so little been heard about democracy and free markets in China, where Secretary Powell asserts, "I submit U.S. relations with China are the best they have been since President Nixon's first visit in 1972,"[14] or about Sierra Leone, Venezuela, the wholesale slaughter in the Sudan, or the disgraceful repression in Peru? Russia now receives almost a free pass on Chechnya. Azerbaijan is so far removed from market democracy that it ranks in 104th place in the Heritage Foundation's 2003 Index of Economic Freedom, yet receives a pat on the back from the administration after holding a Soviet-style presidential election. Uzbekistan has won U.S. favor despite detailed indictments from respected human rights organizations for precisely the abuses that are now used to justify the Iraq war. Indeed, why, at the risk of repetition, was so little heard about North Korea – or, more pertinently, why was evidence about North Korea's nuclear program purposefully delayed in being provided to the American people?[15] The issue here is not absolute consistency – as we have noted earlier, this is neither possible nor necessarily desirable in international affairs – but the ability of the United States to give its various global interests adequate attention on their own merits.

Attention has instead been focused on one region, the Middle East, where, to make them politically palatable, the administration has misrepresented its intentions. The neo-conservative rationale, reflected in endless statements and commentary, has been that only by restructuring the "Arab tyrannies" of the region can U.S. energy supplies and regional security be ensured. Though Secretary Powell has asserted a commitment to multilateralism,

---

[14] Glenn Kessler, "Powell Strongly Defends Bush's Foreign Policy," *Washington Post*, September 6, 2003, p. A15.
[15] John Newhouse, *Imperial America* (New York: Knopf, 2003), pp. 130–32.

neo-conservative decision makers in the vice president's office and Pentagon have advanced a policy that argues that the way to accomplish this is "regime change" – by persuasion or proxy (aid to the internal opposition) if possible, and preemptive military action, if necessary. Thus, one asks, if that is the administration's objective, why not state it clearly? If restructuring the region is practical, if it is a rational goal, why dissemble? Why mislead the American public with yet unproved tales of weapons of mass destruction and terrorist links to Osama bin Laden in Saddam's Iraq when the equation is based on a very different calculation? Why not say that in order to achieve regional security it is necessary to restructure Iraq, Syria, Iran, Sudan, Libya, Yemen, Saudi Arabia, and perhaps the Emirates and Egypt? If this argument can be made persuasively, why not use the immense media apparatus available to the administration and neo-conservative sympathizers to advance it? Why has this proposed policy not been fully detailed by the administration?

The answer is found in their suspicion that Americans would be unwilling, if they knew the real agenda, to restructure the Middle East, to spend hundreds of billions of dollars and countless lives in such an unprecedented undertaking. Leaving aside the fallacy of believing that outsiders can restructure local cultures, the methods chosen to do so have brought, as we have seen, little but disapproval and isolation and a region no less combustible than at the neo-conservative point of entry. Were they to reveal their true agenda, not only would it be rejected as fantastic and impossible, but the neo-conservatives would find themselves out of office.

American Exceptionalism. The conviction that America is an exceptional nation lies at the heart of much American thinking about the rest of the world. This belief in American "exceptionalism" – the idea that America is indispensable to global progress and that American values and institutions are the precondition for progress – is firmly grounded in the extraordinary achievements of American society that, from the earliest days of the Republic, have been the envy of much of the world. Americans' belief in their own exceptionalism has prompted some of the most generous acts of selfless sacrifice for global good in recorded history.

What distinguishes the neo-conservatives is not that they have drawn on this concept but that their discourse seeks to operationalize it in a region – the Middle East – that has followed a different path, in the belief that without their intervention the benighted cultures of the Middle East will remain dispossessed, hostile, and dysfunctional. It is an America-centric view that dismisses the institutions and social mechanisms of local cultures as reflecting inappropriate values – and certainly not the Enlightenment values that have animated the West. It posits that these local characteristics sustain elites whose objectives are antithetical to our own. The mere existence of political institutions grounded in Islamic cultural values is defined as a security threat. All this is seen as threatening American interests, and that threat cannot be eliminated by any means other than restructuring – forcefully, if necessary – their social and political systems. The argument then, however, proceeds to blend this belief in the supremacy of American values with economic, political, and security concerns, to create a new and expanded version of American interests implemented by an aggressive, militarized diplomacy.

This is to learn nothing from previous attempts by similar elite special interests to remake Southeast Asia in the American image or of Europeans to remake the non-European world. It represents a radical departure from the distilled, yet cooperative, diplomacy that, when it has been applied, has produced the greatest advances in American interests, such as the creation of the post–World War II international institutions and the handling of the Cold War endgame. The neo-conservatives have transformed exceptionalism into an aggressive, oppressive quality, which is singularly counterproductive in terms of America's interaction with the world.

The Military and Terrorism. Past administrations, many of them Republican, have successfully employed a range of diplomatic instruments to advance American values and interests, including foreign aid, trade, military agreements of various kinds, and personal relationships, not to mention the closed-door deal making so much a part of decision making within the international institutions such as NATO. Once again, the most successful episodes for American diplomacy, for example, the first Gulf war, have come when the United States has valued consensus and successfully worked within the international organizations to achieve it, notwithstanding the inevitable frustrations and disappointments that are a part of the process. Among the benefits have been expanded economic relations, military and financial burden sharing, intelligence cooperation, and a generally supportive context for American initiatives. Yet focused as they are on Machiavelli and Wohlstetter and conditioned by neo-conservative historians of the classical period, neo-conservative theorists often see military power as the prime factor in relations between states. Furthermore, dismissing the power of sustained, forceful multilateral diplomacy, they see war as the primary way one state imposes its power on another. Persistently failing to grasp the full continuum of warmaking, they emphasize its belligerent, demolition phase, giving scant attention to its reconstruction phase – a phase that we reach if we are lucky;

otherwise this phase becomes one of resistance and insurgency. As we have seen, the failure to address the complexities of the latter following the successful CIA-backed Mujahiddin war against the Soviets in Afghanistan laid the foundation for the Taliban. As for nonstate actors, such as al-Qaeda and their like, neo-conservatives fail to acknowledge how profoundly different this challenge is from that posed by states, essentially in the fact that there is an almost limitless population ready to be recruited to these nonstate actors and to bloody their hands with unconstrained acts of violence – so long as the political cause of their discontent continues. What for us is the last day of combat operations is for our adversaries – remnants, resisters, terrorists, guerrillas, insurgents, nationalists (the name is immaterial) – the first day of their operations. Unless the neo-conservatives accept this difference, "our future may belong to the men with the bloodied hands."[16]

This raises again the fundamental question of why three full years after 9/11 there has not been a full, public debate on how the terrorist threat has been presented and how it should be addressed and whether, for example, there isn't something to be learned from the British. Their distilled response to terrorism in Northern Ireland and on the British mainland, where eventual negotiation and compromise turned terrorists into politicians, cast the challenge not in apocalyptic terms but as a "problem management" issue. Also unexplored is the question, now widely raised, of whether the U.S. effort in Iraq might have inadvertently focused and accelerated terrorist activity by drawing fighters from across the region to resist the coalition (the British Joint Intelligence Committee, in documents now public, warned of this in February 2003).

Rising Anti-Americanism. We have pointed out that the administration's military-based diplomacy has brought a striking rise in world-wide anti-American feeling. When the president travels, he must do so in a locked-down security bubble: eight hours here, sixteen hours there, never more than thirty minutes from an airport, no press conferences, no meeting the people, no seeing of the sights. American representatives overseas tell us that in many small ways their jobs have become more difficult over the past three years. The open doors we experienced in our careers are closing. Poll figures for Europe are particularly striking. Some 64 percent of Europeans condemned the war in Iraq as "not worth the loss of life and other associated costs," while those who believe "it is desirable for the U.S. to exert strong leadership in world

---

[16] John Keegan, *A History of Warfare* (New York: Knopf, 1993), p. 392.

affairs" slipped from 64 to 45 percent from 2002 to 2003.[17] In a related development, there are indications of a global move away from American brands. American market share is under pressure in virtually all regions of the world. Further, as seen in its attempt to garner U.N. support for the reconstruction of Iraq in the U.N., support for American diplomatic initiatives has been elusive.

Thus far unmentioned in these concluding observations is the damage done to American credibility abroad, and the increased difficulty American leaders will have in garnering the support at home needed to address future crises. The irony that neo-conservatives rose to prominence in the late 1960s and 1970s asserting the legitimacy of American force projection in Vietnam is inescapable. After the disillusionment of that war, Americans drew away from military intervention in the wars of liberation, concluding that while nationalist forces could be defeated in set battles, nationalism remained, and the notion of winning opponents' "hearts and minds" was just that – a notion. There were virtually no examples of success in such endeavors, leading both conservatives and liberals to believe that such initiatives, as the neo-conservative agenda demonstrates, remain risky, expensive, dispiriting, and prone to failure.

It was not until the neo-conservatives reformulated the argument in such a way as to link the war on terrorism to regime change in Iraq that the crisp realism that had infused much of the established politico-military discourse in the Nixon-Ford and Reagan years collapsed. It seems certain that one result of the current policy, beyond the upheaval now threatening in Iraq (and likely Egypt, Pakistan, and Saudi Arabia), will be an era characterized by a fractured public trust centering on the government's national security policies and a particular aversion to intervention.

The delicacy of this question is hard to exaggerate. Given the public's limited interest in and knowledge of foreign matters and the relative paucity of analysis in the American media that has brought only a limited understanding of such issues, loss of public confidence is a blunt variable and difficult to reverse even over time. This bodes ill for any number of possible challenges facing the nation. Consider, for example, what difficulties the administration would face in generating public support for military action to address the problem of nuclear proliferation and the deployment of nuclear missiles by North Korea. One could say that it is a Northeast Asia problem and leave it at that. But this ignores the fact that such missiles may one day pose a threat

---

[17] Glenn Frankel, "Poll: Opposition to US Policy Grows in Europe," *Washington Post*, September 4, 2003, p. A15.

to the continental United States, putting the nation's security at risk. In such a situation, it is appropriate to ask whether the public would be disposed to accept U.S. intervention in North Korea, given the unproved claims and flawed rationale surrounding the Iraq war.

Impasse in the Middle East. More broadly, the promised democratic domino effect under which the regime change in Iraq would unleash a new political culture in the Middle East that would somehow transform the dynamics of the Israel-Palestine question shows no sign of materializing. The long-term fragility of the democratic experiment in Iraq – where the country is struggling to avoid either the emergence of a theocratic government under a leader such as Grand Ayatollah Ali Sistani or ethnic fragmentation cascading from Kurdistan – demonstrates how naïve it is to argue, as the neo-conservatives did, that a U.S.-engineered removal of a tyrannical leader can of itself transform a region. Whether the recent, diplomacy-inspired trends toward moderation in Iran and Libya that long preceded the Iraq war can do this remains to be seen. For the immediate future, however, it seems beyond doubt that U.S. actions have stimulated Islamic radicalism in Iraq, Syria, Saudi Arabia, Pakistan, Egypt, Sudan, and on the West Bank and accelerated terrorist designs on the U.S. homeland. Moreover, emigration, failing businesses, and fear have radicalized Israeli politics; it finds itself less stable and certainly less secure in the aftermath of the Iraq war and the downgrading of the administration's commitment to the peace process than before the attack was launched. Policies designed to remove Palestinian Authority President Yasser Arafat while sustaining the struggling Palestinian Authority have come to nothing, bringing the resignation of successive Palestinian cabinets, horrific terrorism, and calls in the Israeli cabinet for Arafat's assassination. Particularly chilling for Washington's neo-conservatives was an Israeli claim they hoped never to hear, namely that the United States undertook the Iraq war in large part to bolster Israeli security; Arafat's assassination, it is thus argued, would be a logical extension of that policy.[18]

The Economy. In January 2000 *Commentary* published twenty-one essays, many written by prominent neo-conservatives, resulting from a symposium on the future direction of American foreign policy. In his contribution, Francis Fukuyama, who is not a neo-conservative, drew attention to a distinctive feature of neo-conservative international thinking, namely the omission

---

[18] Dan Izenberg, "Fanning the Flames," *Jerusalem Post*, September 12, 2003, p. 3.

of any attempt "to come to terms with the global economy or to say anything interesting about it."[19] The charge is accurate. Other than Irving Kristol's 1978 volume *Two Cheers for Capitalism*, the neo-conservative economic lexicon is conventional Chicago-school capitalism with a dash of religious or cultural spice. On international issues, neo-conservatives maintain a generic presumption in favor of free trade, and, ignoring the Chinese example, they believe that market mechanisms lead inexorably to democratic pluralism. Disregarding this and evidence from elsewhere, they, in essence, regard free markets and democracy as one and the same.[20]

These pro-forma references to economic basics aside, neo-conservatives treat economic forces as if they are informed by a self-correcting iron logic. Having asserted a unilateral policy operating within a unipolar world structure, they appear confident that the U.S. economy, flexible and creative, will maintain steady 3 to 4 percent growth over time, despite spiraling deficits, and they ignore Eisenhower's admonition that "there is no defense for any country that busts its own economy."[21]

Moreover, they not only dismiss the increasing interrelatedness of the global economy and the importance of stable, cooperative relations with trading partners, but they appear to disregard China's dramatic expansion that is generating billions of hard currency dollars; resources that can be used to fund the expansion of a high-technology military capability.

The economic world, of course, is not constructed on neo-conservative lines – unipolar, unilateral, and government-dominated, with disputes settled by force and a marginal role for nonstate actors and international agreements. Economic interaction takes place in open, multilateral, and interdependent structures, with American corporate and consumer participation in these structures growing rather than shrinking.[22] U.S. corporations large and small are dependent on the outside world as suppliers, as consumers, as investors, as tourists; as immigrants. The message is obvious. The U.S. business world – multipolar, multilateral, cooperative, interdependent, consumer-driven, and rule-based, with a predominance of nonstate actors – is as different from the neo-conservative world as night from day.

[19] Francis Fukuyama, "American Power – For What?" *Commentary*, January 2000, p. 26.

[20] Amy Chua, *World on Fire: How Exporting Free Market Democracy Breeds Ethnic Hatred and Global Instability* (New York: Doubleday, 2002), pp. 259–88.

[21] Sherman Adams, *Firsthand Report: The Inside Story of the Eisenhower Administration* (New York: Greenwood, 1961), p. 360.

[22] Douglas A. Irwin, *Free Trade under Fire* (Princeton, N.J.: Princeton University Press, 2002), pp. 11–22.

This is not the place to explore this gap in detail. But certain areas strike us as critical and we highlight them in the hope that others will provide their expertise to explore whether foreign policy unilateralism can coexist with economic multipolarity.

1. Can neo-conservative hegemonism be reconciled with market liberalization?
2. Does hegemonism breed protectionism?
3. What is the financial impact of neo-conservative policies?
4. Is the dollar vulnerable to neo-conservative unilateralism?
5. Does unilateralism put U.S. goods and services at risk?

America's business leaders will have useful answers. They live in a world very different from that of the neo-conservatives. The Ford Motor Company accepts the reality of global warming; ExxonMobil speaks of energy "interdependence" and is discreetly supporting good government initiatives in Africa; McDonald's adopts Astérix as its symbol in France. The heads of IBM, Oracle, and Intel have spoken of the need to attract the most innovative minds to America. We suspect their answers would lead in policy directions very different from those advocated by the neo-conservatives.

The Academy. A thoughtful and extensive community of historians, political scientists, anthropologists, economists, and commentators have traditionally provided perspective on government policies – extending from the prosecution of the Vietnam War to the crafting of President Johnson's Great Society to the restructuring of the nation's tax policies under Ronald Reagan to Bill Clinton's "humanitarian interventions." One might ask why thoughtful articles in *Foreign Affairs* and *Foreign Policy* questioning the assumptions that underlie the war in Iraq and our Middle East policy have been so late in coming. Why did we see few, if any, articles questioning the link between Iraq and the terrorist threat to the United States? Where are the anthropologists who know, better than anyone, how difficult it is to reconstruct communities, to rebuild local institutions in accord with local custom; who understand how "knowledgeable ignorance" can inform policy with false assumptions, can fashion the wrong questions, and can draw misleading conclusions? Where are the expert economists who must know that when the president asks Congress for $87 billion for Iraq, the government is borrowing at the rate of $15,000 a second, a million dollars a minute – that it is acting like a person earning $75,000 a year incurring credit card debt as if he or she earns $1 million a year? What effect will government borrowing have not just on interest rates but on the recovery? What effect will this have on our ability to address today's pressing social problems and what impact will it have on our grandchildren, whose debt burden will curtail the infrastructure development and social programs essential to their lives?

In all of this, we rely on the academy for perspective, and until the fall of 2003, there was precious little provided by the major academic journals.[23] Social scientists have been remiss in not demanding that the administration link means to ends – that is, to rational objectives – in the effort to build new Afghani and Iraqi societies. Moreover, military historians and those who have made a study of empire have been strangely silent. An informed debate that places tension in the policy discussion is essential for rational policy.[24]

The electoral process now joined must judge the presidential candidates in some significant part on how they approach this challenge. The debate must consider the outcome of previous attempts by outside powers to remake regions cradle to grave, such as the one under way in the Middle East. If the neo-conservative effort to wrap its Middle East policy in the horrors of 9/11, or the intractable nature of the Israeli-Palestinian conflict, or if the neo-conservative influence on significant parts of the academy have muted the exchange of ideas that has, historically, surrounded major government initiatives, we can only hope this unsettling silence will be short-lived.

The Media. For months the strange silence in the academy was reflected in an equally inert media; fortunately, however, this was not universal. Certainly, some, such as Tim Russert, host of *Meet the Press*, James Wolcott writing in *Vanity Fair*, ABC's Terry Moran, and NBC's David Gregory, challenged administration assertions, posing hard questions on the unproved assertions about Iraq that became more troubling with each passing day. But significant parts of the media – the Washington press corps in particular – seemed frozen in the White House headlights. A case in point is the press conference held at the White House on March 3, 2003, in which the president sought to prepare the country for the war against Iraq. As Wolcott describes it in *Vanity Fair*:

It was a solemn, hollow piece of absurdist theater. Members of the press were marched into the room two by two, like schoolchildren on a trip to the planetarium. Departing from precedent, the President refused to entertain a random volley of questions; instead, he chose reporters from a prepared list, the resulting colloquy so stilted that he couldn't resist blurting out at one embarrassing juncture that the entire evening was

23 Chester A. Crocker, "Engaging Failing States," *Foreign Affairs*, September/October 2003, pp. 32–44.
24 John Gaddis, *Surprise, Security and the American Experience* (Cambridge, Mass.: Harvard University Press, 2004), pp. 107–13.

scripted. . . . Not only were reporters going out of their way to make sure their soft-ball questions were preapproved, but they even went so far as to act on Bush's behalf, raising their hands and jockeying in their seats so as to better give the impression of a spontaneous news conference.[25]

In many of the subsequent stories, exclusively positive images – "calm," "stalwart," and "somber" – were conveyed. The rationale for the war was largely unquestioned.

Journalists who had gained over time a reputation for objective analysis were drawn inexorably to the prevailing frontier atmosphere and bought, whole, the White House recrafted notion of "Wanted Dead or Alive" rough justice for Osama bin Laden and Saddam. Well-educated and cultured cor-respondents went overboard with their images, writing of an America as a "white knight on horseback casting a long, lean shadow down the dusty trail to Baghdad."[26] Others, such as NBC's Andrea Mitchell, openly admired the discipline of the press operation's ability to "stay on message." One CNN commentator admits that the network was "intimidated by the administra-tion."[27] And still others touted the disparaging characterization of those in the administration who expressed doubts as "hand-wringers." In his book *War Is a Force That Gives Us Meaning*, correspondent Chris Hedges of the *New York Times* chronicles the erotic fascination with death to which journalists are susceptible.[28] This may have been what happened on this occasion. Those who adhered to the Marlboro Man, the cool-man-in-a-crisis leitmotif, re-tained access to the White House's version of breaking news, which pleased their editors and apparently most of their readers. That was not the case with critics, who were summarily cut out of the loop. Helen Thomas, dean of the White House Press Corps and a columnist for the Hearst newspapers, provides a case in point. Subsequent to a series of awkward questions rais-ing doubt about the proof of Iraq's weapons of mass destruction, she was removed from her traditional front-row seat in the press room and left un-recognized in later press conferences. Lesser personages raising their hands to ask questions were simply overlooked.

Whether because they were spun into a trance, were fearful of being ig-nored, or suffered an excess of patriotic zeal, the press failed to take a hard, dispassionate look at the administration's rationale for the war. Of equal importance, however, was its unwillingness to confront the fervor of fellow traveling neo-conservative journalists who functioned as enforcers among

[25] James Woolcot, "Round Up the Cattle," *Vanity Fair*, June 2003, pp. 86–98.

[26] Ibid., p. 88.

[27] Paul Krugman, "Lessons in Civility," *New York Times*, October 10, 2003, p. A22.

[28] Chris Hedges, *War Is a Force That Gives Us Meaning* (New York: Public Affairs, 2002), pp. 157–85.

the chattering classes. Using ridicule and ostracism to attack dissenters, neo-conservative strongholds such as the *Weekly Standard*, the *New York Post*, the Fox Network, and the *Wall Street Journal* editorial page effectively stilled the debate. Those questioning the assumptions of the neo-conservative rationale for war faced personal attacks on their integrity laced with allegations of disloyalty.

Not until the presidential primary process began in earnest (when the public's skepticism and anger became a vital political commodity) and the situation deteriorated in Iraq did the White House lose its grip on the elite media and balance seep back into the process. This, of course, casts little virtue on the press as an institution, where a tradition of relative objectivity was preempted by the pressure to retain "inside" sources, a critical asset in covering breaking news. But the media's dispiriting performance testifies to the extent of the neo-conservative reach in the opinion-forming sectors of American society – at least until it was overtaken by the political process.

The Intelligence Agencies

There is a story, perhaps apocryphal, that is related to all incoming recruits into Britain's Secret Intelligence Service. The prime minister of the day once asked the service's chief how he saw his main function. The answer is reported to have been: "To bring you bad news, Sir." The recruits were instructed that bad news did not mean just reports of unexpected new threats, but the courage to deliver news that went against the political grain. They were told that their job was to produce the "truth as they saw it" and to deliver it without fear or favor. The CIA, with its biblical quotation in its entrance foyer – "And ye shall know the truth and the truth shall set you free" – embodies the same ethos.

As the situation in Iraq soured, the Washington investigative machine in characteristic fashion went after the least powerful potential scapegoat, specifically the intelligence community. However, in carrying out any investigations, it will be important to remember that, for the neo-conservatives, weapons of mass destruction were an important but hardly exclusive element in their reasons for going to war. As we have shown, their agenda ranged much more widely toward remaking the face of the Middle East. Had the intelligence agencies reported more cautiously about Iraq's holding of weapons of mass destruction, the neo-conservatives would not have backed off their determination to go to war with Iraq. The intelligence agencies were thus caught in a vise. The extrapolation of the source material that became necessary to buttress the neo-conservative goals now adopted by the administration placed their truth-seeking ethos under enormous strain. The impact of neo-conservative policy is evident not only in America's global standing but also in the damage done to the policy process itself. The intelligence services in both the United States and Britain suffered a loss of credibility that will, among other things, render their contribution to future policy challenges less authoritative and their findings open to debate. In the United States, the stature of the CIA reached a low when its director, George Tenet, testifying before the Senate was forced to admit that his agency's finding that Saddam had obtained nuclear materials from the African nation Niger was not correct. At the same time it was revealed that visits by Vice President Dick Cheney or members of his office to CIA headquarters to examine raw intelligence – that is, information that had not been corroborated, properly caveated, or fully assessed or was incomplete – left some at CIA with the impression that they were being pressured to remove the conditional conclusions from their assessments to make them more categorical.[29] A secretive unit at the Pentagon – the Office of Special Plans – attached to the office of the Undersecretary for Policy Douglas Feith had the same effect, reinterpreting as it did intelligence material not through a rigorous analytic process but in the light of their own ideological preconceptions. On occasions, Feith's office sent its findings straight to friendly media outlets. As one intelligence officer observed, "the easiest intelligence to produce is when you already know the answer. The truth? That may be more difficult." In combination, these activities compromised the core function of intelligence, namely to act as an independent and objective arbiter of information available to the U.S. government.[30] Much of this centered on the intense neo-conservative desire to prove the existence of weapons of mass destruction in Iraq and their claim, so far unproved, that al-Qaeda was harbored and supported by Saddam's regime.[31]

Not since the Iran Contra hearings, when the CIA and the National Security Council were excoriated for their role in the Nicaragua conflict against the Sandinistas, has the intelligence community, then as now bending to political pressure, faced such pervasive public skepticism about their independence and credibility.

---

[29] Walter Pincus and Dana Priest, "Some Iraq Analysts Felt Pressure from Cheney Visits," *Washington Post*, June 5, 2003, p. A1.
[30] Douglas Jehl, "The Struggle for Iraq: Washington Memo; More Proof of Iraq-Qaeda Link, or Not?," *New York Times*, November 20, 2003, p. 18.
[31] Stephen S. Hayes, "Case Closed," *Weekly Standard*, November 24, 2003.

Similar damage occurred in Britain. There the prime minister's office sought to enhance its position with a skeptical electorate on many of the same issues. Downing Street, attempting to heighten the immediacy and magnitude of the threat, claimed that Saddam possessed weapons of mass destruction and could deploy them within forty-five minutes. Carefully conditioned intelligence findings were rewritten to produce politically palatable conclusions. Finally, in September 2002 a U.K. government dossier, "Iraq's Weapons of Mass Destruction," was agreed upon, much to the embarrassment of the prime minister and the intelligence services. The dossier, along with the suicide of David Kelly, the government's lead scientist on weapons of mass destruction issues, eventually brought an unprecedented court of inquiry in which the prime minister was, effectively, placed on trial. The ministers themselves survived to fight another day, but the credibility of the intelligence services suffered enormous damage.

The crux of the problem in both London and Washington is found in the distinction between what the political authorities wanted their respective intelligence services to say about the Iraqi threat and the availability of hard, rigorously sourced intelligence. As Dr. David Kay, a former chief weapons inspector in Iraq, observed in Senate testimony, "we were all wrong."[32] It was largely because of the presumed objectivity and credibility of the intelligence institutions, and their tradition of discretion, that they found themselves in the political vortex. The tragedy is that they succumbed to the political pressure applied. What awaits, at least in the near term, is a future in which the intelligence services struggle to be viewed as authoritative but instead are seen as simply another interest group in the policy mix.

The National Security Council

The intelligence services are not the only institutions that have failed to fulfill their mandate. Through an unfortunate combination of factors, the National Security Council is among the weakest in memory. If the NSC director has three primary functions – first to represent the president's views in policy deliberations, second to coordinate the administration's direction and message on national security matters, and third to ensure that the president's decisions reflect coherent and coordinated recommendations from all of the relevant departments and agencies – the present incumbent has failed in at least the latter two.

[32] Richard W. Stevenson and Thom Shanker, "Ex-Arms Monitor Urges an Inquiry on Iraqi Threat," *New York Times*, January 29, 2004, p. A1.

Strongly held and competing views are standard components of all aspects of the American policy debate, including national security. As noted earlier, this is a highly complex field and unanimity about the best way forward is likely to be rare – indeed, may even be undesirable as signifying lazy group think. So it is quite right that those with knowledge, convictions, and passion speak up. In parallel, it is essential that a coordinating mechanism – the NSC in the post–World War II American foreign policy system – is sufficiently credible to blend these competing inputs into a rational whole. The inability of the NSC to resolve the policy differences between the Pentagon and the State Department, in particular, has been damaging. Allies abroad and supporters of the administration at home have concluded that there are at least two distinct approaches to the nation's foreign relations, one represented by the Pentagon and the other advanced by the State Department. Neo-conservatives in the upper reaches of the Pentagon have advocated unilateral policies that shun the United Nations and NATO at critical points during the run-up to war in both Afghanistan and Iraq and have advanced politically tone-deaf proposals that mispositioned allied governments in Turkey, Britain, and Spain, among others. The stewardship of foreign policy, traditionally located in the State Department, where professional diplomats parse and craft proposals to address local requirements, has been subordinated to military demands, all too often bringing recriminations from those who have been counted on as allies. Substantial responsibility for this rests with the hard-wired neo-conservative network, which includes NSC Middle East director Elliott Abrams, Lewis "Scooter" Libby, Chief of Staff to the Vice President, and Paul Wolfowitz and Douglas Feith at the Pentagon, which consistently prevailed over State Department representatives behind closed doors. Consensus was elusive. The ideological agenda, driven by the neo-conservatives, left little common ground in the NSC from which both the State and Defense Departments could proceed. The fault, however, lies not with the neo-conservatives. "True believers" have a role in all administrations. The fault lies with the NSC.

When differences have emerged in the past, as with the assessment of Soviet military capabilities, NSC directors have created mechanisms such as the "A-Team, B-Team" process to allow opposing factions to develop their ideas fully in the form of real-time conflict scenarios. This would have been one way of assessing the neo-conservative agenda with reference to broader U.S. security interests as war with Iraq was contemplated. This was not to be, however. Instead of receiving a policy proposal from the NSC that integrated the generally differing perspectives reflected by the State and Defense Departments, in the fearsome days of September 2001, the president was left to choose among options, at times bitterly disputed, to the detriment of the administration. What should have been a cooperative relationship, characterized by policy debate and resolution, devolved into a "score-settling" match in which there was a winner and a loser – all of which was made worse by incessant leaking to the press.

A former Republican Cabinet secretary with years of foreign policy expertise said, "The interagency process is completely dysfunctional. In my experience, I have never seen it played out this way."[33] None of this was made easier by the president's reluctance to step in and impose new procedures on the forceful personalities at the top of the State Department and the Pentagon. Nor did the long-standing personal relationship between Donald Rumsfeld and Dick Cheney – partners during the Nixon and Ford administrations – favor a compromise with Colin Powell. Each, a powerful political figure in his own right and a political asset to the administration, dwarfed the NSC director, who was relegated to subordinate status and was unable to place proposed initiatives in a context reflecting nuanced military and diplomatic concerns for presidential decision.

Examples abound. Planning for postwar Iraq is a case in point. Extended squabbling between the State Department, the Defense Department, and the CIA over the type of government Iraq would have and who would lead it were left unresolved. The State Department's plans for a civil administration that would address the everyday concerns of water, electricity, and communications were blocked by Douglas Feith, the Pentagon's Under Secretary for Policy during March and April. Even Ahmed Chalabi, the Pentagon's choice to lead a postwar Iraqi government and the source of so much misleading reporting about weapons of mass destruction and the welcome that the U.S. forces could expect in Iraq, complained that the White House failed to impose a single strategy, leaving a vacuum with no effective Iraqi allies. Meanwhile, the administration spoke with two, sometimes three voices on critical issues, such as North Korea's nuclear threat, Iran's nuclear program, and the prospect of military action against Syria.

There are, of course, precedents in which senior officials have had unequal access to the president and greater or lesser influence on foreign policy – but few instances in which massive confusion surrounded a range of critical policy questions. During the Nixon administration, Secretary of State William Rogers was effectively cut out of the policy process by Henry Kissinger, then the National Security Advisor. In Kissinger's case, however, policy coherence

---

[33] David Ignatius, "A Foreign Policy Out of Focus," *Washington Post*, September 2, 2003, p. A21.

arose from an intellectually rich exchange of views between him and the president. Policy was then imposed on the departments and agencies in weekly meetings at the NSC in which Assistant Secretaries of State, Defense, and Treasury and senior CIA officials were told what the president's priorities were and instructed in how they should be implemented. The distinction is that during the Nixon administration the NSC ensured that the president had the benefit of differing departmental perspectives; departmental differences were not ideologically based and were resolved by the National Security Advisor and his deputies. Most important, with the exception of policy spin provided to the press by the NSC, the debate stopped there and was not carried forward, as it has been now, by a network of agenda-driven activists.

Allies and Friends

The self-evident proposition that the United States cannot allow the nation's security to be subject to external veto has been allowed to cloud discussion of relations with allies and friends. It has inflicted a binary quality on the discussion by making it seem as if the only alternatives are unilateral American action – perhaps with token partners who can be coerced into support of the American objective – or subservience to Fiji or, worse, France. This is nonsense, the main effect of which is to turn allies and friends into either docile yes-men or tiresome critics. This is neither dignified for the allies, whose publics see them as U.S. adjuncts rather than real partners, nor useful to the United States. Countries as various as the United Kingdom, Spain, Turkey, Korea, and Australia have run afoul of their citizens in this regard. The president of Bolivia was forced into exile partly because he was seen as doing the U.S.'s bidding on coca eradication without obtaining the reciprocal benefit in economic aid.

The other side of this approach – the adversarial – deprives the United States of valuable inputs. France, for example, has an invaluable range of experience in the Maghreb countries of northern Africa. Yet the deterioration in relations that has been allowed to arise (through the fault of both sides) between the United States and France deprives the former of this asset. At the height of the Iraq war, the United States created a bizarre distinction between "Old" and "New" Europe. All this did was to complicate relations between, for example, Germany and Poland – when the reality is that it is essential that Poland attracts German investment if it is successfully to integrate itself into the European Union. After all, the United States has no wish to bail out the Polish Central Bank should its fragile currency flounder.

A corollary distortion is that countries have been allowed to become friends simply because they have aligned themselves with one aspect or other of U.S. policy. The new independent states of Central Asia come to mind. In exchange for overflight rights or basing privileges, the United States turns a blind eye to precisely those abuses that the neo-conservatives hurl against their chosen enemies. Similar risks present themselves in Southeast Asia where, in response to counterterror-related assistance from Indonesia, the United States is considering deepening or reinvigorating relations with the military. Given the track record of the military there (even allowing that it has improved), the risks to democracy are palpable.

PART II: LOOKING AHEAD

As noted earlier, there have been previous occasions on which the neo-conservatives have been written off – only for them to bounce back in rein-vigorated form. Nonetheless, so long as the normal checks and balances of the American political process apply, we anticipate that they represent a temporary detour in America's global relations, not a permanent realignment. The damage that has accrued to date is considerable, but the nation, as before, will recover. What is to be expected when American foreign policy regains its balance and direction? The ideas that follow may strike some as rather cautious. In an interview with *Vanity Fair*, Paul Wolfowitz said that he looked down on foreign policy pragmatism that was based on "doing business and being sensible."[34] We beg to disagree. America's foreign relations now have a history approaching 250 years. During that time, most single issue "paradigms" have been tried, and few, if any, have provided the promised illumination. Some of America's least successful interactions with the outside world took place when simplistic, ideological mindsets held sway. The world is simply too complex. The neo-conservative paradigm of "unipolarity" has already had its fateful shortcomings exposed.

Our contention is that American policy has been most successful when it achieved a conjunction of two elements: First, when American moral authority has been deployed in support of identified national interests; second, when the United States has acted in concert with its major allies. These are the two elements on which we draw to establish a framework to address the

---

[34] Paul D. Wolfowitz, from the full transcript of an interview with Sam Tanenhaus, "Bush's Brain Trust," *Vanity Fair*, July 2003.

three major external challenges facing the United States:

- Restoring balance to the conduct of America's international relations whereby national priorities and policy instruments are properly integrated
- Reviving international comity by appreciating the practical limitations of unipolarity
- Avoiding a "clash of the civilizations" that could consume our world in ever more dangerous conflict for generations to come. This will require an openness to nonstate factors such as history, culture, and religion, especially in the Middle East.

There is nothing particularly extraordinary here. Many of our suggestions are already at work in areas where the neo-conservative agenda does not extend. It goes without saying, however, that a return to tried and true ways will not be possible, either in the overall environment in which the United States conducts its foreign relations or in the regional detail, so long as the neo-conservative influence endures. We set out our views on what might be possible if this influence is curtailed.

Balance

Following the defeat of Napoleon in 1815, the Concert of Europe, inspired by Metternich and guided by British Foreign Secretary Castlereagh and French Foreign Minister Talleyrand, devised an intricate system that guided European relations for the century that followed until World War I. With the exception of the Crimean War and other more minor conflicts, peace was generally maintained among the great powers. In essence, the system gave all the great powers a stake in its maintenance. In her remarkable book *The Guns of August*, Barbara Tuchman aptly demonstrates that, until ego, miscalculation, and finally poor communication resulted in World War I, the balance of power remained intact.[35]

With the rise of Nazi Germany in the 1930s and the failure of British Foreign Secretary Neville Chamberlain's efforts to mobilize a balancing force, the notion of "appeasement" entered the modern diplomatic discourse. The specter of "appeasement" – in essence a collapse of principle resulting from the failure to establish and sustain a balance of power – has haunted diplomacy ever since. The neo-conservatives, believing U.S. military power largely obviates the need for balance-of-power diplomacy, have exploited the political symbolism of appeasement to present a Manichean world in which

---

[35] Barbara W. Tuchman, *The Guns of August* (New York: Ballantine, 1994).

selected dictators must be confronted. In this they set aside the important lessons of the Cold War in which containment – the antithesis of appeasement – assembled, in effect, a new balance of power to confront the Soviet Union with great success.

With their ideological antipathy to balance-of-power politics, the neo-conservatives, as we have seen, learned the wrong lesson from Ronald Reagan, fallaciously convincing themselves that he also eschewed balance-of-power politics. In fact, he was able to exploit the Soviet Union's difficulties with China (a legacy from Nixon's rapprochement with China) to great American advantage. On a smaller but nonetheless critical scale, President G. H. W. Bush was able to balance West Germany against France and the United Kingdom to bring about the reunification of Germany. Seduced by the power of U.S. precision weapons (Wolfowitz has spoken enthusiastically about how the Tomahawk cruise missile transformed his thinking), the neo-conservatives have tried to make "balance of power" yesteryear's phrase. It is not. It is a dynamic concept that produces results. It is a principle that American policy might embrace again after the neo-conservatives depart.

We see the notion of balance in two contexts: first, balancing U.S. interests in specific regions and, second, managing the inevitable rise of China, Europe, and India as powerful economic blocks and, at least in China's case, as military powers. What would be involved? Once again, the answer is not breathtaking. Many of the pieces are already in place. For example, the United States balances India and Pakistan, China and Taiwan, the E.U. and NATO, and Chile and Brazil. It surrounds North Korea with Russia, China, Japan, and South Korea. The one exception is the Islamic world, where the United States has lost its instinct for constructing an equilibrium. As a result, the United States risks empowering a tiny minority of Islamic extremists and fundamentalists and risks being feared and reviled by 1.3 billion Muslims spread throughout the globe – several million of whom reside in the United States. This is a highly complex dysfunctionality, given that it is with both state and nonstate actors. Restoring balance to this policy arena will take more than a successful advertising campaign.

More broadly, with the rise of China and the possible drift of Britain toward Europe over time, it is perhaps inevitable that, even having resolved the current dysfunctionality in the Middle East referenced above, today's unipolar world will further rebalance. The challenge for Washington is to accept the fact that no nation has or can dominate global affairs indefinitely. This means that, at a time optimal to American interests, Washington will have to manage the transition to multipolar status so that it is peaceful, secure, and productive. This is a matter that American policymakers will likely engage in the half-century ahead. Its successful outcome will be critical to the nation's security, prosperity, and *primus inter pares* status.

We set out some ideas below, none of which can be considered if the neo-conservatives remain in positions of influence but which may be possible once they have departed.

Nonstate Actors

Having proposed that a return to classic balance-of-power principles provides the most prudent format for America's relations with foreign states, we now turn to the other component of international relations, namely nonstate actors. In the United States today, the best known of these is probably al-Qaeda, an example of a nonstate actor that in a morning's work reordered our national priorities and transformed our lives. The events of 9/11 demonstrated the destructive capacity of nonstate actors. Top policy makers understand this well. Referring to the asymmetrical power in the hands of committed adversaries, Donald Rumsfeld has written that "terrorism is relatively low-cost and deniable and can yield substantial results at low risk and often without penalty. Terrorism can be a great equalizer – a force multiplier.[36] This is right on the mark – as far as it goes.

In fact, however, the range of nonstate actors is vast. It includes religious, ethnic, philanthropic, social, media, professional, commercial, and academic organizations. Nongovernmental organizations, which lie at the interface of the public and private sectors, are important nonstate actors. Trade unions and political parties provide other examples. Taken together, these form an institutional framework often called "civil society." An essential part of this is a realm well known to America's economists, entrepreneurs, and corporate executives, namely a highly interdependent network, animated by consumers around the world making purchase decisions.

What has received inadequate emphasis in recent U.S. policy is recognition that the overwhelming majority of nonstate actors can and do play powerful positive roles. The vast system of affiliations and social organizations that inform the lives of individuals and families tends, naturally, toward minimizing risk and optimizing stability and personal security; in short, evolution rather than revolution. The nonstate actors, mentioned earlier as forming a "civil society," largely facilitate socio-economic investment by individuals,

[36] Donald H. Rumsfeld, "Take the Fight to the Terrorist," *Washington Post*, October 26, 2003, p. B7.

families, colleagues, and friends in stable, predictable relationships that maintain their social and spiritual interests and advance their political and financial security. The neo-conservative policy calculus overlooks this "silent global community" of ordinary people seeking incremental progress, which could function naturally as, perhaps, America's strongest strategic asset.

This is an area where change of emphasis from the neo-conservative focus on states is overdue. The challenge is to determine how best to utilize the natural security/stability – oriented aspirations and the often community-based power of most nonstate actors in support of U.S. objectives. The struggle against terrorism in Colombia, for example, has begun to show slow but discernible progress. Utilizing a range of policy instruments, it has extended beyond the central government in Bogotá to employ local law-enforcement, economic, social, ethnographic, anthropological, and cultural measures that involve both the "civil society" and ordinary people seeking predictable, secure lives.[37] Similarly, if the U.S. engagement in Iraq is to be a long-term success, these are the tools that must be added to the policy mix. In essence, the United States needs to mobilize the "silent, stability-seeking majority" not only in Iraq but also in the wider Islamic community, by giving it a more tangible stake in the ordering of their lives.

On the U.S. side, obtaining these results will require reinvestment in those with local and regional expertise, together with a willingness to respect their advice. Traditionally, these skills have been based among diplomatic and intelligence professionals. But they are never enough – the classic case is the Iranian revolution where proximity to the Shah and Savak, his intelligence service, obscured attention from the rage on the streets.[38] Today, a whole range of nonofficial entities, including charitable and religious entities, are often able to get closer to local sentiments than those who operate from official premises. Their advice will never call the tune, but if there is any truth in the fact that nonstate actors may assume a much increased importance in future, American leaders will need a much wider circle of advisers than the politicized ideologues with whom the neo-conservatives would prefer to populate the State Department and CIA.[39]

---

[37] Hernando de Soto, *The Other Path: The Economic Answer to Terrorism* (New York: Basic Books, 2002).

[38] William Shawcross, *The Shah's Last Ride* (New York: Touchstone, 1989). In a classified study, the British Foreign Office also concluded that its analysis had been overreliant on conversations with the Shah and made changes in the way British embassies develop multisource reporting capabilities.

[39] David Frum and Richard Perle, *An End to Evil: How to Win the War on Terror* (New York: Random House, 2003), pp. 223–34.

International Comity

Having extracted the wrong lessons from their "unipolar world," neo-conservatives have created a crisis in bilateral relations among the Western allies and in the U.N. such that there is now an unprecedented need for the United States to restore an atmosphere of cooperation in global affairs.

Their assumption that the United States dominates a unipolar world system is obviously correct in the military sphere, but elsewhere the assessment is more shaded. The capacity of American adversaries to conduct asymmetrical warfare in the form of terrorist attacks indicates that U.S. military power cannot provide complete security from attack, in all circumstances, to the American people. Claims to hyperpower status in a unipolar world are misleading and worse; they convey the sense that security can be ensured by America's technical military might alone. But that is not the case.

Assuming that the neo-conservative–inspired unilateralism begins to recede under the weight of its own contradictions, the door will once again open to what might be described as foreign policy "best practice," that is, a revitalization of international cooperation that is a precondition of returning the Middle East to a functioning whole, containing the dangers of nuclear weapons proliferation, understanding and combating the terrorist threat, maintaining U.S. interests in Asia, and promoting continued economic openness. This is only to sketch out the issues of major transnational significance.

The time requirements for senior management and resource demands implicit in addressing these various issues are immense. Remember that both the British and French imperial systems were primarily designed to advance their commercial interests. Both ruled with an iron hand, and though they made efforts to improve literacy, there was little inclination, except at the point of independence, to leave democratic government behind. The missionary impulse – the desire to improve the lot of mankind that resonates so loudly today – arrived as something of an afterthought at the end of the nineteenth century when the imperial sunset was well under way. Thus governing tasks were less complex both because their objectives were simpler and because opinion and its expression through the media were not the factors then that they are now.

With today's changed context and the continuing dysfunctionality in bilateral relations among the Western allies, Washington's broader interests can be served only by restoring comity in global affairs. In this context, Boston University professor Andrew Bacevich makes an important point.[40]

---

[40] Andrew Bacevich, *American Empire: The Realities and Consequences of American Diplomacy* (Cambridge, Mass.: Harvard University Press, 2002).

It is that through the 1990s the United States was guided by a strategy that emphasized "openness." Our commitment to global "openness" played to our greatest strengths. We sought the removal of barriers to trade, capital flows, and ideas. The objective was an international order based on the principle of democratic capitalism with the United States the guarantor of order and the enforcer of norms. Given the power of American ingenuity, advanced information processing, communications capability, entertainment, finance, military capacity, and the attraction of democracy, a strategy that effectively employed these attributes would greatly benefit the United States and many other countries. Moreover, from the perspective of national interest, it would sustain American preeminence. This is not simply an academic theory. The rules of international relations are written in such a way – for example, the prominence given to intellectual property protection and market access in the World Trade Organization – that the United States benefits disproportionately from a rules-based global system.

A precondition to global acceptance of these American "exports," however, is the belief in Europe, Latin America, Asia, and Russia that U.S. leadership is accompanied by a respect for international law and that the United States is willing to proceed in concert with the international community, even as it insists on *primus inter pares* status. If the objective is to reacquire workable relations with the international community, there must be the perception that American power is balanced in some manner and that it is deployed in support of internationally accepted norms. The most obvious way is through a reconstituted relationship with the world's international organizations.

We deliberately avoid referring directly to the United Nations. Clearly, in its present form, the U.N. has failed in its primary mission, namely to provide a forum for rational exchange and a mechanism to avert military confrontation. Today the U.N. is as much part of the problem as the solution. But the neo-conservative–advocated corollary, namely that the United States should act outside the framework of the international community, has also been shown to have crucial shortcomings. Doing so robs the United States of legitimacy in the context of global opinion and significantly adds to the human and material costs borne by the United States. The time may have come therefore to step away from the typical neo-conservative binary approach – unilateralism versus multilateralism – and to refashion selected international structures in a manner not unlike that at the end of World War II.

In a post neo-conservative Washington, there would be no shortage of proposals to make the international organizations more relevant. Some, such as former Canadian Ambassador to Washington Alan Gottlieb, believe that the notion of national sovereignty is obsolete. He would eliminate national boundaries, permit only democracies to be members of a new organization that would act against tyrannies with trade and other sanctions. Others advocate a return to "coalitions of the willing" to resolve threats to international security; others would utilize the U.N.'s capacity to assist on health, agricultural, educational, and development problems but see no role for power projection; still others would simply allow it to fade into irrelevance. None of these options fully serves American or indeed international interests.

The challenge for American diplomats is to achieve conditions that permit the United States to utilize a reconstituted successor to the U.N. as an effective instrument of U.S. foreign policy. In such circumstances America would have the advantage of its wealth, moral authority, and power and would enter the discussion of a revitalized and reformed international body with more inherent flexibility and greater stature than others.

Avoiding the Clash of Civilizations

The United States now finds itself in a virtual one-on-one confrontation with Islamic radicalism. Partly as a result of a broken equilibrium in its Middle East policy, the United States has allowed Islamic radicalism to emerge as, for all intents and purposes, the prevailing political voice of the Muslim world. Clearly, U.S. policy is not the only or even the main reason for this state of affairs – the cultural context laid out in the *Arab Human Development Report 2003* makes for grim reading[41] – but it is the variable that is most directly under U.S. control. Given that the threat from radical Islamic groups is tangible and retains the potential to inflict mass death and catastrophic disruption of the economy, this zero-sum confrontation makes no sense. Containing the threat through massed fixed forces in the manner of the Cold War format is not possible. The adversary has no fixed address. Concepts such as "mutual assured destruction" do not apply. And as we have seen too often, when ten terrorist leaders are removed, a hundred are there to replace them. And with a generation of youth whose honor and status is infused with the imagery of martyrdom, the supply of foot soldiers is endless. The sums of money needed are tiny in relation to the damage that can be inflicted.

We have seen in Iraq the emergence of a disturbing and familiar pattern of devastating suicide bombings and attacks, delivered by Iraqis and "foreign jihadists" alike, not dissimilar in form to the tactics now commonplace on the West Bank. Just as overwhelming Israeli power has failed to contain that asymmetrical threat – a fact that senior Israeli commanders have

---

[41] U.N. Development Program, *Arab Human Development Report 2003*.

acknowledged in public – so overwhelming U.S. military power alone does not now, nor will it in the foreseeable future, resolve the problem in Iraq.

Second, U.S. unilateralism, while devastating in the conflict phase of confrontation, fails to offer a context in which the objectives sought – Middle East regional stability and an end to terrorism – can be reached. For its attack on the Taliban regime and al-Qaeda the administration garnered substantial international support and legitimacy, with the result that the peacekeeping and reconstruction efforts are widely shared – albeit still crucially underresourced. Iraq proves the opposite point, with American requests for additional participation receiving lukewarm support. Therefore, the prospects of success will remain limited until the motivations for continuing attacks on American interests are addressed – which cannot occur without reformatting U.S. regional policy. With that review and policy changes that effectively address the root causes of Islamic radicalism, we believe that the United States can gain international support for investment in Middle Eastern regional infrastructure and commerce and a willingness to take security measures that protect the embryonic pluralism, of which we have seen early signs. Only with the sustained commitment of the international community is there hope of nurturing individual enterprises, political factions, parties, and eventual market-democratic forms of government.

Middle East Alternatives

From mid-2003 onward, two initiatives involving prominent Israeli and Palestinian former officials – the Geneva Accord and the People's Voice Initiative – developed practical proposals for peace that briefly illuminated several commonsense approaches to long-standing differences. They started to solicit public support for their proposals. Predictably, neo-conservative analysts and commentators dismissed the process and the proposals, effectively inhibiting the debate in Washington. Instead, we are left with the all-too-familiar zero-sum game of terrorism versus reprisal – perhaps indefinitely. This state of affairs ensures that the region remains intensely unstable, greatly damaging American interests on a global basis.

But other futures are possible. For example, British historian Richard Crockatt asks how to identify common ground between the West and Islam where there are deep differences in culture and religion. This begs the question of how international organizations can accommodate and modify, even neutralize, clashing religious and cultural perspectives.

Must cultural differences be reflected in national policy to the degree that international organizations are rendered dysfunctional? A first step is to examine the kinds of interactions – the categories of interaction – that have given rise to the pervasive distrust, often bordering on hatred, now characterizing relations between Islamic culture and Western nations. Two models can be used to understand Islamic-U.S. relations: a cooperation model and a confrontation model. Both models address the underlying challenge that, as seen by Crockatt, Islam represents a way of life and a religion in which various entities aspire to nationhood, whereas the United States is a modern, diverse nation where church and state are separate. It is hard to imagine how these perspectives could be more different. Yet the stakes are so great that a beginning dialogue must be attempted. What would the grounds be for such a discussion?

The first assumption is that geo-political boundaries today do not mark stable borders in many regions; borders are not hermetically sealed and most nations – with rare exceptions, such as Cold War Albania and modern North Korea – maintain a complex network of relations with each other. Populations and cultures span borders in nearly all countries, and thus multiculturalism should be regarded both as a permanent characteristic of the international environment and as an asset. Second, multiculturalism is increasingly accepted in the United States and in Europe and is a fact in most Islamic countries as well. Third, there is no alternative but to accept different religious beliefs. Neither the non-Islamic world nor the Islamic world should conclude that Islam is "grossly incompatible with other religions." Fourth, pluralism leading to democratic forms of government is possible in Islamic countries, and these conditions lead to modernity.

Large Islamic populations live cooperatively in democratic nations now; some 77 percent of Muslims living in the United States were born in other countries. Moreover, by 2010 the Muslim population will be larger than the Jewish population in the United States. When we ask how Muslims have interacted with mainstream American culture inside the United States, we must acknowledge that there have been few serious confrontations, despite the widely held belief among Muslims that the war on terror is a war on Muslims and despite the fact that the 9/11 attack generated broad condemnation of Muslims by many Americans. What can we conclude from this? First, that America's acceptance of cultural diversity is both broad and deep, that Americans can live comfortably with those professing distinct cultures and religions. Second, that there is nothing in Islam that makes it inherently impossible for Muslims to live peacefully with non-Muslims – though the distinction between majority and minority status, hence power, is quite obviously very important in terms of tolerance and flexibility. Culture, therefore is not the functional issue; it is rather the way in which culture and its assumptions are represented in the political discourse that brings conflict. In his book *After Jihad: America and the Struggle for Islamic Democracy*, New York University professor Noah Feldman sets out this case with considerable learning.[42]

The alternative to this model is the "confrontation model," which has many of the characteristics of the "clash of civilizations." It posits that a clash between the West and Islam is inevitable, as differences are reflected in all aspects of life, from ideology to culture. Islam, in this model, is thought inflexible, intolerant, and resentful of Western advances. Islam is resistant to globalization and instead reflects anger and resentment at the great disparity in wealth when compared with the West. Embattled and isolated, enraged Islamic calls to avenge loss of life have precluded productive contact with Western governments and, instead, employed terrorism to great asymmetrical effect against Western "openness," exacerbating matters further. This is the model presented in effect by Princeton professor Bernard Lewis, the neo-conservative's favorite Arabist, albeit more elegantly and with less bile than some of those, such as Daniel Pipes, who tread in his footprints.

Given this reality, the "confrontation model" holds that the United States, facing a fearsome enemy, must preserve itself by rejecting multiculturalism to preserve the values and ideals that comprise its identity and that have brought progress, freedoms, and the market-democratic system. This perspective asserts that cultural homogeneity is preferable and that it is a precondition to consensus and coherence. It further posits that the vast cultural differences offer no grounds for the resolution of political and economic differences. As we have seen in our analysis of early neo-conservatism, it is instinctively suspicious of multiculturalism.

What are the possibilities for an improvement in U.S.-Islamic relations? Some would conclude the problems are intractable, that the economic, political, and security issues are so great and prospect of solutions so remote that there is no solution. But we would join others in the view that this is largely because the political discourse advanced by governments to their citizens in each sphere presents each party as a culture and nation embattled. This results in a battle of cultures and a political conflict that promotes cultural conflict, that is, a politically inspired confrontation of cultures.

The distinction is important because it may point the way to an alternative strategy that seeks to lower political tensions and build on those limited

---

[42] Noah Feldman, *After Jihad: America and the Struggle for Islamic Democracy* (New York: Farrar, Straus and Giroux, 2003), pp. 38–50.

points where there may be common ground. In Northern Ireland, part of the impetus for religious reconciliation came from the bottom up, from nonstate actors such as women's groups. If we could move away from the assumptions embraced by the neo-conservative agenda, which are antithetical to this prospect, something of this sort might be possible in the Middle East. Indeed, many of the building blocks in terms of citizen initiatives searching for alternative peace options are already in place. The Geneva Accord and People's Voice Initiative have added fresh urgency to the process.[43] We would argue that if it is in the U.S. national interest to invest in nation building, as the neo-conservatives have advocated in Iraq, then it is in the U.S. national interest to address the problem that is perceived to lie at the center of Middle Eastern radicalism: the Israeli-Palestinian dispute.

Proceeding to create a Palestinian nation on the West Bank, a goal accepted in principle by all parties, is the common ground sought in this complex matter. It is a specific endeavor that is central to the U.S. national interest and central to Israeli security, because a viable state on the West Bank is an essential precondition to the restoration of stability in the region. A full commitment to an internationally led initiative – perhaps through the creation of a Special Commission designed for the purpose – with Western, including substantial U.S., financial support would address Palestinian objectives, deny the pivotal rallying point for Muslim radicalism the world over, and deliver to Israel the security and prosperity to which it is entitled.

Clearly, there are no easy solutions to this complex and longstanding issue. Diplomats as a class are neither foolish nor malevolent. If an answer were available, it would have been found. Despite vast efforts by governments and nongovernmental organizations and despite an immense body of work on the subject, substantial questions remain as to whether the United States or others adequately understands the technology of nation building. If the record is any indication, the prospect of success is far from certain – and close to zero unless the nation concerned embraces the rebuilding concept.[44] Efforts such as the Wye River Accords have allocated massive financial provisions in the event of a settlement, but even these have not been enough. The structure of the Middle East challenge, however, leaves no other option if there is to be relief from the inexorable spread of radical Islam and the terrorism it has sponsored. Moreover, the West Bank may be an exception to the caution against nation building in that the creation of a nation

[43] Jackson Diehl, "A Better Road Map," *Washington Post*, October 27, 2003, p. A19.
[44] John W. Downer, *Embracing Defeat: Japan in the Wake of World War II* (New York: W. W. Norton, 1999), pp. 29–30.

there has been a central part of the political discourse and the rallying cry for both secular Arab and Palestinian nationalists and for Muslim radicals since 1948.

Beyond these caveats we would add that the sponsor of a project of this kind cannot be the United States nor, given the recent disappointing history in the region, the West in general. As mentioned above, an international commission might be considered with the specific purpose of integrating and deploying the various skills needed to achieve the objective. Those skills extend well beyond the circle of those who have been tasked in the past. While the effort requires organization and discipline, former generals and terrorism experts, while essential for implementation and security, do not have the scope of experience to direct this effort. Senior decision makers should, instead, include those able to conceptualize the structure and function of the different aspects of the community to be created both in terms of local culture, tradition, and religion and in terms of what will encourage the development of a political environment characterized by pluralism. This means that it is essential to see the evolving state in terms of how local cultural predisposition and social practice might support, over time, movement toward representative government. The skills required are those evinced by social anthropologists, jurists, political scientists, sociologists, and medical, educational, urban planning, and aid experts, as well as those able to create a modern banking system and conflict resolution mechanisms – all of which can take many forms. But the essence is to empower those who appreciate how to integrate local custom, traditions, and prejudice into a political framework that reflects at least some degree of choice. The objective would be to initiate a process that, at a minimum, generates the preconditions for democratic and market development.

Nuclear Proliferation

Nuclear proliferation is both the most urgent and most vexing challenge of our time. The danger is what the 2002 National Security Document calls the "crossroads of radicalism and technology." Virtually all agree on the cataclysmic nature of the problem, yet there is no clear solution or even a provisional agreement on how to proceed. The fear that a new, powerful, easily concealed agent of destruction could tip the balance of power between an aggrieved citizenry and the state is not new. In his 1887 appeal against conviction for an anarchist bomb throwing, Albert Parsons quoted a report of November 1884 by General Philip Sheridan, then commander of the U.S. Army, in which he commented about the emerging weapon of dynamite, saying that "it should be remembered destructive explosives are easily made, and that banks, United States sub-treasuries, public buildings, and large mercantile houses can be readily demolished, and the commerce of entire cities destroyed by an infuriated people with means carried with perfect safety to themselves in the pockets of their clothing." Citing this case, the former British and now E.U. diplomat Robert Cooper has pointed out that nuclear and biological weapons are the dynamite of our time: "For the first time since the Middle Ages, individuals or groups will possess destructive power that puts them on equal terms with the state."[45] As a solution, Cooper proposes an updated imperialism in which the postmodern world allows the premodern world (the polite form of Kipling's "lesser breeds without the law") access to its markets in exchange for a commitment to good governance, specifically commitment to democratic institutions, open markets, and vigorous anticorruption mechanisms. He sees this as a form of voluntary regime change.[46]

The notion that there should be some form of trade-off between renunciation of nuclear and biological weapons and access to first-world markets and other privileges of the "civilized world" has some attractions – even if the imperialist packaging needs to be rethought and care has to be taken lest this concept offers a form of financial reward for bad behavior, precisely the perverse incentives that North Korea and others are exploiting.

However, this idea does little to address the fact that these weapons are being sought in an extensive "black market" by a variety of nonstate actors. Nor does it recognize that the search for these weapons is based on motivations much more complex than that the would-be acquirers are simply evildoers bent on mass murder or simply will be satisfied with an entrance ticket to a privileged club. The motivations are likely to have some or all of the classic components of belligerent action identified by Thucydides some 2,500 years ago, specifically "honor, fear and profit,"[47] which raises a difficulty of the current mix of international institutions. Today, they are divided between those that deal with security, primarily the U.N. Security Council and its subsidiary bodies, such as the International Atomic Energy Agency, and those that deal with development, such as the IMF and World Bank. Princeton professor Harold James has proposed closing this gap through a new institution in which security, development, and economic issues can

---

[45] Roger Cooper, "Civilize or Die," *The Guardian*, October 23, 2003.

[46] Robert Cooper, *The Breaking of Nations: Order and Chaos in the Twenty-first Century* (London: Atlantic, 2003), pp. 65–75.

[47] Donald Kagan, *On the Origins of War and the Preservation of Peace* (New York: Doubleday, 1995), p. 8.

be discussed simultaneously, thus reducing the potential for playing off one against the other.[48] This is worth considering.

Final Words

We are very conscious that none of this will cause our readers to rush into the streets crying "Eureka!" To a great extent, that is our point. The golden mean of American foreign policy does not need to be discovered. It is already there. "We are committed to multilateral institutions because global threats require a global response." These are President Bush's words to the Australian parliament on October 22, 2003. No doubt he had in mind the inching forward on North Korea and Iran brought about by multilateral cooperation. He repeated the sentiments at Whitehall Palace in London on November 19, 2003. "Like 11 Presidents before me, I believe in the international institutions and alliances that America helped to form and helps to lead."

But these words also reflect that the negatives induced by the neo-conservatives are coming home to roost: financial and military resources stretched to the breaking point, moral authority dissipated, allies alienated, adversaries energized and radicalized, the absurd situation that in late 2003 Europeans believed that America and North Korea were equal threats to peace, the nation polarized. Add all this together and we can see clearly that the neo-conservative calculus is irredeemably flawed. Far from making itself safer, America's use of force has, ironically, demonstrated the limits of its force. America's strategic position is weaker. In short, politics on the ground, from London to Beijing, present a controlling reality that has blunted, if not broken, the neo-conservative sword.

The neo-conservatives have had their moment. Sadly, their doctrine of unipolarity has done great damage. They leave a legacy in Middle East policy and the wider struggle against terrorism that, unchecked, could aggravate this damage many times over, not just on foreign policy but on how Americans relate one to another. Their pessimistic notion that American ideals need to be delivered on the back of a cruise missile rather than be allowed to speak for themselves as universalist aspirations has severely distorted America's relations with the rest of the world. Happily, this detour is now coming to an end. Work will be needed to put the cruise missiles back in their packing cases for use only in cases where they can add value

---

[48] Harold James, "The World Needs to Stamp Out Nuclear Blackmail," *Financial Times*, October 21, 2003.

to America's broad interests. Work will also be needed to revive America's moral authority, but it will be inspiring, worthwhile work of the sort that Americans have shown themselves capable for generations. And there will be plenty of help from America's friends, who know that the world works best when they and America are in partnership.

Bibliography

DISSERTATIONS, DOCUMENTS, AND PRESIDENTIAL SPEECHES

"A Clean Break: A New Strategy for Securing the Realm." Institute for Advanced Strategic and Political Studies, June 1996.

"The Dangers of Unilateralism." Congressional Record, May 16, 2001, pp. E813–E814. United States Library of Congress.

Department of Defense News Briefing, September 13, 2001. http://www.defenselink.mil/transcripts/2001/t09132001_t0913dsd.html.

Garcia Estrada, Sol. "Linguistic Foundations of US Foreign Policy after 9/11." Ph.D. dissertation, Centre of International Studies, Cambridge University, July 2003.

Hutton, Lord Brian. "Investigation into the Circumstances Surrounding the Death of Dr. David Kelly." London: Department of Constitutional Affairs, January 28, 2004.

Interview with the President. Weekly Compilation of Presidential Documents. United States Government Printing Office. Vol. 29, no.12, March 29, 1993.

JINSA Report no. 321. Jewish Institute for National Security Affairs, March 26, 2003.

"Prepared Testimony of Paul D. Wolfowitz." House International Relations Committee. United States Congress, February 25, 1998. United States Library of Congress.

"Prepared Testimony of Paul D. Wolfowitz." House National Security Committee. United States Congress, September 16, 1998. United States Library of Congress.

The President's News Conference. Weekly Compilation of Presidential Documents. United States Government Printing Office. Vol. 29, no.19, May 14, 1993.

Project for the New American Century. "Rebuilding America's Defenses: Strategy, Forces and Resources for a New Century." Washington, D.C., September 2000.

Project for the New American Century. "Statement of Principles." Washington, D.C., June 3, 1997.

Remarks by the President to a Special Session of the German Bundestag, May 23, 2002. http://www.whitehouse.gov/news/releases/2002/05/20020523-2.html.

Remarks by the President on Iraq, September 24, 2002. http://www.whitehouse.gov/news/releases/2002/09/print/20020924-1.html.

Remarks by the President on Iraq, Cincinnati Museum Center, October 7, 2002. http://www.whitehouse.gov/news/releases/2002/10/print/20021007-8.html.

Remarks by the President on Iraq in the Rose Garden, September 26, 2002, http://www.whitehouse.gov/news/releases/2002/09/print/20020926-1.html.

Remarks by the President at Louisville, Kentucky, September 5, 2002. http://www.whitehouse.gov/news/releases/2002/09/print/20020905-1.html.

US Admirals' and Generals' Statement on Palestinian Violence. Jewish Institute for National Security Affairs, November 6, 2000.

US Kosovo Diplomacy. Hearing before the Senate Committee on Foreign Relations. United States Senate. 106th Congress, 1st Session, September 28, 1999. United States Library of Congress.

The War in Kosovo. Hearing before the Senate Committee on Foreign Relations. United States Senate. 106th Congress, 1st Session, March 20, 1999. United States Library of Congress.

BOOKS

Albright, Madeleine. *Madam Secretary: A Memoir.* New York: Miramax 2003.

Allin, Dana H. *Nato's Balkan Interventions.* Oxford: Oxford University Press, 2003.

Alterman, Eric. *What Liberal Media?* New York: Basic Books, 2003.

Ambrose, Stephen E. *Eisenhower: Soldier and President.* New York: Simon and Schuster, 1990.

Anderson, Benedict. *Imagined Communities: Reflections of the Origin and Spread of Nationalism.* London: Verso, 1991.

Ansell, Amy E. *Unraveling the Right: The New Conservatism in American Thought and Politics.* Boulder, Colo.: Westview, 1998.

Bacevich, Andrew. *American Empire: The Realities and Consequences of American Diplomacy.* Cambridge, Mass.: Harvard University Press, 2002.

Barber, Benjamin R. *Fear's Empire: War, Terrorism and Democracy.* New York: Norton, 2003.

———. *Jihad vs. McWorld.* New York: Times Books, 1995.

Bardach, Ann Louise. *Cuba Confidential: Love and Vengeance in Miami and Havana.* New York: Random House, 2002.

Barker, David C. *Rushed to Judgment.* New York: Columbia University Press, 2002.

Beck, Sara, and Malcolm Downing, eds. *The Battle for Iraq: BBC News Correspondents on the War against Saddam and a New World Agenda.* London: BBC, 2003.

Benedict, Ruth. *Patterns of Culture.* Boston: Houghton Mifflin, 1934.

Bennett, William. *Why We Fight: Moral Clarity and the War on Terrorism.* Washington, D.C.: Regnery, 2003.

Berkowitz, Bruce. *The New Face of War: How War Will Be Fought in the 21st Century.* New York: Free Press, 2003.

Bert, Wayne. *The Reluctant Superpower.* New York: Macmillan, 1997.

Boot, Max. *The Savage Wars of Peace: Small Wars and the Rise of American Power.* New York: Basic Books, 2002.

Brandon, Ruth. *The Dollar Princesses.* London: Weidenfeld and Nicolson, 1980.

Brennan, Mary C. *Turning Right in the Sixties: The Conservative Capture of the GOP.* Chapel Hill: University of North Carolina Press, 1995.

Brown, Michael, ed. *The International Dimensions of Internal Conflict.* Cambridge, Mass.: MIT Press, 1996.

Bull, Hedley. *The Anarchical Society: A Study of Order in World Politics.* London: Macmillan, 1977.

Burwell, Frances, and Ivo Daalder. *The United States and Europe in the Global Arena.* London: Macmillan, 1999.

Bush, George, and Brent Scowcroft. *A World Transformed.* New York: Knopf, 1998.

Cameron, Fraser. *US Foreign Policy after the Cold War.* New York: Routledge, 2002.

Campbell, C. S. *From Revolution to Rapprochement: The United States and Great Britain, 1783–1900.* New York: Wiley, 1974.

Campbell, David. *Writing Security: United States Foreign Policy and the Politics of Identity.* Manchester: Manchester University Press, 1996.

Cannon, Lou. *Ronald Reagan: The Role of a Lifetime.* New York: Putnam, 1982.

Charters, David, ed. *The Deadly Sin of Terrorism: Its Effects on Democracy and Civil Liberty in Six Countries.* Westport, Conn.: Greenwood Press, 1994.

Chilton, Paul. *Security Metaphors: Cold War Discourse from Containment to Common House.* New York: Peter Lang, 1996.

Chua, Amy. *World on Fire: How Exporting Free Market Democracy Breeds Ethnic Hatred and Global Instability.* New York: Doubleday, 2002.

Cohen, Eliot A. *Supreme Command: Soldiers, Statesmen and Leadership in Wartime.* New York: Free Press, 2002.

Coogan, Tim Pat. *The IRA.* New York: Palgrave, 2002.

Cooper, Robert. *The Breaking of Nations: Order and Chaos in the Twenty-first Century.* London: Atlantic, 2003.

Crockatt, Richard. *The Fifty Years War: The United States and the Soviet Union in World Politics, 1941–1991.* New York: Routledge, 2000.

Daalder, Ivo. *Getting to Dayton: The Making of America's Bosnia Policy.* Washington, D.C.: Brookings Institution Press, 2000.

Daalder, Ivo, and James M. Lindsay. *America Unbound: The Bush Revolution in Foreign Policy.* Washington, D.C.: Brookings Institution Press, 2003.

Dallek, Robert. *Ronald Reagan: The Politics of Symbolism.* Cambridge, Mass.: Harvard University Press, 1999.

Darman, Richard. *Who's in Control: Polar Politics and the Invisible Center.* New York: Simon and Schuster, 1996.

Davis, Richard, and Diana Owen. *New Media and American Politics.* New York: Oxford University Press, 1998.

DeMuth, Christopher, and William Kristol, eds. *The Neo-Conservative Imagination.* Washington, D.C.: AEI Press, 1995.

Devigne, Robert. *Oakeshott, Strauss and the Response to Postmodernism.* New Haven, Conn.: Yale University Press, 1994.

Diamond, Sara. *Roads to Dominion: Right Wing Movements and Political Power in the US.* New York: Guilford, 1995.

Diner, Dan. *America in the Eyes of the Germans: An Essay on Anti-Americanism.* Trans. Allison Brown. Princeton, N.J.: Markus Wiener, 1996.

Dobbs, Michael. *Saboteurs: The Nazi Raid on America.* New York: Random House, 2004.

Dorman, Joseph. *Arguing the World: The New York Intellectuals in Their Own Words.* New York: Free Press, 2000.

Dorrien, Gary. *The Neoconservative Mind: Politics, Culture and the War of Ideology.* Philadelphia: Temple University Press, 1993.

Downer, John W. *Embracing Defeat: Japan in the Wake of World War II.* New York: W. W. Norton, 1999.

Downie, Leonard, Jr., and Robert G. Kaiser. *The News about the News.* New York: Vintage, 2003.

Drawbaugh, Kevin. *Brands in the Balance: Meeting the Challenges to Commercial Identity.* London: Pearson Education, 2001.

Drury, Shadia. *Leo Strauss and the American Right.* New York: Macmillan, 1997.

D'Souza, Dinesh. *Ronald Reagan: How an Ordinary Man Became an Extraordinary Leader.* New York: Free Press, 1997.

Dumbrell, John. *A Special Relationship: The Anglo-American Relations in the Cold War and After.* Basingstoke: Macmillan, 2001.

Ehrman, John. *The Rise of Neoconservatism: Intellectuals and Foreign Affairs 1945–94.* New Haven: Yale University Press, 1995.

Fairclough, Norman. *Language and Power.* London: Longman, 1989.

Feffer, John, ed. *Power Trip: US Unilateralism and the Global Strategy after September 11.* New York: Seven Stories Press, 2003.

Feldman, Noah. *After Jihad: America and the Struggle for Islamic Democracy.* New York: Farrar, Straus and Giroux, 2003.

Ferguson, Niall. *Empire: The Rise and Demise of British World Order and the Lessons for Global Power.* New York: Basic Books, 2003.

Fitzpatrick, John C. *The Writings of George Washington.* Washington, D.C.: U.S. Government Printing Office, 1934–40.

Foucault, Michel. *Power/Knowledge: Selected Interviews and Other Writings, 1972–1977.* Ed. Colin Gordon. London: Harvester Press, 1980.

Friedberg, Aaron L. *In the Shadow of the Garrison State.* Princeton, N.J.: Princeton University Press, 2000.

Friedman, Thomas. *The Lexus and the Olive Tree.* London: HarperCollins, 1999.

Frum, David. *Dead Right.* Toronto: HarperCollins, 1994.

_____. *The Right Man.* New York: Random House, 2003.

Frum, David, and Richard Perle. *An End to Evil: How to Win the War on Terror.* New York: Random House, 2003.

Gaddis, John Lewis. *Strategies of Containment.* New York: Oxford University Press, 1982.

_____. *Surprise, Security and the American Experience.* Cambridge, Mass.: Harvard University Press, 2004.

Gerson, Mark. *The Neo-Conservative Vision: From the Cold War to Culture Wars.* Lanham, Md.: Madison, 1996.

Glazer, Nathan, and Daniel Patrick Moynihan. *Beyond the Melting Pot: The Negroes, Puerto Ricans, Jews and Irish in New York.* Cambridge, Mass.: MIT Press, 1963.

Goodwin, Doris Kearns. *FDR: No Ordinary Life.* New York: Simon and Schuster, 1994.

Gottfried, Paul. *The Conservative Movement.* New York: Twayne, 1993.

Grossman, Gene M., and Elhanan Helpman. *Special Political Interests.* Cambridge, Mass.: MIT Press, 2001.

Haig, Alexander. *Caveat: Realism, Reagan, and Foreign Policy.* New York: Macmillan, 1984.

Halberstam, David. *War in a Time of Peace: Bush, Clinton and the Generals.* New York: Touchstone, 2002.

Halliday, Fred. *The Making of the Second Cold War.* London: Verso, 1983.

Harries, Owen, ed. *America's Purpose: New Visions of US Foreign Policy.* San Francisco, Calif.: Institute of Contemporary Studies, 1991.

Hedges, Chris. *War Is a Force That Gives Us Meaning.* New York: Public Affairs, 2002.

Heymann, Philip B. *Terrorism, Freedom and Security: Winning without Fighting.* Cambridge, Mass.: MIT Press, 2003.

Himmelstein, Jerome. *To the Right: The Transformation of American Conservatism.* Berkeley: University of California Press, 1990.

Hirsh, Michael. *At War with Ourselves: Why America Is Squandering Its Chance to Build a Better World.* New York: Oxford University Press, 2003.

Hitchens, Christopher. *The Trial of Henry Kissinger.* London: Verso, 2001.

Hobart, Mark, ed. *An Anthropological Critique of Development: The Growth of Ignorance.* London: Routledge, 1993.

Hoffman, Bruce. *Inside Terrorism.* New York: Columbia Univerity Press, 1998.

Holbrooke, Richard. *To End a War.* New York: Random House, 1998.

Hollander, Paul. *Anti-Americanism: Critiques at Home and Abroad, 1965–1990.* Oxford: Oxford University Press, 1992.

Hunt, Michael H. *Ideology and US Foreign Policy.* New Haven, Conn.: Yale University Press, 1987.

Hutton, Will. *The World We're In.* London: Little, Brown, 2002.

Irwin, Douglas A. *Free Trade under Fire.* Princeton, N.J.: Princeton University Press, 2002.

Jamieson, Kathleen Hall, and Paul Waldman. *The Press Effect: Politicians, Journalists and the Stories That Shape the Political World.* New York: Oxford University Press, 2003.

Johnson, Paul. *A History of the Modern World.* London: Weidenfeld and Nicolson, 1983.

Judis, John B. *William F. Buckley Jr.: Patron Saint of the Conservatives.* New York: Simon and Schuster, 1988.

Kagan, Donald. *On the Origins of War and the Preservation of Peace.* New York: Doubleday, 1995.

———. *The Peloponnesian War.* New York: Viking, 2003.

Kagan, Donald, and Frederick Kagan. *While America Sleeps: Self-Delusion, Military Weakness and the Threat to Peace.* New York: St. Martin's Press, 2000.

Kagan, Robert. *Of Paradise and Power: America and Europe in the New World Order.* New York: Knopf, 2003.

Kagan, Robert, and William Kristol, eds. *Present Dangers: Crisis and Opportunity in American Foreign and Defense Policy.* San Francisco: Encounter, 2000.

Kaplan, Lawrence F., and William Kristol. *The War over Iraq: Saddam's Tyranny and America's Mission.* San Francisco: Encounter, 2003.

Kaplan, Robert. *The Coming Anarchy: Shattering the Dreams of the Post–Cold War World.* New York: Random House, 2000.

Kaufman, Robert G. *Henry M. Jackson.* Seattle: University of Washington Press, 2000.

Keegan, John. *A History of Warfare.* New York: Knopf, 1993.

Kellner, Douglas. *From 9/11 to Terror War: The Dangers of the Bush Legacy.* Lanham, Md.: Rowman and Littlefield, 2003.

Kennan, George F. *Around the Cragged Hill: A Personal and Political Philosophy.* New York: W. W. Norton, 1993.

Kissinger, Henry. *Does America Need a Foreign Policy?* New York: Simon and Schuster, 2001.

————. *The White House Years.* Boston: Little, Brown, 1979.

————. *Years of Upheaval 1208–9* Boston: Little, Brown, 1982.

Korn, David. *The Lies of George W. Bush: Mastering the Politics of Deception.* New York: Crown, 2003.

Kozodoy, Neal, ed. *The Mideast Peace Process: An Autopsy.* New York: Encounter, 2001.

Kristol, Irving. *Neoconservatism: The Autobiography of an Idea.* New York: Free Press, 1995.

Lacorne, Denis, Jacques Rupnik, and Marie-France Toinet, eds. *Rise and Fall of Anti-Americanism: A Century of French Perception.* Trans. Gerry Turner. New York: Macmillan, 1990.

Laqueur, Walter. *The New Terrorism, Fanaticism and the Arms of Mass Destruction.* London: Phoenix, 1999.

————. *No End to War: Terrorism in the 21st Century.* New York: Continuum, 2003.

Ledeen, Michael. *The War against the Terror Masters.* New York: St. Martin's Press, 2002.

Leone, Richard C., and Greg Anrig, Jr., eds. *The War on Our Freedoms: Civil Liberties in an Age of Terrorism.* New York: Public Affairs, 2003.

Lessor, Ian O., ed. *Countering the New Terrorism.* Santa Monica, Calif.: Rand Corporation, 1999.

Leventhal, Fred M., and Roland Quinault, eds. *Anglo-American Attitudes: From Revolution to Partnership.* Aldershot: Ashgate, 2000.

Lewis, Bernard. *What Went Wrong: Western Impact and Middle Eastern Response.* New York: Oxford University Press, 2002.

Livingstone, Neil C. *The War on Terrorism.* Lexington, Mass.: D. C. Heath, 1976.

Locke, John. *Second Treatise on Civil Government.* Amherst, N.Y.: Prometheus, 1986.

McCullough, David G. *John Adams.* New York: Simon and Schuster, 2001.

Maier, Pauline. *From Resistance to Revolution: Colonial Radicals and the Development of American Opposition to Britain, 1765–1776.* New York: Knopf, 1974.

Mann, James. *About Face: A History of America's Curious Relationship with China, from Nixon to Clinton.* New York: Knopf, 1999.

————. *The Rise of the Vulcans: The History of Bush's War Cabinet.* New York: Viking, 2004.

Matlock, Jack F., Jr. *Autopsy of an Empire.* New York: Random House, 1995.

Mayer, J. P., ed. *Alexis de Tocqueville: Journey to America.* Trans. George Lawrence. London: Faber and Faber, 1959.

McDougall, Walter A. *Promised Land, Crusader State: The American Encounter with the World since 1776.* New York: Houghton Mifflin, 1997.

McMahon, Robert J. *The Cold War.* Oxford: Oxford University Press, 2003.

McNamara, Robert. *In Retrospect: The Tragedy and Lessons of Vietnam.* New York: Times Books, 1995.

Mead, Walter Russell. *Special Providence: American Foreign Policy and How It Changed the World.* New York: Knopf, 2001.

Meyer, Karl E. *The Dust of Empire: The Race for Mastery in the Asian Heartland.* New York: Public Affairs, 2003.

Morris, Edmund. *Theodore Rex.* New York: Random House, 2001.

Moynihan, Daniel Patrick. *A Dangerous Place.* New York: Secker and Warburg, 1975.

————. *Pandemonium: Ethnicity in International Politics.* New York: Oxford University Press, 1993.

Murray, Williamson, and Robert H. Scales. *The Iraq War: A Military History.* Cambridge: Harvard University Press, 2003.

Neal, Mark. *The Culture Factor: Cross-national Management and the Foreign Venture.* Basingstoke: Macmillan Business, 1998.

Newhouse, John. *Imperial America: The Bush Assault on the World Order.* New York: Knopf, 2003.

Nordlinger, Eric A. *Isolationism Reconfigured.* Princeton, N.J.: Princeton University Press, 1995.

Norris, Pippa, Montague Kern, and Marion Just, eds. *Framing Terrorism: The News Media, the Government and the Public.* New York: Routledge, 2003.

Novak, Michael. *On Corporate Governance: The Corporation as It Should Be.* Washington, D.C.: AEI Press, 1997.

Nye, Joseph S., Jr. *The Paradox of American Power.* Oxford: Oxford University Press, 2002.

Offner, Arnold. *Another Such Victory: President Truman and the Cold War, 1945–1953.* Stanford, Calif.: Stanford University Press, 2002.

Owen, David. *Balkan Odyssey.* New York: Harcourt Brace Jovanovich, 1995.

Paine, Thomas. *Common Sense.* New York: Penguin, 1976.

Pells, Richard. *Not like Us: How Europeans Have Loved, Hated, and Transformed American Culture since WWII.* London: Basic Books, 1997.

Petersen, Roger D. *Understanding Ethnic Violence: Fear, Hatred, and Resentment in Twentieth-Century Europe.* Cambridge: Cambridge University Press, 2002.

Phillips, Kevin. *Wealth and Democracy.* New York: Broadway Books, 2002.

Pillar, Paul R. *Terrorism and US Foreign Policy.* Washington, D.C.: Brookings Institution, 2002.

Pipes, Daniel. *Militant Islam Reaches America.* New York: Norton, 2003.

Prestowitz, Clyde. *Rogue Nation: American Unilateralism and the Failure of Good Intentions.* New York: Basic Books, 2003.

Reagan, Ronald. *An American Life.* New York: Simon and Schuster, 1999.

Regan, Donald T. *For the Record.* New York: Harcourt Brace Jovanovich, 1988.

Rehnquist, William H. *All the Laws but One.* New York: Vintage, 1998.

Remini, Robert. *Daniel Webster: The Man and His Time.* New York: W. W. Norton, 1997.

Ricci, David M. *The Transformation of American Politics: The New Washington and the Rise of the Think Tanks.* New Haven, Conn.: Yale University Press, 1993.

Robertson, Geoffrey. *Crimes against Humanity: The Struggle for Global Justice.* New York: New Press, 1999.

Rodin, Judith, and Stephen P. Steinberg, eds. *Public Discourse in America: Conversation and Community in the Twenty-first Century.* Philadelphia: University of Pennsylvania Press, 2003.

Schiller, Dan. *Digital Capitalism.* Cambridge, Mass.: MIT Press, 1999.

Schlesinger, Arthur M., Jr. *The Cycles of American History.* Boston: Houghton Mifflin, 1986.

Schlesinger, Stephen C. *Act of Creation: The Founding of the United Nations.* Boulder, Colo.: Westview, 2003.

Schoenwald, Jonathan. *A Time for Choosing: The Rise of Modern American Conservatism.* Oxford: Oxford University Press, 2001.

Schwartz, Stephen. *The Two Faces of Islam.* New York: Doubleday, 2002.

Shawcross, William. *The Shah's Last Ride.* New York: Touchstone, 1989.

_____. *Allies: The U.S., Britain, Europe and the War in Iraq.* New York: Public Affairs, 2004.

Shultz, George. *Turmoil and Triumph: My Years as Secretary of State.* New York: Charles Scribner, 1993.

Sifry, Micah, and Christopher Cerf, eds. *The Iraq Reader: History, Documents and Opinions.* New York: Simon and Schuster, 2003.

Simms, Brendan. *Unfinest Hour: Britain and the Destruction of Bosnia.* London: Penguin, 2002.

Soto, Hernando de. *The Other Path: The Economic Answer to Terrorism.* New York: Basic Books, 2002.

Steinfels, Peter. *The Neo-Conservatives: The Men Who Are Changing America's Politics.* New York: Simon and Schuster, 1979.

Stiftung, Friedrich Ebert. *America's Image in Germany and Europe.* Papers of a Seminar in Washington, D.C., March 31, 1985.

Stiglitz, Joseph E. *Globalization and Its Discontents.* New York: Norton, 2002.

Strauss, David. *Menace in the West: The Rise of French anti-Americanism in Modern Times.* London: Greenwood, 1978.

Suskind, Ron. *The Price of Loyalty: George W. Bush, the White House, and the Education of Paul O'Neill.* New York: Simon and Schuster, 2004.

Thorpe, D. R. *Eden: The Life and Times of Anthony Eden, First Earl of Avon, 1897–1977.* London: Chatto and Windus, 2003.

Tilly, Charles, ed. *The Formation of Nation States.* Princeton, N.J.: Princeton University Press, 1975.

Tocqueville, Alexis de. *Democracy in America.* Trans. Henry Reeve. London: Oxford University Press, 1946.

Todd, Emmanuel. *Après l'Empire: Essai sur la décomposition du système américain.* Paris: Gallimard, 2002.

Trollope, Frances. *Domestic Manners of the Americans.* London: Century Publishing, 1984.

Tuchman, Barbara W. *The Guns of August.* New York: Ballantine, 1994.

Tucker, Robert W., and David C. Hendrickson. *The Imperial Temptation: The New World Order and America's Purpose.* New York: New York University Press, 1992.

Van Susteren, Greta. *My Turn at the Bully Pulpit: Straight Talk about the Things That Drive Me Nuts.* New York: Crown, 2003.

Viguerie, Richard A. *The New Right.* Falls Church, Va.: Viguerie, 1981.

Weber, Max. *The Protestant Ethic and the Spirit of Capitalism*. London: George Allen and Unwin, 1930.

Weinberger, Caspar. *Fighting for Peace: Seven Critical Years in the Pentagon*. New York: Warner, 1990.

Weinberger, Caspar, and Peter Schweiz. *The Next War*. Washington, D.C.: Regnery, 1996.

Wills, Gary. *Inventing America: Jefferson's Declaration of Independence*. New York: Doubleday, 1978.

Woodward, Bob. *Bush at War*. London: Simon and Schuster, 2002.

Woolsey, R. James, ed. *The National Interest on International Law and Order*. New Brunswick, N.J.: Transaction, 2003.

Young, Hugo. *This Blessed Plot: Britain and Europe from Churchill to Blair*. London: Macmillan, 1998.

Zelikow, Philip D. and Condoleezza Rice. *Germany Unified and Europe Transformed: A Study in Statecraft*. Cambridge: Harvard University Press, 1995.

Index

Abrams, Elliott, 14, 16, 62, 75, 103, 121, 147, 173, 174–75, 198
absolute consistency, 308
academics, intellectuals, and scholars: comprising body of neo-conservatives, 9, 14, 15; early influence of, 41–48; early writings, 45–47; elite as neo-conservative, 46; move from academia to government, 67–68
Action Council for Peace in the Balkans, 93
Adams, John Quincy, 141, 160
Addington, David, 120
Adelman, Kenneth, 12, 75
adversaries: energized and radicalized, 338; instruments for approaching, 298; preempting, 12
affirmative action, 53–54
Afghanistan: follow-up in, 28; jihad against Soviet invasion, 277; nation-building problems, 7; as peripheral, 204, 299; Reagan doctrine, 163; Soviet invasion, 163
Afghanistan war, 32, 139–40, 238, 274; cost of, 28; decision to attack, 152, 205
Africa, 19
agenda-ism, 19
Agresto, John T., 62
Akashi, Yasushi, 88

Albright, Madeleine, 19, 86, 89, 98, 177
Alcove 1, 45, 67, 74
Allen, Richard V., 46, 71, 173
allied cooperation: on Iraq issue, 203; as policy instrument, 28, 324–25; unilateral policies and, 321
allies: alienated, 338; America's image among, 238–39; anti-Americanism and restraint of support from, 232–33, 238; corrective intervention/actions, 323–24; Kristol on European allies, 96. *See also specific countries*
al-Qaeda, 149, 209, 306, 311, 332; bridging the gap between Iraq and, 212–14; link to Iraq, 155, 202, 210; public misperceptions, 193
Alterman, Eric, 190
alternatives: examining, 5–6; resolving cultural conflicts, 333–35; trade-off between radicalism and policies reflecting values and interests, 274–75
Al-Zarqawi, Abu Musab, 212
American Civil Liberties Union, 286, 301
American commercialism, 259. *See also* McDonaldization
American Conservative Union, 301
American Enterprise Institute (AEI), 14, 47–48, 103, 104–5, 108–9

American exceptionalism, 23, 297, 309–10

American hegemony, 146

"American internationalist," preferred term for neo-conservatives, 4

American values and society: changes in, 299–301; character of, 5–6; first-generation neo-conservatism and, 41–55; impact of force on society, 29–30; mutual dependency of liberty and vigilance and, 295; 1960s, 51–55; normal decencies, 300; values as central to diplomacy, 25, 157, 158–61. *See also* Americans; capitalism; civil liberties; democracy; diplomacy; organizing myths; privacy; public awareness

Americanism, 233, 240–41. *See also* anti-Americanism; un-Americanism

"Americanization," 248, 259; McDonaldization and, 257–60

Americans: changing the questions for, 8; feelings of security/threat, 4, 275; limited interest in foreign policy, 303–4, 312–13; psychological change, 3–4; world perception of, 5. *See also* public awareness

Americans for Victory over Terrorism, 19

Anderson, Benedict, 262

Anderson, Marty, 71

Angola, Reagan doctrine, 163

Annan, Kofi, 123

Ansar-al-Islam, 212

anthrax, 145

anti-Americanism, 26, 30, 297; American cultural imperialism, 257–60; Americanism described, 240–41; "Americanization," 248; British attitude/sentiments, 244–47, 262–67; cost in terms of declining approval, 260–62; current, 254–57; distribution of power and, 256–57; in future international relations, 272; international attitude toward America, 232–35; "knowledgeable ignorance," 267–69; "lite," 243;

McDonaldization of society and, 257–60; nationalism and, 261–62; 19th-century sentiments, 239, 244–47; "Orientalism" and, 267, 269–71; Pew poll data, 237–40; polarizing social action in local cultures, 261–62; post-9/11, 2–3, 238–40; post–WW II sentiments, 251–53; precolonial America and, 243–44; revolutionary period sentiments, 239, 244–47; "soullessness," 250; 20th-century sentiments, 248–51; un-Americanism and, 241–43; unipolarity and, 235–37, 297; U.S. military capability expansion and, 260–62. *See also* Americanism

Anti-Ballistic Missile (ABM) Treaty, 126–28, 151, 256

anticommunism: anti-Americanism and, 234; foreign policy and, 55–58

anti-Semitism, 59–60, 72

applicability of force, 30–35

Arab world: boycotts against American goods, 253; Iraq as first democracy in, 148, 155–56, 220; "Orientalism" and, 267, 269–71

Arafat, Yasser, 313

Armitage, Richard, 33, 103, 119, 150

arms control, Reagan administration, 75, 170–71, 179

Asia, 239

authoritarianism, 6

Baath Party, 225

Bacevich, Andrew, 329–30

Baker, James A., 82, 100, 113, 114

balance of power, 325–28; checks and balances, 10, 218, 288, 301; between government and individual, 273; *see also* civil liberties; national security; Kristol on, 77; two contexts, 326

Balkans, 81–86, 158, 180

Barber, Ben, 285

Barnet, Richard, 103

Bauer, Gary, 109, 198

Beauvoir, Simon de, 251

Beirut, intervention in, 165
Bell, Carol, 178
Bell, Daniel, 41, 45, 90, 205
Benedict, Ruth, 261
Bennett, William J., 25, 62, 70, 109, 198
Berger, Peter, 41, 59, 76, 196
Berkowitz, Bruce, 27
Biden, Joseph, 98, 115
Big Brother, 291
bin Laden, Osama, 152, 227, 277, 279–80, 306
biometric devices, 292
Black, Alison, 215
Blair, Tony: on Guantanamo Bay, 290; initial impression of Bush, 132; solidarity with U.S. after 9/11, 229, 263–64
Blankley, Tony, 191
Blix, Hans, 228–29
Bloom, Allan, 62, 66
Bolivia, president's exile, 323
Bolton, John R., 14, 16, 17, 29, 103, 114–15, 122, 123, 127, 147
Boot, Max, 14, 26
Bork, Robert, 62
Bosnia, 84–98
Bosnian Serb Army (BSA), 87–88, 91–92
Bourguet, Christian, 271
Bove, José, 258
boycotts, 254–55
Bremer, Paul, 223
Brinkley, Douglas, 120
Brogan, Dennis, 252
Brooks, David, 67
Bryen, Steven, 62
Brzezinski, Zbigniew, 90, 93n.
Buchanan, Pat, 70
Buchananite wing, presidential administration grievances of, 72–73
Buckley, William F., Jr.: distancing from anti-Semitism, 72; on Moynihan, 44
Burke, Edmund, 244–45
Bush, G. H. W.: balance of power and, 326; China and, 23; Desert Storm, *see* Hussein, Saddam; Persian Gulf War; discontent with, 80–86; domestic policy, 83; early days of administration, 13; Germany and, 158; grievances of Buchananite wing, 72; neo-conservatives in administration, 5; Yugoslavia and Somalia and, 81–86
Bush, George W.: "axis of evil" statement, 139, 208, 238, 264–65; China and, 23–24; declaration of "war on terror," 137–38; election of, 112–13; foreign affairs experience and views, 131–35; humble foreign policy, 133–34, 138; immediate post-9/11 events, 31–35; Limbaugh's effect on presidency, 191; Middle East policy and "Bush doctrine," 20; on nation building, 134–35; October 7 national address on Afghanistan, 32; Pew data on, 237; post-9/11 use of language, 207–8; September 11 national address, 31–32; September 20 congressional address, 32; State of the Union address, 2002, 139–41, 216–17, 238, 264–65; unstated reasons and aggressive approach to Iraq and, 154–56; on use of force, 134; view of military, 135
Bush, Jeb, 104
Bush administration: complaints, criticisms, displeasure with, 129–31; confirmation battles and, 113–16; days preceding 9/11 and, 136–37, 154–55; Defense Department and, 135–36; early unilateralism in, 121–31; EP-3 spy-plane incident, 130–31; foreign affairs and policy, 131–35; ICC and, 121–24; neglected alliances and rough foreign relations, 128–29; neo-conservative empowerment after 9/11, 138–39; neo-conservative rise during, 32–34; neo-conservatives in, 113, 114–16; 9/11 and, 137–38; open letter outlining conduct of war on terror, 149; rejection of AMB Treaty, 126–28; Rumsfeld and Defense

Bush administration (*cont.*)
  Department, 135–36; shift in focus
  from 9/11 to Iraq, 307–8; timidity in
  Middle East, 129–131130; transition
  and staff selection, 117–21
Business Roundtable, 47–48
Byrd, Robert C., 145

cable news, 182, 183, 199, 303
Cambodia, Reagan doctrine, 163
Canada, diminished opinion of U.S.,
  238
capitalism, 314; "vague consensus" of
  five principles, 49, 50–51
Card, Andrew, 137
Carlucci, Frank, 172
"Carnivore" system, 288
Carter, Jimmy, 16, 56–57, 196–97, 197;
  Iran hostage crisis, 271; paradox in
  policy, 57
Carterism, 166–67
Case, Clifford, 62
Casey, Samuel, 198
Castle Rock Foundation, 108,
  109
Ceasar, James W., 235
Center for Middle East Policy,
  107
Center for Security Policy (CSP), 103,
  106
center, or "establishment,"
  underperforming, 304–6
Central America, 5, 16
Central Intelligence Agency (CIA):
  communication with, 226; "public
  diplomacy" media programs, 234;
  yellowcake issue, 213–14
Chalabi, Ahmed, 220–21, 225–26,
  322
Cheney, Dick: compromise with Powell,
  322; ideology parallels to
  neo-conservatism/support of agenda,
  14; 9/11 call from Bush, 137; PNAC
  and, 205; Regional Defense Strategy
  and, 33; staff, 120; during transition,
  113; Wolfowitz and, 117
Chilton, Paul, 230

China, 8, 29, 298, 302, 308; ABM
  Treaty and, 128; EP-3 spy-plane
  incident, 23, 130–31; George Bush's
  relations with, 23–24; Reagan's
  policies, 168–69; Rumsfeld and
  Powell on, 151
Chomsky, Noam, 103, 242
Christian evangelicals/conservative
  groups, neo-conservative
  connections with, 70, 182,
  196–200
Christopher, Warren, 86, 89
Churchill, Winston, 263
citizenship, relinquishment, 289–90
civil liberties, 273, 284, 285–86, 295,
  300; privacy, 3, 273–74, 287, 300
"civil society," 327, 328–29
Clark, Wesley, 205
Clark, William, 173, 174
clash of civilizations, 298, 325,
  331–32
Clear Channel Radio Networks, 184,
  189, 191–92
Clinton, Bill: ICC treaty, 121, 122;
  Mandelbaum on, 100; nation's moral
  ideals and, 23; neo-conservatives and
  policy of, 83–84, 86–90; open letter
  on Bosnia, 90; open letter on
  Hussein's removal, 14, 103,
  146–47, 205; Republican capture of
  Congress and, 109–10; as soft on
  Hussein, 89
Clinton administration: Balkans and,
  81–85; focus on domestic issues, 183;
  "humanitarian interventions," 315;
  indecisive foreign policy, 88–89;
  neo-conservative disenchantment
  with, 86–90, 197–98; *NSS* of 1999
  contrasted with 2002 version, 142;
  PRD-13 and, 86–87; Somalia and,
  85–86
CNN, 185, 193
Coalition for a Democratic Majority
  (CDM), 55, 56, 60–61
Coalition for Constitutional Liberties,
  286
Coats, Daniel R., 117

Cohen, Eliot A., 14, 29, 30, 98
Cohen, William S., 122
Colbert, James, 107
Cold War: embrace of U.S. during, 234;
  moral authority and, 1; U.S. and
  European policy, 25. *See also*
  communism; post–Cold War period;
  Soviet Union, collapse
Combs, Roberta, 198
commercial policy instruments, 28
Committee for Peace and Security in the
  Gulf, 103
communism, 15–16
Computer Assisted Passenger
  Pre-Screening II (CAPPS II),
  294–95
conservatism, restoration of, 7
conservative radio. *See* talk radio/talk
  shows
containment, 133, 143, 147, 164
Cook, Robin, 229
Cooper, Robert, 337
Coors, Joseph, 109
Coors Brewing Co., 109
corrective intervention/actions: allies
  and friends, 323–24; charges against
  neo-conservatives, 296–301;
  intelligence agencies and, 318–20;
  involving center or "establishment"
  performance, 304–6; National
  Security Council and, 320–23; policy
  damage through deceptive agenda
  and, 308–18; public awareness,
  302–4; public trust and, 306–8
cost of war: Afghanistan, 28; Iraq, 28,
  224
counter-Americanism, 237. *See also*
  anti-Americanism
counterculture, 46, 53
counterterrorism, 227–28, 280–81,
  283–84
Cox, Christopher, 121
credibility: damage to, 22, 29, 312;
  restoring and preserving, 8
Croatia, 84
Crockatt, Richard, 241, 242–43, 332,
  333

Cropsey, Seth, 62
Cuba, 5
cultural differences and clashes, 332–36
cultural imperialism, anti-Americanism
  and, 251, 257–60
cultural policy instruments, 28
culture of poverty, 54

Daniel, Norman, 268
Daniels, Mitch, 224
Daniels, Mitchell E., Jr., 153
Dannhauser, Werner, 67
Davies, Merryl Wyn, 256, 257
de Pauw, Cornelius, 243–44
Dean, Howard, 305
Deaver, Michael K., 71
deception. *See* false history; Iraq,
  political discourse strategy for
decision-making process: influence on,
  33–34, 38–39, 224–26, 230–31;
  knowledgeable ignorance and
  "Orientalism" and, 267–71
Decter, Midge, 14, 35, 41, 67, 104
Defense Advanced Research Projects
  Agency (DARPA), 293–94
Defense Intelligence Staff (DIS)
  document, 214–15
Defense Planning Guidance (DPG),
  145–46
Defense Policy Board, 104, 226
defense spending, 27, 163
democracy: humanitarian pursuit
  of/spread of, 76–81, 218–19;
  Kirkpatrick and Abrams on, 175
Democratic Party: culture of
  appeasement, 26; use of force
  and, 26
Dershowitz, Alan, 276
desegregation and ethnicity, 53–54;
  "vague consensus" of five principles,
  49
Desert Storm. *See* Persian Gulf War
détente, 41, 56, 92, 164
deterrence, 143
developing countries, 251, 256–57
Dionne, E. J., 191
diploma tax for emigrants, 60–61

diplomacy: American values as central to, 157, 158–61; as constraint, 4; disdain for, 11; as lost cause, 228–29; new threats and, 280; policy instrument, 28, 297; soft power, 182, 260

discursive manipulation of 9/11, 194–96, 206–8, 306–8

discursive representation of reality and use of frames, 202, 211

Dobriansky, Paula, 147

Domestic Security Enhancement Act (Patriot II), 289–90

Dowd, Maureen, 213

Drucker, Peter, 46

D'Souza, Dinesh, 176

due process, erosion of, 290

Dulles, John Foster, 16

Eagleberger, Lawrence, 100, 172

East Asia, 298

East Timor, nation-building problems, 7

Eastern Europe: during Cold War, 25; diminished opinion of U.S., 238. *See also specific countries*

Eckstein, Yechiel, 199

economic policy instruments, 28

Edleman, Eric, 121

Ehrman, John, 75

Eisenhower, Dwight, 16, 23

El Al flight hijacking, 277

El Kaissoumi, Mahmoud, 255

El Salvador, Reagan doctrine, 163

Empower America, 109, 198

"enemy combatants," 290

Epstein, David, 68

"establishment," or center, underperformance of, 304–6

Estrada, Garcia, 230

Europe: ABM Treaty and, 128; anti-Americanism in, 232–36, 248–53; current anti-Americanism, 254–57; declining U.S. approval, 261; diminished opinion of U.S., 237–40; distribution of power and, 256–57;

divergent perspective on Middle East, 253; McDonaldization of society/anti-Americanism and, 257–60; objection to U.S. socio-political assault, 261–62; post–Cold War relationship with U.S., 94–98; postwar tensions and fear of mass culture, 249–50; resentment over view of developed and underdeveloped world, 251; Weber's distinctions between Europe and America, 249. *See also specific countries*

European Union (E.U.): dialogue and trade as tools of leverage, 96; relations with, 299

evil: "axis of evil" statement, 139, 208, 238, 264–65; "Evil Empire" speech, 16, 75; human capacity for, 56; Vietnam example, 52

Fairbanks, Charles, 107

Fallows, James, 187

false history, 4–5, 35–36. *See also* myths, organizing; Reagan administration; Reagan legacy

Falwell, Jerry, 72, 196, 197

Federal Communications Commission (FCC), 186, 189–90, 191–92

Feith, Douglas, 20, 103, 107, 319, 321; ABM Treaty and, 127; joining Defense Department, 119–20; postwar Iraq plans, 225–26, 322

Feldman, Noah, 334

Felzenberg, Alvin, 109

financial network, 108–10; institutions funding print media, 188

financial resources, 297, 305, 338

First Amendment rights, 287, 289

first-generation neo-conservatism: as philosophical movement, 41–45; "post–Cold War normalcy" and, 100; significance to American values and society, 41–55

Fisher, Joshka, 229

Fleisher, Ari, 125

Foley, Tom, 15

force, use of, 8, 11, 26, 338; Bush on, 134; as default weapon against terrorism, 30–31, 281–82; impact on American values and society, 29–30; international problem analysis and, 29; against Iraq, 147–50; Weinberger's "six tests," 177. *See also* military, unilateral force

Ford, Gerald: AEI and, 47; neo-conservatives in administration, 5

foreign and defense policy, 146–56; the academy and, 315–16; American exceptionalism, 309–10; anticommunism, 55–58; charges against neo-conservatives regarding, 296–99; consensus, 8, 310; global economy and, 313–15; goal to minimize international violence, 31; historical amnesia, 37; humanitarian pursuit of/spread of democracy, 76–81, 218–19; impasse in the Middle East, 313; instruments, 26–31; maintaining the straight and narrow, 24; the media and, 316–18; military and terrorism and, 280–81, 310–11; naïveté in, 57; narrow focus, 43; neo-conservative approaches, 11; "neo-Reaganite foreign policy," 161–62; objection of locals to U.S. socio-political assault, 261–62; policy coherence of the past, 322–23; realism in, 24–25, 77–78; restoring balance in, 325–28; rising anti-Americanism and, 311–13; strategy for revamping, 17–22; successful, 324–25; transition after 9/11, 31–35. *See also specific presidents and administrations*

Foreign Intelligence Surveillance Act (FISA), 287

Foundation for the Defense of Democracy (FDOD), 109, 198

Founding Fathers: on early anti-Americanism, 244; revelance today, 37

Fourth Amendment rights, 286, 288, 300

Fox News Channel, 184, 185–86, 187, 188, 191, 194, 195, 196, 303

France: ABM Treaty and, 128; anti-Americanism, 233, 235, 251, 252; betrayal felt by Americans, 254; Bosnia and, 84–85, 87, 88; diminished opinion of U.S., 238; McDonaldization and, 258; studies on the U.S., 250

Franklin, Benjamin, Weber on, 248–49

Friedberg, Aaron, 14, 300

Friedman, Murray, 59

Frum, David, 18, 32, 139, 189

Fukuyama, Francis, 66, 104, 313–14

Future of Iraq Project, 224–25

Gaddis, John Lewis, 164

Gaffney, Frank, 82, 90, 102, 103, 106

gag orders, surveillance and, 288–89

Garner, Jay, 106

Gellman, Barton, 145

Geneva Accord, 332, 335

Gerecht, Marc, 130

Germany: ABM Treaty and, 128; Black September attack, 36, 277; Bush speech to Parliament, 140; diminished opinion of U.S., 238; postwar embrace of U.S., 253

Gershman, Carl, 76, 80

Gerson, Mark, 188

Gerson, Michael, 188

Gingrich, Newt, 15, 110, 191

Glazer, Nathan, 45, 78; racist charges against, 44, 53

global relations. *See* international affairs/relations

globalism/globalization, 8, 277–78; maintaining U.S. security and, 280; restoring comity and, 329–31

Glynn, Patrick, 88, 89

Goldberg, Jonah, 189

Gorbachev, Mikhail, 75, 170, 179

Gottlieb, Alan, 330

government, purpose of, "vague consensus" of five principles, 49, 54

Graham, Franklin, 199

Great Britain: American mass culture and, 232, 250; anti-Americanism in, 232; attitude/sentiments and "special relationship," 239, 244–47, 250, 252, 253, 262–67; Bosnia and, 84–85, 87, 88; British intelligence and political discourse strategy for Iraq, 210, 213, 214–15; clear and present danger/WMD inspections and, 229; damage to intelligence, 265–66, 320; diminished opinion of U.S., 238; DIS document, 214–15; experience in Palestine, 282–83; in Iraq, 201–2; legitimacy conferred on U.S., 266–67; post-9/11, 264–67; public trust, 264; WMD dossier, 210, 215, 216, 320

Grebe, Michael, 109

Grenada, intervention in, 165, 171, 176

Guantánamo Bay, Cuba, 290

Gulf War. *See* Persian Gulf War

Hadley, Stephen, 216, 217, 321

Haig, Alexander, 165, 172, 173

Haiti, nation-building problems, 7

Halberstam, David, 183

Hannah, John, 121

Harries, Owen, 20

Harrington, Michael, first use of "neo-conservative," 44

Hedges, Chris, 317

Heidegger, Martin, 250

Helms, Jesse, 115, 122, 173

Heritage Foundation, 48, 103, 108–9

Hertog, Roger, 188

Heymann, Philip, 281

Hill, David, 240

Himmelfarb, Gertrude, 41, 52, 67

Hirsh, Michael, 37

Hispanic Broadcasting Network (HBC), 191–92

Hobart, Mark, 268

Hollander, Paul, 242

homeland, impact on, 9, 26

Homeland Security Advanced Research Projects Agency (HSARPA), 294

Hoover Institution, Stanford University, 108

Hudson Institute, 103; Center for Middle East Policy, 107

human rights, foreign policy based on, 18–19

Hussein, Saddam, 189, 194, 195, 306–7; and assertion of U.S. power, 206; case for war against, 80, 203, 204–6, 215; Kuwait invasion, 180; link to/involvement in 9/11, 201, 210, 211; removal of, 81, 147, 230; State-Defense disagreements on, 153–54; WMD and, 213–14; yellowcake issue, 156, 185–86, 213–14, 215–17

Hutton Report, 265

Ifshin, David, 83

Ignatieff, Michael, 79

Ikle, Fred, 173

India, 8, 19

information revolution, 278

Institute for Advanced Strategic and Political Policies, 106

Institute on Religion and Democracy, 56

integration, 53–54

intellectual movement/phenomenon, 10, 15, 46. *See also* academics, intellectuals, and scholars

intelligence agencies, 288, 318–20

intelligence collection, 236, 287. *See also* surveillance

interagency process, dysfunctionality, 321–23

Intermediate-Range Nuclear Forces (INF), 74

international affairs/relations: anti-Americanism in future, 272; avoiding clash of civilizations, 325, 331–32; defining concepts for neo-conservatism, 41; disagreement with tenets, 13; impact of force on American global relations, 29–30; Middle East alternatives, 332–36; nonstate actors and, 298, 311, 327–28; nuclear proliferation and, 299, 312–13, 336–38; post–Cold War relations between U.S. and Europe, 94–98; restoring balance in, 325–28; reviving international comity, 325, 329–31

International Atomic Energy Agency (IAEA), 214

international commission, Middle East and, 336

International Criminal Court (ICC), 121–24; Bolton's arguments, 16; issue as fairness, 256

International Fellowship of Christians and Jews (IFCJ), 199

international legitimacy and credibility, 10, 297, 312

International Monetary Fund (IMF), 256–57

Internet, intelligence collection via, 288

intervention: Clinton's "humanitarian interventions," 315; possibility of future interventions, 230; priorities for, 18; during Reagan administration, 165–66

Iran, 29; hostage crisis, 163, 271; Iran-Contra scandal, 75, 179

Iraq, 146–56; bridging the gap between al-Qaeda and, 212–14; British in, 201–2; cost of war in, 28, 224; Dean and, 305; exit strategy, 304; Feith and postwar Iraq plans, 322; as first democracy in Middle East, 148, 155–56, 220; link to 9/11, 204–6; oil as reason for military action against, 155–56; oil wealth to underwrite reconstruction, 222–24; post-9/11 attention to, 32–34; public perception/misperception, 183, 192–96, 201; reconstruction efforts, 7, 221–24, 305–6; threat as "proven" fact, 201, 306–8; use of force against,

147–50; weapons declaration, 214; *see also* weapons of mass destruction. *See also* Iraq, political discourse strategy for

Iraq, political discourse strategy for: bridging al-Qaeda and Iraq, 212–14; British intelligence and, 210, 213, 214–15; building climate of fear, 208–10; CIA and, 216–17; credibility gap, 213–14; deception's legacy, 230–31, 297–98; diplomacy as lost cause, 228–29; discursive manipulation of 9/11, 194–96, 206–8; faulty evidence, 214–15; harmful influence on real war on terror, 227–28; international cooperation against terrorism and, 227–28; media and, 182–83, 186, 202–3; misperception and deception used to fashion, 201–3; persuasion techniques, 203; polarized identities and, 217–18; postwar government, 219–21, 322; reasons for targeting Iraq, 204–6; reconstruction of Iraq, 7, 221–24, 305–6; remaking the Middle East and, 155–56, 218–19; takeover of postwar decision making, 224–26; template for Middle East, 203, 219–21; U.N. Security Council and, 201, 211–12; unfounded hypotheticals and, 210–11; use of abstract enemy in notional war, 230; yellowcake issue, 156, 213–14, 215–17

Iraqi Governing Council, 221

Iraqi National Congress (INC), 33, 220–21, 225–26

Islam, 20–22, 198–99; Islamic-U.S. relations, 332–36; "knowledgeable ignorance" concept of Muslim world, 268–69; "Orientalism" and, 267, 269–71

Islamic-inspired terrorism, 19, 313

Islamic radicalism, 326, 331–32

isolationism and protectionism, 112, 126

Israel, 24, 58–60, 313; asymmetrical
threats to, 331–32; Bush senior's
policy, 82–83; grievances of
Buchananite wing, 72; Lod Airport
attack, 277; Reagan's policies,
167–68, 170–71; Stern Gang and
Irgun, 276; support and defense of,
41, 199
Israeli-Palestinian dispute, 167–68, 227,
335–36
Italy, 128, 238

Jackson, Henry M. "Scoop," 15, 56,
116
Jackson Vanik Act, 61
Jaffa, Harry, 62
Jaffe, Amy Myers, 223
James, Harold, 337–38
Jamieson, Kathleen Hall, 202
Japan, 19; opinion of U.S., 239
Jefferson, Thomas, 37
Jewish emigration/Soviet Jewry,
60–61
Jewish Institute for National Security
Affairs (JINSA), 58, 103, 105–6,
220
Joffe, Josef, 125
John M. Olin Foundation, 108
Johnson, Lyndon, preempting China,
141
Jones, Tim, 189
Judis, John, 74, 102–3

Kagan, Donald, 14, 36, 104, 281
Kagan, Robert, 67, 211, 218, 221,
235–36, 297, 305, 306; on EP-3 plane
incident, 130–31; on Kosovo, 95;
letter on removing Hussein, 103;
"neo-Reaganite foreign policy," 146,
161–62; PNAC founder, 104; on
Reagan, 169, 170; on transatlantic
relations, 94–95, 95–96
Kampelman, Max, 75, 90, 173
Kaplan, Lawrence, 206, 219–20
Kaplan, Robert, 20
Kay, David, 320
Kelly, David, 264, 320

Kemble, Penn, 56
Kemp, Jack, 15
Kennan, George F., 16, 135, 160
Kennedy, John F., preempting Cuban
missile crisis, 141
Kerry, John, 115
Keyes, Alan, 62
Khalilzad, Zalmay, 103
Kiley, Sam, 187
Kirkpatrick, Jeane, 16, 70, 90, 174–75;
on international obligations and
universal dominance, 78; U.N. and,
46, 57, 75, 173, 174
Kissinger, Henry, 18, 22–23
Klink, John, 150
"knowledgeable ignorance," 267–69,
271, 315
Koestler, Arthur, 276
Korean War, 27
Kosovo, 19, 30, 92, 94–95,
97–98
Kosovo Liberation Army, 276
Kovner, Bruce, 188
Krauthammer, Charles, 14, 76, 77,
78–79, 80, 82, 179
Kristol, Irving, 15, 20; on arming
Saudis, 167; on balance of power, 77;
on Buckley, 44; "coming conservative
century," 72; discussions in
autobiographical collection, 42;
endorsement of Nixon for president,
52, 67; on enhancing democracy,
76–77; as founder, 41, 45;
"godfather" of neo-conservatism, 10;
on ideas, 45; on Israel, 59; on
neo-conservatives, 48; on new
American imperium, 99; on next
generation, 67–68, 99; on Reagan,
71–72; on Reagan's response to
Soviets, 166
Kristol, William, 14, 62, 68, 179,
187–88, 298, 305, 306; Bush and,
112; on Cheney, 120; on China, 131;
on EP-3 plane incident, 130–31; on
European allies, 96; on Iraq, 206,
211, 218, 219–20; on Limbaugh, 191;
"neo-Reaganite foreign policy," 146,

161–62; as one-man think tank, 102; open letters to White House, 103, 198; PNAC and generational handoff, 98–99; PNAC founder, 104; on pseudo-neo-cons, 67; on Reagan, 169, 170

Kurtz, Howard, 187

Kyoto Protocol, 123, 124–26, 256, 258

Laffer, Arthur, 81

Laird, Melvin, 47

Lake, Anthony, 89, 97–98

Langford, Paul, 245–46

language and rhetoric, use of, 13, 300. *See also* discursive manipulation of 9/11

Lasky, Melvin, 45

Latin America, 19, 179, 261

Laurel Lodge meeting, September 15, 2001, 149, 204–6

Laxalt, Paul, 71

Le Carré, John, 208–9, 229

Leadership Council of Exiles, 221

Lebanon, 176

Ledeen, Michael, 29, 44–45, 189, 198, 199, 305

legal responses to terrorism, 283–84, 285–95

Leiken, Robert, 108

Lewis, Bernard, 14, 20, 270, 334

Libby, I. Lewis "Scooter," 14, 16, 67, 104, 120, 145–46, 205, 321

liberalism, 49–55

Libya, intervention in, 165, 176

Lieberman, Joseph, 15

Likud Party, 199

Limbaugh, Rush, 190–91

Linderman, Jan, 255

Lindsay, Lawrence, 224

Lipset, Seymour Martin, 45

locator technology, 292

logic of war, 92–93, 274–75

Lord, Carnes, 62, 68

Lowry, Rich, 189

Luti, William, 226

Luttwak, Edward, 89

Lynde and Harry Bradley Foundation, 108, 109

Malbin, Michael, 68

Mandelbaum, Michael, 100

Mansfield, Harvey, 62

Marcos, Ferdinand, 170

Marcuse, Herbert, 259

McDonaldization of society, anti-Americanism and, 257–60

McDonald's Corporation, 257–58

McGovern, George, 19, 55–56

McGrath, Dean, 121

McNamara, Robert, 31

media and media outlets, 182–84, 299; bias in, 190; changing face of, 184–86; discursive manipulation of 9/11 and, 194–96; echo chamber, 194–96; FCC regulations and, 186, 189–90, 191–92; international affairs coverage, 302; Murdoch and, 184, 186–88; post–Cold War period, 183–86; print media, 188–89; promotion of ideology by, 4–5, 182; public misperception of Iraq, 183, 192–96, 202, 226. *See also* talk radio/talk shows

Meese, Edwin, 71

Melman, Seymour, 45

Mexico, 19

Meyer, Christopher, 132

Meyer, Karl, 38

Middle East: declining U.S. approval, 261; focus on, 308–9; foreign policy, 146–56, 304–6, 338; influencing rather than imposing demise of, 25; Israel's position, 59–60; objection to U.S. socio-political assault, 261–62; peace process, 20–22; policy objectives, 8, 19; political discourse strategy and remaking the Middle East, 155–56, 218–19; Reagan's policies, 166–68; real agenda and, 309; template for, 202, 203, 205–6, 219–21, 226, 297–98; transformation, 306

Middle East Forum (MEF), 108
Middle East Media Research Institute
(MEMRI), 107
military: avoidance of intrusion into
politics, 3; hostility and danger
encountered by, 7; as nation builders,
135; preemptive military action, 11,
12, 69; resources, 338; spending, 27;
successes, 27; terrorism and, 281–85;
tribunals, 290; troops required in
Iraq's aftermath, 220, 222; unilateral
force, 26–31, 90–93, 305; value of,
283
military power, 2, 6–7, 237, 310–11;
asymmetrical, 297, 329; precision
and specialized weapons and, 92–93;
successes, 6–7; technological
capability, 5–6, 63–64, 92–93; U.S. as
world's policeman, 77–78; use in
Middle East, 19. *See also* force, use of;
military, unilateral force
Mitterand, François, 25
moral arrogance, 22–26
moral authority, 1–2, 6–7, 275, 296,
324, 338, 339
moral clarity, 23
Moral Majority, 71–72
moral relativism, 26
morality and moral purpose, 23–26;
religion and, 54–55
Morris, David, 257–58
Moynihan, Daniel Patrick, 15, 16; as
founder, 41, 45; as a
neo-conservative, 44; on Oliver
North, 45; racist charges against, 44,
53; U.N. and, 59; on Vietnam, 52
MSNBC, 188, 189
multiculturalism, 54
multilateral peace keeping, 85–86
multilateralism, 7, 77, 81–82, 92, 256,
338; assertive multilateralism, 7, 89;
Clinton administration policy, 86–90;
Congress and, 97–98; PRD-13 and,
86–87
Muravchik, Joshua, 61, 76, 77, 79–80,
82, 83, 89, 90, 102, 103, 179
Murawiec, Laurent, 20

Murdoch, Rupert, 184, 186–89, 190
Murray, William, 198
Muslim world. *See* Arab world; Islam
Mylroie, Laurie, 204
myths, organizing: American values as
central to diplomacy, 157, 158–61;
basis in reality, 157–58; Reagan
legacy and, 157, 161–62

Naim, Moises, 243
nation building, 7, 28, 335–36
National Missile Defense (NMD), 256
National Public Radio (NPR)/PBS, 193
national security: counterterrorism as
issue of, 280–81, 295; impact on, 9;
restrictions and, 273–75, 295; *see also*
civil liberties; unfunded federal
demands, 3
National Security Council (NSC):
A-Team, B-Team process, 321;
corrective intervention/actions,
320–23; institutional failure and, 218
National Security Strategy (NSS) of 2002,
141–46, 156, 177, 336
national sovereignty, as obsolete,
330–31
NATO, 8, 87–88, 91–98, 158;
Implementation Force (IFOR), 93;
Operation Allied Force, 97
Natsios, Andrew, 223
Near East and South Asia (NESA)
bureau, 226
neo-conservatism: anti-Semitism and,
58–60; anticommunism and foreign
policy and, 55–58; areas with which
to agree/disagree, 15–17;
Balkans and, 81–86; binary
formulation/interpretation, 43, 196,
323; confusion and fracture of
movement, 75–79; defining, 41,
44–45; doctrine, demonstration of,
206; as East Coast intellectual
phenomenon, 9, 15; founders, 41,
45–46; *see also names of specific
individuals*; heroes of, 35–36; Israel
and, 58–60; McGovern and, 19,
55–56; move from left to right,

49–55; new political animal, 100–103, 178–81; as a persuasion, 10; philosophical underpinnings, 48–52; Reagan era, 68–72; strategy, 17–22; *see also* Iraq, political discourse strategy for; Strauss and, 64–68; think tanks and, 47–48; Trotskyism and, 45, 74; U.N. and, 58–60; "vague consensus" of five principles, 49, 52–55; Wohlstetter and, 62–64. *See also* first-generation neo-conservatism; neo-conservatism, ascension of; neo-conservatism, history of; neo-conservative ideology; next-generation neo-conservatism

neo-conservatism, ascension of: Bush administration transition and staff selection, 117–21; Bush foreign affairs and policy, 131–35; confirmation battles and, 113–16; days preceding 9/11 and, 136–37; Defense Department and, 135–36; early unilateralism in, 121–31; G. W. Bush election, 112–13; neo-conservative empowerment after 9/11, 138–39; 9/11 and, 137–38; *NSS* of 2002, 141–46; preemption and, 139–41

neo-conservatism, history of, 7; false history, 4–5, 35–36; origins, 9, 40–47. *See also* myths, organizing; Reagan administration; Reagan legacy

neo-conservative agenda: media and, 4–5, 40; policy damage done by deception, 308–18; preexistence, 4–5, 32–34, 139, 149, 203; securing adoption of, 149–56; specious nature of, 14; unspoken, 17–22

neo-conservative ideology, 4–5, 11–13; as aberration, 7, 10; "American global leadership," 99; areas with which to agree/disagree, 15–17; as fully operational, 230; philosophical underpinnings, 48–52; as special interest, 38, 297; state-against-state conflict as sole policy option, 4–5, 32; substitution for "interests," 5; three common themes/denominators, 11. *See also* force, use of; unilateralism

neo-conservative policy: areas with which to agree/disagree, 15–17; damage from, 302–6; debate over definition, 76–81; *see also* first-generation neo-conservatism; next generation neo-conservatism; as insensitive to global community, 256–57; versus policy based on core values, 274–75

neo-conservatives: academics and scholars, 14; affiliations and associations, 15, 67; Atlantic relations and, 94–98; attitudes, behaviors, and views, 12–13; caricature, 43; charges against, 296–301; "clientitis," 267–68, 267–71; during Clinton administrations, 146–56; composition and identity, 10; confidence trick, 306–8; confrontational postures, 12; difference of temperament with Reagan, 177–78; "Disciples of Strauss," 67; financial network, 108–10; general discussion, 9–10; generational transition in leadership, 98–103, 179–80; identifying early members, 45–47; as "in group" or "cabal," 13–14; influence of, 9, 10, 230; in influential positions, 9, 14, 41–48, 62, 67–68; lack of members among representative branch, 15; links to and involvement in media, 188–89; in media, 14; members and member identifiability, 14–15; network, 103–8; overreach, 72; patriotism, 16; perception of world, 267–71; pessimism, 12, 178, 338; practitioners vs. pamphleteers, 16; remembering everything/learning nothing, 8; as special interest group, 36–39; term as biographical, 44–45; as Wilsonians, 49, 74. *See also names of specific individuals and organizations*

Netanyahu, Binyamin, 20, 106–7
Neuhaus, Richard, 56
New Alternatives Workshop, 63–64

New Right, 54–55, 70–72

next generation neo-conservatism, 43, 60–62, 67–68, 179–81; activist projection of power, 79–81; generational transition in leadership, 98–103, 179–80; links to evangelical groups, 198–99; "Young Turk" faction, 78–79

Nicaragua, Reagan doctrine, 163

Niebuhr, Reinhold, 55–56

Nietzsche, Friederich, 248, 250, 274

Nitze, Paul, 133

Nixon, Richard: China and, 158; endorsement for president, 52; Soviet Union and, 56

Nofziger, Lyn, 71

nonstate actors, 281, 298, 311, 327–28, 337

Normal Trade Relations Act, 61

Norris, Pippa, 202

North, Oliver, 45

North Korea, 5, 19, 23, 29, 210, 211, 298, 308

Northern Ireland, 276, 279, 284, 335

Novak, Michael, 41, 56

nuclear proliferation, 299, 312–13, 336–38

Nunn, Sam, 115

Nye, Joseph, 182, 256

O'Brien, James, 93

O'Connor, Sandra Day, 72

O'Neill, Paul, 154

"Orientalism," 267, 269–71

Orwell, George, 291

Owen, David, 82

Paine, Tom, 245

Pakistan, 19, 299

Parsons, Albert, 336–37

Pentagon: Chalabi and, 225–26; Office of Special Plans (OSP), 226, 319. *See also* U.S. Department of Defense; surveillance

People's Voice Initiative, 332, 335

Peretz, Martin, 103, 188

Perle, Richard, 14, 18; affiliations, 105; arms control, 75; Bush and, 112–13; Defense Policy Board Chairman, 104, 119; Defense Secretary candidate, 115–16; on Europeans after 9/11, 95; on Hussein and Iraq, 147–48, 155; Jackson and, 61–62; on Middle East peace process, 20–21; Mylroie and, 204; on North Korea, 19; open letter to Clinton on Bosnia, 90; open letter to Clinton on Hussein's removal, 103, 147; PNAC and, 104; in Reagan administration, 173, 176; state-on-state war policy, 32–33

Persian Gulf, Reagan's foreign policy, 166–67

Persian Gulf War, 30, 64, 72–73, 81, 92, 150, 310

Pew Research Center, poll data, 237–40, 254–55

Phillips, David, 224

Pipes, Daniel, 160, 199, 334

Pipes, Richard, 82, 173; Team B, 61

Podesta, John, 287, 288

Podhoretz, John, 67

Podhoretz, Norman, 14, 35, 67, 188, 189; *Commentary* refashioning, 52; distinction between neo-conservative interventionism and humanitarian liberal interventionism, 79; effects on *Commentary*, 46, 75–76; as founder, 41; on Israel, 58–60; loss of authority, 75–76; "neo-conservative" as pejorative, 44; PNAC and, 104; on Reagan administration and policy, 165–66, 169–70, 171; on Wilsonian advocates, 77–78

Poindexter, John, 293–94

Poland, 165–66

policy: corrective intervention/actions, 308–18; neo-conservative impact on process, 9, 319; post-9/11, 4

political discourse, 41–42; high reach of, 46–47; humanitarian pursuit of democracy, 76–81, 218–19; institutional power behind, 208;

knowledgeable ignorance and "Orientalism" and, 267–71; "vague consensus" of five principles and, 49, 52–55; as window dressing, 19. *See also* Iraq, political discourse strategy for

post–Cold War period: Atlantic relations, 94–98; neo-conservative development in, 74–81; neo-conservative policy perceived as insensitive, 256–57; relationship with media, 183–86

Powell, Colin: on China and commitment to multilateralism, 308–9; compromise with, 322; example of traditional Republican internationalism, 9; Fisher meeting, 228; Persian Gulf War, 150; rift between Defense and State, 149–53; "smarter sanctions" policy, 154; State-Defense disagreements on Hussein, 153–54; U.N. Security Council presentation, 201, 211–13; Wolfowitz and, 118–19

preemption: Bush policy, 139–41; *DPG* and, 145–64; implications of, 143–44; *NSS* 2002 and, 141–46; preemptive military action, 11, 12, 69. *See also* military, unilateral force; terrorism and, 176–77

presidency, moral clarity and, 23–24

Presidential Review Directive-13, 86–87

print media, 188–89, 199

privacy, 3, 273–74, 287, 300

Project Democracy, 175

Project for the New American Century (PNAC), 33, 103–5; 1997 Statement of Principles, 14, 205–6, 230; focus on Middle East, 19, 219; letter on removal of Hussein, 101, 103; links to social conservatives, 198; neo-conservative involvement, 14; signatories, 103–4

Proliferation Security Initiative, 16

Protestant evangelicals. *See* Christian evangelicals/conservative groups

public awareness: climate of fear and, 208–10; corrective intervention/actions, 302–4; post–9/11 public opinion/debate, 304, 311; an under-informed citizenry, 194, 201, 302–4; an underperforming center, or "establishment," 304–6

public misperception, 192–94, 201. *See also* Iraq, political discourse strategy for

public trust, 203, 306–8; Great Britain, 264; policy damage through deceptive agenda, 297–98, 308–18

Putin, Vladimir, 126–28

racial discrimination, 53–54, 59

radio. *See* talk radio/talk shows

Raynal, Abbé, 244

Reagan, Ronald: balance of power and, 326; difference of temperament with neo-conservatives, 177–78; "Evil Empire" speech, 5, 16, 75; foreign policy, 35–36; in history of neo-conservatism, 35–36; Kirkpatrick appointment to U.N., 46, 57; as non-neo-conservative, 171–72, 178; optimism of, 177–78; "shining city on the hill" metaphor, 260; soft power and, 260; Soviets and, 25, 69, 75, 158, 165–66; unwillingness to use troops/force, 176–77

Reagan administration: arms control, 75, 170–71, 179; cabinet members, 172–75; Carterism, 166–67; Central and South America policy, 171; China policy, 168–69; disenchantment with, 164–67, 179, 197; early years, 162–64; interventions during, 165–66; Israel/Middle East policy, 167–68; neo-conservatives in, 5, 68–72; Soviet grain embargo, 169–70

Reagan doctrine, 163–64, 171

Reagan legacy, 11, 72; misappropriation of, 5; organizing myths and, 157, 161–62

realism, 24–25, 77–78, 100, 139, 312
reality: discursive representation of,
    202; influence of, 207; organizing
    myths' basis in, 157–58; war on
    terror's harmful influence on,
    227–28
Reed, Ralph, 197, 199
Regan, Donald, 162
Rehnquist, William, 273, 300
religion, "vague consensus" of five
    principles, 49, 54–55. *See also specific*
    religious groups
religious fundamentalism, 277
religious right, 54–55, 196–97
Revel, Jean-François, 233, 252, 253
Rice, Condoleezza, 112, 124, 133–34,
    156, 158, 214, 217
Rio Pact, 258
Ritzer, George, 257, 259
Robertson, Pat, 196, 197, 198–99
Robinson, Glen, 189
Rodman, Peter, 103, 120, 147
Roosevelt, Theodore, 35
Rose, Michael, 88
Rosenblatt, Peter, 83
Rostow, Eugene, 75, 90
"roving wiretaps," 288
Rubin, Michael, 108, 226
Rumsfeld, Donald: ABM Treaty and,
    127; Armitage and, 119; Bush
    Defense Department and, 135–36;
    Bush's secretary of defense, 118, 119;
    Chalabi and, 221; compromise with
    Powell, 322; July 9 congressional
    testimony, 33; foreign policy memos,
    154; on ICC, 122; ideology parallels
    to neo-conservatism/support of
    agenda, 14; on Iraq's oil wealth for
    reconstruction, 224; 1998 letter
    calling for Hussein's removal, 14,
    103, 147, 205; rift between Defense
    and State, 149–53; Shineki's troops
    estimate and, 222; State-Defense
    disagreements on Hussein,
    153–54
Russia: ABM Treaty and, 126–28;
    relations with, 299

Said, Edward, 269–71
SALT II talks, 64
Sandalow, David, 125
Sarah Scaife Foundation, 108, 109
Sardar, Ziauddin, 256, 257
Sartre, Jean-Paul, 251
Saudi Arabia, 167, 168
Scaife, Richard Mellon, 109
Schenker, David, 226
Schifter, Richard, 83
Schlafly, Phyllis, 71
Schmidt, Helmut, 25
Schmitt, Gary, 67, 68
scholars. *See* academics, intellectuals,
    and scholars
Scowcroft, Brent, 82, 100, 119, 155,
    213, 227–28
searches: of business records, 288–89;
    of computer hard drives, 288–89; and
    seizure of property, 289; sneak and
    peek, 289
Selznick, Philip, 45
separation of powers, 300
September 11 terrorist attacks (9/11):
    cost of, 34; discursive manipulation
    of, 194–96, 206–8, 306–8; immediate
    response to, 31–35, 304–6; Laurel
    Lodge meeting, 149, 204–6; link to
    Iraq, *see under* Iraq; primary
    purpose, 279–80; signs of change in
    American people/society, 2;
    sympathy/anti-Americanism
    following, 2–3, 238–40; wider
    context of, 277–78
Shakespeare, Frank, 109
Shawcross, William, 22
Shinseki, Eric, 222
Shokraii, Nina, 121
Shulsky, Abram, 67, 68, 226
Shultz, George, 36, 75, 90, 128, 161,
    173–74, 175, 177–78
siege mentality, 3–4
Smith, Gordon, 98
Smith, William French, 71
Smith Richardson Foundation,
    108
social reform, 49, 53–54

soft power, 182, 260
Somalia, 83, 84, 85–86, 88, 89, 90, 97;
    nation building, 7, 135;
    neo-conservative policy conclusions
    and, 74
South Korea, opinion of U.S., 239
Southeast Asia, engagements in, 19, 39,
    52
Soviet Union, 5, 16, 56; collapse, 74–76,
    101, 179–80; *see also* Cold War; grain
    embargo, 169–70; next generation
    neo-conservatism and, 60–62;
    policies allowing military superiority,
    162–64; Team B and, 61
special interest: definitions, 37–38;
    uninformed citizenry misled by, 203,
    303
special interest groups,
    neo-conservatives as, 36–39
Stand for Israel, 199
state sponsors of
    terrorism/state-on-state war, 32–34,
    138–39
statutory measures to combat terrorism,
    285–91, 295
Stead, William Thomas, 248
Steel, Helen, 257–58
Steinfels, Peter, 46
Stockman, David, 69
Strategic Defense Initiative (SDI), 164
strategic developments worldwide,
    298
Strauss, David, 242
Strauss, Leo, 50, 62, 64–68, 178
Sullivan, Andrew, 62
"supply side economics," 42
surveillance: data, 292; Patriot Act and,
    287–89; and "tangible things," 289;
    technology and capabilities, 3, 275,
    286, 291–95, 301;
    "twenty-first-century surveillance,"
    273–74. *See also* searches
Syria, disagreement on, 152

Taft, William, 98
Taiwan, 128, 298
Taliban, 4, 152, 332

talk radio/talk shows, 182, 184, 188,
    189–92, 195, 199; hosts and
    luminaries of, 190–91
Tarcov, Nathan, 68
Tenet, George, 216
terrorism, 274–75; ambiguities, 276–77;
    "asymmetrical warfare," 278, 279;
    brief history of, 275; civilian
    casualties and change in motivation
    for global terrorism, 278–79; coming
    to terms with political nature/causes
    of, 138–39, 282–83; contemporary
    attacks, 277; "democratized," 34–35;
    discriminate/indiscriminate targeting,
    279; global/international terrorism
    context, 140, 144–45, 227–28,
    275–81; legal responses, 283–84,
    285–95; legitimacy for U.S. action
    against, 284, 285; lessons from other
    nations, 276; media and, 279–80; as
    method, not ideology, 282; methods
    of attack, 278–79; military and,
    281–85; mispositioned response to,
    298; multiple acts of 1985, 176–77;
    nations losing status as terrorists,
    276; networks, 280–81; as politics by
    other means, 2382; preemptive action
    and, 176–77; as problem
    management issue, 281, 301; religious
    radicalism and, 277–78; state
    sponsorship, 32–34, 138–39; statutory
    measures to combat, 285–91, 295;
    superterrorism, 280–81; support for
    groups regarded as terrorists,
    276–77; surrender of rights/freedoms
    to battle, 301; "surrogate war," 278;
    surveillance technology to combat,
    291–95; war as right metaphor, 281;
    wider context of 9/11, 277–78
Terrorist Identification Database, 289
Terrorist/Total Information Awareness
    (TIA), 293–94
Thatcher, Margaret, 25, 75, 90, 158,
    171
think tanks, 47–48, 182
Thomas, Clarence, 62
Thomas, Helen, 317

Tocqueville, Alexis de, 246–47
Toobin, Jeffrey, 288
trade and trade agreements, 3
Transportation Security Agency, 294
Trilling, Lionel, 42
Trollope, Frances, 246
Trollope, Joanna, 246
Truman, Harry, 35, 132–33
trust: corrective intervention/actions,
306–8; as elusive, 12
truth, lacking in politics, 14, 156
Tuchman, Barbara, 325
Tucker, Robert C., 76, 77, 166, 168
Turkey, public perception of U.S., 238
Turley, Jonathan, 291

U.N. operation in Somalia
(UNOSOM II), 86
U.N. Protection Force (UNPROFOR),
84–85, 87, 91–94
U.N. Security Council: Iraq and, 201,
211–12
un-Americanism, 241–43
unilateralism: acceptable in absence of
multilateralism, 256; in Bush
administration, 121–31; coexistence
with economic multipolarity, 315;
Congress and, 97–98; early, 121–31;
failure to reach objectives and, 332;
global, 11; moral authority and,
297
unipolarity/unipolar policies, 10, 11,
92, 297, 306, 324, 338–39;
anti-Americanism and, 235–37,
256–57, 297
United Nations: Clinton administration
and, 86–90; criticism against, 57–58,
330–31; Israel and, 59–60; relations
with, 8, 57–58, 329–31; Resolution
1441, 228–29
United Nations Convention on the
Rights of the Child, 258
United States: boycotts against, 254–55;
budget deficits, 3; Bush on role in
world, 131; "confrontational model"
for, 334; global impression of
dominance, 6; global responsibilities,

8; imperialism, 6, 77; inattention to
needs/priorities, 298–99, 308;
international burden, 272;
Islamic-U.S. relations, 332–36;
isolation and polarization, 5, 296;
negative images of, 232–40;
perception of initiatives in light of
McDonaldization, 260; post–Cold
War relationship with Europe, 94–98;
post–WWI tensions and fear of mass
culture of, 249–50; power projection
and intimidation, 5; relations with
outside world, 2–3, 338; relations
with U.N., 57–58, 329–31; rising
economic power, 250–52; value of
international respect/support for, 6;
vulnerabilities as a democracy,
300–301. *See also* Americans
U.S. Department of Defense: Bush
administration secretary and staff
selection, 117–20; policy differences
with State, 149–53, 321–23; TIA,
293–94. *See also* military; Pentagon;
Rumsfeld, Donald
U.S. Department of Homeland
Security, 3
U.S. Department of Justice, 3, 30;
citizenship relinquishment, 290;
undermining freedoms, 300
U.S. Department of State: Future of Iraq
Project and, 224–25; policy
differences with Defense, 149–53,
321–23. *See also* diplomacy; Powell,
Colin
USA Patriot Act, 273–74, 286–91;
Patriot II, 289–90
Utley, Garrick, 302

"vague consensus" of five principles,
49, 52–58
Vance, Cyrus, 89
Vanik, Charles, 61
"Vietnam syndrome," 30, 56
Vietnam War, 52–53; lessons of, 11, 27,
30
Viguerie, Richard, 71
Villepin, Dominique de, 229

war on terror: bureaucratic intrusiveness in daily life and, 3; *see also* surveillance; Fourth Amendment and, 30; harmful influence on reality, 227–28; neo-conservative doctrine as questionable model, 110–11; open letter outlining conduct of, 149

Warrick, Thomas, 225

Washington, George, on factions, 36–37

Washington Institute for Near East Policy (WINEP), 108, 220

Wattenberg, Ben, 76, 80, 84, 102, 148, 155, 179

weapons of mass destruction (WMD), 155–56, 156, 209, 210–11, 213–14, 265; British intelligence on, 210, 213, 320; Krauthammer on, 79; Perle on, 148; public misperceptions, 193, 194, 202; Resolution 1441, 228–29

Weber, Max, 248–49, 250, 253, 259

Webster, Daniel, 160

Weinberger, Caspar, 172, 177

welfare, government intervention in, 49, 54

Weyrich, Paul, 109; Heritage Foundation and, 48

"What the World Thinks in 2002" survey, 238

Whitman, Christine Todd, 125

Wieseltier, Leon, 103

Wilson, Harold, 263

Wilson, James Q., 14

Wilson, Joseph, 185–86, 216

Wilsonianism, 77; neo-conservatives as Wilsonians, 49, 74; Podhoretz on Wilsonian advocates, 77–78; Wilsonian liberalism, 18; Wilsonian promise, 142

Winik, Jay, 74

wiretap law, 288

Wohlstetter, Albert, 61–62, 62–64, 90, 92

Wolcott, James, 316–17

Wolfowitz, Paul D., 14, 16, 321; candidate for appointment, 115–20, 150; on Clinton, 89; at Defense Department, 119–20; *DPG* and, 145–46; on foreign affairs approach, 66–67; on Iraq's oil wealth for reconstruction, 222; long-standing Iraq concern, 32–33; on "a nation at war," 274; open letter to Clinton on Bosnia, 90; PNAC and, 205; post considerations, 118; in Reagan administration, 173; on reasons for Iraq war, 155–56; rift between Defense and State and, 149–53; Shineki's troops estimate and, 222; targeting Iraq and Hussein, 101–2, 103, 147, 204, 205; Team B, 61; on WMD, 202; on Wohlstetter, 64

Woolsey, James, 14, 29, 204

World Trade Organization (WTO), 256–57

World War I: notion of Americanism following, 240; postwar tensions and fear of mass culture, 249–50

World War II: necessity of war and, 27; postwar anti-Americanism sentiments, 250–53

World War IV, 4–5, 29, 274

Wurmser, David, 14, 103, 107

Wurmser, Meyrav, 14, 107, 108

Yaphe, Judith, 225

"yellow press," 7

yellowcake issue, 156, 185–86, 213–14, 215–17

"Young Turk" faction of neo-conservatism. *See* next generation neo-conservatism

Yugoslavia, 74, 81–82, 84–85, 87, 180

Zakheim, Dov, 82, 103, 120

Zelikow, Philip, 146

Zoellick, Robert, 147